Swedish  American Landmarks

Swedish ✚⬥ American Landmarks

Where to go and what to see

by Alan H. Winquist

👑👑👑 Swedish Council of America
👑 Minneapolis, Minnesota

Requests for permission to reproduce material from this work should be sent to Swedish Council of America, 2600 Park Avenue, Minneapolis, Minnesota 55407.

∞The paper used in this publication meets the minimum requirements of American National Standard for Information Sciences—Permanence of Paper for Printed Library Materials, ANSI Z39.48-1984.

Cover designer and design consultant: Janice Mataya, Salt Lake City, Utah
Text designer and compositor: Beth W. Allen, Houston, Texas
Mapmaker and production artist: Lynne Jones, Houston, Texas
Printer: Thomson-Shore, Inc., Dexter, Michigan

00 99 98 97 96 95   5 4 3 2 1

Cover photograph by Ed Cahill of tapestry by Marjorie Pohlmann in Chisago Lake Lutheran Church, Center City, Minnesota

All photographs were taken and provided by the author except the cover photograph and those provided as a courtesy of the following: *page 17*, Vicki Shaner; *page 56*, David Anderson; *page 69*, North Park College and Theological Seminary; *page 86*, Augustana College and Theological Seminary; *page 104*, Cranbrook Academy of Art; *page 134*, Robert Srenco; page 140, Bethany College; *page 176*, Oliver Magnuson; *page 182*, American Swedish Institute; *page 191*, Bethel College and Seminary; *page 219*, Gustavus Adolphus College; *page 233*, Charles A. Lindbergh House; *page 237*, Dewey Bergquist; *page 262, Brady Standard-Herald; page 274*, Utah State Historic Preservation Office; *page 284*, Nordic Heritage Museum; *page 305*, Harry Talbot.

Line drawings appear courtesy of the Swedish American Museum Center of Chicago *(page 63)* and the Swedish-American Historical Society of Wisconsin *(page 114)*.

Library of Congress Cataloging-in-Publication Data
Winquist, Alan H.
    Swedish-American landmarks : where to go and what to see / by Alan H. Winquist.
      p.   cm.
    Includes bibliographical references and index.
    ISBN 0-9609620-3-4
    1. Swedish Americans—History. 2. Swedish Americans—Monuments—Guidebooks.
3. Historic sites—United States—Guidebooks. 4. United States—Guidebooks. I. Title.
E184.S23W53 1995
973'.04397—dc20   94-43200

*To the loving memory of Mother, to my Swedish-American family,
and to my living and departed Swedish relatives*

CONTENTS

FOREWORD

The student who in the late 1970s asked Professor Alan Winquist
if he knew of a guidebook describing Swedish-American historic landmarks had his fingers on the pulse of history-minded
Swedish Americans and Swedes traveling in the United States
who wanted to find and to see Sweden in America. Professor
Winquist realized the importance of meeting this need and
filling the gap in the record. Supported by grants from the Nils
William Olsson Fund of the Swedish-American Historical Society and from Dr. Harold Snyder of Michigan, he undertook the
tremendous task of making an inventory of such landmarks.
During the summers of 1981 to 1983 and the fall of 1982, Alan
traveled all over this country from the Atlantic to the Pacific and
from the Mexican border to the Canadian border. He carried
with him notepads and cameras and collected lots of information and photos, which he then put together into a manuscript.

At the meeting of the Swedish Council of America (SCA) in
Houston in March of 1990, I was elected chairman of the
Committee for Cultural Affairs. I then replaced Glen E.
Brolander, who is now the chairman of SCA. From him I
inherited what Glen called "the next great project of the
committee," which was to publish as a book an inventory of
Swedish-American landmarks in the United States. I, too, saw
the value of such a project and decided to devote my and the
committee's efforts to it. The Winquist manuscript was then
almost ten years old, and we were aware of the necessity to
check and to update facts in it and to transform the manuscript
into a guide. At the October meeting of the council, we decided

to hire a professional editor, Beth W. Allen, to work with the author and coordinate the project.

At the SCA board meeting in San Francisco in April 1991 we decided to test the project's feasibility by editing and laying out the smallest chapter in the book and to let the final decision on publishing depend on the outcome of this test. The editor, working together with the author, brought "The South" to a camera-ready form. Finally, at the SCA meeting in Seattle in the fall of 1992, the board, encouraged by the successful result of the edited chapter, decided to go ahead and publish Alan's manuscript after necessary editing and fact checking. We decided to make the publishing a two-year project.

Between 1992 and 1994 a great number of persons from all parts of the country were asked to check facts in the book and to suggest additions and deletions. Almost 75 percent of those asked responded to our questions, and many of them suggested institutions and other persons as resources. I hereby thank all the persons who took part in this fact-checking activity. Despite thorough checking, we are aware that significant people and places may have slipped through our net. Errors and omissions will be corrected in future editions, and we encourage readers to let us know of any they find in the text.

I will also take this opportunity to thank Count Peder Bonde and the Marcus och Amalia Wallenbergs Minnesfond for their generous contribution to underwriting this book. Count Bonde is the chairman of this foundation, and it was on his recommendation the SCA applied for a grant from it.

Finally, I thank all members of the SCA Committee for Cultural Affairs. During all the work on this project, the committee has unanimously supported it and participated in the project with valuable advice. Thanks also to Christopher Olsson, SCA director for publications, who with lots of work and support has participated in this project. Editor Beth Allen contributed her knowledge and expertise to this project, and I thank her for her assistance in bringing the project to fruition.

Last but not least, Alan must be commended for this great work. It fills a gap in the historical record and, in its guidebook form, leads Swedish Americans, Swedes, and others thirsty for more information regarding Swedish immigration to this country and its impact to the evidence that is still with us today.

BIRGER JANSSON, PH.D., CHAIRMAN
COMMITTEE FOR CULTURAL AFFAIRS
SWEDISH COUNCIL OF AMERICA

PREFACE

Twenty years ago, a student of Swedish ancestry in one of my history classes inquired whether a guidebook had ever been written describing existing historic landmarks, such as pioneer homes, churches, schools, hospitals, monuments, and plaques, relating to Swedish immigrants in the United States. The answer was no, and the plan for such a book began to develop.

During the course of three summers and the fall of 1982, I have traveled from the northeast corner of Maine to San Diego, California, and from Seattle, Washington, to Silverhill, Alabama, searching for noteworthy Swedish-American historic buildings and monuments. It has involved visiting thirty-six states plus the District of Columbia for the purpose of identifying Swedish communities, locating landmarks, interviewing people, taking photographs, and gathering information. This material has been incorporated in this volume, which I hope will be useful both to the tourist and the academic community.

This work contains a description of the most significant landmarks, some photographs, and bibliographic sources. I have included, when appropriate, historical background and interesting anecdotes about the sites. Considerations regarding the book's length forced me to limit descriptions of the sites. The book has five main divisions—Northeast, Midwest, Minnesota, South, and West. (Minnesota, though a state and not a region, required special attention because of its importance.) Within the regional divisions, the landmarks are organized according to states.

As I worked my way across the nation, I was struck by the spectrum of historical sites. Swedish Americans maintain an interest in the accomplishments of their forebears and wish to preserve what has been built in the past. This is particularly true in the Midwest and Texas and to a lesser extent in the East. On the West Coast, perhaps because pioneer history is so recent, interest in the Swedish heritage is not nearly as pronounced.

I focused this survey foremost on the homes, the historic towns, and the churches of the Swedish immigration period (1840s to 1920s) and the Delaware River Valley (1600s, 1700s). When immigrants arrived, their first concern, understandably, was to put a roof over their heads. Some original immigrant homes survive, for example, several log cabins in the Delaware Valley dating from the 1600s and restored nineteenth-century log homes in a number of southern, midwestern, and western states. Several homes of prominent Swedish Americans have been preserved and are now museums. These include Carl Sandburg's birthplace (Galesburg, Illinois) and residence (Flat Rock, North Carolina), the Charles A. Lindbergh House (Little Falls, Minnesota), the residence of the musician and composer Howard Hanson (Wahoo, Nebraska), and the homestead of John Morton (Philadelphia). Homes in unique architectural styles, built by Swedish craftsmen, include the Swan Turnblad Mansion (Minneapolis), now the American Swedish Institute, and the Hovander Homestead (Ferndale, Washington).

Historic towns dominated by Swedish immigrants include Bishop Hill, Illinois; Stanton, Iowa; Lindsborg, Marquette, and Scandia, Kansas; New Sweden, Maine; Scandia and Vasa, Minnesota; and Stromsburg, Nebraska. Other communities that are strongly though not exclusively Swedish may be found throughout the nation. Within these and other towns are a number of residential sections, built and owned by Swedes, currently on or being proposed for the National Register of Historic Places.

Religion played an important role in the lives of many Swedish immigrants. After housing was constructed, the early Swedes frequently turned their attention to a church sanctuary. A large number of the old churches survive, though many have been torn down, and most remaining have undergone major alterations through the years. A notable exception is the New Sweden Lutheran Church in New Sweden, Iowa, which is remarkably unchanged since its completion in 1861. Usually a Swedish community not only organized a Lutheran church, but also Covenant and Baptist congregations and sometimes Methodist and Evangelical Free. I have been mainly interested in churches constructed before 1900 (later on the West Coast), concentrating on those still used mainly by Swedish-American congregations. Buildings sold to non-Swedish groups as well as those constructed after World War I are included here if they played a significant historic role in the Swedish-American community or if they contain unique architectural features, particularly Swedish design. Traditional Swedish architectural styles may be noted in such churches as the old Gethsemane Lutheran Church (Austin, Texas), Trinity Lutheran (Worcester, Massachusetts), and Bethany Lutheran (Lindsborg, Kansas). Elements of modern and traditional Swedish architecture may be seen in some of the churches designed by Swedish architect Martin Hedmark, including Trinity Baptist Church in New York City, Gloria Dei Evangelical Lutheran Church in Providence, and Immanuel Evangelical Lutheran Church in Chicago.

From the early days, the Swedish immigrants were concerned with education, health, and old age, and those concerns are reflected in still-existent colleges, hospitals, and retirement centers. At least sixteen schools of higher learning were established by Swedish immigrants, but only six of these colleges— Upsala (East Orange, New Jersey), North Park (Chicago), Augustana (Rock Island, Illinois), Gustavus Adolphus (St. Peter, Minnesota), Bethel (St. Paul), and Bethany (Lindsborg, Kansas)—still survive. The Frank Carlson Library (Concordia, Kansas) and Ericson Memorial Public Library (Boone, Iowa) are two public libraries named for Swedish Americans. The Swedes were very active in the founding of hospitals. Although most were church-related, the Swedish Hospital Medical Center (Seattle) was spearheaded by an individual Swedish immigrant who had a deep concern for health care in that city. Swedish immigrants also created and nurtured retirement homes and orphanages.

In addition to the church, Swedish-oriented fraternal organizations and clubs, including the Vasa Order of America, the Independent Order of Svithiod, the International Organization of Good Templars, and the Independent Order of Vikings, were important to the immigrants. The Vasa Order's archives are in Bishop Hill, Illinois. Of all the currently active clubs, probably the largest is the Swedish Club of Seattle, which has about four thousand members.

Businesses begun by Swedes stretch from coast to coast. For example, Swedish immigrants John Jeppson and Sven Pålson (Swen Pulson) were involved with the founding of the Norton Company of Worcester, Massachusetts, the world's largest maker of abrasives and grinding machinery. In Chicago, Charles R. Walgreen (1873–1939) began a drugstore business that eventually developed into a nationwide chain. Headquartered in Seattle, Nordstrom, Inc., is another example of an enterprise begun by Swedish Americans that flourished. Nordstrom has among its holdings fifty-two large retail stores in

Alaska, California, Illinois, Maryland, Minnesota, New Jersey, Oregon, Utah, Virginia, and Washington.

Chronicling the immigrant experience with renewed interest in the Swedish contribution to American culture and life are a number of Swedish-American museums. The large, well-established American Swedish Historical Museum of Philadelphia and the American Swedish Institute in Minneapolis are outstanding examples. Chicago's Swedish American Museum Center was begun modestly and recently, but in 1987 it was able to purchase a four-story building that multiplied its square footage significantly. Smaller ones are scattered throughout the country in such places as New Sweden, Maine; Scandia, Minnesota; Andover, Illinois; and Scandia, Kansas. The McPherson County Old Mill Museum and Park (Lindsborg, Kansas) includes a number of Swedish-related buildings. Numerous general interest museums also include displays about Swedes along with other ethnic groups. The Nordic Heritage Museum in Seattle focuses on all five Nordic countries. The Institute of Texan Cultures in San Antonio features over two dozen Texas ethnic groups, including an extensive display of Swedish contributions.

Monuments and statues honoring famous Swedes or Swedish Americans and plaques commemorating historic Swedish-American events officially recognize the Swedish contribution. Plaques erected by state, county, religious, educational, and fraternal groups are widely distributed, but Minnesota, Texas, Nebraska, Pennsylvania, Illinois, Kansas, and South Dakota lead in this type of recognition. Historic plaques may describe an entire Swedish settlement or memorialize particular individual settlers. Church markers may commemorate the beginnings of a denomination, an important conference, or a former church building. College historic plaques are found on the Augustana and Gustavus Adolphus campuses. Markers also depict such specific historic events as the founding of New Sweden in the Delaware Valley and the 1862 massacre of Swedish settlers near New London, Minnesota. Perhaps the most unusual location for a plaque is the summit of Pike's Peak in Colorado, where one honors Lindsborg, Kansas, artist Carl Lotave.

Swedish inscriptions on monuments, plaques, church and educational buildings, and gravestones have also drawn my interest (graves of prominent Swedish Americans are included in this survey). Except for inscriptions in cemeteries, these are not all that common. For example, in the past, frequently church congregations placed Swedish inscriptions over altars or pulpits. During the Americanization process of congregations, particularly in the 1920s and 1930s, when English replaced the

Swedish spoken from the pulpit, most Swedish inscriptions were removed. Very few churches retained them.

Art depicting historical events of Sweden or the Swedish immigrants or works that were important to the pioneers, such as church art by artists Olof Grafström and Birger Sandzén, has been recognized here. I have also attempted to locate sculpture created by Swedish or Swedish-American artists, particularly Carl Milles. Paul Granlund, the Swedish-American sculptor who is the artist-in-residence at Gustavus Adolphus College, has works in many parts of the Upper Middle West.

Sites are generally easily accessible; however, one major problem is that many churches, particularly in the large metropolitan areas, are often closed for security reasons. Tragically, some buildings have been vandalized, and others have been torn down, as, for example, the historic Mariadahl Lutheran Church north of Manhattan, Kansas.

Balancing these forces, though, are individuals or small groups spearheading restoration projects. Taking hold is the idea that certain churches and houses are worth saving, though traditionally Swedish Americans have remained all-too-modest in their preservation efforts, reluctant to memorialize what is so familiar to them. Although my project has been frustrating from time to time, it has always been challenging and stimulating. The best part has been meeting interested people of Swedish extraction who not only can identify the historic sites, but also recount fascinating anecdotes concerning them.

My effort has been to compile a listing that is as accurate and as comprehensive as possible; thus, the work of many local fact checkers was necessary. Despite our best efforts, though, it is inevitable that the record will be incomplete. Also, because time passes, people change and so do places. Call before you go to a site (the phone number is usually listed).

In 1988, Americans remembered the 350th anniversary of the Swedish colony in the Delaware Valley, and not unexpectedly this anniversary rekindled interest in our American forebears in general and Swedes in particular. In 1996 the nation will remember the 150th anniversary of the beginnings of the nineteenth-century Swedish immigration. I offer this guidebook as an aid to those who wish to uncover and learn more about the Swedish-American heritage.

ACKNOWLEDGMENTS

Producing a book like this one, with the research and writing stretching over more than a decade, requires work that never seems to be finalized. Likewise, when it is completed, the list of people who deserve heartfelt thanks for their help is also never ending.

Dr. Harold Snyder of Mancelona, Michigan, and the Nils William Olsson Fund of the Swedish-American Historical Society helped financially with my research. Dr. Nils William Olsson was also kind enough to review the text. I owe both Dr. Snyder and Dr. Olsson many thanks. Warren Feece of Chesterton, Indiana, an alumnus of Taylor University, where I teach, deserves thanks for giving me the idea for this project.

I owe particular acknowledgment to Taylor professor Dr. Jessica Rousselow, of Upland, Indiana, who has been of great support throughout this project.

The following four people gave special encouragement and help: the late Dr. Wesley Westerberg of Chicago; the late Dr. Walter G. Johnson and his wife, Ruth, of Clinton, Washington; and the late Rolf Erickson of Evanston, Illinois.

Dr. Birger Jansson of Houston, chairman of the Swedish Council of America's Committee for Cultural Affairs, provided outstanding support in getting the manuscript published, and Beth W. Allen, also of Houston, lent her superb editing skills to the task. Extremely helpful was Chris Olsson of the Swedish Council of America in Minneapolis, whose conscientious advice was much appreciated.

Dr. Peter Stebbins Craig and Dr. Richard Hulan lent their considerable expertise to reviewing the Delaware Valley section.

Those who were particularly helpful in giving me clues to various historic landmarks and assisting with the research include the late William Ahrendt of Porter, Indiana; David Anderson of New Sweden, Maine; Dr. Philip J. Anderson of Chicago; Dr. and Mrs. H. Arnold Barton of Carbondale, Illinois; Dr. Conrad Bergendoff of Rock Island, Illinois; Glen E. Brolander of Salem, South Carolina; Ann Barton Brown of Philadelphia; the Rev. Thomas G. Bruner of Grassflat, Pennsylvania; Alice Carlson of Millbury, Massachusetts; Tom Carter of Salt Lake City; Esther Chilstrom-Meixner of Philadelphia; James Christianson of Austin, Texas; Siri Eliason of San Francisco; Dr. Paul H. Elmen, of Woodstock, Connecticut; Anna Engquist of Scandia, Minnesota; Carrie Floto of the Bishop Hill Heritage Association in Bishop Hill, Illinois; Marianne Forssblad of the Nordic Heritage Museum in Seattle; Mr. and Mrs. Ted Forssman of Silverhill, Alabama; Mr. and Mrs. Wilbur Gustafson of Oak Lawn, Illinois; Betty Jane Highfield of Chicago; and Selma Jacobson of Chicago.

Others especially helpful include John Jeppson of Brookfield, Massachusetts; Elna Sue Johanson of Whittier, California; Randolph Johnson of Cambridge, Minnesota; Camille Julin of Bridgeton, New Jersey; Nancy Kahlich of Chicago; Alvalene P. Karlsson, the editor of *Nordstjernan* in New York; Bruce Karstadt in Minneapolis; Kerstin Lane of the Swedish American Museum Center of Chicago; Raymond Lane of New York; the late Dr. Emory Lindquist of Wichita, Kansas; the late Rev. Joel Lundeen of the Lutheran School of Theology in Chicago; Bertil Lundh of Seattle; Dr. Brian Magnusson of Fox Island, Washington; the Rev. and Mrs. J. Murray Marshall of Seattle; Dr. Wesley Matson of Minneapolis; Ronald E. Nelson of Bishop Hill; Dr. Byron Nordstrom of Le Sueur, Minnesota; the late Judge William Peterson of Cadillac, Michigan; Karna Olsson of Orano, Maine; Mr. and Mrs. A. John Pearson of Lindsborg, Kansas; Lennart and Lily Setterdahl of Moline, Illinois; Margaretha Talerman of Philadelphia; Mrs. Louis Titus of Holdrege, Nebraska; and Dean Wahlund of St. Peter, Minnesota.

I also thank Taylor University Professor Jerry Hodson and David Nixon, his former student assistant, now a Taylor alumnus, who kindly printed hundreds of my photographs.

Fact checkers across the country responded to the request to help make the text as comprehensive and up-to-date as possible. The following contributed to that effort: Roy Anderson of Burbank, California; Mary J. Bajuniemi of Lake Norden, South Dakota; Barbara Reynolds Barbour of San Antonio; Bonnie Bloom and Jane Wickham of the Swedish Museum of Swedesburg, Iowa; Betty Bruner of Mitchell, South Dakota;

Eiler Cook of Hendersonville, North Carolina; the Rev. Paul
Cornell of Collegeville, Pennsylvania; Donald H. Erickson of
Omaha; Mark Esping and the Folklife Institute of Central
Kansas in Lindsborg; Robert Falk of Omaha; Ross Fogelquist of
Portland, Oregon; Robert Fraser of Warwick, Rhode Island;
Philip Graham of St. Louis; Victor Hedman of Franklin, Wis-
consin; Gerald E. C. Heglund of Jamestown, New York; Dwight
Holcombe of Elk River, Minnesota; Diane Johnson of Groton,
South Dakota; Ronald Johnson of Vermillion, South Dakota;
Florence Leen of New Effington, South Dakota; Marilyn Lorenz
of West Des Moines, Iowa; Dr. Holger Lundin of Terryville,
Connecticut; the late Bert M. Magnuson of Lakeway, Texas;
John Herman Pearson of Swedesburg, Missouri; Perry Pearson
of Winterset, Iowa; Ruby Perez of the Abilene [Texas] Preser-
vation League; Donald A. Peterson of Stanton, Iowa; Rudolph
Peterson of San Francisco; Helen A. Quirk of Hastings, Ne-
braska; Rita Rosedahl of Jamestown; Patricia M. Schroeder of
Park Falls, Wisconsin; sisters Rose and Ruth Setterberg of
Boston; Armer Severin of Rockford, Illinois; the Rev. Larry D.
Smith of Axtell, Nebraska; Pauline Swenson of Mediapolis
Iowa; Les Wassberg of Fargo, North Dakota; Jack Wilson of
Piedmont, South Dakota; and Elaine Winsor of Red Wing,
Minnesota.

In Minnesota, fact checkers especially helpful in reviewing
pages and answering questions were Mark Belay of Stillwater,
Mildrid and Ethel Collins of Vasa, Paul Daniels of Minneapolis,
Helen Fosdick of Lindstrom, Linda Franzen of Minneapolis,
Lynne Moratzka of Scandia, and Marilyn McGriff of Cam-
bridge.

Others in Minnesota who answered questions about sites
were Kris Anderson of Forest Lake, Valorie Arrowsmith of
Cambridge, Irene Bender of Cokato, Sandy Berglund of Afton,
the Rev. Edward Blair of Buffalo, Ethel Bradbury of Nelson,
Ernest Carlson of Minneapolis, Jean Coffey of Hinckley, Joan
Daniels of Stillwater, the Rev. Michael Dobbins of Vasa, Anne
Eklund of Marine on St. Croix, Hazel Gronquist of Scandia,
Barbara Grover of Alexandria, Inez Gunberg of Minneapolis,
the Rev. Allan Johnson of Gibbon, Philip Johnson of Pennock,
the Rev. Robert Kruger of Carver, May Mequire of Center City,
Nancy Moore of Stillwater, Mona Nelson of Willmar, Bill Scott
of Taylors Falls, E. W. Solyst of Kirkhoven, Lynn Strong of
Almelund, David Swanson of Minneapolis, and Holger Warner
of Harris.

Finally, I would like to thank Taylor University for granting
me two sabbatical leaves to research and to write this guidebook
and the members of the history department for their support.

1 The Northeast

DELAWARE

WILMINGTON A guidebook to Swedish-American landmarks may fittingly begin with the city of Wilmington and specifically with Fort Christina State Park (302/739-4266) on Seventh Street adjacent to the Christina River, which flows into the Delaware. It was here on 26 March 1638 that the first Swedes landed in North America, establishing the New Sweden Colony. Nothing remains of the fort built by the Swedes, though the state park, located on the original site, is on the National Register of Historic Places. The park commemorates the expedition led by Peter Minuit and his two ships, the *Kalmar Nyckel* and the *Fogel Grip*. On 27 June 1938, a monument designed and created by Swedish sculptor Carl Milles was dedicated in the presence of President Franklin D. Roosevelt, Crown Prince Gustav Adolf, Crown Princess Louise, and Prince Bertil. It is a hexagon of black Swedish granite surmounted by a stylized wave bearing the *Kalmar Nyckel*. On the granite shaft are inscriptions and bas-reliefs depicting various historical events of the seventeenth century pertaining to the New Sweden Colony.

Along the walk on a brick wall approaching the Milles monument are numerous historic plaques. Also in the park is a log cabin. The plaques read in part: "The log cabin—unknown to

1

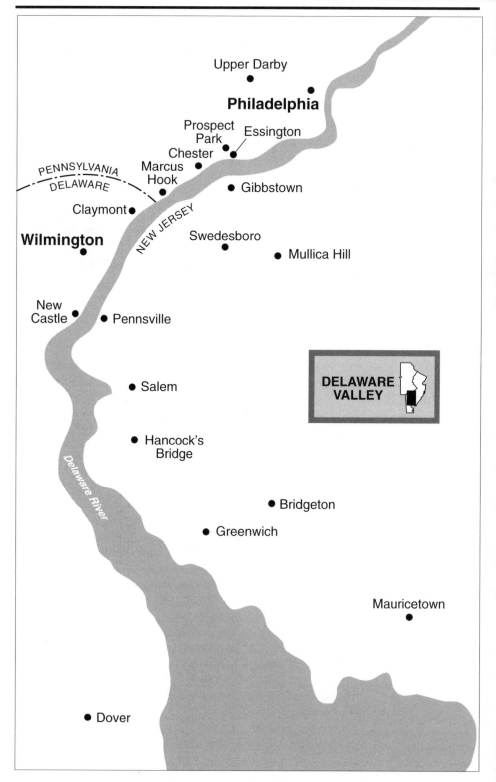

first English, Dutch settlers. Introduced into America from Sweden here at Ft. Christina. Cheap, quickly and easily built, it was an ideal pioneer home. Spread to the Pacific with westward settlement. Several different log construction techniques developed later, some were Swedish, some of other origins.

"This cabin is the early Swedish type with rough-hewn round logs saddle-notched at the ends, chinked with sticks, twigs, and grass-mixed clay. It has one large room with a fireplace and a huge shelf above for extra sleeping and storage space."

Several seventeenth-century Swedish log cabins still stand in the Delaware Valley. This particular log cabin was moved to and reconstructed in the park in 1963.

At the end of Seventh Street at the confluence of the Christina and Brandywine Rivers is the East Seventh Street Park, a historical park opened in 1988. In the park, which is open from 7 A.M. until dusk, stands a partial replica of Fort Christina.

In recent years, a replica of the *Kalmar Nyckel* was being constructed at the Kalmar Nyckel Shipyard, 1124 East Seventh Street (302/429-SHIP), where tours were offered by appointment. The small Kalmar Nyckel Museum Institute at 823 East Seventh Street (302/429-0350) tells in part the history of Wilmington and the Delaware Valley with special emphasis on New Sweden.

Holy Trinity (Old Swedes) Church, at 606 Church Street (Seventh and Church streets), was erected in 1698-99, making it the oldest sanctuary in the United States still standing as originally built and continuing to hold regular religious services (held on Sundays and Wednesdays; call 302/652-5629). The church, listed on the National Register of Historic Places, is open 1–4 Monday, Wednesday, Friday, and Saturday. On Saturday volunteers act as guides. Established in 1638, the church initially conducted services in Fort Christina. In 1667, the Lutheran community built a new church two miles to the south at Crane Hook, which was more convenient for the many Swedes and Finns on that side of the Christina River. The wooden church at Crane Hook was in use for thirty years. Its former site, west of the intersection of Pigeon Point Road with the railroad spur serving the Castlewood Industrial Park, is indicated by a stone marker on the grounds of an oil refinery.

In 1697, three Church of Sweden missionaries—Jonas Aurén, Eric Björk, and Andreas Rudman—arrived, and on Trinity Sunday, 4 July 1699, the present church was consecrated. It remained a Swedish Lutheran congregation until 1791 when it was transferred to the Protestant Episcopal Church. There are seven "Old Swedes" churches remaining in the Delaware Valley in Wilmington; Pennsville and Swedesboro, New Jersey; and Philadelphia, Kingsessing, Upper Merion, and

Construction of Holy Trinity (Old Swedes) Church in Wilmington, Delaware, was completed in 1699.

Douglassville, Pennsylvania—and all were to become Episcopalian in time.

The sanctuary contains some historically significant items, including the original raised, canopied pulpit, made of black walnut and believed to be the oldest in the United States. The brick in the aisles and the hinges on the main door were imported from Sweden. The communion silver was presented to the church in 1718 by Stora Kopparbergs Bergslags Aktiebolag of Falun, Dalarna, the district that Björk served as pastor after he left Delaware.

Graves may be found inside and outside the church. The grave of Peter Tranberg, an early pastor of the Swedish congregation, is just outside the altar rail's center opening. In the cross-aisle is the burial site of Peter Abraham Acrelius, the infant son of the last Swedish pastor of Old Swedes. The child died of whooping cough in 1786. In the south porch under the steps to the balcony is the grave of Carl Christopherson Springer (1658–1738), who was head warden to Pastor Björk. The graveyard surrounding the church contains several graves of historic significance, but most buried in the cemetery were settlers of English descent. Early wooden markers have disappeared.

On the belfry is a plaque noting the Holy Trinity (Old Swedes) Church in 1963 was officially given national historic landmark status. Vice President Lyndon B. Johnson presented this plaque to the church, and Prince Bertil of Sweden along with numerous state and city officials attended the ceremony.

On the opposite side of the cemetery from the church is Hendrickson House, which is open the same hours as the church. The stone house was built in 1690 for Andrew Hendrickson, a young Swedish farmer, and his wife, Brigitta, daughter of Mårten Mårtensson. In 1959, the seventeenth-century house was moved to the present site because its original location was developed for industry. One of the two rooms on the first floor is a gift shop. In the other can be seen the Hendrickson family Bible, the 1722 will of Hendrickson, and a model of the *Kalmar Nyckel* presented to Wilmington by the Maritime Museum of Gothenburg, Sweden. Also on display are paintings of the church and the altar cloth presented in 1950 by the Swedish ambassador to the United States on behalf of the king of Sweden. At age 92, King Gustav V partially embroidered the central cross. The large fireplace contains the original mantel. On the second floor is the church office. Although the house has been extensively restored, the walls are original.

CLAYMONT

On the property of the Robinson House (No. 1 Naaman's Road at Philadelphia Pike, 302/792-0285) at the extreme northeastern tip of the state, stands a small one and one-half–story structure locally known as the "Swedish Blockhouse." This is somewhat misleading, inasmuch as the house is not made of the horizontal timbering that defines a blockhouse in Sweden. Narrow slits in the stonework of the upper level have been interpreted as rifle ports, but they may have had a more prosaic ventilating function. The interior has a Swedish-style corner fireplace to which a separately roofed external beehive oven was attached. Some sources have identified this structure with New

Sweden's last governor, Johan Rising. His residence was built on Timber Island, seven miles closer to Fort Christina and overlooking it from just across the Brandywine River. The blockhouse is listed on the National Register of Historic Places, and authorities believe it may be the oldest surviving building in the state. Nearby on Naaman's Creek is a state historic plaque that claims that in 1655 the local Native American chief deeded the land along the creek to Rising. Gustavus Hesselius and Adolf Ulrik Wertmüller, both noted Swedish artists, lived on plantations on this creek.

NEW CASTLE

The settlement that became New Castle began as Fort Casimir, which was erected by the Dutch in 1651 and taken by the Swedes on Trinity Sunday, 1654. They renamed it Fort Trefaldighet (Fort Trinity), but the Dutch reclaimed it the next year. The state historical marker for the fort is on Chestnut, between Second Street and the Delaware River. English rule, first under the Duke of York and later under William Penn, succeeded that of the Dutch in 1664. New Castle is one of the most important towns in America to have survived with its colonial appearance relatively intact; many fine homes date from the eighteenth and early nineteenth centuries. The pulpit of Immanuel Church (Episcopal) here was frequently occupied by visiting Swedish pastors from its beginning. The oldest part of the present church dates from 1703.

DOVER

In the Delaware Agricultural Museum at 866 North DuPont Highway (U.S. Highway 13) (302/734-1618) is a one-room Swedish-style log house. Seven logs in height, the house has a low entry door, three windows, a loft, and a brick fireplace and is decorated with seventeenth-century furnishings.

NEW JERSEY

SWEDESBORO

What is today southern New Jersey was also part of the colony of New Sweden. Several Swedish historic sites remain, particularly in and around Swedesboro, which was originally called *Raccoon*.

For years, the early Swedes of southern New Jersey crossed the Delaware River to attend religious services in present-day Delaware or Pennsylvania. In 1702, a log structure was built on the banks of Raccoon Creek, and Trinity Episcopal (Old Swedes) Church became the first Swedish Lutheran church in New Jersey. The present two-story red brick Georgian-style structure was built between 1784 and 1786, having been designed by the Rev. Nicholas Collin, who at the time was pastor of this congregation. The church stands at 208 Kings Highway (northwest corner of Church Street and Kings Highway, which is also known as County Road 551) (609/467-1227). The church was topped in 1838 by a five-story tower. The white interior has a balcony on three sides. In the rear of the sanctuary is a Swedish flag and a plaque unveiled by Prince Bertil in June 1938 in commemoration of the three hundredth anniversary of the Swedish settlement on the Delaware. When King Carl XVI Gustaf visited Swedesboro and the church on 8 April 1976, a granite marker with a plaque was unveiled in front of the church describing the construction of the first sanctuary. The church is listed on the National Register of Historic Places.

The VanLear–Schorn cabin, on the churchyard's north end, and the C. A. Nothnagle Log House, both seventeenth-century log cabins, were built by Swedes in the vicinity of Swedesboro. The VanLear–Schorn log cabin was acquired by the Gloucester County Historical Society and moved to the churchyard. It is a twelve- by fifteen-foot windowless cabin that dates from the early eighteenth century. Originally it was located a mile down Raccoon Creek on Swedesboro-Bridgeport Road on land purchased by Mårten Mårtensson, who came to New Sweden in 1654. Because of massive insect damage and weathering, roughly half of the log timbering required replacement. The work was carefully and skillfully done when the cabin was moved to its new site.

The C. A. Nothnagle Log House (406 Swedesboro Road in Gibbstown, New Jersey), listed on the National Register of Historic Places, is believed to have been built shortly after the first Swedish settlers arrived in America. The exact date of construction is not known, though a plaque on the cabin claims that it was built between 1638 and 1643. Leading authorities on the settlement history of Gloucester County consider this impossible and suggest as more probable a date closer to 1680 and either Israel Helm or Benjamin Bramman as the first owner. Attached to the sixteen- by twenty-two–foot cabin of dovetailed, hand-hewn logs is a house built between 1730 and 1750. Privately owned, it contains a corner fireplace and can be seen by appointment (609/423-0916).

PENNSVILLE   A Swedish congregation purchased land and constructed a church, which was dedicated in March 1717. But when the Rev. Nicholas Collin visited the parish in 1770, he noted that the congregation demonstrated few distinctively Swedish characteristics. Twenty-four years later, it became Episcopalian. The present small red brick church, now known as St. George's Episcopal Church, was built in 1808 to replace the earlier Swedish log structure. Immediately south of the Delaware

Memorial Bridge on State Highway 49 (305 North Broadway), the church, which has an adjoining cemetery, may be visited by appointment (609/678-7979). To the east of the main church door is a plaque commemorating the earliest Finns in the United States.

BRIDGETON

In commemoration of the 350th anniversary of the New Sweden Colony, a reproduction of a seventeenth-century farmstead of the type built by the early Swedish colonists was constructed in Bridgeton City Park on Mayor Aiken Drive near Commerce Street (609/455-9785). This crowned the efforts of the New Sweden Company that had begun in 1983 and were successfully completed just in time for the anniversary celebrations. An ongoing organization of volunteers, the company was chaired through its early years by the late Thorsten Karlsson, for whom the museum was a consuming dream. Karlsson, a native of Eskilstuna who became a New Jersey businessman, was active in many Swedish-American causes. Partly through his influence, Bridgeton and Eskilstuna became sister cities.

Called the New Sweden Farmstead Museum, the site features seven log dwellings and outbuildings, including the residence; horse barn; sheep, cow, and goat barn; threshing barn; smokehouse; blacksmith shop with sod roof; and a storage building. The Swedish historic preservation society Riksförbundet för Hembygdsvård was actively engaged in the design (by Gunnar Zetterqvist of Dala-Floda, Dalarna) and furnishing of the farmstead. Zetterqvist also supervised its construction, assisted by Severin Johansson and several American laborers. King Carl XVI Gustaf and Queen Silvia dedicated the museum 14 April 1988 and presented candleholders to the museum for display in the residence. A living history museum, the farmstead teaches seventeenth-century crafts and in the residence displays an eighteenth-century loom and mangles for pressing clothes.

The museum is closed from Labor Day through Memorial Day, except for special tours arranged for schools and similar organizations during May and September. During its open season, the museum welcomes visitors Wednesday through Sunday, and staff members lead hourly tours.

MAURICETOWN

In Mauricetown, at the corner of Second and South streets, is the Caesar Hoskins Log House, an early eighteenth-century dwelling built of dovetailed logs. Privately owned (609/785-1828) and located in the former Maurice River Swedish community, this structure is of interest because of an incised drawing of a schooner on an interior wall. The image is the symbol for the New Sweden Farmstead Museum in Bridgeton.

The Swedish Granary, built about 1650 by Swedes in the Delaware Valley, rests on the grounds of the Cumberland County Historical Society in Greenwich, New Jersey.

GREENWICH

The Swedish Granary found behind the Gibbon House in Greenwich is considered to be the sole surviving example of a farm building erected by the early Swedes in the Delaware Valley. Built of cedar logs, the granary was originally located in the Lower Hopewell Township in the direction of Bridgeton, and it was moved four miles to its present location, the grounds of the Gibbon House on Main, or Greate, Street. This restored mansion is the headquarters of the Cumberland County Historical Society (609/455-8580). A log partition divides the granary into two areas. The structure contains one large front door for wagons as well as a smaller one. The charming town of Greenwich, established in 1675, has been placed on the National Register of Historic Places because of its unique colonial architecture.

MULLICA HILL

Eric and John Mullica, sons of Swedish pioneer Eric Mullica, settled the community of Mullica Hill, which has become a mecca for collectors of antiques and handicrafts. The Mullica family came to America from Sweden, but in the seventeenth century there were recent immigrants there from another Mullica Hill: Mullikannäki, near the present town of Pylkönmäki in central Finland.

HANCOCK'S
BRIDGE

A Swedish log house, which formerly stood within the corporate limits of Salem, was moved to the grounds of the Hancock

House in 1933. This dwelling is preserved to commemorate a massacre by British troops in 1778, unrelated to the early presence of Swedish colonists in Salem County. It stands in the hamlet of Hancock's Bridge, on the southwest side of the Salem–Hancock's Bridge Road, between Front Street and New Street. Remodeled and whitewashed in 1975 when converted to house public restrooms, it retains little of its original residential appearance.

SALEM

Near Salem on the Fort Elfsborg-Salem Road near the Delaware River are two historic markers commemorating Fort Elfsborg. The official New Jersey state plaque notes: "Not far from here on the New Jersey side of the Delaware River in 1643, the Swedes erected an earthwork fort with three angles on order of Governor Johan Printz to control the River. It was commanded by Lieutenant Sven Skute, and was abandoned in 1651." In front of the Elsinboro School is a white stone plaque erected in 1988: "This memorial is presented by the citizens of Gothenburg, Sweden, to Elsinboro Township and the People of New Jersey, from the wall of the original Fort Elfsborg at Gothenburg. It honors those who served 1643–1653 at Fort Elfsborg on Elsinboro Point, and left the lasting legacy of the New Sweden Colony."

EAST ORANGE

Upsala College, at Springdale and Prospect (201/266-7000), was founded in 1893 and named for the Uppsala decree officially establishing the Lutheran creed of the Church of Sweden three hundred years earlier. The first classes were held in the Bethlehem Lutheran Church in Brooklyn. Sixteen students were enrolled during the first year. Dr. Lars Herman Beck was president during the college's first seventeen years, overseeing the move to New Orange (now Kenilworth), New Jersey. In 1924, Upsala moved to its present forty-five–acre campus in East Orange, sixteen miles from New York City. In the fall of 1979, a second campus (Wirths) was opened in Wantage in New Jersey's Sussex County. The school has planned to build a full-service campus there on 240 acres of farmland.

Many of the twentieth-century Georgian buildings on the East Orange campus were designed by Jens Fredrick Larson (1891–1982), who was born in Boston of Swedish-Danish parents. Larson was also responsible for designing other college and university buildings in the United States and overseas, including buildings at Dartmouth (Hanover, New Hampshire), Colby College (Waterville, Maine), Wake Forest University (Winston-Salem, North Carolina), and the Institute for Advanced Study at Princeton University (Princeton, New Jersey). Some Upsala College buildings are named for Swedish Americans or Swedes, including Beck Hall (built in 1949, honoring Upsala's first president), Bremer Hall (a residence hall honoring nineteenth-century Swedish writer Fredrika Bremer), Froeberg North and South Residence Halls (Dr. Peter Froeberg was Upsala's second president and claimed he was the first student to register in 1893), Nelsenius Hall (the Rev. Gustav Nelsenius was the first chairman of the board of trustees), and the Agnes Wahlström College Center (named for a Swedish-born donor). In the lobby of Kenbrook Hall (formerly the Hathaway Mansion, it houses the offices of the president and dean of the college) are photographs of the present king and queen of Sweden; photographs of two former kings; and an eighteenth-century desk, handmade in Sweden, that once belonged to opera singer Blanche Thebom (of Swedish ancestry). In Christ Chapel is the Nicholas Collin Room, named for the Swedish missionary and clergyman of the Delaware Valley in the late eighteenth and early nineteenth centuries.

Upsala was formerly under the Augustana Lutheran Synod until the merger in 1963 when it became affiliated with the Evangelical Lutheran Church in America.

KEARNY

First Lutheran Church, at 63 Oakwood Avenue (201/991-1623), was organized in 1890 and originally called The Swedish Evangelical Lutheran Church of Gustavus Vasa. A frame church had been built in 1891 but was replaced in 1930 by the present brick sanctuary designed by Swedish architect Martin Hedmark (1896–1980). One enters the church through a separate red brick bell tower containing a parabolic arch and a curved hood-shaped base topped by a pointed steeple with a slate roof.

The interior of the sanctuary has a pine ceiling in the shape of a ship's hull. In the center of the ceiling are painted designs reminiscent of modified Viking art. Three wood beams as well as the ceiling over the chancel also include similar stenciled motifs. The raised light wood pulpit trimmed in painted gold is surmounted by a canopy.

BUDD LAKE

The New Jersey Vasa Home and Park (201/691-8383) in Budd Lake is a 126-acre site purchased in 1936. On Wolfe Road, the park contains recreational facilities, summer cabins, and retirement homes operated by the twenty lodges of District 6, one of the more active divisions of the Vasa Order of America.

PENNSYLVANIA

The Swedish-American landmarks of Pennsylvania can be divided between those in the eastern and western parts of the state. In the east, many sites are associated with the seventeenth-century New Sweden colony. In contrast, the history of the northwest region, including Chandlers Valley–Sugar Grove, is part of the nineteenth-century immigration story and intertwines with that of nearby Jamestown, New York.

PHILADELPHIA

INSTITUTES AND MUSEUMS

American Swedish Historical Museum—1900 Pattison Avenue (in Franklin Delano Roosevelt Park). Open Tuesday through Friday 10–4, Saturday and Sunday 12–4. Closed Monday and holidays (215/389-1776).

The American Swedish Historical Museum is one of the two largest museums in the United States devoted to Swedish-American culture (the other is the American Swedish Institute in Minneapolis). The museum, organized in 1926 to preserve and record the accomplishments of Swedish Americans with particular emphasis on the Swedish heritage in the Delaware Valley, was founded and first guided by Dr. Amandus Johnson. Johnson wanted the museum to be a national repository of Swedish culture in the United States—a place where famous Swedes and Swedish Americans from the Delaware colony's times to the present could be immortalized. Although his grandiose plan has not reached complete fruition, the museum contains an impressive, diverse collection.

The museum is housed in the John Morton Memorial Building. This memorial was Swedish America's contribution to the larger sesquicentennial celebration of the Declaration of Independence, of which John Morton was a Pennsylvania signer. In 1926, Crown Prince Gustav Adolf laid the cornerstone. Not only was the year 1938 the three hundredth anniversary of Swedes in America, but it was also the grand opening of the museum, which was attended by Crown Princess Louise and Prince Bertil. The museum's exterior design by John Nydén, a Swedish American from Chicago, is based on the seventeenth-century Eriksberg Manor in Södermanland, Sweden.

In the late 1980s, the museum was reorganized in an effort to make it a more effective educational and cultural center. On the first floor, the impressive grand entrance hall features three large frescoes of historic subjects painted in 1928 by Swedish artist Christian von Schneidau. The ceiling painting illustrates the arrival of Swedish settlers to the Delaware Valley aboard the *Kalmar Nyckel*. One of the two wall paintings depicts John Morton, a descendant of original Swedish settlers, signing the Declaration of Independence and the other features Swedish army officer Axel von Fersen who was present at the surrender of Lord Cornwallis at the battle of Yorktown in 1781.

The American Swedish Historical Museum, designed by John Nydén, was completed in 1938.

In the George and Marion Anderson Wing is a gallery devoted to special exhibits and a Golden Map Room, where visitors may imagine themselves in the middle of the Baltic Sea surrounded by Sweden's seventeenth-century empire. In the Colonial Room, designed originally by Hans Asplund of Stockholm in 1959 and reinstalled in 1988, the theme is the daily life of the Swedish colonists among the Lenape Indians. The Sinnickson family chest came from Sweden in the seventeenth century. Another room, known as the Stuga, is a somewhat idealized view of the interior of a nineteenth-century Swedish farmhouse. Important features of this room are the Swedish corner fireplace, a functioning floor loom, and a seventeenth-century trestle table. The Immigrant Room focuses on nineteenth-century and early twentieth-century Swedes who settled in the Middle West. The photographs are drawn from the museum's extensive collection, which was begun by Amandus Johnson. "The Immigrants" is a bronze sculpture by Charles (Carl) Oscar Haag (1867–1933). The spinning wheel from the 1880s was used by Dr. Johnson's grandmother in Minnesota, and the log cabin model was built in northern Sweden in 1964. The New Sweden Room has small sculptures by Carl Milles entitled "Johan Printz" and "The Printz Group." The John Hanson Room has display cases featuring archaeology at the "Printzhof" on Tinicum Island and artifacts of the type that would have been found in most homes or the fort in the New Sweden colony. These artifacts are on loan from several museums and individuals. Also on the first floor are the gift shop and the Nord Memorial Library, which has twenty thousand volumes available to researchers by appointment.

The second-floor balcony features paintings (members of the Swedish royal family, scenes from Sweden, and the American West) and sculptures (bronze busts of Carl Sandburg and August Strindberg) by well-known Swedish and Swedish-American artists (e.g., Carl Oscar Borg, Birger Sandzén) along with a selection of Swedish furniture. On the second floor is the Kalm-Seaborg Room, featuring Swedish and Lapp costumes and glass by Orrefors and Reijmyre Glassworks. Named for the nineteenth-century Swedish writer and advocate of women's and human rights, the Fredrika Bremer Room is dedicated to the accomplishments of Swedish women, including Bremer (1801–65), author Selma Lagerlöf (1858–1940), and humanitarian nurse Elsa Brändström (1888–1948). The room is furnished as a mid-nineteenth-century Swedish parlor and evokes the feeling of the salon of Lagerlöf's Värmland home at Mårbacka and Bremer's home at Årsta. The Jenny Lind Room contains two works by Carl Larsson (1889–1959), the watercolor "My Bedroom" and a large-scale cartoon for a tapestry called "Kräftfisket" ("Crayfishing"). There are also several etchings by Swedish painter and sculptor Anders Zorn (1860–1920).

The Chicago Room, designed in 1936, features a wood inlay mural by Swedish artist Ewald Dahlskog (1894–1950), portraying the work of Swedish-American bricklayers, carpenters, and architects. Included in the mural are John Nydén, who designed the American Swedish Historical Museum, and Andrew Lanquist, who founded the prestigious Chicago construction firm of Lanquist and Illsley at the beginning of the twentieth century and built Chicago's first skyscraper.

The John Ericsson Room I, designed by Martin Hedmark in 1938, is in an art deco style. Wall murals by Swedish artist Olle Hjortzberg show Ericsson presenting his design for the iron-clad *Monitor* to Abraham Lincoln's war cabinet and the subsequent battle between the *Monitor* and the *Merrimac*. The John

Ericsson Room II, renovated in 1988, features several examples of Ericsson's designs and inventions. The Swedenborg Room highlights the life and work of Emanuel Swedenborg—inventor, philosopher, and theologian.

In addition to school programs, the American Swedish Historical Museum sponsors special events, including Midsommarfest in mid-June, a crayfish party in August, and Lucia Fest and Julmarknad (a Christmas market) in early December.

HISTORIC PLACES

City Hall—Market and Broad streets (215/686-1776).

City Hall occupies all of Penn Square, at the intersection of Market and Broad streets. This square was at the center of the original seventeenth-century Philadelphia city plan, though Market was formerly called High Street. A historic plaque at City Hall commemorates the Swedish settlements on the Delaware River. It lists the four Swedish governors of New Sweden and other prominent settlers.

Near the top of City Hall (below the large statue of William Penn that surmounts the building) is a sculpture of a woman holding a child, representing early Swedish settlers in Pennsylvania. The official flag of Philadelphia is in the blue and yellow of the Swedish flag in recognition of the first settlers to come here.

Governor Printz Park—Taylor Avenue and Second Street (Essington).

The seven-acre park on Tinicum Island (now Essington) on the western shore of the Delaware River, is the site of the capital of New Sweden from 1643 to 1654, making it the first European settlement in what is today Pennsylvania. It consisted of Fort New Gothenburg, a log chapel, simple wood houses for the settlers, and the house of Governor Johan Printz (1592–1663), which was known as the Printzhof. It was built of hewn logs, probably two stories in height. Although none of these buildings survive, the stone foundation of the Printzhof was uncovered in 1937 archaeological excavations and may be seen in the park. Additional archaeological work was done in the late 1980s and early 1990s, and the site is on the National Register of Historic Places. An imposing bronze statue of Printz by Carl Lindborg looks over the level waterfront park on the Delaware. The site is administered by the Pennsylvania Historical and Museum Commission, which erected interpretive display panels and created a paved pathway that functions as a kind of historical hopscotch game for children.

To the east of the park is a yacht club, at whose gate is a large stone monument commemorating Governor Printz. At the main entrance to the clubhouse is a plaque, noting the location of the chapel of Fort New Gothenburg and the burial ground. The large stone beneath the plaque was the step of the chapel. It is not widely known or advertised that this was the first regularly consecrated house of worship for Lutherans in America. Its few surviving artifacts are preserved in Gloria Dei Church in Philadelphia.

A historic marker outside the Tinicum Township Memorial Building on Fourth Street (not far from Governor Printz Park) notes that Tinicum, the first permanent settlement in Pennsylvania, was founded in 1643 by Johan Printz.

Lower Swedish Cabin—Darby Creek—Upper Darby Township, on Creek Road near Dennison Avenue (215/284-0256 or 215/259-4753).
This one and one-half–story log structure, owned by the Upper Darby Township, was constructed in the seventeenth century. Originally the cabin consisted of one twenty- by fifteen-foot room with a corner fireplace and a large stone mantle. At a later date, an addition, also made of logs, was constructed—this part also has a corner fireplace. Earlier this century, the Lower Swedish Cabin's interior was plastered and covered with wallpaper, and electricity was installed. It was owned by a hosiery mill across Darby Creek and was rented to various employees who whitewashed its outer walls. In the 1930s the Upper Darby Township took possession, hoping to preserve the cabin as a historical site.

The Lower Swedish Cabin was placed on the National Register of Historic Places in 1982. Its extensive restoration, begun in 1986, was completed in 1989. A voluntary caretaker organization, The Friends of the Swedish Cabin, maintains it. Nearby, another log cabin known as the Upper Swedish Cabin had managed to survive until the 1980s when a fire destroyed it.

Morton Homestead—100 Lincoln Avenue (on Darby Creek north of Governor Printz Park), Prospect Park (215/583-7221).
From Interstate 95, exit at State Highway 420, and follow signs to Morton Homestead. (State Highway 420 is called Lincoln Avenue in Prospect Park and Wanamaker Avenue in Tinicum Township.)

Administered by the Pennsylvania Historical and Museum Commission and the American Swedish Historical Museum, the Morton Homestead, begun by Swedish settler Mårten Mårtensson, features two seventeenth-century Swedish log houses. For many years, the property remained in the hands of the family, the most famous member being the great-grandson of Mårtensson, John Morton (1727–77), a signer of the Declaration

The Lower Swedish Cabin, built in the seventeenth century, is maintained by The Friends of the Swedish Cabin, a volunteer organization.

of Independence. The homestead is on the National Register of Historic Places.

One part of the Morton Homestead dates from 1654. An adjacent building was constructed in 1698. Both were originally one story. In the late 1790s or early 1800s, the two buildings were connected by stone walls, and a higher roof added, thus creating a half story above the cabins. In 1835, some alterations were made to the upstairs room. The house contains late seventeenth-century furniture. The date 1698 is carved on the fireplace in the newer cabin. The earlier cabin was built of hewn oak logs and fitted together without the use of nails. Wooden pegs hold the timbers in position.

CHURCHES

Gloria Dei (Old Swedes) Episcopal Church—Delaware Avenue at Christian Street (215/389-1513).

The red brick structure of English architectural design was built by Swedish colonists between 1698 and 1703, making it the oldest church in Philadelphia. It is a steep-roofed building featuring a square belfry and small spire (built probably in the

1730s). In the entrance vestibule is a stairway leading to a balcony that extends on three sides of the sanctuary. Gloria Dei was declared a National Historic Site by President Franklin D. Roosevelt on 17 November 1942. It is also listed on the more recent National Register of Historic Places.

The church congregation had its origins in Fort New Gothenburg. A small log church with bell tower was built in 1643 and existed until 1645, when it was destroyed by fire. A larger log church and bell tower was built the following year. Many of the Swedish settlers moved north along the Delaware River to Wicaco (now South Philadelphia), where about 1677 a block house just south of present Gloria Dei was converted into a church. That structure was succeeded by the present church at the end of the seventeenth century.

Gloria Dei has preserved several items from the log church at Tinicum, including the baptismal font and the golden sprays on the front of the lectern. Significant are the two wooden cherubs, brought from Sweden in 1643, on the rear balcony under the organ. Below the cherubs is an open Bible whereon is written in Swedish: "The people who wander in darkness shall see a great light / And over them that dwell in dark lands it shone clearly. Glory to God in the Highest."

Two ship models of the *Kalmar Nyckel* and *Fogel Grip* are suspended from the ceiling. These models as well as the candelabra were given by Carl Milles, noted Swedish sculptor. The wood carving of the angel Gabriel over the pulpit is a replica of an earlier one.

Buried beneath the church floor are several of the early Swedish missionaries, including Andrew Rudman, pastor at the time of the present church's construction. The last of these missionaries—Nicholas Collin—served the church from 1784 to 1831. He was a friend of Thomas Jefferson and Benjamin Franklin (who supplied lightning rods for the church), well educated, and had an interest in science. In June 1777, Betsy Ross was married in Gloria Dei. Jenny Lind gave a religious concert here in 1851. On the left side of the sanctuary are old Bibles, including one presented by the Swedish king and queen in 1926 and a reproduction of the 1541 Gustav Vasa Bible. A small museum in the church compound holds a number of interesting documents associated with the early pastors. The Gloria Dei Church and grounds have been beautifully restored as a result of funds collected in the United States and Sweden.

One of the most famous people buried in the adjacent cemetery is Swedish artist Adolf Ulrik Wertmüller (1751-1811) who came to America in 1794. Also in the graveyard is the Statue of the Seven Johns. It is a seven-sided black granite monolith from Sweden, surmounted by a bronze bust of John Hanson (1715-83), the first president of the United States under the Articles of Confederation, with seven bronze low-relief plaques, the work of local artist and sculptor Carl Lindborg. The seven plaques memorialize Hanson, whose Swedish ancestry is now doubted by serious historians, and six famous men of Swedish descent—Johan Printz (1592-1663); Johan Rising (1617-72), the last governor of New Sweden; John Dahlgren (1809-70); John Nystrom (1824-85), the engineer, inventor, and author; John Ericsson (1803-89); and John Morton (1727–1777).

In 1876, a Maryland Hanson of authentic New Sweden ancestry declared himself in print to have been patriot John Hanson's relative. This report gave to the living Hanson an important kinsman; to the deceased Hanson it gave a huge population of recent immigrants from Sweden, who were as eager to adopt an early patriot as they were to make this country their own.

In 1988, a short scholarly article by a former editor of the *National Genealogical Society Quarterly* was published just as New Sweden celebrated its 350th anniversary. In this article, "John Hanson of Maryland: A Swedish Origin Disproved," George Ely Russell succinctly enumerated ten points of evidence of the fact that the patriot's immigrant ancestor, John Hanson (also spelled *Henson*), was an English indentured servant who arrived in the winter of 1661–62. He lived in Charles County, Maryland, where his numerous documented associations never included the Delaware Swedes or their descendants, including those named Hanson in distant Kent County, Maryland.

Since 1988 historian and genealogist Peter Stebbins Craig has brought to light at least two additional points of evidence from the contemporary records of New Sweden refuting the 1876 Hanson claim. In a complete list of orphans in the colony between 1641–48, he found none of the four allegedly orphaned Hansons brought to America by Governor Printz in 1643. Furthermore, the Hansons who did leave descendants in the colony (and some in Kent County, Maryland) are found in the records of this period as full-grown adults, who were not orphans, not wards of Governor Printz, not brothers to each other, and not named John.

St. James' Church of Kingsessing—6838 Woodland Avenue (215/727-5265).

The stone structure is the sixth oldest church edifice in Philadelphia and the oldest west of the Schuylkill River. The Rev. Carl Magnus Wrangel dedicated the site in 1760 and the Rev. Nicholas Collin served the church from 1786 to 1831. Although constructed in 1762, the building was not dedicated until 1765. In 1844 it became an Episcopalian church, and in 1962 it was declared a historic landmark.

Christ Church (Old Swedes), Upper Merion, and Cemetery— State Highway 23, one-half mile east of Bridgeport (215/272-6036).

Swedes by 1712 had gradually migrated from the Delaware Valley and Philadelphia northwestward along the Schuylkill River to the Upper Merion Township area. They established a village first known as Swedesford, which today is Swedesburg. The original log cabin that housed the congregation and school was built in 1733 on land donated by Gunnar Rambo, a direct descendant of Peter Rambo, a colonist who arrived in 1640. In 1760, Christ Church (Old Swedes), today covered by yellow plaster, was dedicated.

The interior of Christ Church is significant for its stained glass windows depicting various scenes relating to the early Swedes in America. They were installed in 1938 for the three hundredth anniversary of the landing of the Swedes at Wilmington. Another historic memorial is the baptismal font presented to the church in 1876 by Prince Oscar (1859–1953), the second son of King Oscar II, during a visit to the United States. Also in the sanctuary by the front entrance is Prince Oscar's flag (the union flag of Sweden and Norway), which flew on the *Norrköping* when it was anchored in the Delaware River during the prince's visit. Near the baptismal font is a Swedish flag sent in 1960 by the archbishop of Sweden for the two hundredth anniversary of the present edifice.

The oldest grave in the adjacent cemetery is that of Diana Rambo who died in 1744 at the age of twenty-six years. A plaque in the path left of the main door honors the Rev. Nicholas Collin, George Washington, Benjamin Franklin, and Anthony Wayne.

During the winter of 1777 when the Continental Army was encamped at nearby Valley Forge, George Washington and his officers occasionally came to this church for worship services. It is an annual tradition at Christ Church to celebrate Lucia Day (December 13). After the Lucia enters the sanctuary, men costumed as Continental soldiers knock on the church door and the congregation sings "America" in response.

The Bryn Athyn Cathedral Church of the New Jerusalem (Swedenborgian)—Cathedral Road at Huntingdon Pike (Pennsylvania Highway 232), one mile north of its intersection with Pennsylvania Highway 63, in Bryn Athyn (215/947-0266).

Bryn Athyn serves as the episcopal seat of the Church of the New Jerusalem (Swedenborgian). Most of the population of this community is associated with the church and/or its educational institutions. Guided tours of the cathedral are offered to the public seven days a week in the afternoon. Call the cathedral for the schedule.

The most outstanding building in the complex is the Bryn Athyn Cathedral. Groundbreaking for the twentieth-century Gothic and Romanesque edifice took place in 1913, and its dedication was six years later. The original endowment was a gift of John Pitcairn, and the design and construction was supervised by his son, Raymond Pitcairn. The three parts are the church proper (inspired by Gothic architecture of the thirteenth and fourteenth centuries and to a limited degree the fifteenth century), the Council Hall (twelfth-century Romanesque style), and the Choir Hall (also twelfth-century Romanesque). The stained glass windows in the church depict biblical scenes. The cathedral, on one of the highest points in Montgomery County, is an unexpected and spectacular site in the rolling countryide.

OTHER POINTS OF INTEREST

Historic Bartram's Garden—Fifty-fourth Street and Lindbergh Boulevard (215/729-5281).

Historic Bartram's Garden was originally part of the 1100-acre Aronameck plantation granted under English government to Hans Månson in 1669. He sold it in 1681 to his stepson, Peter Peterson Yocum, who in turn sold this part to his brother-in-law Mouns Jones. The inner core of the 1731 John Bartram House was the home of Mouns Jones before he moved to present Douglassville, Pennsylvania, where his later and larger residence is a significant landmark. Remains of a very early cider mill and press on the Bartram property are also believed to date from the period of Swedish occupancy.

John Bartram (1699–1777) is remembered as the first American-born botanist. A founding member of the American Philosophical Society and a close friend of Benjamin Franklin's, he was sought out by Pehr Kalm early in his lengthy stay in America. Seeds and sample plants from Bartram's collection were prominent among those sent by Kalm to Linnaeus in Sweden and among those he later planted in his own study collection in Åbo (Turku), Finland.

Grave of Rear Admiral John A. Dahlgren—Laurel Hill Cemetery, 3822 Ridge Avenue (302/228-8200).

A reddish granite stone marks the grave of Swedish-American Rear Admiral John A. Dahlgren (1809–70), a famous U.S. Navy officer, scientist, scholar, teacher, and author. Other members of the Dahlgren family are buried nearby.

SCULPTURE AND OTHER ART

John Ericsson Fountain—near the Philadelphia Museum of Art (Twenty-sixth and Benjamin Franklin Parkway).

This marble fountain is dedicated to John Ericsson, the scientist and inventor, who was born in Sweden 31 July 1803 at Långbanshyttan in the Swedish province of Värmland and died in his adoptive homeland, the United States, 8 March 1889. On his birthday Filipstad, Värmland, annually celebrates John Ericsson Day with a mock battle on Lake Daglösen by replicas of the *Merrimac* and Ericsson's *Monitor*.

Carl Milles Sculpture—Fairmount Park along the Schuylkill River.

Carl Milles created three angels blowing wind instruments and surmounting large stone columns, approximately thirty-five feet high. Elsewhere in the park near the river stands a statue, presented in 1974 by the Leif Ericson Society of Philadelphia, in honor of the explorer for whom the society is named.

Claes Oldenburg's "Clothespin"—Centre Square at 1500 Market Street.

"Clothespin," the work of artist Claes Oldenburg, stands opposite Philadelphia's City Hall. Oldenburg, born in Stockholm in 1929, became a naturalized American citizen.

CHESTER

Chester is the second oldest settlement in Pennsylvania. Originally called Upland by the Swedes, the city got its new name from William Penn. In the cemetery of the old St. Paul's Episcopal Church (1703), on East Third Street between Welsh and Market streets, is the grave of John Morton (1727–77), marked with an obelisk. Because of age, inscriptions on this and many other stones are almost or completely illegible.

On the northwestern edge of Chester stands one of the most elegant of all the memorials relating to the New Sweden colony: a large red granite monument by the noted Finnish sculptor Väinö Aaltonen, donated to the people of Pennsylvania and the city of Chester in 1938 by the government and people of Finland. It stands in Crozer Park, just southwest of the Kerlin Street exit from Interstate 95. The monument, which has scenes in bas-relief on both faces, has inscriptions in Finnish and English. It honors the many colonists who came from Finland or were Finns living in Sweden (especially in Värmland) just before remigrating to New Sweden.

MARCUS HOOK

First settled by Swedes, Marcus Hook is one mile from the Delaware-Pennsylvania border. A plaque outside Marcus

Hook Municipal Building at the southwest corner of West Tenth and Green streets describes the contribution of the early settlers.

DOUGLASS-VILLE

St. Gabriel's Church and Cemetery on U.S. Highway 422 East, established in 1720, was the first church founded by Swedish Lutherans in Berks County. The first sanctuary, built in that year, was a log cabin, but it was destroyed by fire in 1832. In 1801, the present stone church was built, some forty years after the congregation officially became Episcopalian. The stone church was used by the congregation until a larger Gothic-style church was constructed in 1884 approximately one hundred yards to the west. In that same year the name St. Gabriel's was first employed. From that time until 1959 when it was restored as a chapel, the old stone church was used as a parish house. The building is on the National Register of Historic Places. It contains an impressive raised, canopied pulpit and a balcony on three sides.

The Mouns Jones House (The Old Swede's House) on Old Philadelphia Pike is near St. Gabriel's. The two and one-half–story stone structure is the oldest dated building in Berks County. It was erected in 1716 by Mouns Jones, an early Swedish settler, who, along with fourteen other Swedes in 1701, took up ten thousand acres of land. The first structure built on the site was a small log cabin, the foundation of which still remains. The present twenty-four– by thirty–foot house is constructed of coarse, squared stone and has two chimneys, including one for a corner fireplace. Considerable damage, particularly on the second floor, was caused by a fire in the 1950s, but the structure and grounds have been restored and are now well maintained by the Historic Preservation Trust of Berks County. Since it is located close to the Schuylkill River, the structure was used as a ferry house. It has also been known as Lamb's Inn. It is open only by appointment (215/385-3870).

Jones's name has been a puzzle to some. Jones is an Anglicized version of what his traditional Swedish name would have been—Jönsson. His father, Jöns Nilsson (sometimes called Jonas), arrived in 1642 with Governor Johan Printz. One descendant still living in Pennsylvania has reason to believe the name should be Jonas, not Jones. Historians have noted that county court records consistently spell the last name *Jones* but that his first name appears in several variant spellings. Records of the time were kept in English and sometimes German. In the fall each year, St. Gabriel's and the Historic Preservation Trust of Berks County hold a popular country fair in Jones's name on the church grounds and near the house.

BIRDSBORO

Hopewell Village National Historic Site is six miles south of Birdsboro on State Highway 345 (215/582-8773). A restored ironworks and ironworkers' residential community that includes both eighteenth- and nineteenth-century structures, Hopewell Village National Historic Site is operated by the National Park Service. Hopewell Furnace was founded by Mark Bird in 1771. While the interpretation of this site to the public does not highlight its Swedish connection, Bird's mother was the descendant of New Sweden colonists. Her father, Marcus Huling, was a partner in nearby iron mines forty years before the founding of Hopewell. Her maternal grandfather was Mouns Jones, who is mentioned above.

Bird and his parents were active in the Swedish church that became St. Gabriel's, Douglassville. His sister was the wife of James Wilson, a signer of the Declaration of Independence and the Constitution of the United States. As one of the primary suppliers of American-made cannon to the Continental Army and a founder of other early ironworks in New Jersey, Virginia, and North Carolina (where he died in poverty in 1816), Bird may rightfully be considered alongside John Morton as a genuinely significant player in the struggle for the independence of this country.

HARRISBURG

The State Finance Building, bounded by North Street, Fisher Plaza, North Drive, and Commonwealth Avenue (one block from the Pennsylvania Capitol), has twelve bronze doors designed by Carl Milles. They depict the state's agricultural enterprises (North Street entrance) and its industries, including oil drilling, glass making, steel manufacturing, and coal mining.

GRASSFLAT-LANSE

In central Pennsylvania near the Interstate 80 Kylertown exit are the small mining communities of Grassflat and Lanse. In 1883, thirty Swedish men, who had been part of a migration beginning in 1875 from Dalsland to the coal fields of McIntyre in Pennsylvania's Tioga County, moved farther west and south to the Grassflat-Lanse area. The following year 181 more Swedes arrived. In nearby Peale, a community no longer in existence, the Swedish Evangelical Lutheran Nebo Church was organized in 1884. Gustavus Adolphus, a daughter congregation, sprang up in Lanse shortly afterward, and the congregation built a chapel in 1892. Other congregations were also formed, but eventually some Swedish congregations merged, forming Holy Trinity Lutheran Church of Lanse, which now stands on Lanse Road and holds several items from the old Gustavus Adolphus Church, which was dismantled in 1986. Included in the collection are the 1901 altar painting by Olof Grafström of Jesus praying in the Garden of Gethsemane, the remodeled pulpit, the altar, and most of the altar rail. Several graves in the Grassflat-Lanse Lutheran Cemetery on State Highway 53 have Swedish inscriptions (go north from Interstate 80 on State Highway 53 for a little over two miles, and then go east for one-half mile). In the center is the grave of Pastor P. A. Bergquist (1855–1912), who served all the Swedish congregations in the area. Several early markers give Älvsborg Län, Sweden, as the birthplace. Organized in 1892, the Evangelical Free Church of Lanse has Swedish roots, but its building was constructed in 1977.

PITTSBURGH

At the University of Pittsburgh is the Cathedral of Learning, a Gothic-style building honoring the achievement in learning of various ethnic groups by devoting individual classrooms to single countries. It is bounded by Forbes, Bigelow, Fifth, and Bellefield. One of more than twenty such rooms, the Swedish Classroom combines a peasant cottage atmosphere with murals in the style of the eighteenth-century Hälsingland painter Gustav Reuter. The Bollnäs cottage of Stockholm's Skansen inspired a hooded brick fireplace, which is a central feature of the room. Murals feature biblical events and personifications of virtues. Swedish sculptor Carl Milles was the university's advisor in creating the room.

CHANDLERS VALLEY–SUGAR GROVE

The first Swedes in northwestern Pennsylvania were connected with the story of the New Sweden, Iowa, colony, which was organized in 1845 by Peter Cassel. His glowing letters about Iowa encouraged additional Swedes to emigrate in 1846; however, when they arrived, they were robbed of their money and left stranded in Buffalo, New York. Two young girls with the group, one seven years old and the other nine, were offered homes by families in Warren and Sugar Grove. These girls—the first Swedish-born persons to come to that area—arrived in December of 1846, and the centennial of their arrival is commemorated in a Chandlers Valley park by a monument unveiled in 1946, bearing the biblical inscription, "A little child shall lead them." In the fall of 1848, some members of the party began to arrive in Chandlers Valley–Sugar Grove, Pennsylvania, where the men became woodsmen and proceeded to acquire farms. The settlement became known as Hessel Valley for three brothers from Hässleby, Småland. Later, Swedes worked in the area's oil fields.

The Chandlers Valley–Sugar Grove area became a center from which Swedes spread to various parts of western Pennsylvania and western New York, particularly Jamestown. By 1870, Swedes were actively engaged in that city's developing furniture business. By 1930 there were about eight thousand Swedish-born people.

With the exception of the churches established in the Delaware Valley in the seventeenth century, the Hessel Valley Lutheran Church on Brown Hill Road in Chandlers Valley (814/489-0228) is the oldest Swedish Lutheran Church in the eastern part of the United States, having been organized in 1854. Thus it is the "mother" church of the New York conference of the former Augustana Synod. In 1856, the Rev. Jonas Swensson of Unnaryd, Småland, became pastor (a year later, his son, Carl Aaron Swensson, the founder of Bethany College, Lindsborg, Kansas, was born in Chandlers Valley).

In 1883, the congregation decided to build a brick church, and two years later, the edifice was completed. The church has a high central steeple and windows in the nineteenth-century Gothic style. The altar painting of the Ascension is original to the building. Above the chancel is the inscription: *"Tror Du På Guds Son?"* ("Do you believe in the Son of God?"). A large Victorian chandelier dating from the 1870s, formerly used for kerosene lamps, hangs in the center of the sanctuary. The chair used by King Carl XVI Gustaf on his 1976 visit is to the right of the altar. Also on the right wall is a picture of the king, a Swedish flag, and a plaque noting the visit. Over the door leading to the basement is a bronze plaque giving a brief history of the congregation. In the basement Sunday School room is a glass case displaying various historical mementos.

The move of the Lutherans to nearby Sugar Grove in 1883 partly explains why thirty persons met in November of that year to explore the possibilities of organizing a separate church. This group became the Evangelical Free Church of Sugar Grove Township (later the Sugar Grove Mission Covenant Church). Three years later, a small white clapboard sanctuary with a steeple was built at Jackson Run and Youngsville Road (814/489-3044). It is adjacent to the Covenant Cemetery and across the road from the Lutheran Cemetery. Nearby is a small Methodist graveyard. Two miles west of the Hessel Valley Lutheran Church, up a gravel road, is the former Swedish Methodist Episcopal Church (the congregation has disbanded). Originally it was near the old Methodist cemetery.

MOUNT JEWETT

Mount Jewett, separated from Chandlers Valley and Sugar Grove by the Allegheny National Forest, is home to the octagonal Nebo Evangelical Lutheran Church, which dates from 1887. The members had organized one year earlier. Reportedly patterned after Ersta Kyrka in Stockholm, the church has an altar painting of the Ascension by Birger Sandzén. In 1950 this congregation merged with Mount Jewett's Zion Lutheran to form St. Matthew's Lutheran (13 Main Street). In the fellowship hall of St. Matthew's is an Olof Grafström painting of the Good Shepherd formerly located in the Zion church. The faithful gather at the old Nebo church for three annual services—Easter sunrise, Ascension Sunday, and the Swedish festival service on the second Sunday of August.

KANESHOLM   Lebanon Lutheran Church (three and one-half miles east of Kane and off U.S. Highway 6) is the "mother" church for several Pennsylvania Swedish Lutheran congregations in McKean County. Lebanon Lutheran was organized in 1870, and the present sanctuary, a white frame structure with a short steeple, was constructed in 1871 and 1872.

KANE   Tabor Lutheran Church (at the corner of Greeves and Dawson) is an old congregation with Swedish roots. Emmanuel Mission Church at Edgar and Biddle (814/837-8760) was built in 1902, twenty-four years after the church was first organized.

WILCOX   The Nazareth Lutheran Church in Wilcox was organized in 1875, and the present white frame church was built in 1881 with windows and a high steeple in the popular nineteenth-century Gothic style. Eleven other Lutheran congregations in northwestern Pennsylvania founded by Swedes remain active, and most retain their old church buildings.

MARYLAND

NORTH EAST   North East, a geographic neighbor of Wilmington, is shown on a 1731 Swedish map of the eastern United States as the only town in Maryland, because its church was the only one in that colony regularly served by Swedish clergymen. The church, St. Mary Anne's Episcopal, was organized in 1702 as North Elk Parish (of the Church of England). Its original resident pastor was Jonas Aurén from Ekshärad, Värmland, whose marriage to a local Swedish girl is the first entry in the church book. Aurén was a remarkable man who also taught school, was a surveyor, and operated one of the very few printing presses in America before his death in 1713. As a memorial to his service, Aurén's home church in Sweden commissioned the Ekshärad master blacksmith Alan Sjöberg to create a hand-wrought iron candlestick, which was presented to St. Mary Anne's Church in 1988 in his honor.

The present church building, on its original and lovely waterfront site, dates from 1742. In recent years the congregation has hosted or participated in several events commemorating its early Swedish and Finnish ties. One possible explanation of the odd name (there being no saint named Mary Anne) is that the Värmland Finns who had settled this area and attended the church referred to it by the common Finnish church name *Marian Kirkko* (Mary's Church).

ELKTON

Seven miles from North East in the Cecil County seat of Elkton, a dilapidated stone shell is all that remains to mark the late seventeenth-century residence of John Hansson Steelman at Elk Landing. An Indian trader and interpreter prominent in the history of both Maryland and Pennsylvania, this son of New Sweden colonists was the wealthiest Swedish American for much of his career. Through a combination of donations and loans, Steelman advanced about one-third of the cash to finance the construction of Holy Trinity (Old Swedes) Church in present Wilmington. The pastor there, Eric Björk, referred to Steelman as his *"svärfaders svåger":* he was the brother-in-law of the pastor's father-in-law. Steelman's family and several neighbors (Elkton was known as Swedestown at least until 1710) were nominally parishioners of the Swedish church in Delaware, but most Cecil County Swedes were active in Anglican parishes closer to their Maryland homes.

ANNAPOLIS

At the U.S. Naval Academy (410/267-6100), the contributions of Rear Admiral John A. Dahlgren to weapons development are recognized. Dahlgren's father came in 1806 from Sweden to Philadelphia where he later served Sweden and Norway as consul. Dahlgren Hall, a large stone structure, formerly serving as an armory and drill area, is named for the rear admiral. Today it is an activity center for the midshipmen, and a plaque outside the doors note Dahlgren's accomplishments. Outside the building are two heavy armaments—a Dahlgren rifle, which is a thirty-pound rifle invented by the rear admiral, and a 25-mm machine gun presented to the U.S. Navy by the Swedish Navy. Over the entrance immediately inside Dahlgren Hall hangs a portrait of Dahlgren, who has also had three naval ships named for him. In the Naval Academy museum's Civil War display are Dahlgren's frock coat, his pearl-hilted sword, and models of the various guns he invented.

WASHINGTON, D.C.

In Potomac Park, directly south of the Lincoln Memorial (where Constitution Avenue NW ends at the Potomac River), is a monument to John Ericsson (1803–89), Swedish-born builder of the *Monitor*, the first modern warship clad in iron. Unveiled 29 May 1926 before President Calvin Coolidge and Crown Prince Gustav Adolf, the monument depicts Ericsson seated above an inscription recognizing his building of the *Monitor* and the revolution in navigation caused by his invention of the screw propeller. On the statue, labor, adventure, and vision are represented, respectively, by a man, a Viking warrior, and a woman.

In the Great Hall of the Supreme Court Building (1 First Street NE; for information, 202/479-3298) is a bust of Earl Warren, whose mother was born in the province of Hälsingland and whose father was from Norway. Warren served as the fourteenth chief justice of the U.S. Supreme Court from 1953 to 1969. At the National Air and Space Museum (Sixth Street at Independence Avenue; for information, 202/357-2700) prominently displayed is Charles Lindbergh's *Spirit of St. Louis*, the first aircraft flown solo across the Atlantic. At the National Museum of American History can be found Swedish-American artifacts, but exhibits change regularly. In Leutze Park in the Washington Navy Yard is a plaque in the northwest corner describing the early history of this important Washington, D.C., landmark. U.S. Navy Rear Admiral John Dahlgren, a Swedish American born in Philadelphia, was twice commandant of the Navy Yard (1861-62 and 1869-70). At 1611 Sixteenth Street NW is the Church of the Holy City (Swedenborgian) and, as part of it, the Swedenborg Information Center. The Gothic-style stone church is the national church of the Swedenborgians.

At the U.S. Holocaust Memorial Museum (100 Raoul Wallenberg Place, 202/488-0400), Swedish diplomat Raoul Wallenberg (1912–47?) is honored by the naming of the museum's street and featured in the exhibit on those who rescued Jews from the Holocaust. Wallenberg saved the lives of thousands of Hungarian Jews during World War II. In 1981, the U.S. Congress granted him honorary citizenship.

NEW YORK

NEW YORK

Most Swedes and millions of other European immigrants first set foot on American soil in New York City. Although most of the Swedes continued westward, many also stayed. No other urban center except Chicago had more Swedish-born inhabitants than New York City. By 1910, there were about thirty-five thousand Swedish-born, about half living in Brooklyn. Important immigrant churches were established in New York to help ease the transition from the Old Country to the New Land.

INSTITUTES AND MUSEUMS
Ellis Island National Monument and Statue of Liberty National Monument—New York Harbor. Take Circle Line Statue of Liberty Ferry from either Battery Park in Lower Manhattan or Liberty State Park in New Jersey. Call 212/269-5755 for schedules and fares.

It was through Ellis Island, a 27.5-acre plot of land in New York Harbor that over 12.5 million immigrants (70 percent of all immigrants between 1892 and 1924) were admitted to the United States. Because over 100 million Americans today claim to be descended from these 12.5 million, Ellis Island and its buildings have been preserved as a fitting memorial to the largest voluntary immigration in world history.

In 1890, the federal government took over from the state of New York the processing of immigrants, resulting in the move from Castle Garden to Ellis Island. It remained the central depot for immigrants until 1924 when quotas were adopted, resulting in the inspection process being conducted overseas rather than in New York City. Ironically, after 1924 Ellis Island became a detention and deportation center and for a while also served as a military hospital and Coast Guard station. It was abandoned between 1954 and 1965, when it became part of the Statue of Liberty National Monument. From 1976 to 1984, guides conducted tours of the crumbling buildings, but then it closed for restoration. Since 1990 this national monument has featured an outstanding museum, attracting large numbers of tourists to its interpretation of the immigrants' first steps in the new land.

Work on the main building restored its turn-of-the-century French Renaissance style and its baggage, legal inspection, hearing, dormitory, medical inspection, and immigrant aid rooms. Restored to its 1918–24 appearance is the second-floor Registry Room, where as many as five thousand people were processed daily. Exhibits tracing American history and displaying thousands of items brought by immigrants to the United States help visitors appreciate immigration's complexity and the immigrant's plight. Visitors may view a film or play, or listen to an audio tour. Outside stands the Wall of Honor bearing the names of more than 480,000 individuals and families who immigrated to the United States, many of whom passed through Ellis Island. About two-thirds of all the immigrants from Europe and Asia went west; one-third stayed in New York.

A short distance away the Statue of Liberty, designed by Alexandre-Gustave Eiffel and given to the United States by France in 1876, holds her torch 152 feet above ground, persevering as the symbol of American freedom for people around the world. A two-year renovation was ended in 1986, and now visitors can take a glass-walled elevator to the statue's pedestal, where museum exhibits retell the story of immigration and explain the statue's restoration.

New Jersey has restored the Central Railroad of New Jersey Passenger Terminal, which is part of Liberty State Park, opposite Ellis Island. The terminal is open occasionally to the public.

United Nations—First Avenue between East Forty-second and East Fiftieth streets.
Swede Dag Hammarskjöld (1905–61) served as the United Nations' second secretary-general from 1953 until his tragic death in 1961 in the Congo (Zaire). His great work for international peace and justice is recognized in and around United Nations Headquarters.

The Dag Hammarskjöld Library, funded by a $6.6 million Ford Foundation gift, is on Forty-second Street east of First Avenue (southwest corner of the United Nations complex). Dedicated 16 November 1961, the library has in its main reading room near the main desk a portrait of the former secretary-general that was donated by the governments of Argentina and Sweden.

North of the library and west of the Secretariat Building is a fountain with the sculpture "Single Form" by Barbara Hepworth. In 1964, this twenty-one–foot abstract bronze sculpture standing on a granite base was erected in memory of Hammarskjöld. A portrait of him by Swedish artist Bo Beskow (1906–89) hangs on the north wall of the Secretariat lobby.

The plaza on East Forty-seventh Street between First and Second avenues is named in honor of Hammarskjöld. (Nearby is the Raoul Wallenberg Walk.) At Second Avenue and Dag Hammarskjöld Plaza is the Dag Hammarskjöld Tower (240 East Forty-seventh Street), a condominium and apartment complex. At the entrance, on the southwest corner of Second Avenue and Hammarskjöld Plaza, is a bust of the former secretary-general by Carina Ari, a Swedish sculptor, ballerina, and choreographer.

Outside the Meditation Room at the United Nations, Dag Hammarskjöld and Count Folke Bernadotte (1895–1948) are both recognized by plaques. Near the bluish stained glass window by Russian painter Marc Chagall in a glass case is a book inscribed in French by Chagall—"To all who served the purposes and principles of the United Nations Charter, for which Dag Hammarskjöld gave his life—Marc Chagall, 15 May 1963." Within the small Meditation Room are two gifts from Sweden— a large iron ore slab in the center of the room and an abstract painting of various geometric shapes, also by Beskow.

The Economic and Social Council Chamber was designed by the Swedish architect Sven Markelius and furnished by the government of Sweden. The burgundy window curtains came from Märta Måås-Fjetterström's studio in Båstad. The marble floor was donated by Sveriges Stenindustriförbund. Markelius left the ceiling unfinished to represent the ongoing work of the council. He was one of eleven members of an international team of architects who worked on the plans for the U.N. Headquarters. The other two major councils—Security and Trusteeship—were designed by Norwegians and Danes, respectively.

HISTORIC PLACES

Castle Clinton National Monument—Battery Park (southern end of Manhattan Island).
From 1855 to 1890, Castle Clinton was the principal immigrant depot, having more than seven million immigrants pass through it—the "Gateway to the New World." Originally it was a harbor fortification during the War of 1812, but it was never tested. In 1824, the structure was leased by New York as a place of public entertainment. Performers included Jenny Lind, whose 1850 appearance at Castle Clinton was arranged by P. T. Barnum.

In the twentieth century, when it was known as Castle Garden, it was for a time a New York City aquarium, but in 1950 it was designated a national monument. Only the lower part of the original structure remains.

Swedish Cottage (The Cottage Marionette Theatre)—Central Park, near Seventy-ninth Street and Central Park West (close to the Delacorte Theater at 81 Central Park West) (212/988-9093).
Part of the Swedish exhibition at the 1876 Centennial Exhibition at Fairmount Park in Philadelphia was a timbered Swedish-made schoolhouse. After the exhibition closed, the City of New York purchased the building for fifteen hundred dollars and moved it to Central Park. In 1947, the Parks and Recreation Department's Marionette Theatre touring company began using it for its workshop and headquarters. Since 1972, when it became a marionette theater, contemporary and classical shows, enchanting to the young and the young at heart, have been offered throughout the year.

New York City sites honoring John Ericsson (1803-89), Swedish designer of the naval vessel _Monitor_.
The John Ericsson Society, founded in 1907, has been active in furthering interest in Ericsson's life and accomplishments. The John Ericsson statue erected in 1903 in Battery Park depicts the Swedish inventor holding blueprints of the _Monitor_ in his right hand and a model of the ship in the left. On the marble base are scenes from the Civil War and a brief biographical sketch. Annually on 9 March, the anniversary of the 1862 Civil War

This statue of John Ericsson was erected in Battery Park in 1903. In one hand is a model of the Monitor, *and in the other are the blueprints for it.*

battle between the *Monitor* and the *Merrimac,* a special ceremony of remembrance takes place near the monument. Also Ericsson's birthday (29 July) is commemorated.

On the west side of lower Manhattan, just south of Canal Street, is Ericsson Place, a one-block stretch of Beech Street between Hudson and Varick streets, where Ericsson lived and died at number 36 (the building no longer exists). After he died, Ericsson's remains were taken to Sweden for burial in Filipstad, Värmland.

Three sites are noteworthy in the Greenpoint section of Brooklyn, where on 30 January 1862 the *Monitor* was launched. In Monsignor McGolrick Park, which is bounded on one side by Monitor Street, stands the impressive bronze *Monitor* memorial monument. It commemorates the Battle of Hampton Roads (9 March 1862) between the *Monitor* and *Merrimac;* the men of the *Monitor;* and its designer, John Ericsson. Rising from a nine-foot square base, the figure of a sailor strains at a hawser (a heavy rope for mooring or towing). On West Street near its intersection with Calyer Street, a historic plaque notes the spot where the *Monitor* keel was laid 25 October 1861, and about six months later it was launched. An intermediate school in the area is named in Ericsson's honor (John Ericsson Intermediate School, 424 Leonard, Brooklyn [718/782-2527]).

Long Island sites honoring aviator Charles A. Lindbergh, Jr.

At Roosevelt Field in Garden City, near the spot where Lindbergh took off in 1927 for the first transatlantic solo nonstop flight from New York to Paris, is a monument honoring that feat. A thirty-foot abstract stainless steel sculpture, dedicated 20 May 1981, is at the Old Country Road entrance to the Roosevelt Field Shopping Mall, near JCPenney. Lindbergh Park in Huntington is the site of the annual Midsummer Day festival celebrated by Long Island Swedish Americans.

Augustana Lutheran Home—1680 Sixtieth in Brooklyn (718/232-2114).

Founded in 1908 at the Bethlehem Lutheran Church, Augustana Lutheran Home preceded the Swedish Home for the Aged *(Solhem)* at 20 Bristol Avenue on Staten Island by only one year. In 1912 the Swedish Home purchased a residence formerly occupied by the Vanderbilts as its new site.

CHURCHES

Gustavus Adolphus Lutheran Church—155 East Twenty-second Street (near Third Avenue) (212/674-0739).

Gustavus Adolphus was one of the main Swedish immigrant churches in New York City, having been organized in 1855.

During its early years, the congregation was beset by several problems, the first being a theological dispute. This resulted in the formation of what would be identified as Bethesda Covenant Church, which became a large immigrant church in midtown Manhattan. The Bethesda church building no longer exists, but the present small congregation continues to meet at the Church Center for the United Nations (777 United Nations Plaza). Gustavus Adolphus also had debt problems and was rocked by frequent pastoral changes. The "golden age" for the congregation, however, was the forty-seven–year ministry of Dr. Mauritz Stolpe, which began in 1891.

Four years before his arrival, the cornerstone was laid for the present church sanctuary, a turn-of-the-century Romanesque stone building. The sanctuary was designed by the same architect responsible for the old Metropolitan Opera House, and the curved balconies are reminiscent of those found in an opera house auditorium. A noteworthy Tiffany window is on the ceiling of the sanctuary. The congregation has preserved the old marble baptismal font with a Swedish inscription. In 1926, Crown Prince Gustav Adolf and his wife, Crown Princess Louise, attended a morning service, leaving a signed Bible and chasuble now worn by the pastor on special occasions. In 1994 about 25 percent of the Gustavus congregation was of Swedish-American extraction.

Trinity Baptist Church—250 East Sixty-first Street (on the south side between Second and Third avenues) (212/838-6844).

Trinity was organized in 1867 as the First Swedish Baptist Church of New York (the name was changed to Trinity in 1942). The congregation worships in a sanctuary that was designed by Swedish architect Martin G. Hedmark and built in part by Swedish craftsmen.

The church has a towering straight-edged brick front facade with a stepped gable described as late Scandinavian Art Nouveau. At the top of each side tower is a miniature Swedish bell steeple made of lead-coated copper. Each steeple is different: one represents a bell tower in Västergötland, the other a tower in northern Sweden with a distinctive Russian influence. At the base of the central tower are two black marble cornerstones imported from Sweden that were a gift from Mrs. A. K. Fernstrom of Karlshamn. The decorative iron work on the front oak doors is also of Swedish origin.

Creating "an atmosphere of rustic strength and austerity," according to one account, the narthex ceiling has a fresco painted by Olle Nordmark, a Swedish artisan. A circular dome tops the square sanctuary. Nature's colors—tan, brown, and red in the birch, oak, brick, and polished marble appointments—

predominate. Stairway railings curve like vines, and columns are entwined with grapevines sculpted in relief. Hedmark designed Expressionist stained glass windows, which were executed by Sten Jacobson, another Swedish craftsman. At one time the inscription "God bless you" in Swedish was visible on the rose window at the rear of the sanctuary, which portrayed the hand of Christ.

The architect, Hedmark, was born in Sweden and graduated from Tekniska Högskolan (Stockholm) in 1921. He and another architect worked on Engelbrekt's Church, Stockholm, and in 1923 Hedmark alone designed the Boo Church on Värmdö, an island near Sweden's capital city. Hedmark then came to the United States and designed several churches on the East Coast and in Chicago and one of the John Ericsson rooms in the American Swedish Historical Museum in Philadelphia. He eventually left the United States and returned to Sweden, where he died in 1980.

The Salvation Army Central Citadel Corps—221 East Fifty-second Street (between Second and Third avenues) (212/758-0763).
The Salvation Army's Citadel Corps, organized in 1888, maintains its strong Swedish heritage. The Corps, known as *Tvåan*, has had several locations in Manhattan. The present building was erected in 1940, and on the west side of the front door is the inscription, *"Frälsnings Armén Tillbedjen Herren i Helig skrud"* ("The Salvation Army Prays to the Lord in Holy Raiments").

The Church of Sweden—5 East Forty-eighth Street (on the north side between Fifth and Madison avenues) (212/832-8443).
The only Swedish Seaman's Church in the United States, the Church of Sweden was organized in 1873. In 1978, the church moved to its present facility, formerly owned by the New York Bible Society. With a plaque inside the front door the church honors Raoul Wallenberg, who heroically during World War II saved thousands of Jews from the Holocaust horrors. The facility has become a cultural and social center for visiting Swedes and Swedish Americans.

Other churches of Swedish background in Manhattan include the Lexington United Methodist Church at 150 East Sixty-second (212/838-6915), which was organized in 1882, and the Rock Church (Swedish Pentecostal) at 153 East Sixty-second (212/838-2724). The churches stand almost directly across from each other on Sixty-second Street between Third and Lexington avenues. The New Church (Swedenborgian) is at 112 East

Thirty-fifth Street, between Park and Lexington avenues (212/ 685-8967).

Bethlehem Lutheran Church—490 Pacific (southwest corner of Third Avenue and Pacific Streets) in Brooklyn (718/624-0242). Bethlehem Lutheran is the second Swedish Lutheran "mother" church in New York City. It has been said that some ten thousand children were baptized in this church who later moved west with their parents. The congregation was organized 15 April 1874, and the present Romanesque light brick building with its tall tower was constructed twenty years later. Over the main door in marble is the inscription, "Swedish Evangelical Lutheran Bethlehem Church."

The church sanctuary contains an outstanding raised hand-carved wood pulpit depicting various Christian symbols. Above the pulpit are the words, *"Predika Ordet"* ("Preach the Word"). There are stained glass windows throughout the sanctuary, including one in the front of the east balcony of Olaus Petri. There is stenciling on the walls near the ceiling. On the altar is a copy of Bertel Thorvaldsen's sculpted Christ. The altar cloth was embroidered by King Gustav V in honor of the congregation's seventy-fifth anniversary.

Bethlehem Lutheran Church was the cradle for two of the strongest institutions of the former Metropolitan New York Synod of the Augustana Lutheran Church—Upsala College (East Orange, New Jersey) and the Augustana Lutheran Home (Brooklyn). Plaques in the rear of the church describe these historic events.

Former Immanuel Swedish Methodist Episcopal Church (today Immanuel and First Spanish United Methodist Church)—424 Dean Street (on south side between Fourth and Fifth avenues) in Brooklyn (718/622-8296). The light brick church and its congregation is of direct lineage from the first Swedish Methodist church organized in the world. At one time there was a bronze plaque in front of the church noting that in 1845 Olof Gustaf Hedstrom (1803-77) organized the oldest Swedish Methodist Episcopal church in the world in the *John Wesley,* also called the *Old Bethel Ship,* anchored at a pier in the Hudson River. When Hedstrom died in 1877 (he is buried in Green Wood Cemetery in Brooklyn where on a gray granite obelisk surmounting the grave is the inscription "Founder of Swedish Methodism"), a group of Norwegians brought the *Old Bethel Ship* to Brooklyn, but it was not successfully used again as a floating chapel. The Norwegians purchased the property and kept the name, even though the floating chapel was sold in 1895 as scrap. Today there is a church on Fourth Avenue and Fifty-sixth Street in Brooklyn called Bethelship Norwegian United Methodist Church. In its sanctuary is a large painting of the *Old Bethel Ship*.

Not far from Bethlehem Lutheran and Immanuel Swedish Methodist Episcopal churches is Atlantic Avenue, which in the past was known as "Swedish Broadway." At one time nearly all the stores were run by Swedish merchants.

Salem Lutheran—450 Sixty-seventh Street (between Fourth and Fifth avenues) in Brooklyn (718/748-4024).

Located in the Bay Ridge section of Brooklyn, the Salem Lutheran congregation was established in 1904. The present cut stone English Gothic–style church was built between 1934 and 1945. In the sanctuary is a stained glass window of Gustavus II Adolphus. Opposite the church in a small park is a monument to Leif Eriksson dedicated in 1939 by Crown Prince Olav of Norway. The monument is a replica of a runestone found in Tune, Norway.

JAMESTOWN

First Lutheran Church in Jamestown memorializes Gustavus II Adolphus in this stained glass window.

At least seven Swedish-speaking congregations were established in Jamestown, beginning in 1852 with the Swedish Methodist Church (today called Epworth Christ United Methodist Church). The largest congregation (and thus the largest building) belongs to First Lutheran at 120 Chandler, which was organized 26 July 1856. It is the only Swedish church in the United States designated a cathedral. It was an outgrowth of the Hessel Valley Lutheran congregation. In 1864, Dr. Carl O. Hultgren became the third pastor, beginning a thirty-one–year ministry in the church. As a result of an increased membership plus the idea that there should be one service in which all the communicants could worship together, the decision was made in 1892 to begin the construction of a great Romanesque sanctuary. Aaron Hall, a local architect and contractor who had designed the Governor Fenton Home was in charge of constructing the enormous church, which was not completed until 1901, the delay due in part to the economic depression of the 1890s.

The cruciform church is 136 feet long and 64 feet wide, and its highest tower stands 153 feet and its lower one 96 feet. Seating 1300, the spacious sanctuary, soaring sixty-five feet to the ceiling, features a large raised pulpit with canopy, stenciling on the ceiling and chancel walls, and large stained glass windows, including one in the east transept memorializing Gustavus II Adolphus. In the rear of the sanctuary a plaque placed by the New York Conference of the Augustana Evangelical Lutheran Church commemorates the church. The church bell bears a Swedish inscription.

On the second floor of the Memorial Chapel, adjacent to the church office, is the Heritage Room, where sometimes the altar and altar rail, candelabra, and hymn board from 1866 are displayed. Pictures of former pastors and the old church remind visitors of former times. The parsonage stands across the street from the church and was built from the same rough stone and in the same nineteenth-century Romanesque style.

At the Fenton Historical Center at 67 Washington Street (open Monday through Saturday 10–4; 716/483-7521) is the collection of the Fenton Historical Society housed in the Italian villa–style mansion of former Governor Reuben E. Fenton. Used by the society since its inception in 1964, this impressive building features exhibits on life in Jamestown and Chautauqua County. Its library has the finest genealogical records in southwestern New York. In the basement is the Jennie Vimmerstedt Swedish Heritage Room, which commemorates the contributions of Vimmerstedt, an indefatigable, dedicated worker who was probably Jamestown's most honored citizen. The room, which is a replica of a Swedish *stuga*, was designed and executed by wood-carver Russell Chall and contains authentic Swedish items.

In recognition of the 1976 visit of King Carl XVI Gustaf, the museum has on display a chair made specifically for the king by the Union National Furniture Company of Jamestown, a mural of the palace and Riksdag, and a place setting from the 1976 royal luncheon held in the Jamestown Municipal Building. Swedish immigration memorabilia—an immigrant's trunk; a knife made from wood from Holy Trinity in Wilmington, Delaware; and numerous other items—complement the royal visit exhibit.

In the former living room of the Fenton mansion is a secretary made by the Lindblad Brothers Furniture Company of Jamestown and an Ahlstrom Company piano of 1875. In the stairway hang pictures of Jamestown citizens selected as outstanding. Two Swedish Americans—Roger Tory Peterson, the famed ornithologist, and Samuel Carlson, a former Jamestown mayor (Jamestown has had eight mayors of Swedish ancestry)— are among the group. In the staircase to the third floor is a bag of greetings dropped by Charles Lindbergh, Jr., to Mayor Carlson as he flew over the city on 1 August 1927. The tower of the Fenton Mansion affords a good view of the city, including First Lutheran Church.

The Fenton Historical Center has been making plans to expand so it could include exhibits on the city's industrial life. Up until a few decades ago, at least forty furniture establishments were headed by Swedish Americans. They were also involved with the manufacturing of steel building material and equipment.

The First Covenant Church at 520 Spring Street was organized in 1878 (an 1897 building was destroyed by fire in 1950). Now the congregation meets in an attractive 1952 colonial-style structure. The church's history exhibits are collected in its Heritage Room. A second Covenant church, Zion Covenant, was originally located two blocks from First. Now outside central Jamestown at Fairmount and West Ellicott, the church celebrated its centennial in 1994. The Epworth Christ United Methodist Church congregation, which was founded as a Swedish congregation, meets in a church at Foote and Chandler built in 1891 of red brick. Located across the street from First Lutheran, the red brick building of the former First Swedish Baptist Church (now Hillcrest Baptist) was constructed in 1907.

Though it does not have a Swedish cemetery, Jamestown has said farewell to many of its Swedish citizens at Lakeview Cemetery. One of the more interesting graves at this lovely place is that of the Rev. Hultgren, the long-time pastor of First Lutheran. His grave is near the main entrance and a lengthy Swedish inscription marks it.

The Jamestown Vasa (known as Thule Lodge) and Vikings are large and active Swedish lodges. They have their own downtown buildings and also operate facilities on or near Lake Chautauqua for various summer activities. Each lodge supports a Swedish folk dancing group, and the Viking Lodge, divided into Ingjald Lodge (for men) and Diana Lodge (for women), is known for its Viking Male Chorus. The Norden Club, the Norden Women's Club, and the American Scandinavian Heritage Foundation also are active.

Swedes in Jamestown founded the Gustavus Adolphus Children's Home, the Lutheran Retirement Home, and the Covenant Home for the Aged. The children's home and the retirement home are now part of an ecumenical campus called Lutheran Social Services (715 Falconer Street) that also includes a Presbyterian facility.

The Salvation Army broadcasts a religious program, largely in Swedish, each Sunday morning over radio station WKSN. A weekly one-hour radio program entitled "Swedish Hour" that begins at 9 P.M. each Sunday on WJTN is hosted by Polar Star honoree Gerald Heglund, who plays light classics, dance music, anthems, and religious songs and reports news from Sweden and Swedish America.

NEW ENGLAND

The first group of Swedish immigrants that came to New England arrived in Brockton, Massachusetts, in 1851. Nineteen years later, fifty-one Swedish settlers headed for the extreme northeast corner of Maine to establish the colony of New Sweden. Beginning in the 1870s and rapidly increasing during the remainder of the nineteenth century, large numbers of Swedes settled in Worcester, Massachusetts, particularly attracted by the Norton Company (a grinding machinery and abrasives concern that was founded in 1885) and various steel industries. Many of the early Swedes who came to Worcester were from Skåne, particularly in and around Höganäs. One such Swede was John Jeppson, who came to Worcester in 1869 and by 1885 was superintendent of the Norton Emery Wheel Company. His son, George Jeppson, eventually became chairman of the board of Norton Company. By the late 1880s, there were some five thousand Swedes living in Worcester, mainly in the Belmont Hill, Greendale, Vernon Hill, and Quinsigamond Village sections of the city. By 1920, the Swedish-born and second-generation population made up about one-fifth of Worcester's population. Other Massachusetts cities with considerable Swedish populations included Boston (particularly in the Dorchester and Roxbury sections) and its nearby communities of Beverly, Lynn, Waltham, and Newton. In Rhode Island, the majority of Swedes settled in and around Providence.

In the 1870s, there were also Swedish immigrants who went to Portland, south of Hartford and near the Connecticut River, attracted by employment opportunities at the sandstone quarries and the silk mills in nearby Middletown. Other Swedes in the Connecticut Valley settled close by in Cromwell and New Britain. Swedes also settled in Bridgeport and New Haven. Some Swedes were drawn to farming possibilities in northeast Connecticut, particularly in the Woodstock Township. But with the exception of Woodstock and New Sweden, Maine, the Swedish population in New England generally has been concentrated in the cities and other industrial areas.

CONNECTICUT

DARIEN   The Convent of St. Birgitta and the Vikingsborg Guest House, at Tokeneke Trail and Runkenhage Road (203/655-1068), is the only convent in the United States of the worldwide order of the Sisters of St. Birgitta (Bridget), founded by Saint Birgitta of Sweden (1303–73). Maria Elisabeth Hesselblad, born in Fåglavik, Västergötland, in 1870, became a Roman Catholic convert and joined this order because of the high regard she had for Saint Birgitta. Mother Elisabeth was instrumental in breathing new life into the order, one achievement being the reintroduction of the Sisters of Saint Birgitta into Sweden for the first time since the Reformation. Just before her death in 1957, she obtained

Vikingsborg, a mansion nestled at the head of a rocky cove on Long Island Sound. The property belonged to a Swedish evangelist, who had immigrated to New York, and his wife. They used it as a meeting center and a missionary rest home. Mother Elisabeth obtained the property from their children.

Nine sisters from India, Italy, and Mexico reside here and wear the full fourteenth-century-style habit. The nuns offer twelve rooms to guests and prepare three meals daily. The house features antique furniture, a library with books in several languages, a chapel, and sun porches overlooking the sound.

NEW HAVEN

Berzelius Hall at the corner of Temple and Trumbull streets and Whitney Avenue (near the campus of Yale University) is a large white granite building that carries the name of famed Swedish chemist Jöns Jacob Berzelius (1779–1848). The structure is used by a Yale society.

NAUGATUCK

Salem Lutheran Church at 14 Salem (203/723-0246) was organized in 1887 and the church dedicated in 1888. An old Covenant congregation is Hillside Covenant at Hillside and Elmwood (203/729-2444).

WASHINGTON DEPOT

Trinity Lutheran Church was organized in 1872 and its building dedicated in 1897. Salem Evangelical Covenant is an old Covenant congregation, and stained glass from the former sanctuary decorates the windows in its new building.

NEW BRITAIN

First Lutheran Church, at 77 Franklin Square (203/224-2475), has a large, impressive early twentieth-century Gothic sandstone building, the dream of the congregation's dynamic pastor Sven Gustaf Ohman, who served the church from 1895 (fourteen years after the church's founding) to 1922. Having been inspired by Uppsala Cathedral in Sweden, Ohman decided to use design elements of that structure in First Lutheran. The church originally had two soaring spires above the present towers when completed in 1906, but these had to be removed in 1938 because of structural weaknesses. The Swedish bell bears an inscription from Psalms in Swedish.

The impressive interior is noted for its vaulted ceiling, large stainedglass windows depicting various scenes from Christ's life (also small windows at the rear of the sanctuary portraying Gustavus Adolphus and Martin Luther), a large balcony on three sides, and three altar paintings by Olof Grafström (1855–1933). Twice the sanctuary was remodeled.

Constructed in 1897, the three-story brick Vega Hall at 57 Arch Street was the former headquarters of the Vega Benefit

Society, which now meets at First Lutheran Church. Visible under the roof line is an elaborate ship sculptured in stone.

The Klingberg Family Centers, at 370 Linwood Street (203/224-9113), were founded by the Rev. John Eric Klingberg. Born into a poor Västmanland family, Klingberg came to the United States and worked in a steel mill near Chicago before earning a theology degree at the University of Chicago. Remembering his difficult, poverty-stricken childhood, Klingberg in 1903 founded an orphanage in New Britain. It remained nondenominational though closely connected with Swedish Baptists. Today it is a residential treatment facility for emotionally troubled children. The site's oldest building was constructed in 1920.

Buried in Fairview Cemetery, whose office is at 110 Smalley Street, is Swede Nils Pearson (1850–1938), founder of the Vasa Order of America, a Swedish-American fraternal group that sponsors activities promoting Swedish culture. Pearson's grave is marked with a reddish granite memorial stone. First organized in 1896 in New Haven, the Vasa Order of America now has more than three hundred lodges and twenty-five thousand members in the United States, Sweden, and Canada.

HARTFORD

Emanuel Lutheran Church, 311 Capitol Avenue (203/525-0894), was organized in 1889 and the building dedicated in 1924.

MIDDLETOWN

Christ Lutheran Church at 300 Washington Street (203/347-6068) is opposite the campus of Wesleyan University. This light brick church was built in the Gothic style in 1958. The congregation, organized in 1891, has an altar painting (1910) by Olof Grafström of the crucifixion.

CROMWELL

Cromwell is famous for the extensive nurseries and greenhouses of Andrew N. Pierson (Anders Nils Persson) (1850-1925), from Håslöv, Skåne. Pierson, head of A. N. Pierson's, Inc., became known as the "Rose King of America." The town of Pierson, Florida, was named for one of his brothers who was a citrus grower.

Also located in Cromwell is a large complex run by the Evangelical Covenant Church of America. It includes the Children's Home of Cromwell, Covenant Village of Cromwell, Pilgrim Manor (a retirement center), and the East Coast conference headquarters of the Covenant Church of America.

PORTLAND

Zion Lutheran Church at 183 William (203/342-2860) was organized in 1874 and is the oldest Swedish Lutheran congregation in Connecticut. The first sanctuary was built in 1877, but a fire destroyed it before it was completed. The second church building at 13 Waverly Avenue was dedicated in 1879 and is currently owned by another congregation. In 1968, the Lutherans built a new sanctuary on William Street, opposite the old Swedish cemetery, which yields a wonderful view of the Connecticut River Valley. An altar painting by artist Olof Grafström of Christ in Gethsemane (1901) hangs in the fellowship hall.

EAST HAMPTON

Bethlehem Lutheran Church at 1 East High (203/267-4272) was organized in 1899 and the building constructed in 1900. This church was originally Congregational.

MANCHESTER

Emanuel Lutheran Church was organized in 1881 and the church dedicated in 1923.

WILLIMANTIC

Ebenezer Lutheran Church at 96 Oak (203/423-2193) was organized in 1889 and the church building dedicated in 1894. Except for its steeple, it is almost an exact replica of the former Zion Lutheran Church in Portland, about thirty miles away.

WOODSTOCK

A charming town in an idyllic setting in northeastern Connecticut, Woodstock first attracted Swedes in 1871. Initially Swedes came to Woodstock as a result of the cranberry interests of Dr. George Bowen, who hired three Swedes who had just arrived in New York in 1871. Apparently one of the Swedes, Carl Anderson, was such a success that Bowen asked him to invite his friends and relatives to join him in Woodstock as indentured workers. Although the cranberry business did not become profitable, the Swedes did become successful local farmers. By the early 1900s about one-fifth of the local population was Swedish. Names of the area's roads testify to the Swedish influence.

The Evangelical Covenant Church at 24 Childs Hill Road (203/928-0486) was originally organized for Swedes by Swedes. Although there was a Congregational church in Woodstock, none of the Swedish immigrants became members. It has been said that the Swedes were obliged to sit in the church's balcony during the services because the established residents did not want the newcomers in close proximity. In response, the Swedes organized their own church—the Swedish Evangelical Mission Congregation of Woodstock (the name later changed). The first Swedish service was held in 1875; fifteen years later, the congregation was offered the blacksmith shop on Woodstock Hill. The building was remodeled and dedicated in 1892.

The Quasset School on the east side of State Highway 169, behind the Woodstock Elementary School, was used as a school from 1748 until 1945, and Swedish children attended. It claims to be the oldest existing one-room school in the United States.

Referred to as the "Swedish Cemetery" in Woodstock, Elmvale Cemetery was begun in 1906.

NORTH GROSVENOR DALE
The congregation of Emanuel Lutheran Church on Main Street (203/923-9418) was first organized in 1882, and the brick building with its tall steeple was dedicated in 1897. This is one of the oldest Swedish church buildings still surviving in the state. Its members were mainly workers in the local cotton-weaving company.

RHODE ISLAND

PROVIDENCE
Organized in 1889, the Gloria Dei Evangelical Lutheran Church at 15 Hayes Street (401/421-5860) is probably the most outstanding Swedish church architecturally in Rhode Island. At one time there were seven Swedish churches in the city. Two blocks from the state Capitol, the church, on the National Register of Historic Places, was designed by Martin Hedmark and dedicated in 1928. It has been said that Hedmark was influenced by Gripsholm Castle in Mariefred, Sweden, in designing the church's exterior. The combination of brick and limestone facing is used on the circular corner towers with their small windows and sheet metal caps. A Viking ship, symbolic of the Church sailing through the ages, is used as a weathervane on the left tower. The highest part of the dramatic edifice contains a stepped gable.

On the doors leading into the nave from the narthex are small metal medallions of people who have greatly influenced the Swedish Lutheran Church—St. Ansgarius, St. Botvid, St. Eric, St. Birgitta, Martin Luther, and Olaus Petri. The sanctuary can perhaps best be described as Art Nouveau. It is marked by an array of Christian symbolism. The stained glass windows have Swedish inscriptions honoring the contributors. The window to the right of the altar depicts the Last Supper from a perspective above the table. At the top of the window is the inscription, "Given for you for the forgiveness of sins" in Swedish. The eight-sided raised pulpit with a canopy has a wood panel in gold leaf with the image of the Rev. J. E. Morton (1869–1913), a popular pastor during the first decade of the twentieth century. Morton died in Sweden and is buried in Svenljunga, where the Gloria Dei Church along with a congregation in Gävle has erected a monument in his honor.

There were Swedish Lutheran congregations in other Rhode Island towns, including East Greenwich (First Lutheran is the oldest Swedish Lutheran congregation in the state, having been organized in 1874); Pawtucket (Trinity Lutheran was organized in 1893 and its building constructed in 1896); and West Warwick (Emanuel Lutheran was organized in 1893 and its building constructed in 1896). Covenant congregations are found in Cranston, East Greenwich, Pawtucket, and West Warwick. The Scandinavian Home in Cranston is run by a corporation.

Several Providence Swedes were instrumental in organizing the Mayflower movement for the purpose of raising money for the Swedish National Sanatorium (today called the Swedish Medical Center) in Denver. The Berkander Plant in Providence, founded by George Berkander, made little mayflowers (celluloid wood anemonies) that were sold to raise the money. This sale follows the Swedish custom of making and selling mayflowers in May and using the proceeds to pay some health costs.

MASSACHUSETTS

This survey of Massachusetts begins with Worcester in the central part of the state and, after a brief mention of Orange, Holden, and Shrewsbury, moves to Boston, whose satellite cities are covered by beginning with Quincy on the south and moving clockwise around Boston. Last, two towns on Cape Ann, Rockport, and Pigeon Cove, whose granite quarries drew Swedes, receive attention.

WORCESTER

CHURCHES

Trinity Lutheran Church—73 Lancaster Street (at the corner of Lancaster and Salisbury streets, opposite the Worcester Art Museum) (508/753-2989).

The Trinity Lutheran Church congregation was begun on 1 January 1948 as a result of the merger of three congregations, including the Swedish First Evangelical Lutheran Church organized in 1881. Since the merger involved over two thousand communicants, a new larger sanctuary was needed. George Jeppson was appointed the chairman of the building committee and Jens Fredrik Larson, known for his work at Upsala College (East Orange, New Jersey), was selected as the architect. His design employs both Swedish and New England architectural features. The exterior of this impressive church is faced with cream-colored brick trimmed with limestone. The curved base of the tower is of seventeenth-century Swedish design. The tower above it is of New England Georgian design.

Trinity Lutheran Church, designed by Jens Fredrick Larson, and its octagonal Christ Chapel combine Swedish and New England architectural features.

The nave of the large sanctuary is of cream-colored brick penetrated by arches of the twentieth-century Norman style supported by limestone columns. The sanctuary is believed to contain the only decorated ceiling of its kind in the United States—128 plywood panels depicting through symbolism the Old and New Testaments. They were painted by Arthur Covey, who was influenced by the bright color in some of the most important church paintings in Sweden found in the ceiling of a small thirteenth-century church in Dädesjö, Småland, as well as the decorations in Swedish provincial houses. Hanging from the ceiling are eight Swedish-designed silver chandeliers of clustered lotus leaves. Throughout the church nave are commemorative plaques (one for the nineteenth-century immigrants, another for George Jeppson), and the cornerstones of the three churches that merged in 1948. Behind a glass is a golden crown worn by the brides of the church.

The altar and reredos are a modification of a design by Nicodemus Tessin (1654–1728) for the Cathedral of Kalmar, Sweden, which his father designed. (The altar was completed and installed at Kalmar in 1712.) It is made of carved oak, is free standing, and contains a painting of Christ in Gethsemane by Olof Grafström. The three stained glass windows were given by John and Thilda Jeppson for the old First Lutheran Church (the two former sanctuaries are now a Lebanese-American Roman Catholic Maronite Church on Mulberry Street and the Church of Our Lady of Fatima on Belmont Street). King Gustav V embroidered an altar cloth—it was dedicated by the Swedish archbishop in 1948. The baptismal font is a replica of a medieval font dating from about 1200 in the old church of Träne, Skåne, and is made from stone from the quarry that furnished the stone for the Cathedral of Lund.

The exterior of the Parish House reflects the manor house type of Swedish architecture. The door and entrance on the Lancaster Street side was inspired by one designed by Ernst Torsten Torulf (b. 1872), a Swedish architect. In the Parish House is the Olander Memorial Library, honoring a former pastor of the 1950s. It contains a number of rare old Bibles. Also in the Parish House is the 360-seat Jeppson Hall that includes stained glass from the First Lutheran Church.

On 26 May 1959, the octagonal Christ Chapel was dedicated. It was inspired by the work of Swedish architect Nicodemus Tessin the elder (1615–81), who built several eight-sided churches in Sweden. The stained glass windows are from the First Lutheran Church. The altar cross is made of ground quartz crystal and brass by Lars Fleming (b. 1928) of Stockholm, who was the silversmith to the king. The altar paraments were embroidered in Lund, Sweden. The Jeppson family was responsible financially for this lovely chapel.

Bethlehem Covenant Church—46 Greenwood Street (corner of Greenwood and Halmstad streets in Quinsigamond Village) (508/752-1459).
The congregation of Bethlehem Covenant Church is an offshoot (organized in 1894) of the Salem Square Church (now the Salem Covenant Church, 215 East Mountain Street) made famous by the Rev. John Alfred Hultman (1861–1942), known for his church concerts throughout the United States. The Rev. Hultman was a singing evangelist called *Solskenssångaren* ("the Sunshine Singer"). The present church was built in 1901. Near the Bethlehem Church is the old Swedish Methodist Church (Quinsigamond United Methodist Church, 9 Stebbins Street) and former Emanuel Lutheran (now the Quinsigamond Village Community Center). In Quinsigamond Village, Emanuel Lutheran is now at 220 Greenwood Street, and the Salvation

Army is at 884 Millbury Street. The local Roman Catholic church, at 3 Wiser Avenue, is called St. Catherine of Sweden.

Zion Lutheran Church—41 Whitmarsh Avenue, Greendale (508/853-2009).

Zion Lutheran Church has included many employees of the Norton Company (near the church are a number of large three-story homes formerly owned by Swedes). The congregation was organized in 1914, and the sanctuary dedicated in 1920. In 1948, groundbreaking for Faith Chapel took place with the Swedish archbishop Erling Eidem in attendance. The architect was Martin Hedmark of Sweden.

Historically, the most interesting feature of the chapel is the light pastel fresco on one side wall. It is the history of this Greendale congregation. From right to left are depicted an experienced potter, representing John Jeppson (see page 40), peacefully working in front of his Skåne home near a church with a stepped gable; two trees, a willow (on the wind-twisted trunk is a Viking looking toward the potter) and an elm (with a Native American, looking to the left at a New England valley, and Abraham Lincoln, who symbolizes integrity and love of freedom); a white New England–style church and homesteads in the valley; and an angel of peace carrying the banner, "Peace be with you." The angel looks down on a blond worker at the Norton Company. At the top of the fresco are the hands of God blessing the valley and its people, churches, and homes.

Belmont Street Baptist Church—25 Belmont Street (next door to the Church of Our Lady of Fatima) (508/753-0312).

Organized in 1880 as First Baptist Church, this congregation originally built its sanctuary at the corner of Eastern Avenue and Mulberry Street.

Epworth Methodist Church—64 Salisbury Street (across the street from the Worcester Art Museum and Trinity Lutheran Church) (508/752-2376).

Swedish immigrants organized this church in 1885 as the Thomas Street Methodist Episcopal Church.

OTHER POINTS OF INTEREST
Norton Company—One New Bond Street (617/853-1000).

As late as 1914, about 75 percent of the workers of this large company were of Swedish extraction. On the fourth floor of the administration building at the Greendale location is Norton Hall. On the walls is a unique family tree showing the founders and all employees who have worked for the company for twenty-five years or more. A great number of the employees, particularly during the early years, were Swedish or Swedish American. Norton Company now has eighty plants throughout the world. Murals in Norton Hall depict various aspects of the company's operations, and glass cases show its numerous products.

In earlier years, Norton Company built single-family houses for its employees. Before World War I, these houses were sold to the workers for $1500. When the first village was built on Indian Hill Road, Theodore Roosevelt was present at the dedication. Other houses were constructed on Ararat and New Bond streets.

Other efforts of Swedes included a hospital. On 1903, the Swedish National Federation was organized. At its 1921 meeting, it was proposed that a Swedish hospital be established, and the following year the Fairlawn Hospital, now Fairlawn Rehabilitation Hospital, was opened.

Lutheran Home for the Aged at 26 Harvard Street (508/754-8877) was established in 1920 as the Swedish Lutheran Home. Five years later, the Jeppson Building, the first part of the existing structure, was constructed.

At 370 Main Street the former Skandia Bank and Trust Company, originally known as the Skandia Credit Union, was opened in 1915. It started as a credit union, and after fifteen years secured a bank charter. Owners have included Guaranty Bank and Trust Company, New England Bank, and Fleet Bank.

In Old Swedish Cemetery (154 Webster Road) and New Swedish Cemetery (on Island Drive, which is opposite 240 Webster Street) lie the pioneers of Worcester's early era. Upon entering the Old Swedish Cemetery, the visitor faces a marble monument "in memory of those Swedish pioneers of Worcester who in 1885 founded this cemetery." Probably the most imposing of the monuments is the Jeppson family marker. Viking ships and part of the Twenty-third Psalm decorate the vertical stone whose border has a swirling Viking motif. Not far from the Jeppson monument is a marble seat in memory of Pehr G. Holmes (1881–1952), mayor of Worcester and a member of Congress.

To the right, immediately upon entering the New Swedish Cemetery, is a monument erected in 1967 by the Vasa Order of America in memory of their deceased members. At the southwest end is a large stone honoring former residents of the Lutheran Home for the Aged.

SCULPTURE AND OTHER ART

Three works by Carl Milles—"Man Riding Fish" (a fountain made of pewter), "The Sun Glitter," and "Head of Nereid"— have been collected by the Worcester Art Museum at 55 Salisbury

(508/799-4406). At 327 West Boylston Street, in front of Norton Company Plant II, is Milles' "Eagle," a war memorial made of black granite.

ORANGE

Originally known as the Swedish Lutheran Church, Bethany Lutheran Church (62 Cheney Street, 508/544-3541) was organized in 1889 and the present church built in 1896. Orange is northwest of Worcester, near Athol.

HOLDEN

Immanuel Lutheran Church, at 346 Shrewsbury Street (508/829-4416), is the largest of the Swedish congregations located in communities near Worcester. Its building was built in 1948.

SHREWSBURY

The Scandinavian Athletic Club at 435 Lake Street (508/757-3948) is the last of numerous Swedish clubs in and around Worcester. It erected a large clubhouse in the early 1920s, which today is rated as one of the best and largest of private sports facilities in the Worcester area.

BOSTON

The Isabella Stewart Gardner Museum, housed in the Venetian palace–style former home of Isabella Stewart Gardner (280 The Fenway, 617/566-1401), contains an art collection that includes a number of works by Swedish artist Anders Zorn (1860–1920). Of special interest is a portrait of Gardner that Zorn painted in Venice. A long-time friend who introduced Zorn to patrons and helped him arrange exhibits in Boston, Gardner first met Zorn at the Chicago World Columbian Exposition in 1893 when she purchased his *The Omnibus*, now also part of the museum's collection. Open to the public are both Gardner's collection and her turn-of-the-century home.

Two churches in the Boston metropolitan area have Swedish roots. The first, Resurrection Lutheran (formerly Emanuel Lutheran) Church, at 94 Warren Avenue (southeast corner of Warren Street and Kearsarge Avenue) in Roxbury (617/427-2066), was organized in 1873, and the large stone twentieth-century Romanesque church with a tall tower (designed by architects Carl Enebuske and Hilding Hanson) was constructed between 1923 and 1934. Over the front door, under a statue of Christ, is the inscription in Swedish, "Come to me all ye who are heavy laden."

The second, Covenant Congregational Church, at 455 Arborway in Forest Hills, grew from a meeting 1 November 1881, when twelve men met in a home in Cambridge and signed the organizational document making them charter members of the Scandinavian Free Church of Boston. Later it became known as the Swedish Congregational Church and Covenant Congregational. In 1936, the present sanctuary was dedicated. Built in a Romanesque architectural style, the church has a modified stepped gable on the bell tower reminiscent of southern Swedish design.

QUINCY

Organized in 1889, Salem Lutheran Church, an originally Swedish church that became Faith Lutheran Church in 1974, dedicated its present structure at 201 Granite Street in 1894 and enlarged it in 1909.

BROCKTON

The "mother" church of the former Augustana Lutheran churches of New England, First Lutheran Church at 900 South Main Street (508/586-9021) was organized in 1867, but its roots go back to 1853 when the first service was conducted by Olof Gustaf Hedstrom (1803–77), founder of Swedish Methodism. The present structure was dedicated in 1923 with Swedish Archbishop Nathan Söderblom in attendance.

Gethsemane Lutheran Church at 906 North Main Street (508/586-7975) was organized in 1895 and the church building dedicated in 1923.

NORTH EASTON

Covenant Congregational is an old Covenant church in North Easton (508/238-6423).

ATTLEBORO

The First Evangelical Covenant Church at 841 North Main (508/226-6221) is an old Covenant church in Attleboro.

WEST NEWTON

As a result of the 1907 visit of Sweden's Prince Wilhelm to Boston, the Swedish National Union was founded. In 1911, it became the Swedish Charitable Society of Greater Boston, Inc., for the purpose of establishing and maintaining a home for aged and incapacitated Swedish Americans in the area and providing charitable social assistance. In 1917 the Home for Aged Swedish People (now the Swedish Home for the Aged) at 206 Waltham Avenue (617/527-9751) was established. In 1926, Crown Prince Gustav Adolf and his wife, Crown Princess Louise, visited the home as did King Carl XVI Gustaf in 1976. At the right of the front door is a historic plaque placed there at the 1917 opening. In 1991 the society voted to allow any persons of Nordic heritage —not only Swedes—as residents.

CAMBRIDGE

Faith Lutheran Church (formerly Augustana Lutheran) at 311 Broadway (617/354-0414) features a central tower and was constructed in the Gothic style and dedicated in 1909. The congregation was officially organized in 1892.

Also in Cambridge is the Church of the New Jerusalem (Swedenborg Chapel) at 50 Quincy Street (617/864-4552). The Swedenborgian church's general convention headquarters is in nearby Newton near the Swedenborg School of Religion (617/262-5918). The Swedenborgian Book Store is in Boston at 79 Newbury Street (617/262-5918).

WALTHAM

By 1885 there was a growing number of Swedes in the Boston suburb of Waltham. Two congregations were formed: the Swedish Lutheran Church, now known as First Evangelical Lutheran, and the Swedish Free Mission, which became the Covenant Congregational Church. In 1894, the Swedish Free Mission constructed a building on Central Street, but in 1950 the congregation, wishing to relocate, began holding services in the lovely Gothic-style stone church of the Waltham Church of the New Jerusalem (Swedenborgian). In 1960, the church, at 375 Lexington Street (617/893-7717), was sold to the Covenant congregation. The First Lutheran congregation worships in a twentieth-century English Gothic church designed by Hilding Hanson and built in 1927 at the corner of Eddy and Weston.

On United Nations Day, 24 October 1961, the Waltham Junior Chamber of Commerce erected a plaque on reddish Swedish granite on Waltham Common (on the east side near Elm Street) honoring Dag Hammarskjöld's life with the words, "In tribute for service and sacrifice to the cause of world peace."

WOBURN

Lutheran Church of the Redeemer (617/933-4600) on Forest Park Road was organized in 1893 and its building dedicated in 1897. It was called the Swedish Evangelical Lutheran Church.

MEDFORD

On the campus of Tufts University, two buildings are named for Swedish Americans. Arthur Anderson Hall (Tufts College of Engineering) takes its name from the former chairman of the university board of trustees who was Boston's Swedish consul and had a successful career in the insurance business. The Nils Yngve Wessell Library is named for Tuft's president from 1953 to 1966. A Carl Milles bronze casting of an elephant welcomes visitors to a library courtyard fountain. Inside the library is a reduced copy of "Man and Pegasus" by Milles. Also at Tufts in the Barnum Museum is a collection of Jenny Lind memorabilia.

MALDEN

Organized in 1893, First Lutheran Church at 62 Church (617/324-7133) was dedicated in 1897.

PIGEON COVE Cape Ann, northeast of Boston, was known for its quarries of granite, the stone used to build the Bunker Hill Monument in Boston and to pave the streets of several eastern cities, including New York. Swedes and Finns were attracted to the area by employment possibilities. The first Swede arrived in 1879. Most of the early Swedish quarry workers lived on Pigeon Hill Street or in the immediate vicinity. In the early 1890s, three Swedish churches were built. The former Swedish Lutheran Church in Pigeon Cove (20 Stockholm Avenue) is now a private residence. In 1891, the Swedish Methodists built a church at 147 Granite Street. Today the building is used as a silversmith's studio. Down the block at 111 Granite Street is the former Swedish Evangelical Church (Mission Covenant), built in 1894. Today the former Covenant church has been converted into an attractive private residence. Although none of the former Swedish congregations currently exist in Pigeon Cove, there are Lutheran and Covenant churches with Swedish roots in nearby West Peabody, Beverly, and Lynn.

ROCKPORT In Rockport at 18 Broadway is the Vasa Order's Spiran Lodge, which was chartered in 1906. The Vasa Order still meets regularly in the hall and has Swedish festivals.

VERMONT

Vermont attracted few Swedish settlers, but still existing are several churches of Swedish heritage. In Brattleboro, the entire congregation of Trinity Lutheran Church at 43 Western Avenue was originally from Dalsland. The altar rail is believed to be designed after the one found in the Tisselskog Church in Dalsland. (Some other Dalsland natives settled twenty miles north of the Vermont border in Waterville, Canada's first Swedish settlement.) In Proctor, St. Paul's Lutheran Church was organized in 1890 by Swedes who were employed by the Vermont Marble Company. They built a sanctuary in 1894. In Rutland, an Augustana Lutheran congregation was formed (Salem Lutheran), as was a Covenant congregation, and in nearby Center Rutland, a former Covenant church, whose building won a place on the National Register of Historic Places, was nurtured by Swedes.

NEW HAMPSHIRE

Like Vermont, New Hampshire had only a scattering of Swedish settlers. Evidence of their settlement remains today in Gethsemane Lutheran Church in Manchester at 65 Sagamore

Street. Organized in 1882, the congregation erected its building in 1887. Holy Trinity in Portsmouth and Concordia in Concord were Augustana Lutheran congregations. Bedford has a Covenant congregation. Near Peterborough, the Covenant church created a conference center and summer campground called Pilgrim Pines. Berlin, near White Mountain National Forest in northern New Hampshire, has a sizable Lutheran church that maintains in its archives the contribution of its Swedish members. Swedes in Berlin were known for ski jumping.

MAINE

MONSON

Monson is nineteen miles northwest of Dover-Foxcroft, the largest town in central Maine. The Monson area slate quarries first drew Swedes in 1874 and 1875. Once there, the Swedes established two churches—a Swedish Mission Church, which was built in 1890 and later became the Lutheran Church, and a Swedish Methodist Church, which was built in 1892. Both churches had Swedish ministers and conducted services in Swedish. The Swedish Lutheran Church on Wilkins Street was a frame building with a central steeple. In recent times it was a hostel for Appalachian Trail hikers, but later it was sold at auction. The former Swedish Methodist Church on Water Street is a small clapboard structure that has been sold to another congregation.

The small Monson Town Museum (on Main Street above the town office) opens its doors mid-June through early September 1–4:30 daily except Sunday. The Welsh were the first ethnic group to arrive, followed by Swedes and later Finns. Today the Swedes have for the most part moved out, leaving behind many tombstones with long Swedish epitaphs. Persisting, however, is an interest in kick sledding, which Swedes first introduced to Maine. The sleds were manufactured in Monson for a while. The museum has two kick sleds on display, and the community still sponsors kick sled races.

CARIBOU

Built in 1938, the Nylander Museum, 393 Main Street, honors Olof O. Nylander (1864–1943), the Swedish-American botanist and geologist. A Ystad shoemaker's son, Nylander began as a house painter but became a self-taught geologist. In 1893, he discovered fossils in Chapman Plantation, Maine, and became employed with the U.S. Geological Survey.

Nylander contributed articles to numerous geological and scientific magazines in various parts of the United States. He collected fossils, minerals, and shells in many areas of Maine. Upon his death, they became the property of the City of

Caribou. This museum houses Nylander's extensive geological, marine life, and natural history collection.

Nylander is buried in the Caribou City Cemetery, where the Ketch-Nylander stone lists family members.

NEW SWEDEN   New Sweden is located in the extreme northeast corner of Maine in the Aroostook Valley, an area of vast stretches of pine and birch-covered hills and mountains, of crystal clear lakes, and of potato agricultural enterprises. Swedish settlement dates from late summer, 1870. In June, twenty-two men, eleven women, and eighteen children set sail from Gothenburg for Halifax, Nova Scotia. The prime mover was William Widgery Thomas, Jr., a native of Portland, Maine, who had been the American consular agent in Gothenburg between 1863 and 1865 and later served as American minister to Stockholm. Thomas believed that the hardy Swedes he saw leaving for points west in the United States also would be ideal for settling the frontier of his home state of Maine. Thomas advertised in the Swedish press, offering in the Aroostook Valley one hundred acres of land per family, land grants he had persuaded the state legislature to supply. The emigrants were required to pay for the journey to America, they had to be in good health, and they had to present letters of recommendation concerning their moral character. Thomas was particularly interested in attracting Swedish farmers who had additional skills in other fields such as carpentry and tailoring.

The first group of Swedes came from several provinces, Skåne being the one producing the most. They arrived too late to plant and harvest any crop during the first summer; only a good crop of turnips was harvested the first year. The settlers spent their time building a central gathering hall, known as the Kapitoleum, where they lived during the first long winter. They had expected log cabins to have been built before their arrival, but they found only six had been constructed by the state of Maine. By 1873, some twenty-two thousand acres of land had been cleared. The population grew to six hundred, including many new arrivals from Jämtland. This contingent decided to build their log cabins immediately north of New Sweden, calling their settlement Jemtland. To the west of New Sweden is a township called Westmanland, which was being settled as early as 1879. In 1881, a few Swedish immigrants moved north from New Sweden. Fourteen years later the township of Stockholm was organized. Mainly because of the vast timber resources and the construction of a new lumber mill, Stockholm expanded industrially between 1900 and 1910.

New Sweden and the surrounding area prospered during the late nineteenth and early twentieth centuries. In the early

The New Sweden Historical Museum is a replica of the Kapitoleum, the earliest Swedish settlers' first home.

sixties one could still hear Swedish spoken, Swedish food prepared, and Swedish songs sung and dances danced. In 1970, the town observed its centennial, stimulating even greater interest in its Swedish heritage. In the vicinity of New Sweden are several geographic features named for the early Swedish settlers, including Fogelin Hill and Pond, Gelot and Jacobson Hill, and Stockholm Mountain.

There are no motels or restaurants either in New Sweden or Stockholm. Travelers should arrange overnight accommodations in the neighboring town of Caribou, where there are motels and bed and breakfast inns.

At the New Sweden Historical Museum on Capitol Hill Road, visitors are welcome daily mid-June until Labor Day. Call for information (207/896-3018). The building itself is a replica of the old Kapitoleum, which immigrants used as their first home and the community eventually used as a place of worship, a school, a store, a community hall, and the office of the commissioner of immigration. In later years, the historical society converted it into a museum, but on 30 June 1971 a fire destroyed it. Three years later, thanks to a special fund collected in the United States and Sweden, the present replica was dedicated. Displays feature the area's historical collection saved from the fire, including photographs of early settlers, hand-hewn skis, the original altar rail and pews from Gustaf Adolph Lutheran Church, various farm implements, and a portrait of New Sweden's immigration commissioner, W. W. Thomas, in Stockholm.

Two markers near the museum—a state plaque on a large boulder in front and a granite monument inscribed *"Mina Barn I Skogen"* ("My children in the forest") in front and toward the west—recognize New Sweden's heritage. North of the museum is the restored Lindsten Stuga, an immigrant log cottage dating from 1894. Another Swedish homestead that has been restored is the Larson-Ostlund House, which also has a potato cellar.

The Gustaf Adolph Lutheran congregation was organized in 1871, and the present sanctuary on Capitol Hill Road (207/896-3068) was built in 1880. The stained glass in the balcony is in memory of the early pioneers. The church bell was from W. W. Thomas. In March 1871, eight settlers organized the First Swedish Baptist Church (now called First Baptist Church of New Sweden), making it the oldest congregation in New Sweden. The first church building was erected in 1892 but destroyed by fire ten years later. The present building dates from 1902. The stained glass windows are memorials to Swedes of New Sweden. The Evangelical Covenant Church was organized in 1886 with seventeen charter members. The attractive white clapboard church was dedicated in 1891, and ten years later the high steeple was given by W. W. Thomas. The colored windows are memorials given by Swedes of the congregation.

The New Sweden Cemetery is east of the New Sweden Historical Museum and includes the graves of the early Swedish settlers. Adjacent to the cemetery to the northwest in a grove of trees is a granite monument "in loving memory of the first Swedish pioneers laid at rest here 1871–1875." There is also a very small Swedish cemetery on State Highway 161 one-half mile south of the New Sweden–Woodland town line on the east side of the road. Other cemeteries may be found in Westmanland, West Jemtland, and Rista.

New Sweden claims nearly thirty log houses built by pioneer Swedes, though none of the original state-built cabins survives. The privately owned Timmerhuset ("the log house") is the only structure in New Sweden listed on the National

Register of Historic Places. A one and a half–story dwelling, it was built sometime between 1871 and 1873. The interior has been totally restored, and the hand-hewn logs can be seen in the living room, which has a cathedral ceiling. The front of the house formerly had an exterior balcony, as do homes in northern Sweden. This characteristic has been preserved in the upstairs interior balcony.

W. W. Thomas Memorial Park, beyond the museum, is named for the founder of New Sweden. Here and at other sites on the weekend nearest 21 June, the annual Swedish Midsummer festivities, including an interdenominational community worship service and Swedish folk dancing and singing, take place. Beyond the park is the restored Lars Noak Blacksmith Shop.

WEST-MANLAND

The Westmanland School House is a one-room, white clapboard schoolhouse built in 1925 (take West Road west three miles from the New Sweden Historical Museum; turn north on Westmanland Road and travel one mile to the schoolhouse, which is on the west side of the road). The interior walls and pressed metal ceiling are painted white. Today it is used as the town hall for the township of Westmanland. Almost directly east of the school is the Westmanland cemetery with old stone markers.

On the east side of Westmanland Road, less than a mile north of the schoolhouse and cemetery, is a restored privately owned log house (the logs may only be seen on the interior). The cabin was probably built in 1880 by Carl August Peterson, an early Swedish settler. Later the family of Algot Andersson (he was the first person born in Westmanland) lived in the house. On the west side of West Road is a farmhouse, the drive leading to the farm being lined with birch trees. Between the house and barn (built in the 1870s) is a log house built by A. G. Ohlson, another early Swedish settler, in 1871. Less than a mile north is a large white frame Victorian home. Behind is a small white clapboard structure that was once the Westmanland post office.

JEMTLAND

The small Jemtland Cemetery is located on West Jemtland Road, and Jemtland's other cemetery (at Rista) is two-tenths of a mile east of Fort Kent Road (on the north side). The West Jemtland Cemetery is on the north side of the West Jemtland Road, almost a mile from Fort Kent Road. Also, on the Fort Kent Road, about one-half mile north of Rista Road, was the Everett Larsson Store, where the community Sunday School was held.

STOCKHOLM

The Stockholm Historical Museum was opened in 1976 in a 1901 building that housed the first store in Stockholm. It is on

North Jemtland Road, east of State Highway 161, north of New Sweden. Among the museum displays are the Swedish flag given to the town by King Gustav V marking the seven hundredth anniversary of Stockholm, Sweden; items from the Fogelin store and family; a Stockholm centennial quilt depicting buildings in the town; old photographs; skis and sleds; a lumbering display; and a schoolroom and old kitchen displays.

The white clapboard First Baptist Church, on North Jemtland Road in between State Highway 161 and the Stockholm Historical Museum, is the oldest church building in town, constructed in 1905. Trinity Lutheran Church (formerly called the Oscar Frederick Evangelical Lutheran Church) was organized in 1906 and constructed in 1907.

On the east side of North Jemtland Road, on top of a hill overlooking Stockholm, is the cemetery containing graves of the early Swedish settlers. At the north end of the cemetery is a fine view of the pine forests and the town of Stockholm in the valley.

2   The Midwest 🇺🇸

ILLINOIS

Illinois drew the greatest number of Swedish immigrants—even more than Minnesota—from the mid-1840s on because many Swedes chose it as their original destination. Chicago, Rockford, Rock Island, Moline, Galesburg, and other parts of Cook, Winnebago, Rock Island, Knox, and Henry counties developed into Swedish strongholds. But it was Carl Sandburg's Chicago—"Hog Butcher for the World, / Tool Maker, Stacker of Wheat, / Player with Railroads and the Nation's Freight Handler; / Stormy, husky, brawling, / City of the Big Shoulders"—the commercial distributing center for all the Middle West, where Swedes created struggling new communities and from which were sprung second-stage immigrants who went to new destinations throughout the Midwest and West.

CHICAGO

The first Swedes arrived in Chicago in the 1840s, and by 1900 the city had forty-nine thousand Swedish-born, whose ninety-six thousand children swelled their ranks. At the time, only Stockholm, the capital of Sweden, could boast more Swedes and their children.

At first the Swedes settled in Swede Town, just north of the Chicago River, establishing several churches there, but the

61

Great Chicago Fire of 1871 wiped out that settlement, reducing four of the churches to ashes. The next Swedish settlement was farther north in the Lake View district around Belmont Avenue (3200 North). By the 1890s, the Swedes moved into the area surrounding Clark and Foster Avenues (5200 North), which became identified as Andersonville. There were also Swedish settlements on the south side (Twentieth and Twenty-first streets; Buffalo Avenue between Eighty-sixth and Eighty-eighth, known as Englewood); on the northwest side (Irving Park and Logan Square); west side (Humboldt Park); and the far south side (Grand Crossing, Pullman, Roseland, and Indiana Harbor). In nearby Evanston, north of the city, was another Swedish community.

Swedish architects, contractors, carpenters, and engineers were in part what made Chicago Sandburg's "City of the Big Shoulders." Estimates of the buildings built by Swedes range from 35% in 1928 to 75% in 1948. Research funded by the Swedish American Museum Center has shown that Swedish architects helped shape Chicago and nearby Evanston: Eric Edwin Hall (born in 1883 in Östergötland) designed Chicago Stadium, "the home of the Bulls and Blackhawks," built in 1929; Lars Gustaf Hallberg, Sr. (born in 1844 in Vänersnäs, Västergötland), designed what is now Kendall College and was formerly the Swedish Theological Seminary in Evanston; John A. Nydén (born in 1878 in Småland) founded in 1907 the John A. Nydén Company and was responsible at the time of his death in 1932 for perhaps one-third of the buildings in Evanston (he is buried at Memorial Park Cemetery in Evanston); Arthur F. Hussander designed school buildings, including Lindblom High School.

Swedish and Swedish-American builders executed plans that changed Chicago's skyline forever. They included Henry Ericsson (b. 1862 in Småland) and Andrew Lanquist (b. 1856 in Ving, Västergötland), who in 1891 erected the Monon Building, considered Chicago's first skyscraper. In 1904 Lanquist organized and became president of the Lanquist & Illsley Company, responsible for the Wrigley Building and several additional downtown buildings. Other builders included Henry Ericsson's brother John (b. 1868 in Småland), John Adolph Lindstrom (b. 1883 in Västergötland), Louis M. Nelson (b. 1867 in Värmland), Nils Persson Severin (b. 1861 in Skåne), Eric E. Skoglund (b. 1878 in Närke), and Erik Peter Strandberg, Sr. (b. 1860 in Jämtland).

In Chicago, the Swedes founded or helped to establish five colleges and seminaries (two—North Park and Trinity—still remain in or near the city), two hospitals, a number of Swedish-language newspapers, and two national societies (Svithiod,

Vikings) as well as many local ones. Four Swedish churches—
Lutheran, Covenant, Methodist, Baptist—had homes for the
aged. Two Swedish-founded church denominations—the Evangelical Covenant Church of America (originally known as the
Mission Friends) and the Baptist General Conference (formerly
Swedish Baptist Church)—continue to have their headquarters
in the Chicagoland area. Today, along with Minneapolis–St.
Paul, Chicago retains a central position among Swedish Americans.

INSTITUTES AND MUSEUMS
**Swedish American Museum Center of Chicago—5211 North
Clark (312/728-8111). Open 11–4 Tuesday through Friday, 11–
3 Saturday and Sunday, and closed Monday.**

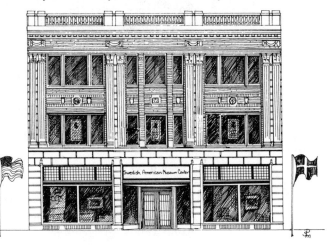

*The Swedish American
Museum Center of
Chicago draws visitors
with art, artifacts,
classes, and concerts
and other cultural
events.*

This museum sprang from seeds of effort planted by local
residents, generally as a result of the 1976 U.S. Bicentennial.
Originally located on the west side of Clark Street, the museum
moved after the Swedish American Museum Association of
Chicago purchased in 1987 the four-story building on the east
side of Clark. King Carl XVI Gustaf and Queen Silvia officially
dedicated the center on 19 April 1988. "The Dream of American
Swedish Immigration to Chicago," the museum's permanent
collection display, features Swedish immigrants' trunks, linens,
tools, and kitchen utensils from the late nineteenth and early
twentieth centuries, and elements of the museum's jewelry
collection complement displayed folk costumes from Skåne.

The center plans to open a children's section in the basement
with the theme "From Vikings to Volvo" and offer educational
programs in adjacent classrooms for schoolchildren. Temporary
exhibits of Swedish contemporary art on the first floor are
expected to attract young and old alike. Other additional plans
include development of a third-floor lending library of

contemporary Swedish literature and a noncirculating collection of reference works.

Concerts, cultural events, and classes draw visitors to the center year-round. The "Linnea Recitals," a three-concert series featuring the music of Swedish and Swedish-American composers, combine art, music, and ethnicity to create a unique experience. At the Midsummer celebration during Father's Day weekend in June, four blocks of North Clark are closed to traffic. The center celebrates *julmarknad* with an arts and crafts festival the first weekend of December and a Christmas café and the Lucia festival on December 13. At 5 P.M. the procession assembles and proceeds west on Foster Avenue to Ebenezer Lutheran Church, where the main celebration takes place. Then the crowd heads back to the center for *glögg*. The center also opens its doors to those seeking Swedish language lessons or folk dancing classes.

Nobel Hall of Science—Museum of Science and Industry, Fifty-seventh Street and Lake Shore Drive (312/684-1414).

The Nobel Hall of Science at the Museum of Science and Industry commemorates Swedish inventor Alfred Nobel (1833–96) and is dedicated to the American Nobel laureates in physics, chemistry, and physiology/medicine.

HISTORIC PLACES

Andersonville—bounded by Peterson (north), Broadway (east), Lawrence (south), and Damen (west).

Andersonville is the only remaining Chicago district that is distinctively Swedish, though the area now is quite ethnically mixed. A neighborhood in a city of neighborhoods, Andersonville has a pulse that can be felt on Clark Street north of Foster Avenue. A plaque on the southwest corner of Foster and Clark identifies the location of the former Andersonville School, from which the area took its name. Several restaurants and businesses with Swedish roots or featuring a Swedish decor are located along Clark Street, but these are only an echo of the strong Swedish commercial offerings—Gustafson's Haberdashery, Hedstrom's Shoes, Johnson Brothers' Grocery, for example—that formerly drew Chicagoans to Andersonville, six miles north of downtown, by horse-drawn streetcars. Today Svea Restaurant, owned by Kurt Mathiasson, a force behind the rejuvenation of Andersonville and the establishment of the Swedish American Museum Center, recalls with its traditional Swedish dishes the days when Swedes were the largest ethnic group in Andersonville. Annually Andersonville celebrates Midsummer Day festivities, which thousands attend, and enjoys a Lucia festival at the museum and the Ebenezer Lutheran Church.

CHURCHES
St. Francis Church—2514 West Thorndale (northeast corner of Thorndale and Maplewood) (312/561-8189).
The first group of Swedes to arrive in Chicago came in 1849. Among early arrivals was Gustav Unonius (1810–1902), who migrated to the United States from Sweden in 1841 and was ordained an Episcopalian priest in 1845. He founded the Swedish-Norwegian St. Ansgarius parish in Chicago and became its pastor in 1849. Nine years later he returned to Sweden after conflicts with recently immigrated Scandinavian Lutherans. A church Unonius built on Indiana (today Grand) near Wells Street with financial assistance from Jenny Lind burned during the 1871 fire. A second, erected in 1872 on Chicago Avenue, was razed in 1920 after also burning. In 1929, the present church was built farther north, and in the 1940s the name of the parish was changed from St. Ansgarius to St. Francis. Over the main door of this light red brick church is inscribed in stone "Jenny Lind Memorial Chapel," and the cornerstone reads, "AD 1849–1929." Nothing inside the church is of Swedish origin.

One item remaining from the mid-nineteenth century is the beautiful silver Jenny Lind communion chalice and paten presented by the famous Swedish singer to St. Ansgarius Church, on which is the inscription, *"Gifven till den Skandinaviska Kyrkan St. Ansgarius Chicago af en Landsmaninna A.D. 1851"* ("Gift to the Scandinavian Church St. Ansgarius Chicago from a Fellow-Countrywoman A.D. 1851"). The chalice and paten, kept at the Episcopal Church Center (65 East Huron), are used on special occasions at St. Francis Church.

Immanuel Evangelical Lutheran Church—1500 West Elmdale Avenue (northwest corner of Elmdale and Greenview) (312/743-1820).
This is the "mother" church of Chicago's Swedish Lutherans. The congregation was organized in 1853 by the Rev. Tuve Nilsson Hasselquist (1816–91), who was the first president (1860–70) of the Augustana Synod. The first pastor was the Rev. Erland Carlsson (1822–93), a powerful preacher and strong advocate of temperance. The present church building, dating from the early 1950s, is the fifth in the congregation's history, earlier ones having been located on Superior Street and at Sedgwick and Hobbie streets. The modified Gothic-style church of red brick, trimmed with Indiana limestone, was designed by the firm of Adolph Hanson and Einar Olson. On the lawn outside the church are three 1886 bells, with Swedish inscriptions, from a former sanctuary. Inscriptions on two of the bells read, *"Glädjens med dem som glade äro och gråten med dem som gråta"* and *"Ära vare Gud i höjden."*

Many of the interior appointments are attributed to Swedish architect Martin Hedmark and to Swedish-American craftsmen. The church sanctuary and adjacent Lanquist Chapel have numerous historic reminders. At the rear of the sanctuary are five stained glass windows depicting five historic events that occurred at Immanuel Lutheran, including the first classes of Augustana College and Theological Seminary from 1860 to 1863; the organizing of Augustana Hospital in Chicago by Immanuel members in 1882; the establishing of seven Chicago daughter congregations; and the founding in the late 1800s of the Augustana Women's Missionary Society, with special recognition to Dr. Emmy Evald. There are four wood statues on the north side of the sanctuary representing St. Birgitta; the shadowy and somewhat legendary twelfth-century king of Sweden and patron saint, Erik IX; Nathan Söderblom, archbishop of Sweden; and Pope John XXIII. The chancel is said to be of Swedish style, and the ends of every pew are painted in floral designs reminiscent of Swedish folk art.

The Lanquist Memorial Chapel, to the south of the main sanctuary, is in memory of Andrew and Elsa Lanquist. Andrew Lanquist (1856–1931) was one of Chicago's major building contractors, responsible for such structures as the Wrigley Building (410 North Michigan Avenue) and Wrigley Field (1060 West Addison). The chapel's ceiling, embellished with frescoes depicting the heavenly host, has chandeliers from AB Orrefors Glasbruk. The frontal on the altar was handmade by Solvig Westerberg of Sweden who is known for her artistic embroideries. The baptistery contains a silver flagon used in the congregation's former church sanctuaries. The stained glass windows represent scenes from the history of Immanuel.

On the north side of the main sanctuary, on the same level as the rear balcony, is the St. Ansgar Room, named in honor of the ninth-century missionary to Sweden. A stained glass window and a small altar commemorate the missionary. On the north wall are depicted various churches associated with St. Ansgar's ministry. In Founders Hall, also to the north of the main sanctuary, are stained glass windows with the coat of arms of the various Swedish provinces.

Ebenezer Lutheran Church—1650 West Foster Avenue (northeast corner of West Foster and North Paulina) (312/561-8496).

One of the daughter congregations of Immanuel Lutheran, Ebenezer is faced with rusticated limestone and topped by a tall silver spire and a shorter one. The church, founded in 1892, dedicated the building in 1912. The sanctuary with its high vaulted ceiling contains two large Gothic-style stained glass windows. The ornate Gothic-style altar includes a statue of Christ (patterned after Bertel Thorvaldsen's Christ in Vor Frue Church in Copenhagen), and on either side of the altar are two paintings of the life of Christ. High above the exterior Foster Avenue door is carved *"Svenska Ev. Lutherska Ebenezer Kyrkan"* (the English inscription is on the Paulina Street side).

A second daughter congregation of Immanuel Lutheran is Salem Lutheran (318 East Seventy-fourth, 312/783-7776). Its former sanctuary, designed by a Swede and dedicated in 1885, is at 2819 South Princeton Avenue (on the east side of Princeton between Twenty-eighth Place and Twenty-ninth Street).

Other Churches
Another older Chicago Swedish church building is the former Trinity Swedish Evangelical Lutheran Church at the northeast corner of Seminary and Barry (one block south of Belmont). It is a red brick edifice with Gothic-style windows and a soaring steeple. The cornerstone notes the date, 11 September 1887, when the church was founded. The stained glass window over the front door has the inscription, *"Svenska Ev. Lutherska Trefaldighets Kyrkan 1896"* ("Swedish Evangelical Lutheran Trinity Church 1896").

The "mother" church of the north side Chicago Covenant churches was originally identified as the North Side Church, and its roots go back to 1868. Many of its early members were associated with Immanuel Lutheran. Later it became First Covenant at 280 North Franklin. That building is now gone, having been closed in 1976. Other early Mission Friends (Covenant) groups in the greater Chicago area merged with various congregations, and the early buildings have generally disappeared. An exception is the church building of the former Englewood Covenant Church on the northeast corner of West Fifty-ninth and Carpenter streets, which was constructed in 1898. Over the Carpenter Street door is a floral stained glass window with the words *"Svenska Missions Kyrkan."* The former Edgewater Covenant Church (northeast corner of Bryn Mawr and Glenwood) dates from 1909.

The Addison Street Baptist Church at 1242 West Addison (between North Magnolia and North Lakewood) (312/935-2357) was the first Swedish Baptist church in Chicago. On the east side of the large red brick building is a cornerstone—"First Swedish Baptist Church AD 1911." The former Edgewater Swedish Baptist Church (southwest corner of Hollywood and Glenwood) dates from 1910.

The sanctuary of All Saints Lutheran Church at 3311 West Thorndale (northwest corner of West Thorndale and Spaulding) (312/539-6432) was constructed in the 1930s, and the sanctuary contains a triptych altar painting (dated 1918) by Emil Zoir, an internationally known Swedish painter born in Gothenburg in 1861. He studied in Paris and at the Institute of Fine Arts in Boston and died in Sweden in 1936.

SCHOOLS

North Park College and Theological Seminary—3225 West Foster Avenue (312/583-2700).
As early as 1884, the Rev. Erik August Skogsbergh (1850–1939) began a school first in his home in Minneapolis and shortly thereafter in the basement of the Minneapolis Swedish Tabernacle. At the 1891 annual meeting of the denomination, Skogsbergh and David Nyvall (1863–1946) proposed that it become a training school for the denomination's pastors. On 19 September 1891, the Covenant school was born. In Chicago in 1893, thirty-one men formed a real estate group known as the Swedish University Land Association. It acquired ninety acres of land on and around Foster Avenue, an area known as North Park, for the purpose of dividing it into 725 lots for housing. The association offered a donation of eight and a half acres of land to the Covenant school with a contribution of twenty-five thousand dollars for a building. The group saw the school as a focal point for a new Swedish community. The offer was accepted. The school became known as North Park College, and today it is a four-year liberal arts college with a graduate theological seminary. It enrolls about 1450 students.

To encourage better understanding between the United States and Scandinavia, North Park in 1982 launched the Center for Scandinavian Studies and began cooperating with Södra Vätterbygdens Folkhögskola in Jönköping, Sweden, in an exchange program. It also has a nursing exchange program with the College of Health and Care in Jönköping. The center is housed in Caroline Hall, which was designed by noted Swedish-American architect John A. Nydén and built in 1925. In addition to having a significant collection of books in Swedish, the school also maintains the archives of the Evangelical Covenant Church (Nyvall Hall) and the archives of the Swedish-American Historical Society (Caroline Hall).

On the south side of Foster Avenue at North Sawyer is what is called Old Main (3235 West Foster Avenue). Construction began in the summer of 1893, the contractor being J. A. Modine, one of the founders of the Swedish University Association. When this building was completed the following year, it was one of the very few structures in the largely rural area of North Park. Old Main is a three-story brick building surmounted by a lighted cupola that served as a guide in the 1920s for early aviators. Architecturally the building is an example of "aca-

Old Main at North Park College was completed in 1894 and for eight years housed the entire school.

demic" Georgian Revival style. Over the porch and under the third floor window is inscribed "SEMC College," meaning Swedish Evangelical Mission Covenant College, the original name of North Park. The cornerstone verse in Swedish is from Psalms 111:10: *"Herrens fruktan är vishetens begynnelse"* ("The fear of the Lord is the beginning of wisdom"). During the first eight years, until Wilson Hall was completed in 1901, the entire school was housed in Old Main. Later it was the home of North Park Academy, a secondary school that closed in 1969. Renovations completed in 1987 have converted it to the central administrative offices for the college. In 1982, the building was listed on the National Register of Historic Places.

Nyvall Hall, built in 1947 and named for the first president of North Park College and Theological Seminary, houses the Covenant Archives and Historical Library. Located on the second floor, north end, this room contains a collection of written records and memorabilia associated with the history of the Covenant church. Significant memorabilia include the Skogsbergh round pulpit used in the Mission Tabernacle built by Skogsbergh in 1877 (it was located at Thirtieth and LaSalle but torn down in 1960 to make way for the Dan Ryan

Expressway); hymn writer and minister Nils Frykman's rocking chair; the collapsible portable organ used by J. A. Hultman, the "Sunshine Singer," from the 1890s to 1942 on his concert tours in the United States and Sweden; a lectern made by Algoth Ohlson, former North Park president; and two large Rörstrand urns of King Oscar II and Queen Sophia. In the stairwell at the east end of the archives are two large wood plaques with biblical verses inscribed in Swedish; they were carved by Axel Larson of the Covenant church of Cambridge, Massachusetts, in 1921.

In addition to the Covenant Archives, Nyvall Hall houses the seminary and the Isaacson Chapel. The chapel is in a simple dignified Georgian style. In the foyer of the chapel is a memorial plaque and a picture of John Isaacson (1875–1939), founder of Isaacson Steel in Seattle and a generous contributor to the Covenant church. Isaacson was born in Medelpad, Sweden.

Nearly all the buildings on campus are named for Swedish Americans. Wilson Hall, the second oldest building on the campus, was dedicated in 1901 and later named for a North Park science teacher. The "Old Gym" was constructed in 1915. Its construction, along with that of Wilson Hall, was funded by money from Alaskan gold claims. The Modine Learning Center honors Arthur B. Modine—scientist, inventor, industrialist, and philanthropist and son of Swedish University Association member J. A. Modine. Parts of the center include the Carlson Tower (named for Paul Carlson, martyred Covenant missionary who served in the Congo) and Wikholm Laboratories (named for Donald Wikholm, a professor of chemistry). Other campus buildings named for Swedish Americans include Caroline Hall, Lund House, Wallgren Memorial Library, Burgh Hall, Ohlson House, Sohlberg Hall, Anderson Hall, and Hanson Hall. Connected to Hanson Hall is the new Anderson Chapel, dedicated in October 1993 and donated by builder Harold Anderson. Caroline Hall's architect was John Nydén, who also designed Philadelphia's American Swedish Historical Museum.

A bronze statue of Lina Sandell (1832–1903), famed Swedish hymn writer, is to the east of Hanson Hall. Created by artist Axel Wallenberg, the original statue stands in the Fröderyd Church in Småland, and the plaster cast of the statue is in the narthex of Immanuelskyrkan, Stockholm. Another bronze is at Mount Olivet Lutheran Church in Minneapolis.

The Covenant church's main bookstore, Covenant Bookstore, is on the northwest corner of West Foster and North Kedzie.

Sawyer Avenue, leading north from North Park's Old Main, was the most important north-south street in the 1890s and the first to be developed for residential use by the Swedish University Land Association. By 1897, five buildings in addition to Old

Main stood on it. Large frame houses, many with interior oak flooring and woodwork, soon lined the street, housing faculty and students. C. A. Björk, the first president of the Covenant church, built the first house—a three-story frame building at 5240 Sawyer—in 1894. In 1896, Axel Mellander, a professor of theology (one wing of Nyvall Hall is named in his honor), constructed a residence at 5226 North Sawyer (the house, supposedly built in the shape of a cross, has been extensively remodeled). Swede John Hagström, early pastor, writer, and inventor, built at 5223 North Sawyer; there, on the second floor lived A. F. Boring, an early local photographer. The top half of the house burned in 1909. J. A. Modine built a house at 5308 North Sawyer, and his son-in-law, North Park Professor C. J. Wilson, lived in that house and in one at 5302 North Sawyer.

Lutheran School of Theology at Chicago—1100 East Fifty-fifth Street (312/753-0700).

When the Lutheran Church in America was created in 1962 as a result of the merger of the Augustana Lutheran (Swedish), United Lutheran, American Evangelical Lutheran (originally Danish), and the Finnish Evangelical Lutheran (Suomi Synod), the Augustana Theological Seminary in Rock Island, Illinois, was closed and its facilities became part of the Augustana College campus. The Lutheran School of Theology at Chicago, built in 1967, now is one of seminaries of the Evangelical Lutheran Church of America. In the archives and library (third floor) are paintings of the early presidents of Augustana College and Theological Seminary. The school owns an altar cloth embroidered by King Gustav V.

OTHER POINTS OF INTEREST
Swedish Covenant Hospital—5145 North California Avenue (312/878-8200).

In the 1880s, two Swedish hospitals were founded in Chicago—Augustana (1884) and Swedish Covenant (1886). The idea for Swedish Covenant began with Henry Palmblad from Gränna, Sweden. In Chicago, Palmblad was burdened by the appalling health conditions among the newly arrived immigrants. At the first annual meeting of the Covenant church in Princeton, Illinois, in 1885, Palmblad spoke strongly of the need for a health facility. The following year, the Home of Mercy was opened. There is a historic plaque on the California Avenue side of the hospital between Foster and Winona.

In 1891 and 1903, two buildings were erected. The North Wing was completed in 1918, which is still in existence at the southeast corner of Foster and California. The South Wing was constructed in 1928 and in more recent times has been modernized. From the late 1940s to the present, additional facilities have been constructed. Swedish Covenant also includes a school of nursing. Immediately east of the hospital on Foster Avenue is the Covenant Home at 2725 West Foster Avenue. The Evangelical Covenant Church of America administers twelve retirement communities nationwide.

Evangelical Covenant Church of America (Administration Building)—5101 North Francisco Avenue (312/784-3000).

The Evangelical Covenant Church of America has its roots in the great religious revivals that swept Sweden between the 1840s and 1870s. Members of the pietistic wing of the Church of Sweden, the Mission Friends, formed in 1878 the Swedish Mission Covenant under the leadership of Paul Peter Waldenström (1838–1917). In the United States, several mission societies were formed, and in 1885, two rival synods were merged into the Swedish Evangelical Mission Covenant Church in America, which was later changed to its present name. The church's administration building dates from 1947.

Former Swedish Club of Chicago—1254–1258 North LaSalle (on southwest corner of LaSalle and Goethe).

The only significant structure in the old Swede Town section on the near North Side that has a Swedish connection is the former Swedish Club, which incorporated three buildings dating to the 1860s. Listed on the National Register of Historic Places, they have served in more recent years as private residences.

Former Cafe Idrott—3206 North Wilton.

The inscription "The Cooperative Temperance Cafe 'Idrott'" is still visible on this building on North Wilton near West Belmont. By the turn of the century, it was a well-known meeting and eating place for many of Chicago's Swedes. Immigrants gave this address to relatives in Sweden, knowing new arrivals could receive mail there until they were settled. Another similar outpost was at 5248 North Clark. Near the former Cafe Idrott, at 929 West Belmont, is the popular Ann Sather Restaurant, which identifies itself as Chicago's Swedish Diner. A plaque outside the door notes that it is the last of the Swedish restaurants in the area, which until the 1940s was predominantly a Scandinavian community. Other Ann Sather diners are at 5207 North Clark and 1329 East Fifty-seventh.

Landmarks honoring Carolus Linnaeus (Carl von Linné)

In 1885, a large statue by the sculptor Johannes Kjellberg (1836–85), commemorating the Swedish botanist Carolus Linnaeus (1707–78), was unveiled in the park named Humlegården in

Stockholm. Eight years later, at the time of the Columbian Exposition, the city of Chicago received a bronze copy, and it was originally placed in Lincoln Park. But in 1976 the statue was moved to the University of Chicago (5801 South Ellis Avenue) because of traffic pattern changes and increased vandalism in Lincoln Park. The large statue, on the north side of the Midway, east of Ellis Avenue and immediately south of the Harper Library (1116 East Fifty-ninth), originally also included four pewter muses at the four corners of the base, each representing a scientific discipline. (The Swedish sculpture in Humlegården includes the four allegorical figures.)

In September 1983, a bronze sculpture by Robert Berks was dedicated at the Chicago Botanic Garden (near the Education Center, off Lake Cook Road in Glencoe, 708/835-5440). It depicts a young Linnaeus collecting plants with his notes lying on the ground. He is kneeling, studying a rose that is about to be placed in his collection case. Surrounding the twelve-foot Linnaeus are clusters of flowers also made of bronze. Behind him is a toad about to capture an insect.

The Carl von Linne Elementary School (3221 North Sacramento Avenue, near Belmont, 312/534-5262) is named for the famed Swedish scientist. In the lobby opposite the main office is an impressive bust of Linnaeus by Carl J. Nilsson

Sculptor Robert Berks created this bronze image of young Linnaeus collecting specimens with his notebook nearby.

donated in 1937 by the Swedish Cultural Society of Chicago in cooperation with a number of Chicago's Swedish leaders. The pedestal is made of Swedish marble. In Room 211 is a charming wall mural by artist Ethel Spears depicting the eighteenth-century Swedish botanist's life.

Robert Lindblom Technical High School—6130 South Wolcott Avenue (the school is bounded by Wolcott, West Sixty-first Street, West Sixty-second Street, and Winchester) (312/535-9300).

Robert Lindblom (1844–1907) emigrated from Sweden to the United States in 1864, settled in Chicago in 1877, and made a fortune as a grain dealer. He became president of the Chicago Board of Trade and served on the Chicago Board of Education. In 1893, he was one of the principal backers of the Columbian Exposition. A couple of blocks to the west of the high school is Lindblom Park (6054 South Damen Avenue; 312/776-8788), which is also named in his honor.

Peterson Park—5601 North Pulaski Road (312/463-5839).

Per (Pehr) August Peterson (1830–1903) came to the United States via Canada in 1852 from Sweden and in 1856 began a nursery in Chicago. A Chicago District Park, Peterson Park, is named for Peterson, who was known for planting trees along Lake Shore Drive and was at one time the largest landowner in Chicago. Peterson Avenue is also named for him. The Mary Gage Peterson School at 5510 North Christiana Avenue (312/534-5070) (bounded by Catalpa, Kimball, Christiana, and Bryn Mawr) is named in honor of Peterson's wife, who was not Swedish.

Former Swedish Engineers Society—503 Wrightwood (on the southwest corner of Wrightwood and Hampden).

The Swedish Engineers Society was founded in 1908 and used this outstanding baroque mansion (built in 1896 by Francis Dewes, noted brewer and collector of Old World art) as its headquarters for a number of years after it purchased the building in 1920. The mansion was designated a Chicago landmark in 1974.

Carl Sandburg Residence—4646 North Hermitage.

Swedish-American writer Carl Sandburg lived in this three-story residence from 1913 to 1916, but no plaque marks it and it is still a private residence. (On Chicago's near north side at 1355 North Clark Street [also identified as North Sandburg Terrace] is the Carl Sandburg Village, a modern condominium complex.)

Queen of All Saints Basilica—6280 North Sauganash Avenue (between North Lemont and North Keene avenues) (312/736-6060).

Queen of All Saints Basilica is a large Gothic-style Roman Catholic basilica noted for its lovely stained glass windows identifying significant Christian saints. St. Birgitta of Sweden is depicted in the second window from the narthex end of the basilica on the west side. Clearly visible is a yellow cross on a blue field.

Cemeteries

No cemeteries in Chicago are specifically Swedish, but Rosehill (5800 Ravenswood Avenue at Rosehill Drive, 312/561-5940), Graceland (4100 North Clark at Irving Park, 312/525-1105), Mt. Olive (3800 North Narrangansett, 312/286-3770), and Oak Hill (West 119th and South Kedzie, 312/445-5401) contain the graves of many Swedish Americans. Johan A. Enander (1842-1910), buried in Oak Hill, was the first editor and owner of *Hemlandet*, a leading nineteenth-century U.S. Swedish Lutheran publication. His monument, imported from Sweden, is in the form of a runestone. In the southwest corner of Montrose Cemetery (5400 North Pulaski, 312/478-5400) are the simple graves of David and Louise Nyvall. David Nyvall (1863–1946) was the first president of North Park College and Theological Seminary, and his wife, Louise (1857–1940), was E. August Skogsbergh's sister. In October 1991, a commemorative stone was placed at the grave during the centennial celebration of North Park.

SCULPTURE AND OTHER ART

Besides the two sculptures of Carolus Linnaeus mentioned above, one at the University of Chicago campus (5801 South Ellis Avenue) and the other at the Chicago Botanic Garden (near the Education Center, off Lake Cook Road), are other works and monuments created by or celebrating Swedes. Swedish philosopher Emanuel Swedenborg is honored by a monument on Outer Drive (east side), just north of Fullerton Avenue at the boat lagoon, which is on the west side of the Outer Drive. Clearly visible from the Outer Drive is the stone obelisk with an inscription quoting Franklin D. Roosevelt: "In a world in which the voice of conscience too often seems still and small there is a need of that spiritual leadership of which Swedenborg was a particular example."

The Art Institute of Chicago (111 South Michigan Avenue, 312/443-3600) exhibits Carl Milles' "Four Tritons Fountain" in the McKinlock Court, the location of the Garden Restaurant.

At the northwest corner of West Washington Street and South Jefferson Street is the 1977 abstract "Batcolumn." The metal work by Swedish-American sculptor Claes Oldenburg is approximately eight stories tall.

On the front facade of the Tribune Tower (435 North Michigan Avenue), to the north of the main door, a stone from the Royal Castle in Stockholm is imbedded in the wall along with stones from other internationally known buildings and structures. Across Michigan Avenue is the Wrigley Building (410 North Michigan), built by Lanquist and Illsley Construction Company, which was founded in 1904 with Lanquist named as president.

EVANSTON

Former Swedish Theological Seminary—southwest corner of Orrington and Lincoln.

Evanston was the site of a Swedish Methodist seminary. The Swedish Theological Seminary began in Galesburg, Illinois, in 1870, moved to Galva, Illinois, in 1872, and then went to Evanston in 1875, where it operated until 1934. The dark reddish brick building has a cornerstone with the year 1907. Kendall College (2408 Orrington Avenue) eventually acquired the school property.

Pioneer Place and the Swedish Retirement Association—2320 Pioneer Road (bounded also by Colfax, McDaniel, and Grant) (708/328-8700).

In 1894, the Swedish Societies' Central Association was organized in Chicago for dispensing charity to needy countrymen. In 1908, the organization's name was changed to the Swedish Societies' Old People's Home Association. One year later the present property was purchased and the cornerstone laid for the first building. In 1923, a larger facility was constructed and dedicated in the presence of Nathan Söderblom, the Swedish archbishop. This building still stands and is called "Pioneer Place." On the Grant Street door are commemorative plaques. In October 1975, the Robert E. Landstrom Manor building was opened.

Immanuel Lutheran Church—616 Lake at Sherman (708/864-4464).

Immanuel Lutheran was organized in 1888, and the nineteenth-century Gothic light brick building with its tall steeple was built ten years later. The interior has been modernized except for the old stained glass windows. At 1101 Church (the northwest corner of Church and Oak) is the small Evangelical Covenant Church of Evanston with 1910 marked on its cornerstone.

DEERFIELD

In 1884, a group of Mission Friends was organized at Boone, Iowa, independently of what became the Covenant church. The group was first known as the Swedish American Mission Society and then became the Evangelical Free Church of America. Another group, of Danish and Norwegian origin, also merged with it in 1952. In 1995, the group's Trinity College (2077 Half Day Road) and Trinity Evangelical Divinity School (2065 Half Day Road) in Deerfield became Trinity International University. Before 1963, the school was in Chicago, and about ten years after moving to Deerfield, the college separated from the seminary. Though the new campus has buildings named for Swedish-descended donors, the Evangelical Free Church does not demonstrate as strong a tie with its Scandinavian heritage as do some other denominations. The denominational headquarters is in Bloomington, Minnesota.

ARLINGTON HEIGHTS

The Baptist General Conference International Center (2002 South Arlington Heights Road, 708/228-0200) is headquarters for the Baptist General Conference, formerly known as the Swedish Baptist Conference. The modern brick building, dedicated in 1981, features a stone in its lobby taken from the Village Creek, Iowa, home of Eric Sandman. There early plans were made for the Swedish Baptist Conference, which was founded in 1879. In the reception area is a 1923 painting depicting a mid-nineteenth-century baptism in the Mississippi River at Rock Island, Illinois. The conference's archives are at Bethel Seminary in St. Paul, Minnesota.

GENEVA

Geneva hosts an annual Midsummer Festival in Good Templar Park, showcasing its Swedish heritage, still evident in gift shops and a restaurant.

BATAVIA

The Holmstad at 831 Batavia Avenue is an Evangelical Covenant church retirement center.

JOLIET

Salem Village, formerly Salem Home for the Aged, at 1314 Rowell Avenue, came to Joliet from Stony Island and Ninety-fifth in Chicago. It was founded by the Augustana Lutherans.

ROCKFORD

In 1852, about thirty immigrants from Sweden came to Rockford. Others followed, and by 1930 about ten thousand Swedish-born lived in the city, constituting about 25 percent of the inhabitants. Among sizable North American urban areas, only Jamestown, New York, had a larger percentage of Swedes.

In the late 1800s, Rockford, like Jamestown, emerged as a furniture center. In 1875, fifteen Swedes founded the Forest City Furniture Company. Other companies such as the Central Furniture Company and the Union Furniture Company made Rockford by 1885 the second leading furniture-producing center in the United States. In addition, Rockford Swedes contributed to making the city a leading producer of tools and dies, and hardware. Three early leading Swedish industrialists were Per August Peterson (1846–1927), who came to Rockford at the age of six and made a name for himself in Chicago as well as in Rockford; John Nelson (1830–83), the inventor of the automatic knitting machine; and Levin Faust (or Fast) (1863–1936), known for his machine and tool production.

Swedes generally settled in East Rockford, particularly along Kishwaukee Avenue. Seventh Street, an artery parallel to Kishwaukee, included the old Swedish business district. Later Fourteenth Avenue (Broadway) took its place. The corner of Seventh Street and Fourteenth Avenue was the heart of the Swedish business district. Rockford Standard Furniture is one of a few reminders of the manufacturing era that saw furniture factories prosper on Railroad Avenue between Seventh and Eleventh streets.

INSTITUTES AND MUSEUMS

Erlander Home Museum—404 South Third Street (southeast corner of Grove and Third Streets) (815/963-5559). Open 2–4 Sunday; open other days by appointment.

The Swedish Historical Society of Rockford operates the fourteen-room Erlander Home Museum. During the late 1980s and early 1990s the first floor of the museum was restored, and the exterior underwent renovation. Once the home of John Erlander (1826–1917), one of Rockford's first Swedish settlers, the large two-story brick house was built in 1871. Five years later the Union Furniture Company was organized in this house, with John Erlander as president and Per Peterson as secretary. Though Erlander's daughter Mary lived in the house after his death, the house was acquired from her in 1952 and made into a museum. Sweden's Prime Minister Tage Erlander, who was related to these American Erlanders, attended the 6 April 1952 dedication. For many years the connection between the prime minister and his American relatives had been broken. When Wisconsin relatives contacted him in Sweden, he discovered he had cousins in the United States of whom he had not known until then.

Fine examples of furniture made by the Union, Central, and Excelsior furniture companies, all owned and run by Swedes, are on display. In a downstairs parlor is the first piano made in Rockford by the Haddorff Piano Company. In another first floor

The fourteen-room Erlander Home Museum, operated by the Swedish Historical Society of Rockford, holds many examples of fine furniture made in Rockford's Swedish-American–owned companies.

parlor is a bronze plaque inscribed with Carl Sandburg's tribute to Swedish settlers. Visitors may also see a nineteenth-century Swedish *kakelugn* (ceramic tile oven), one of the first knitting machines developed by John Nelson, and a Haddorff dolcette. Though shaped like a grand piano, a dolcette varies from a piano by having vertical strings and only forty-four keys. Failing to become popularly accepted, only two were ever produced in Rockford—the one in the Erlander Home and another now in the Smithsonian.

Rockford Museum Center and Midway Village—6799 Guilford Road (815/397-9112).

Winnebago County Swedish-American life and achievements in industry are highlighted in the Rockford Museum Center. The American Union of Swedish Singers displays memorabilia, dating from its organization in 1892. A Swedish farm model, patterned after the boyhood home of Carl Severin, a Rockford

Products Corporation superintendent, depicts the life he lived in the country of Kalmar Län, Småland, before immigrating to the United States in 1913. Throughout the museum are articles donated by Rockford Swedish Americans, but there are no exhibits devoted exclusively to Swedish contributions. King Carl XVI Gustaf visited the museum in 1976.

In another area of the museum complex, visitors may view the small single-engine airplane that Colonel Bert R. J. Hassell (1893–1974) and a companion attempted to fly from Rockford to Stockholm in 1929 to prove that the shortest route between those cities was along the great circle connecting them. The plane crashed in Greenland, but the two men were rescued. After being retrieved in the 1960s, the aircraft was brought to the museum. A resident of Rockford and an employee of Rockford Products Corporation, Hassell was born in Wisconsin to parents who had emigrated from Värmland.

The Rockford Industrial Building affords visitors a history of the industrial firms of the area. Since many were begun by Swedes, this section may particularly appeal to visitors interested in Swedish-American achievements.

HISTORIC PLACES

Lake-Peterson Home—1313 East State Street (adjacent to SwedishAmerican Hospital, which can be reached at 815/968-4400).

This nineteenth-century Gothic revival house was built by lumber dealer John H. Lake in 1873 and later became the home of Per Peterson, a Södra Ving, Västergötland, native, Rockford commercial leader, and financial supporter of the SwedishAmerican Hospital. A founder of the Union Furniture Company, Peterson eventually became the dean of Rockford furniture manufacturers and one of the most important figures in the industrial and commercial development of the city. At the time of his death in 1927, Peterson was president of more than a dozen industrial firms. A niche between the first and second floors on the spiral staircase holds a sculpted bust of him. The home, owned by SwedishAmerican Hospital since 1919, is listed on the National Register of Historic Places.

SwedishAmerican Hospital—1400 Charles Street (815/968-4400).

On 17 July 1918, SwedishAmerican Hospital opened as a fifty-five-bed facility (this building still stands). The following year, the school of nursing was established. Today SwedishAmerican Hospital is a regional health care center with such specialty departments as an Alzheimer's clinic, a home health care service, and a center for weight management.

Faust Landmark—618-32 East State Street (corner of State and Third streets).
Now part of the East Rockford Historic District, this former hotel was named for Levin Faust, one of its principal investors. Faust started as a penniless Swedish immigrant but subsequently amassed a large fortune. Ericson, Benson Construction Company built the eleven-story building in 1927. No longer a hotel, it is used for low-cost housing. It is down the street from the Lake-Peterson Home.

CHURCHES
First Lutheran Church—225 South Third Street (northwest corner of Third and Oak streets) (815/962-6691).
First Lutheran, a large Gothic-style brick structure with two tall steeples, is known as the "mother" church of at least seven other Swedish Lutheran congregations in Rockford. First Lutheran was organized in 1854, and the founding pastor was Erland Carlsson. The first church and parsonage were built in 1856, and the second in 1869. The church was rebuilt in 1883 and then remodeled in 1928. The impressive walnut altar, altar rail, and pulpit were made by Rockford Central Furniture Company (the president was a member of the congregation). In the back of the sanctuary are artifacts from the church history: a *psalmodikon* used by the first congregation, a velvet heart used on the pulpit of the second church, and the cornerstone box from the second church.

Zion Lutheran Church—925 Fifth Avenue (815/964-4609).
Zion Lutheran is probably the most Swedish of current Rockford Lutheran congregations. The red brick Gothic-style church and its steeple were completed in 1885. In the Fellowship Hall are memorabilia from former times, including the old church sign written in Swedish.

Emmanuel Lutheran—920 Third Avenue at Sixth Street (815/963-4815).
The cornerstone of Emmanuel, a light brick church, bears the dates 1882 (the year Emmanuel was organized) and 1922 (the year the sanctuary was built).

Salem Lutheran Church—1629 Sixth Street (northwest corner of Sixteenth Avenue and Sixth Street) (815/964-5131).
The Salem Lutheran congregation was organized in 1907 and its building erected in 1911. The front exterior of the reddish brick church wall is inscribed, "Swedish Evangelical Lutheran Salem Church South Park." The church building is topped with a pair of spires.

St. Anskar's Episcopal Church—4801 Spring Creek Road (815/877-1226).
St. Anskar's is named for the ninth-century missionary to Scandinavia.

Other Churches
At 714 Third Avenue (the northeast corner of Third and Kishwaukee avenues) stands a reddish brick structure with a cornerstone identifying it as a former Covenant church building—Swedish Evangelical Lutheran Mission Society of Rockford—which was organized in 1888. The First Evangelical Covenant Church has moved to an impressive modern building, built in 1966, at 316 Wood. The former Swedish Baptist Church was located on the northeast corner of Fifth Avenue and Eighth Street.

SCHOOLS
Schools named for Rockford Swedish Americans include those honoring inventor and manufacturer John Nelson (623 Fifteenth, 815/229-2190), former mayor Henry Bloom (2912 Brendenwood Road, 815/229-2170), screw manufacturer and Swedish Pioneer Centennial chairman Swan Hillman (3701 Green Dale Drive, 815/229-2835), former schoolteacher Maud Johnson (3805 Rural Street, 815/229-2485), and former school board president Clifford P. Carlson (4015 River Lane, 815/654-4955).

OTHER POINTS OF INTEREST
Scandinavian Cemetery—1700 Rural at Prospect (815/965-6625).
A number of locally renowned men are buried in this beautifully maintained cemetery, including P. A. Peterson, Levin Faust, John Erlander, John Laurentius Haff (pastor of First Lutheran) (1862–96), Henry Bloom (pharmacist, politician, mayor) (1884–1969), and August Erickson (Covenant minister). Haff's monument, which identifies him as *Joel* Laurentius Haff, was erected by the congregation in 1903 with the Swedish inscription "*Saliga äro de döda som i Herren dö*" ("Blessed are the dead who die in the Lord").

P. A. Peterson Home for the Aging—1311 Parkview Avenue (815/399-8832).
When P. A. Peterson died in 1927, he bequeathed substantial funds to various charitable institutions, including this home. The original building still stands, but it has been expanded.

PECATONICA   Several old Swedish Lutheran congregations still exist in towns surrounding Rockford. The oldest is the red brick First Lutheran

Church of Pecatonica, which was organized here in 1857. The congregation built this church in 1881.

THE QUAD CITIES

Swedes who settled in the Quad Cities—Moline and Rock Island, Illinois, and Bettendorf and Davenport, Iowa—helped make the area the greatest center in the United States for the manufacture of farm implements (see map, page 84). Deere & Company, known for its billion-dollar farm, construction, and lawn machinery and equipment business, is the most outstanding example. The Quad Cities is the third most important urban settlement for Swedes in Illinois, behind Chicago and Rockford. Here are listed sites of importance in the cities of Moline, Rock Island, and Davenport.

MOLINE

Lutheran, Methodist, and Baptist churches in Moline have Swedes in their histories. First Lutheran Church at 1230 Fifth Avenue (southwest corner of Thirteenth Street and Fifth Avenue) (309/764-3517) was organized in 1850 by the Rev. Lars P. Esbjörn, who also led the founding of the church in Andover. Generally early members were unskilled laborers, and later many were employed by such companies as Deere & Company. Young women were hired as maids, laundresses, cooks, and nursemaids. In 1853, the Mississippi Conference of the Lutheran Church, later known as the Illinois Conference of the Evangelical Lutheran Augustana Synod, was organized in the first sanctuary of First Lutheran. A large historic plaque honoring this event is located directly in front of the church.

In 1875, the decision was made to build a new church—a Gothic-style red brick building, which is still in use. Some members, objecting to such an extensive program, left the congregation to form Gustav Adolph's Church in Moline. This congregation eventually joined the Mission Covenant Church. (The former church is on the corner of Fifth Avenue and Tenth Street.) Over the front door of the red brick building is the inscription, *Missions Tabernaklet.* The Covenant congregation has relocated to 3303 Forty-first Street.

The first service in the new church was held 13 October 1878. The impressive sanctuary has a balcony on three sides supported by Corinthian columns. Stained glass windows were added in 1945. Local artist F. A. Lundahl rendered the altar painting depicting the Ascension.

Continued use of Swedish in church services brought about tensions, resulting in congregational splits, including one producing Trinity Lutheran, which was formed in 1916. Despite the schism, First Lutheran was in the forefront in organizing

Lutheran Hospital, now part of Trinity Medical Center (501 Tenth Avenue, 309/757-3131), four years later.

In the lobby of Bethany Baptist Church, organized in 1876, is a historic plaque noting that in 1852 in Rock Island the first Swedish Baptist Church in the United States was organized under the leadership of Gustav Palmquist (1812–67), one of three pastors who laid the foundation of the Swedish Baptist Church in the United States. In addition to Palmquist, who was from northern Småland, were two others—Fredrik Olaus Nilsson (1809–91) from Halland and Anders Wiberg (1816–87) from Hälsingland. Bethany is located at 701 Thirty-eighth Avenue (corner of Seventh Street and Black Hawk Road), and the congregation worships in a modern sanctuary.

The Bethel Methodist Church at 1201 Thirteenth (southwest corner of Thirteenth Street and Twelfth Avenue) is an offspring of the Victoria, Illinois, Methodist church. The present red brick building dates from 1910.

In Riverside Cemetery (Sixth Avenue and Twenty-ninth Street; for information, call 309/797-0790) are the graves of two early presidents of Augustana College and Theological Seminary—Tuve Nilsson Hasselquist and Olof Olsson. From their graves near the Deere Cross is a good view of the Mississippi River. Lars P. Esbjörn, Augustana's first president, returned to Sweden, and he is buried there.

Deere & Company, the world's largest producer of farm equipment, has its headquarters on John Deere Road in Moline, and though not founded by Swedes, many Swedish immigrants have been employed in this company, which in the early 1990s had $7 billion–dollar annual sales and 36,500 workers. Established in 1837, the company is also a leading manufacturer of construction, forestry, and landscaping equipment and an insurance and credit carrier. Designed by Eero Saarinen (1910–61), the son of Finnish architect Eliel Saarinen (1873–1950), the company's headquarters (309/765-8000) offers to visitors a display of the company's products and lovely surrounding grounds.

ROCK ISLAND

The Scandinavian Evangelical Lutheran Augustana Synod was organized in 1860 at Jefferson Prairie, Wisconsin. The minutes state that "the Augustana Synod shall establish and maintain a Theological Seminary, which for the present will be located in the city of Chicago." The Rev. Lars Esbjörn was named the first president of the Augustana Theological Seminary, the oldest Swedish educational institution in the United States. It was called Augustana in honor of the 1530 Augsburg Confession (in Latin, *Confessio Augustana).* The college was organized in 1863.

From 1863 to 1875, the school was located in Paxton, Illinois, under the leadership of Rev. T. N. Hasselquist. Two of the four great pioneer leaders of nineteenth-century Swedish Lutheranism in the United States—Esbjörn and Hasselquist—were presidents of Augustana. The other two— Erland Carlsson (1822–93) and Eric Norelius (1833–1916)—were Lutheran leaders who chaired Augustana's Board of Directors. On 22 September 1875, Augustana College and Theological Seminary (Seventh Avenue and Thirty-eighth Street, 309/794-7000) opened its doors in Rock Island, fifteen years after its founding. At that time the college enrolled ninety students. Today about two thousand students attend classes on the 115-acre campus.

On a stone bench behind Old Main a plaque notes that the stones are from the foundation of the first building of Augustana College and Theological Seminary in Paxton. A tablet by the west entrance of the College Center identifies it as where the cornerstone of the first college building in Rock Island, known as the first Old Main, was discovered when the building was razed in 1935. The Bell Tower, a replica of a Swedish *klockstapel,* is made from its beams, and the bell is also from that building.

The present Old Main (on Seventh Avenue between Thirty-fifth and Thirty-eighth streets), originally called Memorial Hall, was begun in 1884 and was the largest undertaking for any

Old Main, begun in 1884, was completed in 1893, but students and faculty began using the building in 1888.

Swedish group in the United States up to that time. With the college and seminary rapidly expanding in the early 1880s, it was determined that the first Old Main was inadequate and that an additional, larger building needed to be constructed. The board of the college wanted a Renaissance-style building; one member expressed the wish that the building also include a dome for an American look. Former college president Conrad Bergendoff (b. 1895) has suggested that the design of Augustana's Old Main may have been influenced by the Renaissance-style Main Building at Uppsala University in Sweden, which had been completed in 1879.

The Old Main building project was accomplished, thanks in part to a gift of twenty-five thousand dollars from P. L. Cable, president of the Rock Island and Peoria Railroad. The architect was L. G. Hallberg of Chicago, a graduate of Chalmers Polytechnic Institute in Gothenburg. In 1888, students and faculty were able to move into the building, though it was not completed until 1893. Since that time, Old Main, listed on the National Register of Historic Places, has undergone major changes. For example, the need for additional classrooms and offices forced the elimination of the east wing chapel. In Old Main today, the visitor can still see the stained glass windows in the stairwell at the second floor level given by the Young People's Society of the First Lutheran Church of Galesburg, Illinois. Cable Hall, also on the second floor, honors the building's benefactor. On the third floor was Olof Grafström's art studio.

Grafström (1855–1933) was born in Medelpad, not far from Sundsvall, and studied at the Royal Academy of Art in Stockholm. He came to the United States in 1886 and first lived on the West Coast. After teaching for a few years at Bethany College in Lindsborg, Kansas, he arrived at Augustana in 1897 and taught in its art department until his retirement in 1926. Grafström returned to Sweden for the last six years of his life. He was responsible for at least two hundred altar paintings in various Lutheran churches throughout the United States. He also painted landscapes. Many of his paintings are in the school's permanent art collection along with works by Birger Sandzén and Carl Milles. The college's gallery director (309/794-7231) can help visitors locate any of these on campus.

Following completion of a new college library in 1990, Denkmann Memorial Library on Seventh Avenue, which had been dedicated in 1911, was renamed Denkmann Memorial Hall and extensively remodeled. In it is what Augustana claims is the oldest department of Scandinavian studies of any U.S. college or university, having offered courses in Swedish language, literature and culture since 1860. Also in the building is the Swenson Swedish Immigration Research Center (309/794-

7204), founded in 1981 by an initial gift from Mr. and Mrs. Birger Swenson. Birger Swenson was from 1945 to 1962 the general manager of Augustana Book Concern, a Swedish-American publishing house.

The Swenson Center is a national archives and research center for the study of Swedish immigration to North America and the role of Swedish immigrants and their descendants in American society. Its extensive holdings include a microfilmed collection of Swedish-American newspapers; the Gustav Swan, Nils Olsson, and O. A. Linder special collections; and, in the archival collection, rare Swedish-American imprints. The center's collection of church and embarkation records assists persons researching their family histories.

Grants from three Swedish foundations with ties to the Wallenberg family paid the cost of remodeling a portion of the former Denkmann Library for use by the Swenson Center. In recognition of these gifts, the former main reading room on the second floor was converted to an auditorium and named Wallenberg Hall. An inscription retained on the wall reads, *"Bättre börda bär ingen med sig på färden än kunskap mycken,"* which means, "A better burden cannot be carried on a voyage than much knowledge."

The Augustana College Library has an extensive collection of Swedish books, including a collection donated by Sweden's King Charles XV. Presented to the college in 1860, the year of its founding, the collection encompasses thousands of volumes in many languages and on many subjects. Many of these books' bindings bear monograms of the Swedish monarchy. The Swedes in America Collection includes early volumes about the New Sweden Colony in the Delaware Valley, one of which is a 1696 catechism in both Swedish and the Delaware Indian language. Also of special local interest are works written by and about Swedes who settled the Midwest and those who founded Augustana College.

Sorensen Hall is the former site of the Augustana Book Concern, which was the largest Swedish publishing house in the United States. Sorensen Hall houses a portion of the college's administrative offices together with classrooms and offices for several academic departments. Founders Hall was part of the former Augustana Theological Seminary until the 1962 merger creating the Lutheran Church in America. (The Lutheran Church of America seminary moved to Chicago in 1967.) Founders Hall, built in 1923 and remodeled in 1967, is used mainly for college administrative offices. It honors the first three presidents of Augustana—Esbjörn, who was president 1860–63; Hasselquist, 1863–91; and Olof Olsson, 1891–1900. A stained glass window in the stairwell leading to Ascension

Chapel depicts four historic sites of collegiate Lutheran learn-ing—Springfield (Illinois State University was a Lutheran institution serving English and German Lutherans), Chicago, Paxton, and Rock Island. The Carl E. Swenson Hall of Science includes the Fryxell Geological Museum, developed by Dr. Fritiof Fryxell, founder of Augustana's geology department. Swenson was an inventor who left a significant bequest to the college. Outside the building is a large boulder inscribed with the names Lindahl and Udden. Josua Lindahl (1844–1912), a native of Halland, Sweden, taught natural sciences from 1878 to 1893 at Augustana. His student, Johan August Udden, who was from Västergötland, succeeded him, coming to Augustana from Bethany College. In 1911, Udden left for The University of Texas in Austin, where he became famous in oil exploration. Ericson Field and Stadium, on the site of former science build-ing Ericson Hall, is named for Iowa State Senator Charles J. Ericson (1840–1910), who gave thirty thousand dollars to Augustana in 1901 for a professorship in Swedish.

Other campus buildings named for Swedish Americans include Carlsson Hall (named for the Rev. Erland Carlsson), Bergendoff Hall of Fine Arts (Dr. Bergendoff, president from 1935 to 1962), Wallberg Hall (Marie Wallberg), Abrahamson Hall (editor L. G. Abrahamson), Mauritzson Hall (Jules G. Mauritzson, professor of Swedish and a dean), Wald Hall (Arthur E. Wald, a dean), Andreen Hall (Gustav A. Andreen [1864–1940], president from 1901 to 1935), Westerlin Residence Cen-ter for Women (J. M. Westerlin), Erickson Residence Center for Men (Knut E. Erickson, vice president and treasurer), Jenny Lind Hall (nineteenth-century Swedish singer Jenny Lind), I. M. Anderson House (I. M. Anderson, professor of Greek), and Esbjorn House (C. L. E. Esbjorn, professor of German). On the third floor of the College Center is the Hammarskjöld Room, named for the United Nations secretary-general from Sweden.

| DAVENPORT, IOWA | The Putnam Museum (1717 West Twelfth at Division, 309/324-1933) is a lovely modern museum featuring exhibits focusing on the Quad Cities' immigrants, including Swedes. |

ANDOVER

Listed on the National Register of Historic Places is the Jenny Lind Chapel in Andover at Sixth and Oak streets, a site recog-nized as a shrine of Swedish Lutheranism. The Rev. Lars Paul Esbjörn (1808–70), a Swedish state church minister, led the founding of the Andover Lutheran congregation on 18 March 1850. The chapel, dedicated on the first Sunday of Advent (3 December 1854), was named for Swedish soprano Jenny Lind, whose gift of fifteen hundred dollars made its construction possible. Three years in building yet soon outgrown by its congregation, the Jenny Lind Chapel stood over one hundred years before being restored in 1975.

From the outset, the chapel faced challenges. Delays in its original construction were caused mainly by a cholera epidemic, and the coffins required for the cholera victims claimed the wood intended for the chapel's steeple. No steeple ever was erected. The church's basement was transformed into a hospital and immigrant home.

Built by the Andover Lutheran congregation founded in 1850, the Jenny Lind Chapel was dedicated in 1854. No steeple was erected because the wood intended for it had to be used for coffins to bury cholera victims.

The chapel's plain but dignified interior complements the special occasions for which it is still used—an annual worship service in Swedish, summer vesper services, a Founders Day service, and a Christmas service. A kerosene lamp used by the early church is in the sanctuary, which features a pulpit centered above the altar. Originally a large opening in the floor permitted people in the basement to hear the service. Now the basement houses a small museum exhibiting artifacts from the congregation's history.

The cemetery next to the chapel contains many graves of Swedish pioneers and Civil War soldiers. One of the most touching gravestones is that for the two-year-old daughter and eleven-month-old son of Anders and Catrina Peterson. Under a bas-relief of a girl and boy whose hands are clasped the inscription reads, "Not dead but sleeping."

Near the Jenny Lind Chapel is the Augustana Lutheran Church, a large, impressive brick church with a high steeple. Dedicated in 1869, it is of solid masonry construction, and its dimensions rival those of churches the immigrants left behind in Sweden. A central pulpit stands above the altar. Beautiful dark wood appointments and wall stenciling above the altar stand out in the sanctuary, which has a high ceiling and a rear balcony. Also near the Jenny Lind Chapel is the second Swedish Methodist congregation organized in the Midwest, Andover Methodist Church. The small white clapboard church was built in 1854.

The work of the Rev. Esbjörn and his wife is commemorated by a historical marker on the south side of State Highway 81 on the west end of Andover. Near the marker are the graves of cholera victims.

Near State Highway 81 on Locust is the Andover Historical Museum (formerly the Rehnstrom home). Call (309/476-8594) for hours. The white clapboard structure, built about 1860, was originally a boarding house. Some of the men who built the Augustana Lutheran Church stayed here. It became a museum in 1970 and is operated by the Andover Historical Society. The interior furnishings are from the late 1800s and all donated by Andover residents.

The Andover Orphan's Home, one mile southwest of Andover, was organized in 1863 by the Swedish Lutherans. The original building burned and was replaced by the present brick structure between 1905 and 1910. The facilities are now used by Lutheran Social Services of Illinois as a conference center. Swedish immigrants who came to Andover often first stayed in the A. E. "Brick" Anderson House, or Brick House, at the corner of Osco and Cambridge roads. Built in the 1850s and greatly altered over the years, the house is now a private residence.

NEW WINDSOR

New Windsor's inhabitants are largely people of Swedish ancestry. The Calvary Lutheran Church congregation was organized in 1869, and the church building was constructed in 1876. Generally of nineteenth-century Gothic revival style in vertical board and batten construction, the church boasts an impressive ninety-five–foot steeple. Inside, the altar bears the inscription, *"Helig, Helig, Helig"* ("Holy, Holy, Holy").

New Windsor suffered a fire in 1898, but the Opera House in the east business block survived. At the northeast corner of Main and Fifth is the brick mercantile building dated 1911.

BISHOP HILL

In the 1840s the first three Swedish colonizing efforts took place in the United States territory since the ill-fated New Sweden attempt on the Delaware River in the mid-seventeenth century: Gustav Unonius's New Upsala colony at Pine Lake, Wisconsin, in 1841; New Sweden, Iowa, in 1845; and Bishop Hill Colony in 1846, the largest of the three. The last is listed on the National Register of Historic Places.

Eric Janson (1808–50), the leader of the Bishop Hill colony, was born Erik Jansson in Biskopskulla, Uppland, not far from Uppsala. By the time he had settled in Hälsingland in the early 1840s, Janson was convinced all religious books except the Bible were superfluous, even harmful, and that simplicity was the only way to salvation. To him, the Swedish church had seriously strayed from its mission. When the authorities attempted to suppress what was regarded as fanaticism, Janson and others decided to look to America as a haven. He sent Olof Olsson, his most influential associate, to scout land possibilities in western Illinois. Eventually a site about 160 miles west of Chicago was selected during the summer of 1846. In that year, some twelve hundred men, women, and children sailed for the United States and arrived at Bishop Hill in the fall, walking the distance from Chicago. (*Bishop Hill* is the English translation of Janson's birthplace, Biskopskulla.) They built dugouts where the bleachers now rest on the town's central ball field. Ninety-six died during the first winter from inadequate food and shelter. With the coming of spring, crops were planted and the business of organizing and building a settlement commenced. But problems—including a cholera epidemic, weariness with the communal life-style, and disillusionment with Janson's messianic claims—still plagued the community. Many transferred their religious loyalties to the newly founded Swedish Methodist Church in nearby Victoria, Illinois. The Bishop Hill Colony shrunk to between six and eight hundred.

During the fifteen years Bishop Hill existed as a Jansonist communal colony, twenty large commercial buildings were erected, many in classical style, and some fifteen thousand acres of land were put into farm production. After Janson was murdered in 1850, management of the colony passed to a seven-member board of trustees, though for a time Jonas Olsson (brother of Olof Olsson) ruled with a firm hand. From 1853 to 1861 economics motivated the colony rather than religious zeal. The colonists excelled in producing linen, furniture, wagons, brooms, and farm products. A hotel was opened. In the 1850s,

Bishop Hill became a major center of commerce between Rock Island and Peoria, but in the early 1860s, the colony dissolved and the property was divided among its members.

Of the original buildings built between 1846 and 1861, sixteen survive. Of these, nine are open to the public. The State of Illinois, through the Department of Conservation, operates two of them—the Colony Church and the Bjorklund Hotel. The school is operated by the Old Settlers' Association, and the other buildings belong to the Bishop Hill Heritage Association or private owners. A visitor is always amazed by the size of the buildings. Though no longer standing, one building, known as "Big Brick," had a length of two hundred feet and a width of forty-five. It was a communal apartment with ninety-six rooms and several halls in its three floors, basement, and attic. The structure burned in 1928. The Bishop Hill buildings generally were made of kiln-dried bricks. The exception was the first building, the Colony Church. The church's basement level was made of sun-dried adobe bricks, strengthened with straw, and the rest was frame.

The Colony Church was erected in 1848. Since at first there was a housing shortage, colonists decided that this structure should be a combination apartment-church. The basement and

Immediately after construction, the Colony Church building served as both lodging and house of worship for the Bishop Hill colonists. Now the former first-floor apartment units house a museum.

first floor each had ten rooms where twenty families were lodged, one family per room. The first-floor rooms have been made into a Bishop Hill museum with displays focusing on life in the colony.

On the second floor is the sanctuary where a thousand people—men on the right, women on the left—worshiped. The white walls contrast sharply with the black walnut pews. The pulpit panels were painted by Olof Krans, the colony's artist, to resemble marble. The church is not Swedish in design, but the wood and wrought iron chandeliers are copies of brass chandeliers the colonists had known in Swedish churches. The spindles in the railing in front of the pulpit were turned by the colony's women.

The Steeple Building, completed in 1854, has been a home, school, general store, bank, newspaper office, doctor's office, and telephone exchange.

The Steeple Building, erected in 1853 and 1854, is a striking contrast to the unembellished exterior of other Bishop Hill structures. Its classical architectural style, its colonnaded front, its pediments near the crest on two sides, and its symmetrical clock tower are unique. In the tower is a one-handed clock installed in 1859 and operated by two sets of weights attached to ropes in a chute that extends the entire height of the building.

Although the Steeple Building was originally intended as a hotel, it never served that role. Parts of the building have served as a communal home, school, general store, bank, newspaper office, doctor's office, and telephone exchange. In the early 1960s it was converted into a museum; the various rooms contain memorabilia from the late nineteenth and early twentieth centuries. A tour of Bishop Hill should start at the Steeple Building in order to begin with an audiovisual introduction to the colony.

Early visitors to the colony were first accommodated in "Big Brick," but soon the commune's leaders realized a regular hotel was needed. In the 1850s, Bishop Hill became the overnight stop on the stage route between Peoria and Rock Island. The Bjorklund Hotel was built between 1852 and 1860 and has been restored by the state of Illinois. It is a three-story structure with a large cupola on top. On the first floor is a dining room with adjacent bar, men's parlor, ladies' parlor, pantry, and kitchen. Eleven guest rooms are on the second floor, and a large ballroom, awaiting restoration, is on the third. The hotel was owned by the colony and managed by Sven Bjorklund, who remained its manager even after the colony disbanded. His name remains associated with the hotel.

The colony's schoolhouse, completed in 1861, was the town's educational center until 1951 when a new school was erected nearby. Mary Sandburg, sister of author Carl Sandburg, was a teacher in the school from 1899 to 1901. Her brother visited her a few times in Bishop Hill, coming by train from Galesburg.

The colony store, erected in 1853, was for many years a center of daily community life, selling a large stock of groceries, dry goods, and other general merchandise. Folks were drawn to the store not only by the merchandise but also by the Bishop Hill Post Office, which occupied the right front corner of the building for about one hundred years. Drawing visitors to the store more recently has been the Bishop Hill Heritage Association Museum gift shop, which continues to operate as a general store. The shop contains the original shelving and fixtures.

Other original buildings in Bishop Hill open to the public include the Colony Apartment House (built 1855), the Colony Blacksmith Shop (1857), the Colony Administration Building (1856), and the Colony Carpenter Shop (1851). The Colony Dairy (1855), the Colony Administration Building (1856), the Colony Hospital (1855), the Colony Meat Storage Building (1851), and Eric Janson's house are all private residences. At the south edge of Bishop Hill is the Bishop Hill State Historic Site Museum containing more than seventy-five paintings of Olof Krans. They depict original settlers and early life in the colony.

One block south of the Steeple Building is the Vasa Order of America Archives, erected in 1973 and 1974 to serve as the national archive and historical building for this fraternal group that works to perpetuate Swedish culture and traditions in America. A library, exhibit area, records room, and storage area are housed in the building. Having more than three hundred lodges, the group is divided nationally into about twenty districts.

In the Bishop Hill Park are two historic landmarks: a monument and plaque "dedicated to the memory of the hardy pioneers" and a statue honoring the Bishop Hill Company that fought during the Civil War. In the nearby Bishop Hill Cemetery is the grave of Eric Janson, marked with a stone obelisk, and the graves of many of the early colonists. Three miles northwest of Bishop Hill in a district called Red Oak the original log house of the colonists was built (it does not survive). Also located there is a marker erected in 1882 in memory of colonists who died during the first winter. The same year a similar marker was erected on a colony farm three miles southeast of Orion in memory of seventy Bishop Hill colonists who died of cholera. No buildings survive from that farm. On an island in Rock Island, Illinois, some Bishop Hill colonists are buried who were also victims of cholera. These colonists had run a fishing station there.

Twenty gift shops, five museums, and four restaurants dot Bishop Hill, but the town offers no overnight accommodations. Lodging may be found in Kewanee, Galesburg, and Geneseo. The Bishop Hill Heritage Association (P. O. Box 1853, Bishop Hill, Illinois 61419, or 309/927-3899) will provide additional information for travelers. Throughout the year, guides will, by appointment, accompany visitors on a tour of the historic district. In September, Old Settlers' Day (the second Saturday) and Agricultural Days *(Jordbruksdagarna)* (the last full weekend) feature crafts, music, and folk dancing. Also popular near Christmas are the *Julmarknad* and the Lucia nights.

GALVA

Although founded in 1853 by two New Englanders, Galva was shaped largely by the Bishop Hill colonists. Seventy town lots were owned by the colony.

It was from Galva that the Bishop Hill Colony shipped and received goods by railroad, and the 150-foot-long Bishop Hill Colony warehouse, on the west side of Exchange Street on the south side of the Chicago, Burlington, and Quincy Railroad tracks, was erected in 1855. Passengers heading for the colony could stay overnight at the Bishop Hill Colony Boarding House (415 Southwest Third Street), now an apartment building, before going on to the colony.

Several houses in Galva have ties to the colony. The Olof Johnson House (408 Northwest Fourth Street), listed on the National Register of Historic Places, was the residence of Olof Johnson, one of the trustees of Bishop Hill after Janson's murder in 1850. Johnson was the chief liaison between the colony and Galva. He was accorded the honor of naming the town after the Swedish seaport of Gävle from which many colonists sailed. In time, the name was changed to Galva, which was presumably easier for English-speaking people to pronounce. The Jonas Erickson House (421 Northwest Fourth Street) on the same street was also owned and named for a Bishop Hill trustee. At 17 Northwest Fifth Street is a home that was formerly the Bishop Hill Mission Church, a Covenant church built in the 1880s near the Colony Church in Bishop Hill and moved to Galva shortly after 1900.

Churches in Galva include the Swedish Methodist Church (now Grace Methodist), which was organized in 1867 by the Rev. A. J. Anderson, then a pastor in Bishop Hill. Two years after the Methodist congregation was organized, Messiah Lutheran Church was begun, whose congregation now worships in a sanctuary erected in 1915 and 1916 on the same site as the original church. In the Galva Cemetery outside town are buried many Bishop Hill trustees. Olof Krans (1838–1916) and his family are probably the best known of the Swedes buried there.

VICTORIA

Methodists here claim Victoria as the birthplace of Swedish Methodism, and as testimony they point to a red granite monument on the west end of town on the south side of State Highway 167; however, most Methodists recognize the *Old Bethel Ship*, a floating chapel in New York harbor, as the first congregation, even though it was organized on a ship and not on land. Olof Gustaf Hedstrom (1803–79) established Swedish Methodism in New York City in 1845 and Jonas Hedström (1813–59) began the Illinois work in 1846.

The Victoria Swedish Methodists built their sanctuary in 1854, but it was replaced in 1909 by a red brick building, which is still in use. The Swedish group merged with an American Methodist congregation, and they now worship together as a United Methodist church. A handmade wooden pulpit, its base the shape of a lyre and its top a closed Bible, remains the only item in the church commemorating the founding Swedes.

WATAGA

Faith Lutheran Church was built in 1876. The nineteenth-century Gothic Revival white frame church is of vertical board and batten construction. Organized in 1853 by the Rev. T. N. Hasselquist, the congregation built its first church in 1860, which was struck by lightning and burned.

GALESBURG

Swedes first came to Galesburg as a result of dissatisfaction in the Bishop Hill Colony, which was thirty miles to the northeast.

The town became a railroad center and attracted Swedish immigrants seeking employment. By 1912, more than one-third of the city was Swedish by birth or descent. A State of Illinois historic marker near the junction of U.S. Highway 150 and State Highway 97 (in a small rest area and not far from exit 54 from Interstate 74) summarizes the early history of Galesburg, including the Swedish immigrants' contribution.

First Lutheran Church at Water and Seminary is one of the oldest congregations of the former Augustana Synod and one of the earliest congregations of Galesburg, though the sanctuary now used was built in 1928. The third oldest Swedish Methodist Church in the Middle West was organized in Galesburg.

In town at 331 East Third Street is the Carl Sandburg Birthplace (309/342-2361), which is open daily 9–5. Owned by the State of Illinois and operated by the Illinois State Historical Library and the Illinois State Historical Society, the Carl Sandburg Birthplace was the first home of the well-known Swedish-American author. Sandburg's father, August, had been attracted to Galesburg by employment opportunities with the Chicago, Burlington, and Quincy Railroad. Although he could read, he never learned to write. He married a Swedish woman, and together they had seven children, including Carl. About four years before Carl was born, the Sandburgs bought the workman's cottage on Third Street, but they moved a year and a half after he was born, seeking larger accommodations for their growing family. They moved in turn to several houses on East South and Berrien streets.

Since Carl Sandburg's birth 6 January 1878, the house has changed considerably. When it was first constructed, rough vertical siding clad the structure, and the interior was unplastered. Newspapers were pasted over the cracks to reduce drafts. After the Sandburgs moved, the new owner (who was a carpenter) put clapboard on the exterior and had the interior walls plastered. He also added a room to the rear. The cottage appears today much as it looked after these changes were made.

Few Sandburg family possessions remain in the house. Photographs of August and Clara Sandburg and the family Bible (Carl was confirmed in the Swedish Elim Lutheran Church in Galesburg) are on view. The crowded bedroom with its trundle bed, the absence of indoor running water, and a single wood stove for cooking and heating reflect typical living conditions of a working class family of a century ago.

The cottage's rear room, formerly the Lincoln Room and now the Sandburg Room, is devoted to Carl's literary accomplishments, especially his monumental Lincoln biography. Rare editions of Sandburg's early poetry (published in Galesburg), an autographed collection of his books, and the typewriter he used to write *The Prairie Years* and the *Rootabaga Stories* are on display. Behind the house is Remembrance Rock, named for Sandburg's only novel, under which are Sandburg's ashes. Also in Galesburg is Carl Sandburg College at 2232 South Lake Storey Road (309/344-2518).

SPRINGFIELD Lindbergh Field, northwest of Springfield, was the city's first airport, but it is no longer used. In April 1926, Charles A. Lindbergh, Jr., assisted in selecting the field. For a while, he flew mail to Springfield on the St. Louis–Chicago route until he began preparing for his historic 1927 transatlantic flight. In August 1927, the field was named to honor this aviator who was first to cross the Atlantic alone nonstop by plane.

MONTICELLO In the University of Illinois's Allerton Park, between Champaign and Decatur, is Carl Milles's sculpture "The Sun Singer." Castings made from the same mold may also be found at the National Memorial Park, a private cemetery in Falls Church, Virginia, and on the waterfront near the Royal Palace in Stockholm.

PAXTON In 1863, Augustana College and Seminary moved from Chicago to Paxton as the result of a land agreement made with the Illinois Central Railroad. Dr. Tuve N. Hasselquist was appointed president of the college at the time of the move. He replaced the Rev. Lars Esbjörn, who had headed the school when it was in Chicago. The school remained in Paxton until the fall of 1875 when it was relocated to Rock Island, Illinois. On 22 September 1957, a marker was dedicated on the former site of Augustana College and Seminary at the corner of Summer and Park, opposite Glen Cemetery.

Augustana's move to Paxton brought an influx of Swedish immigrants to the area. In June 1863 they organized in Hasselquist's home the First Lutheran Church. In 1907, the present church (the third sanctuary) at the southeast corner of College and Orleans was built. The second church was moved to nearby Pells Park where parts of it were made into the present park pavilion. The third church is a large red brick structure that originally had two spires. Olof Grafström's "Crucifixion" (c. 1910) hangs behind the altar. In the "Master Chapel" in the sanctuary's rear are two stained glass windows depicting Hasselquist and Martin Luther. The sacristy has pictures of all the former pastors as well as an old communion set. The Evangelical Covenant Church (at the northwest corner of Union and Orleans) was organized in 1878 as the result of a split from First Lutheran.

INDIANA

PORTER

In the late 1840s and early 1850s, young Swedish men in Chicago were attracted to northwest Indiana by employment opportunities, thanks in part to a saw mill that had been established by the son-in-law of Joseph Bailly, a French-Canadian fur trader. In 1858, the Rev. Erland Carlsson of Chicago organized the Swedish Lutheran Church of Baillytown (Augsburg Lutheran Church) with thirty-one charter members. In 1864, this congregation erected its first sanctuary in Porter, about a mile northeast of Baillytown. The log church is now gone, as is the second church, which burned in 1933. The present handsome stone church—Augsburg Evangelical Lutheran Church—resting on the foundations of the second sanctuary, was completed in 1938 at 100 North Mineral Springs Road (219/926-1658). On the front lawn is the Swedish-inscribed bell of the second church. The cemetery, to the south, contains many Swedish graves. In the church's basement is a well-organized archival room that includes a Hillstrom organ made in nearby Chesterton. Carl Oscar Hillstrom, born in Stockholm, moved his organ factory from Chicago to Chesterton in 1880 and made it the main industry in town, producing thousands of organs before the factory closed in 1920.

The Swedes wanted their children to have an education as well as maintain their language and some of the customs from the homeland. Swedish was taught during the summer months when the children were not in regular school. Across the road from the old Swedish cemetery (north side of Oak Hill Road, about one-tenth mile east of the intersection with U.S. 12) was a small unused tool shed on the property of Frederick Burstrom. During the summer of 1880, this building was moved near to the Swedish cemetery and renamed Augsburgs Svenska Skola (Augsburg's Swedish School). Today it is known as the Burstrom Chapel and Svenska Skola.

Residents used the building as a public school for five years, until 1885 when Porter County built a local school. Afterward it was used solely as a Swedish-language summer school until the 1920s. A small tower was added to the building, though when is unknown. Under its roof, the community also gathered for midweek prayer meetings and vesper services.

In the 1930s the building fell into disuse and thereafter deteriorated. Because of the efforts of local people, in 1970 restoration began. Though a 1992 storm damaged this work, the building underwent repair again. A granite historic marker stands near the front door.

The old cemetery has the graves of many early Swedes, including Jonas Asp, who initially encouraged his fellow

Under the roof of the Burstrom Chapel and Svenska Skola Swedish-American children learned Swedish and gathered with their families for prayer services.

countrymen to settle in Porter County, and Frederick Burstrom, who was Porter County's first trustee.

At Indiana Dunes National Lakeshore (219/926-7561) is Chellberg Farm, the homestead of Anders and Johanna Kjellberg (the name was anglicized to *Chellberg*), now part of the U.S. Department of Interior's National Park Service. The farm is on Mineral Springs Road, between U.S. 20 and U.S. 12, and the grounds are accessible year-round. Call the park office to determine when the farmhouse is open. Christmas is celebrated at the farm Swedish style, and the farm supports other activities throughout the year.

The Chellbergs left Sweden in 1863 and settled on this eighty-acre farm in 1874. Anders Chellberg was a tailor and farmer who served the Augsburg Evangelical Lutheran Church as a deacon and lay preacher. Three generations of Chellbergs made their living from the farm, where they grew wheat, oats, corn, and rye. The farm produced milk and butter, particularly after 1908 when the South Shore Railroad provided faster transportation to the Chicago market.

The brick farmhouse, built in 1885, replaced a frame house that burned. The barn, constructed in 1880, has a frame held together by wooden pegs. Six other structures stand on the restored farm, which has been used by the Solar Energy Research Institute for a renewable energy demonstration. A visitor's center assists guests.

LA PORTE

Bethany Lutheran (corner of First and G streets) is the oldest Swedish Lutheran congregation in northwest Indiana, having been organized in 1857 by Erland Carlsson. The first church was built in 1860 and the present one in 1883. A red brick Gothic-style structure with a tall central spire, the church has a sanctuary that has been extensively remodeled. In the basement is a small heritage room. Nine other Augustana Lutheran congregations were organized in Indiana before 1900: First Lutheran in Attica (1858), Augsburg in Porter (1858), Augustana in Hobart (1862), Augustana in Elkhart (1873), Bethel in Gary (1874), Immanuel in Donaldson (1876), Bethlehem in Chesterton (1879), Gloria Dei in South Bend (1880), and Zion in Michigan City (1887).

On the northeast corner of Indiana and Maple is the New Church Swedenborgian, which was constructed in 1859. Probably the most prominent Swedenborgian in the state of Indiana was John Chapman, who is now much better known as "Johnny Appleseed."

West of La Porte on Route 50 South, just north of State Highway 2, is the Carmel Chapel, a small simple white clapboard structure that was built in 1872. This is the oldest Swedish Lutheran sanctuary in northern Indiana. Inside is a wall map displaying the Swedish settlement in the area as it looked in the year 1896. Only one annual summer service is held in this chapel. A well-kept cemetery has graves of those early Swedish settlers.

DONALDSON

In Donaldson, a small northern Indiana community nine miles west of the intersection of U.S. 30 and U.S. 31, are two churches of Swedish origin—the modern Covenant church building inside town and the older white clapboard Immanuel Lutheran Church, which is northwest of town off U.S. 30. South of Immanuel is a Swedish cemetery.

ATTICA

Swedes from the Gränna district in western Småland settled in or near Lafayette (Tippecanoe County) as early as the 1840s. Many moved on to Waseca County, Minnesota, in 1857. First Lutheran Church at 204 East Pike Street (corner of East Pike and South Brady, 317/764-4364) is a white clapboard church whose congregation was organized in 1858 by the Rev. Erland Carlsson.

OHIO

Ohio attracted relatively few Swedish immigrants, certainly in comparison to other midwestern states. Those who came generally settled in Cleveland, Akron, and Youngstown. They also came to Ashtabula, where in the late nineteenth century there was a section in the eastern part of the city known as "Swedetown." Swedish Lutheran and Covenant congregations were organized in all four cities, the largest being Bethlehem Lutheran Church in Cleveland Heights, now within the scope of metropolitan Cleveland.

CLEVELAND HEIGHTS

Bethlehem Lutheran Church began as a mission church sponsored by the Home Mission Board of the Augustana Synod's New York Conference. The congregation was organized in 1885 (the oldest Swedish Lutheran congregation in Ohio is Capernaum Lutheran in Ashtabula, which was founded in 1881), and the first church built in 1890 at 434 Central Avenue. A second sanctuary was constructed in 1903 at 7505 Wade Park Avenue adjacent to Cleveland's "Swedetown," roughly bordered by Superior Avenue NE, East Seventy-ninth, Lexington Avenue NE, and Fifty-fifth. Swedish Baptist, Covenant, Methodist, and Salvation Army congregations were also located in Swedetown. In 1953 Bethlehem Lutheran's second church was sold to the Avery African Methodist Episcopal Church, and one year later the large stone Gothic-style sanctuary at 2740 Mayfield Road was dedicated. The architects for this impressive church were Adolph Hanson and Einar Olson of Chicago.

URBANA

Urbana University (One College Way) covers a 128-acre campus on the southwestern side of Urbana. Although founded in 1850 by followers of the Swedish philosopher, theologian, and scientist Emanuel Swedenborg (1688–1772), the school today has only an informal relationship with the Church of the New Jerusalem in the USA. The Swedenborg Memorial Library, built in 1968, contains a Swedenborgian book room. A campus chapel has portraits of Swedenborg. In town at 330 South Main Street is the Romanesque Urbana Swedenborgian New Church and Wedding Chapel, with the year 1880 on its cornerstone.

MICHIGAN

In introducing Swedish-American landmarks in Michigan, it is important to divide the state into its two natural parts—the Lower Peninsula and the Upper Peninsula. In the Lower

The "Orpheus Fountain" by Carl Milles can be seen at Cranbrook Academy of Art, where he was resident sculptor from 1931 to 1951.

Peninsula, Swedes first came in 1853 and 1854 to Lisbon, north of Grand Rapids and now known as Kent City, though industrial opportunities in the Detroit area eventually drew others there. Additional early Swedes settled near the river mouth logging centers of Saginaw and Bay City, at Alpena, and along the western coast from Muskegon to Manistee. In rural Osceola County, Tustin was founded in 1871 by about eighty Swedish families whose men were employed as laborers on the Grand Rapids and Indiana Railroad. These families who homesteaded Tustin originally called it New Bleking after Blekinge in their homeland. Because nearby Cadillac was a large sawmill and lumbering town after the Civil War, it became the funnel through which passed most of the new Swedish immigrants who came to settle and work in northern Michigan after 1865.

Beginning in the 1860s a larger concentration of Swedes settled in Michigan's Upper Peninsula. Initially the iron mines were the principal source of employment, but after they were depleted, the Swedes stayed and turned to other of sources of employment—lumbering, farming, and railroad construction. Ishpeming, in the center of an iron ore region, became a leading center for Swedes. Other communities included Escanaba, Iron Mountain, Norway, St. Ignace, Skandia, and Skanee. The Upper Peninsula also attracted settlers from Finland, some of whom were Swede-Finns. In Hancock on the Keweenaw Peninsula is Suomi College.

BLOOMFIELD HILLS

The architecture and art of the magnificent campus of the Cranbrook Academy of Art at 1221 North Woodward (810/645-3000) (about ten miles north of Detroit's city limits) was greatly influenced by two men—Finn Eliel Saarinen and Swede Carl Milles. From 1931 to 1951, Milles was the resident sculptor at Cranbrook. Today the Cranbrook Educational Community owns the largest collection of Milles sculpture outside Sweden. The outdoor sculptures include "Fountain of Jonah and the Whale," "Orpheus Fountain," "Triton Pool," "Europa and the Bull," and "Siren with Fishes." There are also a number of Milles's works in the Cranbrook Academy of Art Museum (810/645-3312; weekends, 810/645-3319). Another Milles work, "Sunday Morning in Deep Waters," a fountain, is on the University of Michigan's campus at Ann Arbor. It is on the main quadrangle near the Burton Memorial Tower.

Finnish architect Eliel Saarinen (1873–1950) was first asked to draw plans for the Cranbrook Educational Community in 1924 by its founder, financier George C. Booth. In the following years, Saarinen was, by turns, chief architectural advisor, president of Cranbrook Academy, and a departmental director. It was he who persuaded Carl Milles, his good friend, in 1931 to be the resident sculptor at Cranbrook. The Swedish sculptor was director of the sculpture department until 1951. Also working at Cranbrook were Saarinen's son, wife, and daughter. An institute recognized as being on the cutting edge of art, architecture, and design, Cranbrook brought together arts and crafts with a synergy that redefined to some degree American design.

SAWYER

At the beginning of the century, the Swedish Baptist churches of the Chicago area formed the Illinois Sunday School Union. One of the concerns was the need for city children, particularly of poor families, to spend part of their summer vacation in rural surroundings. Beginning in 1905, farmland was purchased in Sawyer, southwestern Michigan. Bethany Beach has now grown into a large summer religious conference center as well as a community of permanent year-round residents. The community's center is the Tabernacle, which was built in 1924. Ecumenical services have been held at Bethany Beach since 1906, the year the first tabernacle was constructed.

HARBERT

Along the southeastern shore of Lake Michigan in Harbert was where the Carl Sandburg family in the late 1920s began spending part of their summers. Listed on the National Register of Historic Places, the Sandburg House on Birchwood Court (still a private residence) later became the family's year-round house. Here Sandburg wrote the volume of poetry, *The People, Yes,* and completed the Pulitzer Prize–winning biography *Abraham Lincoln: The War Years.*

GRAND RAPIDS

The Swedish Covenant congregation was organized in 1880, and three years later its first sanctuary at Broadway and First streets was built. In 1895, the second church, a red brick edifice, was constructed. The interior's woodwork reflects the skilled craftsmanship of the Swedes who were engaged in the city's furniture business. In 1961, the building was sold to another congregation. The 1895 cornerstone is located in the foyer of the present modern Evangelical Covenant Church at 1933 Tremont Boulevard NW.

The Bethlehem Lutheran congregation was organized in 1873, and the present large light brick sanctuary at 330 Crescent NE was built in 1932 in the Heritage Hill Historic District.

KENT CITY

The congregation of the Mamrelund Lutheran Church (4085 Lutheran Church Road NW, between Sparta and Kent City) is important historically because it was the first Swedish church in

Michigan. The congregation was organized in 1866, and six years later, the present site was selected for a church building. At the turn of the century, the church was enlarged, but it was torn down to make room for the new sanctuary completed in 1979. The colored windows in the present edifice are from the old sanctuary.

BIG RAPIDS

Immanuel Lutheran Church, 325 Linden Avenue, is the result of a merger of Swedish and Danish congregations. On the northeast side of town was a section called Swede Hill where the first Swedish Lutheran sanctuary, which no longer exists, was located. In 1932, a historic plaque was erected in a small park on Baldwin Street (two blocks east of North State Street) to commemorate the Swede Hill settlement. Swedes came to the high bluffs above the Muskegon River as early as the 1870s and 1880s. They found work on the Grand Rapids and Indiana Railroad and in lumber camps, sawmills, and factories.

**TUSTIN–
LE ROY**

Three miles south of the Wexford-Osceola County line and west of U.S. Highway 131 in a rest stop is a historic marker, "Unto a New Land." This official State of Michigan marker describes the coming of Swedish Heritage Week in Michigan, which was proclaimed by Governor William Milliken, himself descended from Swedish pioneers who had settled in the Kent City area.

In nearby Tustin at 308 East Church Street is the white frame Augustana Lutheran Church. In 1872, the Rev. Josiah Tustin, rector of St. Mark's Episcopal Church of Grand Rapids, organized an Episcopal congregation known as St. Johannes' Church of New Bleaking (later changed to New Bleking and ultimately to Tustin). Few Swedes, however, showed much sympathy for the Episcopal Church, and in 1874 a group broke away to form the Swedish Evangelical Lutheran Church of Tustin. In 1938, St. Johannes' Church officially closed.

Also in Tustin near the church is Hoaglund Hardware, housed in the former bank building at 107 East Church Street. In a former potato warehouse across from the post office on Howard Street is the local museum. Frequently many early Swedish settlers grew potatoes in the summer and logged in the winter. There is a Swedish Baptist Church in town. The former Covenant church is now a private house, its congregation having merged with the local Presbyterian church. Outside Tustin are several cemeteries with numerous Swedish graves, including Burdell Township Cemetery (about one mile west of Tustin on Twenty Mile Road [Marion Road], just west of U.S. 131), Sherman Township Cemetery (approximately four miles north and east of Tustin on Twenty-one Mile Road [Ina Road]), and Maple Hill Cemetery (about 2.5 miles south of Tustin on Mackinaw Trail [old U.S. 1311]).

The Zion Lutheran Church of Le Roy was constructed in 1902, and for forty-six years was located approximately five miles south of town. Originally the congregation was known as the Swedish Evangelical Lutheran Emanuel Church. The small Covenant church originally was used by a Swedish Baptist congregation. It was built in the late 1870s or early 1880s. In 1890 the Covenant congregation was organized in Le Roy. Southwest of town is the Dewings Cemetery where Swedes are buried.

CADILLAC

The original sanctuary of Zion Lutheran Church, which was organized in 1874, stands on the corner of Shelby and Nelson, but it is now owned by another religious group. This building had been on the corner of Nelson and Simons, but it was moved in 1909 when the second church, a red brick structure with a tall steeple, was constructed. It, too, is now owned by another church. Zion's present sanctuary was built in 1973 at 350 Pearl Street, and in a small chapel are the altar objects from the former sanctuary.

Other churches with Swedish links in this community include the Swedish Christian Mission Church, the Free Methodist Church, and the Swedish Baptist Church. The Swedish Christian Mission Church was organized in 1880, and the next year the congregation built a church building that was not replaced until 1913, when the red brick Covenant church was built. One block west on Pine Street is the Free Methodist Church, the predominantly Swedish congregation having been organized in 1870. The Swedish Baptist Church was organized in 1883, and later it was renamed Temple Hill Baptist Church. The old church, constructed in 1888, is one block north of the old Zion Lutheran Church on North Simons Street. The present Baptist congregation built a new sanctuary at 1601 West Division.

The Gotha Society, operating as a mutual aid and fraternal society, constructed a building at 422 North Mitchell Street that it used for about forty years, but now the building is owned by the American Legion.

About four miles south of Cadillac is the Lutheran cemetery in Clam Lake Township, the graveyard for the former Swedish Lutheran church at Hobart, which disbanded in the early twentieth century.

GILBERT

Trinity Lutheran Church at 2780 North Forty-first Road in Gilbert (south of Manton) was constructed in the late nineteenth century and continues to have a Swedish congregation. Gilbert was a sawmill town on the Grand Rapids and Indiana Railroad.

JENNINGS

The town of Jennings northeast of Cadillac was a lumbering community that attracted a number of Swedish immigrants from 1882 until the early 1920s when the timber reserves petered out and people moved away. St. John's Lutheran, the community's church, which was similar in appearance to Gilbert's Trinity Lutheran, was moved to a new site south of Lake City, but it was eventually demolished. The old Lutheran cemetery at Jennings continues to be maintained.

LUDINGTON

Emanuel Lutheran Church, East Danaher and Lavinia streets, was organized in 1874, and the present sanctuary was built near the turn of the century.

MANISTEE

Completed in 1870, the white frame Our Savior's Historical Museum Church at 304 Walnut (616/723-0077) is the oldest extant Danish church in the United States and the town of Manistee's oldest house of worship. Listed on the National Register of Historic Places, the church bears on its front exterior a historic plaque. A number of Swedes helped build the church, then called Our Saviour's Evangelical Lutheran Church, and attended services there. Across the street is the red brick Evangelical Covenant Church (349 Third Avenue, 616/723-7173), with its cornerstone reading "Swedish Ev. Mission Church 1882 AD 1913." In 1970, three congregations, including the Swedish Messiah Lutheran, merged to form Good Shepherd Lutheran Church. Worship is conducted in the former Messiah Lutheran Church, a brick structure at 521 Cypress with Gothic-style windows and a central steeple .

The Manistee County Historical Museum (425 River Street, 616/723-5531) has a large collection of local artifacts and memorabilia. The material is not sorted according to ethnicity, but much was contributed by Swedes.

ST. IGNACE

In St. Ignace, the gateway to the Upper Pennisula, stands the Zion Lutheran Church at 999 South State Street (906/643-7870), which was organized by Swedes. The sanctuary was built in 1957. The building provides a view of the Straits of Mackinac, and Mackinac Island is visible to the east.

BREVORT

The small white frame Trinity Lutheran Church on U.S. 2 in town, whose congregation was organized by Swedes, is near a scenic beach on the north shore of Lake Michigan and not far from the Mackinac Bridge. Its Olof Grafström altar painting, "The Good Shepherd," is dated 1912. Brevort annually hosts a Swedish Midsummer Day festival.

ESCANABA

The sanctuary of Bethany Lutheran Church in Escanaba (202 South Eleventh, 906/786-6642) is perhaps the most impressive of all the Swedish church sanctuaries of northern Michigan. Built in 1912, the large brick church (the third building of the congregation), features two towering spires. Stained glass windows depict not only Christ and the children but also the pine-covered hilly landscape near Skandia in the Upper Peninsula. Three windows, now in the Fellowship Hall but formerly at the rear of the sanctuary, each portray Swedish leaders—King Gustavus Adolphus (1594–1632); Dr. Tuve Hasselquist, the Swedish Lutheran leader in America; and the Rev. Carl Olander, pastor of the Zion Lutheran Church of Marinette, Wisconsin, who presided at the 1879 organizational meeting of Bethany Lutheran.

NORWAY

Bethany Lutheran Church in Norway (815 Iron) began in 1880, and the sanctuary still in use dates from the late 1880s. The whitewashed frame building was first located in the hills above Norway, but it was moved to town in the early 1890s. The bell tower and chancel were additions. Above the Iron Street door is a stained glass window with the inscription "Swedish Lutheran Church." A couple of blocks away is the white frame Covenant church, whose congregation was organized in 1883.

AU TRAIN

Two miles south of Au Train and State Highway 28 in the Hiawatha National Forest stands the Paulson House (906/892-8293) on Route H03. Swedish pioneer and homesteader Charles Paulson built the two-story log house in 1882 on the shores of Au Train Lake, constructing first a single story and adding a second-floor dormer later. Built of cedar logs, some as long as thirty-four feet, cut at the site, the home was one of the first farmhouses in Alger County. The Paulson family lived in it for over fifty years. In 1968, restoration began. The original rough-hewn subfloor in the living and dining rooms was exposed, and the exterior white washing removed. Listed on the National Register of Historic Places, the cabin now houses a museum of pioneer furnishings and implements and a gift shop. The Alger County Road Commission owns the privately maintained cabin.

SKANDIA

The light red brick Emanuel Lutheran Church at 9812 U.S. 41 sits surrounded by woods. An old structure with transparent

Gothic-style windows, the church has a sanctuary featuring a small 1913 altar painting of Christ by Olof Grafström.

ISHPEMING

Bethany Lutheran Church was organized in 1870, making it the oldest original Swedish Lutheran church in the Upper Peninsula. Today the congregation worships in a facility (715 Mather) dating from 1962. On a separate tower hangs the 1912 bell with the Swedish inscription, *"Hör Gud ännu sin nåd dig bjuder! Se, templets portar öppna sig."*

Also in Ishpeming is the National Ski Hall of Fame (788 Mather, 906/486-9281) This two-story museum, near Bethany Lutheran, traces the history of skiing, emphasizing Norway's and Sweden's importance in developing the sport. Outstanding skiers are also featured.

SKANEE

Skanee is in an isolated area to the east of Keweenaw Peninsula in the most northern area of the Upper Peninsula. Lumbering and dairy farming attracted Swedes to the area. Zion Lutheran Church (906/524-6450) was organized in the late 1880s and is Baraga County's oldest congregation. The white frame sanctuary was constructed in 1892 and is the county's oldest existing house of worship. The impressive large altar painting is by Olof Grafström and dated 1900. Two miles to the west lies a cemetery with Swedish graves.

WISCONSIN

The first identifiable Swedes in Wisconsin were Carl Friman (descendants changed the spelling to Freeman) (1781–1862) and his family from Västergötland, who settled in 1838 in Racine County near Genoa City and what is today New Munster (see map, page 112). By 1900, only sixty-two years later, nearly forty-nine thousand Swedes lived in Wisconsin, according to the Swedish American Historical Society of Wisconsin.

One of those immigrants, Gustaf Unonius, a young graduate from Uppsala University, arrived in Milwaukee in 1841 with his wife and two friends. He established a colony at Pine Lake, some thirty miles west of Milwaukee, and named it New Upsala, creating the first organized nineteenth-century Swedish settlement in the United States (New Sweden, Iowa, holds the distinction of being the first permanent Swedish settlement of the nineteenth century). Although some Swedes responded to his positive letters, the colony was unsuccessful. After entering an Episcopalian seminary at Nashotah a few miles southwest of Pine Lake, being ordained, and serving as a

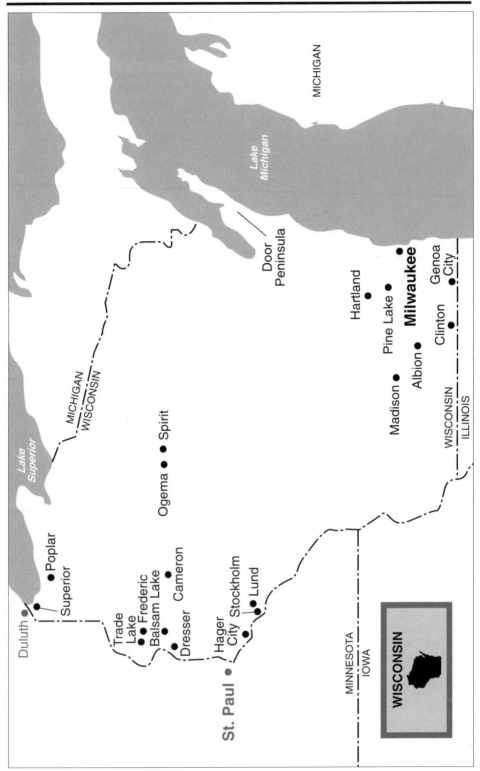

minister to three Wisconsin congregations, Unonius moved on in 1849 to Chicago where he served St. Ansgarius Church until 1858, when he returned to Sweden permanently.

Northwest Wisconsin attracted a significant number of Swedish immigrants, and a sizable percentage of people in Burnett, Polk, Douglas, Pierce, Pepin, and Barron counties are of Swedish ancestry.

MILWAUKEE

By the 1840s, Milwaukee, Wisconsin's largest city, was drawing Swedish immigrants. In the early 1900s, Swedish Americans had numbers great enough to support three Swedish-language churches, a lodge (Independent Order of Vikings), and a unit of the Swedish society Framat. At the southwest corner of Scott and South Tenth Street stands the original building of the Swedish Congregational Church (later Mission Friends–Covenant). Olaf Rehnquist, grandfather of Supreme Court Chief Justice William Rehnquist, helped found the congregation.

Swedish artist Thorsten Lindberg's work from the 1930s may be seen in the Milwaukee Auditorium (West Kilbourn Avenue and North Sixth Street), where his historical murals decorate the walls of large meeting halls. The Milwaukee County Historical Society, the Milwaukee Public Museum, and several county park system administrative buildings also hold Lindberg's work.

At the Milwaukee City Hall (East Wells and North Water Street) Swedish-American author Carl Sandburg served in 1910 as private secretary for Emil Siedel, Milwaukee's Social-Democratic mayor. John Olaf Norquist, elected Milwaukee's mayor in 1988, is of Swedish descent.

GENOA CITY

In a community park and under the roof of a freestanding log structure open on the sides, the Swedish-American Historical Society of Wisconsin erected a mounted plaque recognizing Carl Friman as the first identifiable Swedish immigrant to Wisconsin. Friman, who settled on eighty acres he purchased near Genoa City, emigrated in 1838. The Friman farm site is nearby, and several Friman descendants attended the dedication in 1988, the 150th anniversary of Friman's arrival. Freeman Street in Genoa City is named in honor of Adolph Freeman, Carl's son, who Anglicized the family name.

PINE LAKE

In 1948, the Wisconsin Swedish Pioneer Centennial Commission commemorated the founding of New Upsala by Gustaf Unonius (1810–1902) by erecting a marker at the junction of State Highway 83 and County Highway K. Two years after Nashotah House, an Episcopalian seminary, was founded, thirty-

This log structure shelters a plaque honoring pioneer Carl Friman, who is recognized as the first Swede to settle permanently in Wisconsin. Friman settled near Genoa City in 1838.

three–year–old Unonius was accepted as a student, and, subsequently, he was the seminary's first graduate. On the library's second floor at the head of the staircase is a picture of Unonius, and in its collection are some of his papers. The seminary has preserved two wood buildings dating from the 1840s that would have been familiar to Unonius—the Blue House, originally the dormitory, and the Red Chapel, still used occasionally for religious services. Near these buildings in 1991 the Swedish-American Historical Society of Wisconsin erected a monument memorializing the 150th anniversary of Unonius's immigration to the United States and recognizing Unonius as Nashotah House's first graduate.

St. Anskar Episcopal Church, whose 1968 sanctuary stands at 31340 Hill Road in Hartland (414/367-2439), combines two former congregations, including Holy Innocents. In Holy Innocents Cemetery (Highway C west of Pine Lake) in the northwest corner is one of the earliest graves in the county, that of K. N. Peterson (or Bengt Pettersson) (1797–1845), who came to Pine Lake in 1842. St. John's Lutheran Cemetery in Stone Bank, a small crossroads community on Highway K north of Pine Lake, also contains graves of Swedes. Five or six miles north of Stone Bank on Roosevelt Road is St. Olaf's Lutheran Church, which was organized and served by Gustaf Unonius.

North of Holy Innocents Cemetery off Route C and on Oakland Road (near the south end of Pine Lake) is a restored log cabin that was originally built in 1849 by John O. Rudberg for his recently arrived Danish bride. Later Rudberg added wings and a clapboard exterior to the original structure. It became a large frame house that eventually was converted to a hotel. When the house was being torn down in 1951, the cabin was rediscovered. Believed to be the only log cabin that has survived near Pine

Lake from the early New Upsala settlement, it was subsequently moved and restored. It remains a private residence.

CLINTON	In the Jefferson Prairie settlement near the Wisconsin-Illinois line and east of Beloit, the Scandinavian Evangelical Lutheran Augustana Synod was organized 5 June 1860. In the cemetery near the Lutheran church, which was established by Norwegians, is a large stone marker commemorating the founding. In 1894, the synod replaced *Scandinavian* with *Swedish* in its name.

ALBION

In 1843, two years after the New Upsala settlement was founded at Pine Lake, Thure L. Kumlien (1819–88) from Västergötland led a group of colonists to the Lake Koshkonong area. From 1865 to 1870, Kumlien taught natural history at Albion Academy. The school no longer exists, but Kumlien Hall, its main building, built in 1853, is now used as a local museum. On the two-story light-colored brick building is an official Wisconsin historic marker outlining the academy's history and a reference to Kumlien as a "world famous naturalist." Kumlien and his family are buried in the town cemetery.

Although Kumlien's settlement was not permanent, members of the party remained in the area. One of these was Carl Edvard Abraham Reuterskiöld (1796–1847) from Västmanland. He arrived in 1843 with his wife and seven children, and he and his family are buried in the Busseyville Cemetery in Jefferson County, northwest of Lake Koshkonong on State Highway 106 (about five miles east of Albion). A small curious stone inscribed "Abraham—Royal family of Sweden" marks the grave site, but Reuterskiöld was not royalty.

MADISON

On the state capitol grounds outside the East Wing (Pinckney and East Main streets, near King Street) is a statue commemorating Hans Christian Heg, who was born in Norway in 1820 and died in the Civil War battle at Chickamauga in 1863 (capitol tours: 608/266-0382). Heg was colonel of the Fifteenth Wisconsin Volunteers, or Scandinavian Regiment, during the war. Swedes, including surgeon A. F. Lindsfelt, Lt. Col. Kiler K. Jones, and Capt. Charles Gustafson, were among the regiment's nine hundred men, one-third of whom were killed on the field or died of wounds.

STOCKHOLM
AND LUND

In 1851, Eric Peterson (1822–87) of Karlskoga, Värmland, sighted the wide Mississippi River with its towering bluffs south of Red Wing, Minnesota (today that part of the river is known as Lake Pepin). Two years later, his brother arrived with a group of settlers and founded the community of Stockholm. In

June 1856, the first Swedish Lutheran congregation was organized in the area, but eleven years later, the congregation split. Two churches were built: one in the village of Stockholm and the other in the country some six miles inland. Around the turn of the century, the congregation in the country constructed a large stately red brick church with a soaring steeple, calling it the

The red brick Sabylund Lutheran Church with its soaring steeple stands about six miles outside Stockholm.

Sabylund Lutheran Church. The striking sanctuary has a Gothic-style white altar with a statue of Christ. The chancel wall is painted with white clouds on a blue background, and the wall on either side of the altar has a cross and chalice motif on a red background. Other walls are stenciled with various designs. A cemetery is adjacent to the site.

A number of Lutherans in the Lund area became Mission Friends, and a church was organized in 1874. The present

Gothic-style white frame Lund Mission Covenant Church dates from 1904 and is the second sanctuary of the congregation. A nearby Moravian church is an offshoot of this congregation.

HAGER CITY

Svea Lutheran Church was organized in 1875 near Red Wing, Minnesota, and two years later the sanctuary was built.

DRESSER

Bethesda Lutheran Church on Sand Lake in Dresser is a daughter congregation of Chisago Lake Lutheran Church in Center City, Minnesota. Bethesda Lutheran's Swedish heritage seems more apparent than that of other churches in northwestern Wisconsin. Over the main door of this red brick church is the inscription "*Sv. Ev. Luth. Bethesda Försam's Kyrka Byggd. AD 1888 Församlingen Stiftades 21 April AD 1872*" ("Swedish Evangelical Lutheran Bethesda Parish Church built A.D. 1888. The parish was founded 21 April A.D. 1872.") Set in a lovely location adjacent to Sand Lake, the church stands immediately north of a Swedish cemetery established also in 1872.

BALSAM LAKE

Polk County Museum (715/485-3161, ext. 269), a well-organized museum begun in 1976, is housed at 300 Main Street in the former Polk County Courthouse, built in 1899. The exhibits on the area's ethnic and religious heritage are open to the public daily Memorial Day weekend through Labor Day. Swedes are featured in one display, and Swedish congregations have contributed to the collection.

The Polk County Historical Society has been active in placing historic plaques throughout the county, and a number of the historic sites are of interest to Swedish Americans. The museum offers a complete directory to them.

FREDERIC

In 1873, Grace Lutheran, originally known as the Swedish Evangelical Lutheran Church of West Sweden, was founded. In 1931 electricity was installed in the 1884 sanctuary. Though most of the gas lamps were replaced, the congregation still maintains two old ornate chandeliers, the larger made of brass and the smaller of wrought iron. To the east and north of the church is the cemetery. The small community of West Sweden at one time had a creamery, dance hall, blacksmith shop, school, large merchandise store, and church. Only the last has survived.

TRADE LAKE

Zion Lutheran Church in Trade Lake is the oldest Swedish Lutheran congregation in northwest Wisconsin, having been organized in 1870. Grace Lutheran in Frederic is its offshoot. Zion's present red brick church with its tall steeple and Gothic-style windows was completed in 1914. In the adjacent cemetery, Swedish names predominate. The church is located at what local people call "Four Corners." At one time there were three Swedish churches—Lutheran, Baptist, Methodist (now in Atlas)—at this crossroads.

Additional old Swedish congregations in Burnett County include Bethany Lutheran (which has a contemporary building) and Siren Covenant in Siren; Trinity Lutheran (a small white frame church) in Falun; and Bethany Lutheran in Grantsburg. Although the congregation has disbanded, the old Mission Church in Trade Lake is being maintained by a group of interested local people. The Trade Lake Mission congregation was organized in 1886. Property was purchased in the same year and the present white frame church made of hand-hewn timber was built shortly thereafter.

Other old Swedish congregations in Polk County include United Covenant Church, Clear Lake; Immanuel Lutheran Church, Clayton; Fristad Lutheran Church, Centuria; Atlas Methodist Church, Luck; and Faith Lutheran Church, Balsam Lake. In nearby Washburn County, the lovely Salem Lutheran Church in Shell Lake has recently been torn down. The congregation saved the stained glass windows and incorporated them in the newly built church located at the corner of Second Street and Eighth Avenue.

Southwest of Trade Lake in an isolated part of western Wisconsin known as "The Barrens" (across the St. Croix River from Chisago County, Minnesota) is the Old Settlers' Cemetery. On the grounds, a group of Swedes began a congregation in 1878 and built a church, completed in 1881, known as the Sterling Swedish Lutheran Church. The church is gone, but a small chapel, constructed in 1984, is the site's sentinel. To get to the cemetery from Trade Lake, take County Road 48 west five miles to County Road 87 and turn south. At the north end of Cushing, turn west on Evergreen Avenue. Follow Evergreen 4.6 miles west through several bends and turns to the Trade River. Take the bridge spanning the river to the Old Settlers' Cemetery, which is to the left.

CAMERON

The Barron County Historical Musem (museum, 715/458-2080; manager, 715/458-2841), an impressive open-air museum exhibiting more than twenty historic buildings, includes two structures of Swedish origin. Open 1–5 Thursday, Saturday, and Sunday 1 June through Labor Day, the museum is about four miles east of Barron and one mile west of Cameron on County Highway W. The fourteen– by twenty-four–foot Hedin Log House was built about 1890 by native Swede A. P. Hedin (1865–1941). Hedin lived in the log house with his Swedish wife, five sons, three daughters, and a grandmother until 1909, when they moved to larger quarters. The log cabin had only a kitchen-dining room, a bedroom, and a loft that slept six people. Before 1967, the log cabin was on a farm in the nearby township of Stanfold. Only a few items in the cabin originally belonged to the Hedin family: the religious and song books in the kitchen hutch, the butter churn, and a large cast-iron scalding pot.

The white frame Ebenezer Lutheran Church, where weddings are still held, was built in 1908 between the towns of Poskin and Almena. The congregation was organized in 1908 as the Swedish Evangelical Lutheran Ebenezer Congregation of Poskin, Wisconsin, but later it disbanded. In 1972, the sanctuary was moved to the museum. Original items still found in the church include two pews, a hymn board, communion service pieces, and two velveteen collection pouches on long poles.

OGEMA

One mile outside Ogema is the one-room Lars and Charlotta Ek Log Home, built in the 1880s or 1890s by this couple, who moved to Wisconsin from Bällefors, Skaraborg, Sweden. Ek bought the land in 1881 after coming to Ogema from Chicago shortly before. Now cared for by the Ogema Historical Society, the house is opened annually for the Ogema Christmas Tree Festival and sometimes for other holidays. Because of remodeling the house had been masked it until it was rediscovered in the 1970s.

The Gothic-style frame First Evangelical Lutheran Church in Ogema was built in 1900, and the Olof Grafström altar painting is dated 1905. On the west side of Ogema is the town cemetery, where many stones bear Swedish names.

SPIRIT

Around 1878, a Swede named Charles Hilmar Olson, who worked on a boat that brought immigrants to Michigan's Upper Peninsula, heard about the giant white pine stands on the Spirit River in north-central Wisconsin. Because he was more interested in logging than sailing, Olson brought his family and friends, including Albin Johnson, to the area. The one and one-half–story Albin Johnson Log House was built in 1885 in one of the last-settled regions of Wisconsin. The Johnsons lived in the structure only briefly. In 1972 it was moved to the Roy Meier farm and converted into a local museum. To see the log house, drive east on State Highway 86 for 3.7 miles and then south on County Road Y for four miles. The farm is on the east side of the road, near the German Lutheran Church.

SUPERIOR

Many Swedes settled in this most northwesterly section of Wisconsin. In particular they came to Superior, a city with several churches of Swedish background, including Pilgrim Lutheran, Zion Lutheran, and First Evangelical Covenant. Superior and nearby Duluth, the "Twin Ports," drew immigrants to the shipping trade. Superior's airport is named for Richard I. Bong (1920–45), a Swedish American who as an American fighter pilot in World War II shot down forty Japanese aircraft (see below). Superior was also the birthplace of Irvine Lenroot, U.S. Senator 1918–26, whose parents were Swedish.

POPLAR

In Poplar, about twenty miles east of Superior, are a museum and markers honoring Major Richard I. Bong, who shot down forty Japanese aircraft in World War II. Called "America's Ace of Aces," Bong is remembered by an official state marker on the north side of Route 3 in a rest area at the west end of town, a school named in his honor, the nearby Lockheed P-38 Lightning Fighter Monument, and the Richard I. Bong Memorial (715/392-2773 or 800/942-5313), which is a small museum dedicated to Bong and other World War II veterans. The museum, on U.S. 2, exhibits Bong's medals and awards and a P-38 fighter plane. Bong's father was born in Dalarna and was brought to Wisconsin when he was six years old. Bong is buried in the Poplar Cemetery on Cemetery Road off Route 2.

DOOR PENINSULA

Door Peninsula, jutting into Lake Michigan, was to a great extent settled by Nordic immigrants, with Norwegians and Icelanders (on Washington Island) predominating. Towns such as Ellison Bay, Sister Bay, and Ephraim have a distinctly Scandinavian atmosphere and feature Nordic restaurants and gift shops. Because of its scenic beauty, Door Peninsula attracts tourists from across the Middle West.

IOWA

Iowa is significant in the history of Swedish immigration in part because within its border in southeast Jefferson County was the first permanent Swedish settlement of the nineteenth century (see map, page 121). New Sweden was established by Peter (Per) Cassel (1790–1857), a well-to-do farmer, who in 1845 brought with him seventeen Swedes from Kisa Parish, Östergötland. A year later, a second party heading for New Sweden lost its way and eventually settled along the Des Moines River, north of Des Moines, at a location identified as Swede Point, later renamed Madrid. Boone, Hamilton, and Webster counties in central Iowa with towns including Boone, Boxholm, Stratford, Dayton, Harcourt, Gowrie, and Fort Dodge attracted a large number of Swedish settlers.

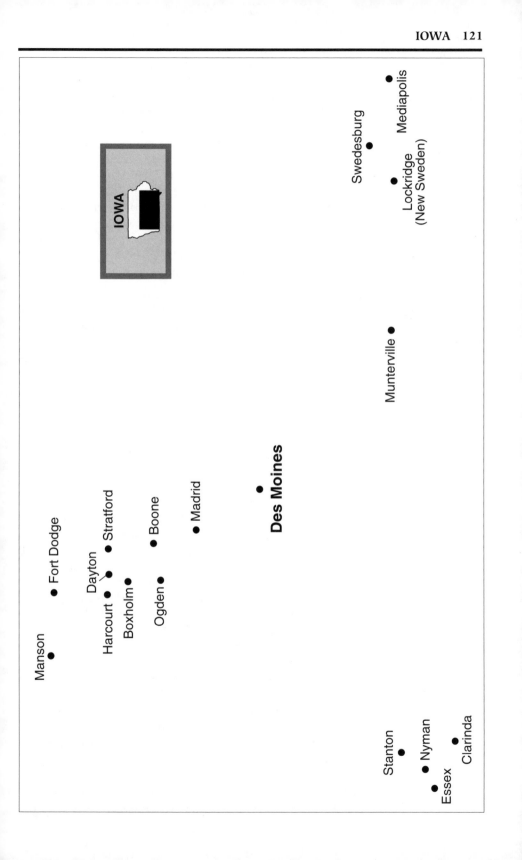

Across the southern tier of counties are other pockets of Swedish settlements, including the southeastern city of Burlington, Swedesburg in Henry County, Munterville in Wapello County, and towns in Montgomery and Page counties in the southwest. Besides the congregations specifically mentioned below, several old Swedish Lutheran congregations in southeastern Iowa carry on, though the early buildings no longer survive: Messiah Lutheran of Burlington (organized 1859), First Lutheran of Chariton (1869), First Lutheran of Ottumwa (1871), First Lutheran of Centerville (1881), and First Lutheran of Keokuk (1883). The most important Swedish settlement in the southwest part of the state is Stanton, founded by the Rev. Bengt Magnus Halland (1837–1902) from the province of Halland. (For Davenport Iowa, see page 89.)

LOCKRIDGE (NEW SWEDEN)

New Sweden can really be described as a neighborhood rather than a town because it was never incorporated, never had stores, and its population never amounted to more than a few hundred. But the community's historic significance in the history of Swedish immigration to the United States is far-reaching. The "Swedish Highway," a gravel road, historically has unified the various churches and farmsteads in New Sweden. It runs west from County Road 40 through the New Sweden Historic District, which itself is about three miles northwest of Lockridge.

On the south side of the Swedish Highway is the New Sweden Chapel, undoubtedly the most significant existing structure in New Sweden. The fifty- by thirty-foot white frame church is basically unchanged since its construction in 1860 (the Lutheran congregation was organized in 1848). It has a two-tiered steeple with a spire, and the lower part of it contains a bell manufactured in St. Louis before the building's construction. Inside, the visitor is struck by the sanctuary's elegant simplicity. The simple wood pulpit, altar and rail, hymn board, plaster walls with wainscoting, and floor are original to the building.

Hanging from the walnut ceiling are two early light fixtures, each containing four kerosene lamps (now supplied with electricity). An old Victorian couch is behind the pulpit. A large altar painting by Olof Grafström was added to the sanctuary near the turn of the century. The edifice replaced a smaller log church, built in 1851, thanks to a gift of three hundred dollars from a fund to which Jenny Lind had generously contributed.

The building has been placed on the National Register of Historic Places. In 1948, in honor of the one hundredth anniversary of the congregation, about three thousand people gathered at the church with Prince Bertil and the Archbishop of Sweden in attendance. The building is recognized as a historic shrine of the former Augustana Lutheran Synod. Many settlers, who died of cholera or diphtheria in the early years, are buried in the cemetery south and east of the chapel.

In 1944, the New Sweden congregation merged with the First Augustana Lutheran Church of Lockridge, which now owns the New Sweden Chapel and Cemetery. Four summer services are held annually in the chapel.

In 1850 a theological dispute resulted in the organizing of the Swedish Methodist Church, the first in Iowa, by the Rev. Jonas Hedstrom, brother of Olof Gustaf Hedstrom, founder of Swedish Methodism in the United States. Jonas Hedstrom conducted an aggressive and successful campaign for members in New Sweden. The white clapboard Methodist church, which replaced in 1871 a church built of logs, stands one mile west of New Sweden Chapel on the south side of the Swedish Highway. Additions have been made to the structure through the years. In the important cemetery to the church's east are buried early pioneers, including Cassel and Danielson family members, many of whom were converted to Methodism. Peter Cassel, New Sweden's leader, was a convert. A tablet in the churchyard identifies the pioneers buried in the cemetery.

The Swedish Baptist Cemetery, one-quarter of a mile east of New Sweden Chapel, on the north side of the Swedish Highway, shared its location with the New Sweden Baptist Church. Although claims have been made that this is the first church built by Swedish Baptists in the United States, the first Swedish Baptist congregation was organized in 1852 in Rock Island, Illinois.

Not part of the historic district but offering a view of the life there is the Fairfield Public Library Museum in Fairfield, twelve miles west of Lockridge on Route 34. A loom, an iron-banded chest, and photographs and paintings connected with the community are exhibited.

SWEDESBURG   Eleven miles east of Lockridge and nine miles north on U.S. 218 is the small community of Swedesburg. Swedish settlers came to the area, then called Freeport, after Pastor Hakan Olson of the New Sweden Lutheran congregation made a trip here in the 1860s. Impressed by the land, Olson encouraged people from New Sweden and Biggsville, Illinois, to establish a colony. The first Swedish settlers, the S. P. Swenson family, came in 1864. In 1866, a congregation was organized under the name of Swedish Evangelical Lutheran Congregation of Freeport, Iowa. The red brick church, built in 1927, is the third sanctuary on the site.

In 1986, the Swedish Heritage Society in Swedesburg was founded, and four years later it purchased four buildings. In 1991, with a Dala horse over the front door, the society opened the Swedish Museum. Exhibits feature a portrait of the immigrant farmers of the 1860s, the leadership of the Swedesburg church in the colony's growth, and the early pioneers. The museum's library contains genealogical records and histories by local writers. Renovation of a second building in 1992 produced a redesigned and reconstructed Swedish *stuga*—and a typical country store from the 1890s will be recreated from a third building. The society celebrates both Midsummer and Lucia Day annually.

MEDIAPOLIS

Swedish immigrants near the southeastern Iowa community of Amityville founded Immanuel Lutheran Church in 1868, and in 1872 they constructed the congregation's first building. As time passed, the Swedish population grew and shifted from the country into Mediapolis. By 1892 so many members had moved from Amityville to Mediapolis that it seemed wisest to build a new church in Mediapolis. Now at 606 Orchard in Mediapolis (319/394-3600), the congregation worships in a building constructed in 1954. Eventually, the church in Amityville was closed, but its cemetery is still well maintained. In 1993 this congregation celebrated its 125th birthday.

MUNTERVILLE

Munterville Lutheran Church, on old Highway 34 six miles northeast of Blakesburg, was organized by Swedish settlers in 1856 by about fifty charter members who called the Rev. Magnus Fredrik Hokanson as minister. In 1865 the congregation built a church and marked off a cemetery on five acres donated by Peter Anderson, an early church supporter. When the members erected (1898 to 1901) the building where it still worships, they used the lumber from the original church to construct the Parish Hall, which has since been moved to another location and converted to a farmhouse. Just before the eighty-fifth anniversary of the church, the congregation added the memorial belfry from stones gathered from members' farms and in it hung the original (1866) church bell. Immediately behind the church are the graves of the organizer of the congregation, the Rev. Hokanson (1811–93), and his wife, Anna. The Rev. Hokanson served the church 1848 to 1856. This crowded cemetery contains many stones bearing Swedish names.

DES MOINES

Pastor Hakan Olson, president of the Iowa Conference of the Lutheran Augustana Synod, organized the First Lutheran Church in November 1869. The first small church was built in 1871 at Sycamore and Front Streets (now East First and Grand Avenue) (515/244-8913). It was replaced by a red brick structure, still in use today, completed in 1887 at 511 Des Moines Street. First Lutheran with its tall Gothic-style spire is on a rise about four blocks from the Iowa state capitol, which was also built about the same time. It has been said that some of the stone used for the church's foundation walls were stones rejected for the capitol construction.   Many Swedes emigrating to Des Moines at this time constructed homes in the community surrounding the church. The church remodeled its spacious sanctuary in 1927, retaining few of the early furnishings.

The Rev. A. P. Westerberg, a pastor of the church in the early twentieth century, presented to the Iowa Conference of the Augustana Synod in the winter of 1909 a plan for creating the Iowa Lutheran Hospital. In March 1910 the hospital's board met for the first time. Construction of the first building began in 1913, and other facilities were added in the 1920s, 1940s, 1960s, and 1970s. Today Iowa Lutheran Hospital (University at Penn, 515/263-5612) is a major health facility.

Two works by Swedish-American sculptors stand in Des Moines. Carl Milles's bronze sculpture "Pegasus and Bellerophon," completed in 1949, complements a lovely reflecting pool in the central courtyard of the Des Moines Art Center (4700 Grand Avenue, 515/277-4405). Another "Pegasus" can be found in a Malmö, Sweden, park. "Crusoe Umbrella," a sculpture by Claes Oldenburg, is at Nolen Plaza between Locust and Walnut streets, about a dozen blocks west of the Iowa state capitol.

MADRID

The fascinating story of how Swedes first arrived in central Iowa, northwest of Des Moines, focuses on Anna Larsdotter Dalander (1792–1854), a widow, the leader of forty-two Swedish immigrants. As a result of Peter Cassel's glowing reports to Sweden about southeastern Iowa, Dalander in 1846 led a group to join the New Sweden settlement. But they followed the wrong river—the Des Moines rather than the Skunk—and arrived in Boone County. Five years later, Dalander platted Swede Point, which was later renamed Madrid. Other ethnic groups were attracted there as well.

The house believed to be the first frame residence erected in Madrid is the Carl and Ulrika Dalander Cassel House at 415 West Second Street. Built in 1862, the one and one-half–story house is closely connected with the Cassel and Dalander families who were chiefly responsible for the early Swedish immigration to Iowa. Carl Cassel (1820–1902), son of New Sweden pioneer leader Peter Cassel, constructed the house. On 21 April 1848, Carl Cassel married Anna Dalander's daughter, Ulrika, in probably what was the first Swedish marriage in Iowa. He became active in politics and served as a county supervisor. He was also a charter member of St. John's Lutheran Church in Madrid.

The Carl and Ulrika Dalander Cassel House, which is listed on the National Register of Historic Places, is made of native black walnut covered by painted clapboards. It has been described as combining elements of Greek Revival and Swedish vernacular architecture. According to the National Register of Historic Places Inventory—Nomination Form, the Swedish architectural features include "broadside orientation, projecting eaves, and a medium pitched gable roof." The same report also noted that "Cassel reverted to the architectural traditions of his native land" when several years later he built a one-story addition to the west end of the house. Exterior alterations have been minimal, though steel siding has been added and the front porch, once removed, has been restored. Only a one-story wood frame storage shed remains of the outbuildings formerly around the farmhouse.

Inside the house is a central hall with doors at either end. This typical arrangement of rooms in early homes has persisted despite a number of remodelings. Woodwork and flooring are original. Carl Cassel lived in this house for forty years until his death in 1902. It remains a private residence.

Cassel and his wife, Ulrika, and her mother, Anna Dalander, are all buried in the Dalander Cemetery, whose entrance is marked by a granite monument (about one mile north of North Street on a gravel road that intersects North three-quarters of a mile west of the Madrid Home). The Elk Rapids–Cole Cemetery is nearby.

The brick sanctuary of St. John's Lutheran Church at 414 West First (north of Cassel's house) dates from 1924, but the congregation was organized by the Rev. Magnus Fredrik Hokanson in 1859, as noted on the cornerstone. Inside the sanctuary is an altar painting (1899) by Olof Grafström. Grafström's painting and the church's two large stained glass windows had hung in the former church.

The Iowa Lutheran Home was planned in 1904 and dedicated four years later, but in 1948 fire destroyed it. A new building was completed in 1950, and additions subsequently have been made. Now known as the Madrid Home, the interdenominational center serves the elderly in a facility still having some Swedish tone.

The only location in the area still retaining the name Swede Point is Swede Point Park, which is situated on high ground above the Des Moines River a short distance from the Dalander Cemetery.

The Madrid Historical Museum attracts visitors at 103 West Second Street (call 515/795-3249 for hours). Within the block and near the library are a doll museum and a replica of a coal mine, a remembrance of the industry that brought many to the region.

BOONE

Boone has landmarks for two of its own, Swedish descendant Mamie Doud Eisenhower (1896–1979), who was born in Boone and became the wife of the thirty-third president of the United States, and Charles John Alfred Ericson (1840–1910), a Swede who became a successful Boone businessman and Iowa state senator. At the Mamie Doud Eisenhower Birthplace at 709 Carroll (515/432-1896), visitors can tour the home belonging to Mamie Eisenhower's paternal grandparents. She was baptized in 1896 in the old Evangelical Free Church (that church building no longer exists). Her maternal grandparents were Carl and Marie Carlson, who were both born in Sweden. Carl Carlson was the head miller at Boone's Reed Flour Mill, and his brother Joel was vice-president of a Boone bank and active in the Evangelical Free Church.

Though Mamie Eisenhower lived just nine months in the house, moving to Cedar Rapids and then to Denver, the museum's aim is to emphasize the former First Lady's background; therefore, considerable Swedish memorabilia is displayed. The house, after five years' restoration work, was dedicated in June 1980.

The Ericson Memorial Public Library at 702 Greene Street (southwest corner of Seventh and Greene, 515/432-3727) was built by Ericson and dedicated in 1901. Born in Vimmerby, Småland, Ericson was president of the City Bank of Boone, which he helped found in 1872; a six-term state senator; and a benefactor of Augustana College in Rock Island, Illinois. The library is listed on the National Register of Historic Places.

Boone is the home of the mother congregation of the Evangelical Free Church in America, founded in 1884. Though the building used by the congregation was built in 1971, the 1900 cornerstone of the old church rests in the lobby (1407 Kate Shelley Drive, 515/432-7690). The Evangelical Free Church Home, begun in 1912 as Frikyrkans Ålderdoms Hem (The Free Church's Home for Old People), at 112 West Fourth, was built after the mid-1960s. Its original cornerstone, inscribed in Swedish, is part of memorabilia displayed, including photographs and early twentieth-century door plates.

The Lutheran congregation in Boone—Augustana Lutheran Church at 309 South Greene—was founded in 1877. Housed in a new building, the congregation now displays its Olof Grafström altar painting (1906) in the Fellowship Hall.

Boone County Historical Society and Culture Center (515/432-1907) is located at 602 Story.

OGDEN

The "mother" Lutheran congregation of the Boone area, organized in 1868, is Swede Valley Lutheran Church (515/275-2164), located five miles south of Ogden on U.S. Highway 169. The white frame church with a high steeple is picturesquely situated on a knoll out in the country. Outside the main entrance is a memorial to the Rev. A. W. Edwins (1871–1942), founder of the Augustana Lutheran Mission to China, whose stone reads, "Buried at Sea."

A daughter congregation in Ogden is Immanuel Lutheran (119 Southwest Second Street, 515/275-2164), which was organized in 1914. Also in Ogden is Mission Covenant, constructed the same year Immanuel was organized.

BOXHOLM

Boxholm is named for the Swedish village in Östergötland where its first postmaster, John B. Anderson, was born. Twenty-one men and women organized the Lutheran church in Boxholm in 1886, and in 1888 the congregation, with much volunteer labor, built a church in the country. But in 1911 the sanctuary was moved to its present location on U.S. Highway 169 in the center of Boxholm. Services were conducted in Swedish until 1924.

Swedish Methodists built the Boxholm United Methodist Church in 1886 three-quarters of a mile southeast of town, but moved it to town at the turn of the century. Swedish and German groups eventually merged, forming the present congregation.

Early Swedish pioneers of the area are buried in Lawn Cemetery near Boxholm.

STRATFORD

Stratford is on the eastern edge of the largest (in area) Swedish settlement in Iowa, including the towns of Dayton, Harcourt, Lanyon, Boxholm, and Pilot Mound.

John Linn, born in Småland in 1826, immigrated at age twenty-three to Swede Point. From there he and his wife continued up the Des Moines River to a location southwest of Stratford called Swede Bend, the third oldest Swedish settlement in Iowa. Soon other Swedes arrived, coming up through the bottomland of the Des Moines River with teams of oxen.

The John Linn House (twenty-four by twenty-six feet), built in the 1850s, is made of trough-grooved logs. A staircase leads from the four-room first floor to the second floor and its low sloping ceiling. A local farmer presented the house in 1981 to the Stratford Historical Society, which uses it occasionally, and it was moved in 1983 to Bellville Road (last paved county road at the west end of town, two blocks north of State Highway 175) and Tennyson Avenue.

After Linn was converted to Methodism, he preached and organized churches, including the South Marion Methodist Church (founded in 1854), the second Swedish Methodist congregation in Iowa. In 1861, the first sanctuary was built in Swede Bend. This building was later sold to the Mission Church (the Mission Covenant had its beginnings in 1868 in Swede Bend). Eventually the building was moved to Twin Lakes Bible Camp in Manson, Iowa, where it is regarded as a historic landmark. At the first sanctuary's original site is a marker identifying the spot as the location of the first church of the Evangelical Covenant Church in America. It is about one and one-half miles east of the Des Moines River on County Road R21 (also identified as the Dragoon Trail, an Iowa Historical Trail).

In 1877, the Methodists dedicated the South Marion Methodist sanctuary (still in use in the early 1980s), three miles to the east of the former one. The white clapboard structure with a high steeple was saved from a 1936 windstorm, though alterations were made afterward. In the South Marion Cemetery, about one and one-half miles from the church, is John Linn's grave.

In 1859, with forty charter members, the Stratford Evangelical Lutheran Church was organized by Pastor Magnus Fredrik Hokanson. In 1893 a white clapboard church with a tall Gothic-style steeple was completed and in the 1980s still in use. A Baptist congregation was also organized in Swede Bend, having been founded in 1856. In 1979, the congregation relocated to the town of Stratford and the former buildings were torn down.

The Swede Bend Schoolhouse, originally located one-eighth of a mile from the old South Marion Methodist Church (the first Covenant sanctuary), now stands in Izaak Walton Park (about three miles west of Stratford on the north side of State Highway 175). Built at the turn of the century, the schoolhouse was a place of learning until 1946. Now it is the clubhouse of the Izaak Walton Club, a conservation group. Also still standing at 801 Shakespeare and listed on the National Register of Historic Places is the former State Bank of Stratford, which was founded by local Swedish Americans and constructed in 1918.

DAYTON

One of the oldest Covenant mission congregations in the area survives in Dayton. Emanuel Lutheran was organized in 1868. On Main Street in downtown Dayton can be seen the former Opera House, restored and reopened as a restaurant. The northwest corner of the town cemetery on State Highway 175 contains the oldest graves, many with Swedish names. In nearby Gowrie, Zion Lutheran was organized in 1871.

HARCOURT   Settlers organized the Mission Covenant Church in 1888, and the same year built its sanctuary at South Wood and East Second. Three years later, Lutherans organized Faith Lutheran on Ash Street and constructed its white clapboard church building. The dark shingled steeple is surmounted interestingly by an unfolded lily. The altar painting of Jesus and his flock (1912) is by Olof Grafström. Settled by Swedes, Harcourt has preserved several original mercantile buildings. Between Harcourt and Lanyon, which is on County Road P46, is the Lost Grove Cemetery.

FORT DODGE   Swedes helped settle Fort Dodge, and a section of the city was known as Swedetown. Leif Ericson Park honors the well-known Scandinavian.

Built in 1861, the first Mission Covenant church in the United States is preserved at Twin Lakes Bible Camp in Manson.

MANSON   The Twin Lakes Bible Camp in Manson preserves on its compound the first Mission (Friends) Covenant church in the United States. Organized on the Fourth of July 1868 at Swede Bend, the congregation was led by Carl August Svenson Björk (1837–1916), a native of Lommaryd, Småland. Greatly influenced by the *läsare* ("readers" or "pietist") movement, Björk left Sweden in 1864 to come to Swede Bend to join his brother. When the local Lutheran church split, Björk persuaded a group meeting in the home of Peter Englund to form the first Mission Covenant congregation. Built by Methodists in 1861 and sold to Björk and his group in 1874, the structure served the Swede

Bend Covenant congregation until it was relocated to Manson on the Fourth of July 1976, America's Bicentennial.

STANTON

In Stanton, which is sixty miles southeast of Omaha, Nebraska, over half of the population still claims to be of Swedish ancestry. The city retains the air of a Swedish settlement with some business district signs written in Swedish, Swedish decor in a number of buildings, and the Stanton water tower in the form of a Swedish coffee pot. A southwest Iowa landmark, the coffee pot was created in the 1970s at a time when millions of American television viewers watched actress Virginia Christine, known as Mrs. Olson, endorse Folger's coffee with a comforting, respect-inspiring Swedish accent. Christine, whose real name was Virginia Rickett Kraft Feld, was born in Stanton.

Stanton's water tower turned Swedish coffee pot is an Iowa landmark.

Stanton, known as the Halland Settlement, was established by Pastor Bengt Magnus Halland (born Johansson) (1837–1902), who had come from Sweden to Illinois in 1856 and was ordained eight years later. Early in 1869, he toured southwest Iowa and became convinced of its suitability for colonization. A land agent for the Burlington Railroad, Halland advertised for "non-drinking" and "God-fearing Swedes." Immigrants from Sweden as well as from Andover, Illinois, flocked to the area, paying six to eleven dollars per acre. In 1870, Halland organized three Lutheran congregations—Fremont in Nyman on 19 May, Mamrelund in Stanton on 25 May, and Bethesda in Clarinda on 26 December.

At the center of the "Little White City" (Stanton's nickname) stands Mamrelund Lutheran Church (410 Eastern Avenue, 712/829-2421), a very large and impressive stone building. The congregation began with a small sanctuary in 1870. Thirteen years later, the "First Big White Church" was erected; however, in 1938 after the building was struck by lightning, only the bell and four church record books were saved from the ensuing fire. Dedicated in 1941, the new white Indiana stone edifice is crowned with a towering spire visible from the town's outskirts. The sanctuary features symbolic stained glass windows and lovely woodwork on the ceiling, balcony, pews, and Gothic-style altar. In a room south of the sanctuary is an altar with the scripture from Psalms 29:2: *"Tillbedjen Herren i Helig Prydnad"* ("Worship the Lord in the beauty of holiness"). The same inscription was over the main altar that burned in 1938. Nearby is a picture of Halland, who is buried in Stanton Cemetery (near the water tower, at the end of Frankfurt) along with other Swedish pioneers.

Also established by Pastor Halland was the Swedish Evangelical Lutheran Orphan's Home of Iowa. He was convinced of the need for a home for Swedish orphans. Located a mile and a half south of Stanton, the home's first building was constructed in 1881. Over time other facilities were added, but the home closed in 1938. Only two barns remain standing.

Northeast of Stanton past old Highway 34 is Tabor Lutheran Church, a white frame church with a cornerstone bearing the date 1898. The 1908 altar painting is by Olof Grafström.

NYMAN

The congregation of Fremont Lutheran Church was the first of three to be organized by the Rev. Bengt Magnus Halland in 1870. The first sanctuary, which also served as a parsonage, was built the following year. The site was approximately one-half mile north of the present church. A cemetery, remnants of which still remain, was established nearby. The old church later became part of a farmhouse and is located north of the present parsonage. Between 1875 and 1880, the congregation erected a new sanctuary. On 1 January 1902, though, the building burned to the ground. Before that year was over, the new white frame Gothic-style sanctuary had been completed. The 1902 altar painting is by Olof Grafström.

ESSEX	The Faith Evangelical Covenant congregation worships in a clapboard structure at 212 Alice Street built in 1926. It was the sanctuary of the Fremont Evangelical Covenant Church (originally Svenska Lutherska Missionsföreningen, chartered in 1876) until the two congregations were consolidated in 1991.
CLARINDA	Bethesda Lutheran Church, built in 1877, remains the oldest Swedish church sanctuary in southwestern Iowa. Remodeled in 1928, the white frame structure is topped by a central steeple.

MISSOURI

Relatively few Swedes were drawn to Missouri, principally because the state was well populated when the Swedish immigration was in full swing. By 1930, more than one-third of Missouri's Swedes were living in Kansas City. Bucklin in north-central Missouri became a Swedish rural settlement. Other Swedes clustered in St. Louis and in southwest Missouri, particularly in and near Verona in Lawrence County and Globe, which drew enough Swedes to organize a Swedish Methodist Church. Swedish Baptists formed churches in several Missouri communities, including Swedeborg in Pulaski County.

ST. LOUIS

Two Carl Milles fountains grace public spaces in St. Louis. In Aloe Plaza, "Meeting of the Waters," also known as "Wedding of the Rivers," was the first monumental fountain designed by Milles for an American city. (Aloe Plaza is opposite Union Station on the north side of Market Street between Eighteenth and Twentieth streets.) The Mississippi River is symbolized by a twelve-foot male figure riding a dolphin escorted by four tritons. He is meeting his bride, the Missouri River, attended by four sea nymphs. The plaza and fountain were dedicated in 1940. In Laumeier Sculpture Park (12580 Rott Road, 314/821-1209) is Milles's sculpture "Folke Filbyter," an equestrian statue that is a replica of one standing in the central square in Linköping, Östergötland.

The oldest operating greenhouse west of the Allegheny Mountains is the Linnean House in the Missouri Botanical Garden at 4344 Shaw (314/577-5100). Honoring Swedish botanist Carolus Linnaeus (Carl von Linné) (1707–78), the Linnean House was completed in 1882, having been built by Henry Shaw, the garden's founder. Because he could see the Linnean House from his home, Shaw made it the most ornate of the three greenhouses. The main entrance is graced by three busts: the central one is of Linnaeus flanked by two nineteenth-century American botanists, Thomas Nuttall and Asa Gray. Shaw

The Linnean House at the Missouri Botanical Garden was completed in 1882 and restored in 1977 (© 1975 Srenco Photography).

originally built the Linnean House as an orangery, but it has had several different uses. As a result of a 1977 restoration made possible by funds from several sources, including the Swedish Council of St. Louis, today the Linnean House is the dramatic setting for the garden's camellia collection. The Missouri Botanical Garden's library (314/577-5155) has a collection of rare books containing nearly every edition and translation of Linnaeus's writings as well as works by his students and colleagues. The botanical garden also features the Milles Sculpture Garden, which includes "Two Girls Dancing" (1917), "Sun Glitter" (1918), "Orpheus Fountain Figures" (1936), and "Angel Musicians" (1949–50).

Aviator and Swedish American Charles A. Lindbergh, Jr. (1902–74), who piloted the first nonstop transatlantic flight from New York to Paris, is honored at the Jefferson Memorial in Forest Park. A bust of Lindbergh, dated 1939, in the collection is inscribed, "In flying, I tasted a wine of the gods." Lindbergh contributed items from his historic flight to the collection of the Missouri Historical Society (314/746-4599) in appreciation for the support organizing the construction and flights of the *Spirit of St. Louis* that came from St. Louis citizens. A main north-south artery west of the city is called Lindbergh Boulevard.

Two other St. Louis Swedish landmarks worth noting are the former Swedish National Society Building at 1157 Kingshighway Boulevard and the Gethsemane Lutheran Church, which was founded in 1894 by Swedish nail makers. The church's sanctuary, built in 1961, stands at 3600 Hampton.

KANSAS CITY

Kansas City has the distinction of owning Carl Milles's last work, "St. Martin of Tours," which is part of the William Volker Memorial Fountain in front of the Nelson-Atkins Museum of Art at 4525 Oak (816/751-1278). The fountain was completed eight months before Milles died in Stockholm in 1955. Bishop St. Martin of Tours is portrayed sharing his cloak with a beggar. The fountain was dedicated in 1958.

Founded in 1906 by Swedish Lutherans, Trinity Lutheran Hospital, at Thirty-first and Wyandotte, was originally called Swedish Hospital. In 1915 the hospital was moved to its current location, which is the highest point in Kansas City. The hospital merged with the Salem Lutheran Home for the Aged, which was also begun by Swedish Lutherans. A marker on Wyandotte honors the area's Scandinavian pioneers.

Three Lutheran churches are of note. First Lutheran Church at 6400 State Line Road in Mission Hills is the "mother" Swedish Lutheran congregation in Kansas City. This is its fourth location after moving from 416 West Fifteenth Street to 1238 Pennsylvania Street to Thirtieth and Benton. The present impressive church building includes a memorial chapel that contains an altar painting by Olof Grafström.

A daughter congregation is Immanuel Lutheran, which was organized in 1899. Its original members worked mainly for the railroads and meat-packing companies. Immanuel Lutheran is at 1700 Westport Road. In former times, Swedes assembled wagons on Westport Road, preparing to move on to points farther west. The red brick building in use dates from the 1920s. Another daughter congregation of First Lutheran is Messiah Lutheran, founded in 1894. Its building at Granview Boulevard and Twelfth Street was built in 1914.

Other buildings of interest to Swedish Americans include the Kansas City Power and Light Building, the U.S. Federal Courts Building, and the City Hall (701 North Seventh). These three are among many built by a company owned by Godfrey G. Swenson (1876–1946), who was born in Vimmerby, Småland, and became a successful building contractor in Kansas City.

BUCKLIN

This community's history involves the story of Olof Olsson (1841–1900) who left Värmland in 1869 with approximately two hundred fifty parishioners, friends, and other fellow believers for central Kansas. When the second group of Olsson's party arrived in Chicago, N. S. Ornsdorf, a Swede who had already settled in Bucklin, persuaded them to come to Missouri to make some money before starting out for central Kansas. One hundred three were persuaded. Once in Missouri, the Swedes decided to stay permanently and to purchase land north and south of Bucklin.

In 1870, the settlers decided to organize a Swedish Lutheran congregation. There were thirty-three charter members, all but three from Värmland. By 1875, the congregation reached 195, its highest membership. In that year, a local Swedish farmer donated an acre of land nine miles north of Bucklin and a church was built. In 1878, thirteen families left for Kackley, near Scandia, Kansas, later to be followed by others. Two years later, discontent in the church caused a split and the founding of a Swedish Covenant Church about three miles south of the Lutheran church (North Swede Church). By 1927, the Lutheran services were discontinued.

The little white frame church has not been altered significantly since it was built. For example, it has the original walnut altar rail and flooring. A cemetery association, which meets annually, was organized in 1927 to maintain the church as well as the adjacent cemetery. Some stones have Swedish inscriptions.

Mission Covenant Church (also called South Swede Church), a small white clapboard church with a short steeple, was built in

1880. Like the Lutheran group, this congregation eventually dwindled. The last services were held in the early 1950s, though the Sunday School continued to meet until 1960. Its cemetery association was organized in 1963. Both the north and south churches have held centennial celebrations, and the cemetery associations oversee the properties' upkeep. Both church yards continue to have interments.

In the vicinity of Bucklin, old farmhouses built by the early Swedish settlers are still standing.

SWEDEBORG   Largely settled by Swedes in the last three decades of the nineteenth century, Swedeborg grew up with the railroad interests. The south central Missouri city was originally called Woodend. The 1890 log school south of town, the school that replaced it in 1891, and early church buildings have given way to twentieth-century facilities. But two cemeteries, St. John's (Swede) Cemetery (on Pulaski County Road BB about one mile off Missouri Route 133 west and north of Swedeborg) and the Bethlehem Cemetery (about three and one-half miles south of Swedeborg) hold many markers with Swedish names and remind those in the present of the contributions of the past.

KANSAS

In 1855, John A. Johnson from Horn Parish in southern Östergötland moved to Kansas. By making his home on the eastern shore of the Big Blue River, about twenty miles north of Manhattan, he became the first Swede to settle in the state. Eight years later, he organized the Mariadahl church, the oldest Swedish Lutheran congregation west of the Missouri River.

During the 1850s and 1860s, other Swedish settlements were established at Axtell (northeast Kansas), Clay Center, Lawrence, Enterprise, and the Scandia area in Republic County (north-central Kansas), but the most extensive Swedish colony was in the Smoky Hill River Valley of central Kansas, centering around Lindsborg (see map, page 138). The first Swede probably arrived in the valley in 1864, and two years later seventeen additional Swedes homesteaded in the area. In 1868, two independently organized Swedish groups in Illinois initiated efforts to promote immigration to the Smoky Valley—the Swedish Agricultural Company of McPherson County in Chicago and the Galesburg Colonization Company in Galesburg. Affiliated with the Chicago organization, Pastor Olof Olsson (1841–1900) of Sunnemo, Värmland, brought a group of more than one hundred Lutheran men, women, and children in 1869 (some two hundred fifty left Sweden, but half the group stayed in Bucklin, Missouri). The Galesburg Company bought more

than thirty-eight thousand acres of land and settled more than two hundred families in the valley during 1869. Among this number were settlers led by Pastor A. W. Dahlsten (1838–1919).

Lindsborg was the last of the Swedish religious settlements in the United States. In 1879, the twenty-one-year-old Rev. Carl Aaron Swensson (1857–1904) arrived in Lindsborg as pastor of Bethany Lutheran Church. He founded Bethany College in 1881. Although the majority of people in the Lindsborg area have their ancestry in Värmland, other provinces are represented, as the names of such neighboring communities as Falun and Smolan clearly demonstrate. The area known locally as the Smoky Valley includes an area bordered on the north by Salina, on the east by Roxbury, on the south by McPherson, and about five miles west of Marquette on the west.

Because Lindsborg is at the center of Swedish life in Kansas, this survey of Kansas will begin there and sweep around the towns of the Smoky Valley. Then before covering the cities of Kansas's eastern half, including Manhattan and Lawrence, we will look west along U.S. Highway 40 at towns from Ogallah to Weskan.

LINDSBORG

Of the three thousand inhabitants in Lindsborg, about two-thirds claim to be of Swedish ancestry. Lindsborg has maintained a strong Swedish heritage, and the town prides itself on being "Little Sweden, U.S.A.," adopting the Dala horse as its symbol and using it on the town seal. Dala horse signs appear on the lampposts and on city vehicles. Many residents also have these symbols hanging from their porches. Some businesses advertise in Swedish. In Bank IV of Lindsborg are displayed Dalecarlian-style paintings by Lindsborg artists including Rita Sharpe and her husband, the late Robert Walker. Paintings by Birger Sandzén, Maleta Forsberg, and Lester Raymer are hung in the bank lobby. Downtown has a Scandinavian air about it, and shops featureSwedish gifts, food, books, and maps.

Among the distinctly Swedish traditional events Lindsborg celebrates are Lucia; Midsummer; and its own festival of tribute to Swedish pioneers, the biennial *Svensk Hyllningsfest* (Swedish Homage Festival), held in conjunction with the Bethany College homecoming. Celebrated mid-October in odd-numbered years, *Svensk Hyllningsfest* has since 1941 paid tribute to the Swedish pioneers who came so far to settle this small town in the Kansas heartland.

Renowned as an art center, Lindsborg is famous for its art studios throughout town. To aid visitors, the Chamber of Commerce at its 104 East Lincoln office (913/227-3706) offers a complete list of artists' studios. In addition to Bethany College faculty member and later artist-in-residence Birger Sandzén

(1871–1954), many other gifted artists have worked in Lindsborg, attracted by the supportive artistic community. Some who have taught at Bethany include Olof Grafström (1855–1933), Carl G. Lotave (1872–1924), and Margaret Sandzén Greenough (1909–93). Others who have taught at Bethany are Oskar Jakobson, Lester W. Raymer, Annie Lee Ross, Charles B. Rogers, John Basher, Rosemary Laughlin, Carl W. Peterson, and Raymond Kahmeyer. Numerous artists have settled in Lindsborg. Gustav Nathanael Malm (1869–1928) assisted with many town-and-gown projects, including the Bethany Oratorio Society. Malm's daughter, Alba Malm Almquist, is noted for oil and watercolor landscapes. Though impossible to name all, others include Signe Larson (religious paintings), Oscar Gunnarson (landscapes), Anton Persson (wood carvings), Carl Peterson (landscapes), Maleta Forsberg, and Robert Walker (Swedish Dalarna peasant motifs). Lindsborg's reputation as an art and music center and especially its Easter week Messiah Festival have earned it the name "Oberammergau of the Plains," identifying it with the German city known for its centuries-old Passion play.

INSTITUTES AND MUSEUMS

McPherson County Old Mill Museum and Park—120 Mill Street (913/227-3595).

The history-rich McPherson County Old Mill Museum and Park complex comprises two parts: first, an open-air museum with free-standing structures and, second, the old mill, museum, and log cabin. The structures in the open-air museum include the Swedish Pavilion, the first classroom building of

Built in Sweden, the Swedish Pavilion was shipped in pieces to the 1904 Louisiana Purchase Exhibition in St. Louis. Afterward at Bethany College it was used as an infirmary and for classrooms. It was relocated and rededicated in 1976 at McPherson County Old Mill Museum and Park and now houses historical exhibits.

Bethany College, a former Lindsborg railway station, the first McPherson County above-ground structure, the workshop of the Erickson brothers, an old school, and storefronts. Two buildings—the Swedish Pavilion and the old mill—are on the National Register of Historic Places.

Designed by Ferdinand Boberg (1860–1946) and built in Sweden, the pavilion is a reproduction of a Swedish manor house, containing a large main room and two wings. Workers reassembled it in St. Louis for the 1904 Louisiana Purchase Exposition. Afterwards, William W. Thomas, Jr., the American minister to Sweden and Norway, purchased the building and donated it to Bethany College. It was moved in sections by railway flatcars to Lindsborg. At Bethany it first served as an art exhibition hall and museum. Later part of the structure was used for classrooms for gymnastics, home economics, and art. One wing was the school's infirmary. In 1969, the Swedish Pavilion was moved to its present location and renovated. The Swedish coat of arms was restored and hung inside rather than outside as originally conceived. New chandeliers were made to approximate the original ones. It was rededicated on 17 April 1976, by King Carl XVI Gustaf. Inside are historic exhibits.

Bethany College's first classroom building (Academy Building), built in 1879, now houses a library, including many Swedish Bibles and other books written in Swedish, and numerous historical items from the college's history.

The Union Pacific Depot, for years after it was built in 1880, was a stopping place on the line between Salina on the north and McPherson on the south. In 1975, the station was moved to the park. Nearby is a Santa Fe engine, built in 1900, one of only about four dozen steam engines of its kind on display in the United States.

The first above-ground building in McPherson County was erected in Sweadal in 1869 from lumber hauled from Leavenworth, Kansas. It served the community as the post office under the supervision of Major L. N. Holmberg, postmaster. In 1870, citizens met in this building and formed McPherson County, and under its roof the first county election was held. In 1872, the county seat was moved to Lindsborg.

Sweadal, about four miles southwest of Lindsborg, was founded by Holmberg, a Stockholm native and a Civil War veteran, but never platted. Holmberg constructed an octagonal tower known as Holmberg's Castle. Today only the brick foundation remains of this rather unusual structure. Approximately five hundred feet from this watchtower are the remains of an old white house, whose basement was a former two-room dugout dating from the early 1870s. The holes in the walls were for bed and table supports.

The Erickson Brothers Workshop belonged to John and Charles Erickson, pioneer developers of automatic telephone systems. Anders Erickson, their father, who had emigrated from Värmland in 1869, was a mechanic, blacksmith, and a fine metal and wood craftsman. Finding his sons also similarly gifted, he set up this cabin as a shop for them next to his own. Here the brothers worked on a variety of projects, including a horseless carriage and a player piano. In the small building they invented in 1895 the first workable telephone dial. John Erickson was credited with 115 patents, and Charles had 35. A friend, Frank A. Lundquist, also obtained numerous telephone patents.

The West Kentuck School, erected in 1903 and used through the 1951–52 school year, belonged to the school district, which was organized in 1874. The first class met in a sod house, and it was not until six years later that the first frame building was constructed.

A livery stable and a farm implements display are part of a recreated example of pioneer storefronts.

The Smoky Valley Roller Mill, constructed in 1898, is the second mill built for the community on Smoky Hill River, and its nineteenth-century machinery is in excellent condition. The first mill, a frame structure, was destroyed by fire.

Eleven thousand artifacts pertaining to natural and pioneer history, Native Americans, and Swedish heritage fill the rustic Old Mill Museum, erected in 1968. The community's culture and crafts may be seen in the woodcarvings by Lindsborg artist Anton Pearson, cement sculpture by local artist Oscar Gunnarson, and a chiffonier by Lindsborg pioneer farmer Andrew Rosander. A painting of the Swedes landing in Germany during the Thirty Years' War is the work of Olof Grafström. Johan August Udden's Native American collection and the Bethany College natural history collection highlight the area's sociological and geographic history. A Swedish *stuga*, Swedish folk costumes, and a corner fireplace bespeak other Scandinavian contributions.

A log cabin, built of cottonwood by August Olson about 1870, was erected over a dugout and later became part of a six-room house. Originally seven and one-half miles southwest of Lindsborg, the cabin was moved in the early 1960s to its current site. Interior furnishings are from pioneer days.

Folklife Institute of Central Kansas—118 South Main (913/227-2007).
Organized in 1989, the Folklife Institute of Central Kansas seeks to research, identify, and present for appreciation the folk art and folklore of central Kansas. A Swedish-American research project undertaken with the help of National Endowment for the Arts grants investigated the *ljuskrona* (a Swedish chande-

lier), and a similar grant allowed the institute to study Smoky
Hill River Valley woodworking traditions. The institue is open
by appointment only.

HISTORIC PLACES

**Hoglund Dugout—one mile west of Lindsborg on Highway 4,
three-quarters of a mile north on the gravel road, and then about
three hundred feet east of the road; or two miles south of Smoky
Hill Cemetery on a gravel road, just past a little bridge and over
a creek.**

The original Swedish settlement in Lindsborg was at the south
side of what has come to be known as Coronado Heights. At first
the settlers built dugouts into the creek or river bank with only
buffalo hide or blankets covering the doorways. More permanent dugouts were constructed in the sides of hills or on flat
ground and lined with stone that usually had been chiseled by
hand. In western and central Sweden are similar cellarlike
structures called *jordkulor*. The Hoglund Dugout, approximately
twenty feet by ten feet, is one of few that have survived. Clearly
visible is the stone wall around the dugout. The doorway faced
east. The dugout now is the property of the Smoky Valley
Historical Association, which intends to leave it as it is. Probably
the family moved to a more substantial house after a year or so
in the dugout; one corner of an old stone house is nearby.

**Rostad House—three-quarters of a mile east of Elmwood Cem-
etery, two-fifths of a mile north on a gravel road, and then visible
on the road's west side.**

On the way between Elmwood and Rose Hill Cemeteries is the
first log cabin built in McPherson County. Today it is part of a
larger private residence, though the logs may still be seen in the
kitchen.

**C. R. Carlson House—northwest corner of Washington and
Lincoln.**

C. R. Carlson, one of the founders in 1876 of the Evangelical
Swedish Mission Church, forerunner of First Covenant Church
across the street, owned this brick house now used for commercial purposes. Carlson, who owned thousands of acres in the
area, was formerly a member of Bethany Lutheran. The house
is noted for its hand-carved woodwork and spiral staircase.

Fridhem ("Peaceful Home")—southwest corner of East Swensson
and North Second streets.

Built in 1879, this early parsonage was home to the Rev. Carl
Aaron Swensson and his family and today is part of Bethany
College.

CHURCHES
Bethany Lutheran Church—320 North Main (913/227-2167).
One of the most outstanding Swedish landmark churches in the
United States, Bethany Lutheran Church in Lindsborg bears a
strong resemblance to the cathedral in Karlstad, Sweden.
Although made in 1874 of brown sandstone quarried near
Coronado Heights north and west of the city, the church in 1904
was plastered with stucco and painted white. Above the church
a spire soars 125 feet. The Bethany congregation is the third
oldest Lutheran church in the area (Freemount Lutheran was
organized four days before Salemsborg Lutheran in 1869),
having been founded by the Rev. Olof Olsson two months after
the others. Olsson was later McPherson County's first
superintendent of schools, a state legislator, and a professor of
theology and president of Augustana Seminary in Rock Island,
Illinois.

The first services of the Bethany Lutheran congregation
were held in the homes of settlers and in the Community House
(or Bolagshuset) of the Swedish Agriculture Company at the base
of the butte known as Coronado Heights. (The first Swedish
Agriculture Company was organized in Chicago. It purchased
more than thirteen thousand acres of McPherson and Saline
County land from the Union Pacific Railroad.) In 1869, the first
church sanctuary was erected less than one mile northwest of
present-day Lindsborg, and the first services in the church were
on 1 January 1870. That church, made of stone and sod and
measuring thirty-four feet by thirty-six feet was one and one-
half miles south of the Smoky Hill Cemetery (see below) and on
the south side of Coronado Heights. A commemorative marker
was erected in 1993. All that remains from the first church are
some foundation stones from the first building and a simple
handmade table now in the sacristy of the present church. After
a lengthy debate, the congregation decided in 1874 to build the
second and present church in the town of Lindsborg. Six years
later the steeple was added. The transepts were constructed in
1904. Bethany Lutheran's services were conducted in Swedish
into the 1920s.

Above the front doorway is the Swedish inscription of
Revelation 3:11 and John 1:29 along with the construction dates.
Higher up on the steeple is, in Swedish, "The Word of God is
forever." In 1904, several stained glass windows and three
chancel paintings were installed. G. N. Malm, a local artist, was
commissioned to do the center altar painting, and Birger Sandzén
executed the other two large ones. All three paintings as well as
the stained glass window above the altar are in memory of the
Rev. Carl A. Swensson and portray biblical events that took
place in or near the village of Bethany.

Bethany Lutheran Church's spire soars 125 feet. The church was completed in 1874.

The Luther window now located in the organ pipe room in the balcony is in memory of the Rev. and Mrs. Olof Olsson. Both bells in the tower have Swedish inscriptions, and the larger one, dated 1881, bears a brief early history of the congregation. In the Hoglund Room are old gas lamps, made from the original sanctuary oil lamps, and a portrait of Olsson, which was a gift from Värmland honoring the congregation's centennial anniversary. In the south transept are the old communion vessels and hymn board. The last pews in each transept are original ones. Malcolm Esping, a local craftsman, in 1964 made the mosaic inlay of the church seal placed in the cement walk leading to the church's front door. The church art clearly reflects the strong artistic tradition in Lindsborg.

It was in the church sacristy that Bethany College was founded 15 October 1881. The first performance of Handel's

Messiah was presented 28 March 1882. Mrs. Carl A. Swensson had directed the rehearsals since December 1881, and Pastor Olof Olsson returned from Rock Island to serve as organist.

Evangelical Covenant Church—102 South Washington at Lincoln (913/227-2447).

A group of immigrants from Östergötland settled on tracts of land later called Rose Hill northeast of present-day Lindsborg. In 1874 they organized and built the first Covenant church in Kansas. When a theological dispute arose in the Bethany Lutheran congregation that same year, C. R. Carlson, a friend of Olof Olsson, left with fifteen others and joined the Rose Hill group, forming the Evangelical Swedish Mission Church. In March 1876, the Rose Hill Church was dedicated, but in August a tornado destroyed it.

After the 1876 disaster, the congregation rebuilt in town, completing in 1878 a unique brick church with an onion dome. In 1905 a north wing and bell tower were added. Disaster struck again when the building began crumbling in the early 1920s because the local brick had not been fired correctly. In 1926 the congregation built the present Gothic-style red brick church.

Other Churches

Other churches with Swedish links in Lindsborg include the Messiah Lutheran Church, the First Baptist Church, and the former Swedish Methodist Church. Messiah Lutheran (402 North First) was organized in 1908 as an English-speaking congregation. In 1911 it built a red brick sanctuary still standing adjacent to the Bethany College campus. G. N. Malm was commissioned to do the altar painting. According to its cornerstone, First Baptist Church (913/227-2360) at the northeast corner of Lincoln and Washington streets was organized in 1880 as the Swedish Baptist Church, and its brick sanctuary was built in 1918. The former Swedish Methodist church at 202 South Second Street is now a private residence. The church now meets at 224 South Main (913/227-3326).

SCHOOLS
Bethany College—421 North First (913/227-3311).

Bethany College was founded in 1881 by the Rev. Carl Aaron Swensson. The first year there were ten students and two teachers—Swensson and Johan August Udden. Originally the school was an academy, but in 1886 it became a four-year college with the right to confer baccalaureate degrees. On campus is a statue of Swensson with an inscription noting that he was born in Sugar Grove, Pennsylvania, in 1857 and that he was Bethany's president until his death in 1904. The statue, unveiled in 1909, depicts Swensson wearing his academic robe with the Royal Order of the North Star.

The first college classroom building, a sixteen- by twenty-four–foot two-room frame structure, had been constructed in the late 1870s and purchased by Swensson in 1882 for five hundred dollars. It was originally located where the present Lindsborg elementary school now stands. It was moved to the campus (Presser Hall's present site), and an addition was built. When Presser Hall was erected, the building was moved to another part of the campus and used for storage. In 1969 the Smoky Valley Historical Society moved it to McPherson County Old Mill Museum and Park (see above).

Old Main was demolished in 1968, but the college built Old Main Court with two capitals from the former structure and the cornerstone—"Bethania 1886." Near the athletic field is the historic bell purchased in 1882 and placed in the first college building.

Presser Hall is a 1,900-seat auditorium where the annual *Messiah* oratorio and other concerts are performed The Bethany Oratorio Society, organized by the Rev. and Mrs. Swensson in 1881, is now a three hundred–voice chorus and a large orchestra. Its *Messiah*, part of Lindsborg's annual Holy Week Festival (between Palm Sunday and Easter), is the longest-running uninterrupted annual rendition of Handel's masterpiece performed in the United States. It began in 1882.

Pihlblad Memorial Union was dedicated in 1964 and honors Dr. Ernst F. Pihlblad and his wife, Marie, who was the sister of Victor Sjöström, a motion picture director. Dr. Pihlblad (1873–1943) was president of Bethany College from 1904 to 1941. Additional buildings on campus honor other Swedish Americans or Swedish-American cultural ties: the Wallerstedt Social Science Center and the Wallerstedt Library-Information Center (Alvar G. Wallerstedt was a businessman and financier from Lindsborg), Nelson Science Hall (Ludvig Nelson was a mayor of Lindsborg), Kalmar Residence Hall, Anna Marm Residence Hall (Anna Marm was a professor of mathematics), Alma Swensson Residence Hall (Alma Swensson, founder Swensson's wife, helped initiate the annual *Messiah* performances), Hahn Physical Education Building (Ray D. Hahn was a former coach), and Anderson Athletic Field and Anderson Memorial Tennis courts (E. T. Anderson was an Emporia, Kansas, cattleman, banker, and businessman).

Today the coeducational institution, which is affiliated with the Evangelical Lutheran Church of America, has about 725 full-time students and 54 full-time faculty members.

OTHER POINTS OF INTEREST

Bethany Home—321 North Chestnut (913/227-2721).
Bethany Home, a cheerful senior citizens home, features paintings throughout rendered by local artists. In the dining room, a Signe Larson painting depicting a Swedish country scene with people in folk dress attracts admiration. Metal liturgical objects made by Malcolm Esping are in the chapel.

Swedish Timber Cottage—125 North Second (913/227-2183).
The Swedish Timber Cottage, a pine log house built in Dalarna of Swedish timber, constructed by hand, and roofed with red concrete tiles from Västergötland, was brought to Lindsborg and reconstructed after every element had been numbered and dismantled. Home to the Anderson Butik and Anderson Scandinavian Tours, the cottage has Swedish wall and ceiling wood paneling. Dean and Charlotte Anderson, carrying on the family business Dean's father started, sell gifts, maps, food, and decorative items from Sweden in the *butik*, and if you crave more, you can sign up for a custom tour of Sweden.

Smoky Hill Cemetery—three miles northwest of Lindsborg, south of Coronado Heights. (From West Swensson Street, go north on Burma Road two miles, turn left on Coronado Heights Road, and travel west less than one mile. The cemetery is on the north side of the road, immediately before the entrance to Coronado Heights Park.)
Near the southeast corner of Smoky Hill Cemetery is a monument to Olof Olsson's mother (Olsson himself is buried in Riverside Cemetery, Moline, Illinois; his parents and his two infant sons are buried here). Other early Swedish settlers are buried here with Swedish inscriptions on their graves.

Elmwood Cemetery—east of Lindsborg (seven-tenths of a mile east of Bethany College campus on East Swensson, which becomes McPherson County Road 1067).
A twenty-foot obelisk marks the graves of Carl Aaron Swensson (1857–1904) and the members of his family. Artists Birger Sandzén, Gustav Nathanael Malm, Lester Raymer, and Margaret Sandzén Grennough are buried here, as is Bethany College president Dr. Peter Ristuben, who died in office in 1989.

Rose Hill Cemetery—go east two miles from the corner of Coronado Heights and Burma, turn left on Fairchild Road, travel one-half mile north, and turn west to enter cemetery.
Dotted with stones bearing Swedish inscriptions, this cemetery has a granite marker commemorating the Rose Hill Mission Covenant Church, formerly located about a half mile south, which merged with another Lutheran congregation in Lindsborg.

SCUPLTURE AND OTHER ART
Birger Sandzén Memorial Gallery—Bethany College Campus, 401 North First (913/227-2222).
Among the buildings on the Bethany College campus is the Birger Sandzén Memorial Gallery (open 1–5 Wednesday through Sunday). This gallery is dedicated to and houses the works of Birger Sandzén (1871–1954), Lindsborg artist and Bethany College professor. Sandzén was born in Västergötland, the son of a pastor. He attended Lund University and studied for two years with noted Swedish artist Anders Zorn before going to Paris. Sandzén joined the faculty at Bethany in 1894, and for almost six decades served the school. He also gave voice lessons; sang tenor solos at various *Messiah* performances; and taught French, German, architecture, and sculpture. He lived at 421 North Second Street, where he also had a studio. In 1940, Sandzén received the Knight of the Royal Order of the North Star from King Gustav V. In 1946, he retired from teaching at the college and became an artist in residence as well as professor emeritus.

Sandzén developed a love for America, particularly the natural wonders of western Kansas and the mountains of Colorado. He was fascinated by old houses and the early pioneers of the land. The one-story brick gallery, dedicated in 1957, displays Sandzén's extensive watercolors, oils, and prints. Although this is the largest Sandzén collection, his works may also be found in numerous local churches and national and international museums (Nelson Gallery, Kansas City; Brooklyn Museum; Santa Fe Museum; and the National Museum, Stockholm). In the outer courtyard is Carl Milles's "Little Triton," Milles's only major work in Kansas. Sandzén and Milles were personal friends, and inside the museum are seven plaster of Paris plaques by Milles—models for bronze panels on the doors of the State Finance Building in Harrisburg, Pennsylvania.

NEW
GOTTLAND

The early Swedish settlers who referred to the area as *"nytt gott land"* ("new good land") gave the town its name. The first permanent settlers arrived in 1871, and a year later the Rev. Olof Olsson organized the New Gottland Lutheran Church. The present sanctuary was erected in 1910. Signe Larson painted the picture over the altar.

MCPHERSON

Swedish Lutherans and German Mennonites, in addition to other groups, settled McPherson, the McPherson County seat. Lindsborg silversmith Malcolm Esping created a life-size statue of Christ for Trinity Lutheran Church, 119 North Elm (316/241-0424), and other metal liturgical objects. Swedish Americans also organized Countryside Covenant at 940 East Northview Road (316/241-4499). Central College, at 1200 South Main in McPherson (316/241-0723), formerly was known as Walden College, and briefly in the early 1900s it existed as a Covenant school. Central College's Science Hall, with a cornerstone date of 1904, was Walden's main building.

The imposing McPherson County Courthouse (Maple and Kansas streets) opened its doors in 1894. Swedish immigrant A. G. Linn, at the request of the county commission, supervised the brick and stone work on the building. Linn also helped construct the Heceta Head Lighthouse on the Oregon coast near Florence. McPherson City Museum exhibits feature some Swedish objects, including Swedish immigrant Anna Larkin's wood carvings.

FREMONT

In the late summer and early autumn of 1868, the Galesburg Company was formed in the Swedish Lutheran Church, Galesburg, Illinois. The company received from the Kansas Pacific Railroad twenty-two sections of land in southern Saline and northern McPherson counties. The Galesburg group met on 12 June 1869 to organize a congregation. Although this community to the southwest of Lindsborg is called Fremont (after explorer and soldier John C. Frémont, who lived 1813–90), the congregation elected to spell its name Freemount. The first church, made of brown sandstone hauled from nearby hills, was erected in 1870. It is the oldest public building in McPherson County and currently is used as a local museum.

Almost immediately the church proved too small, and a large structure was built in 1881. The interior was a copy of First Lutheran Church in Moline, Illinois. A bolt of lightning struck the high steeple on 7 June 1926, and the church burned to the ground. In the museum are some memorabilia from this second church. Made of red brick, the third church was completed the following year. In the church basement is a large Swedish-inscribed stone that had been over the front door of the 1881 church and weighed more than one ton. During the 1926 fire, the stone fell to the ground and miraculously remained intact. Translated, the inscription reads, "Watch your step in God's house. God, we foresee Thy goodness upon Thy temple." The main sanctuary of the church built in 1927 has an altar painting by Sandzén. Graves at the north end of the adjacent cemetery have stones bearing Swedish inscriptions. The home south of the church was formerly the parsonage. It was built in the 1880s.

MARQUETTE

Although founded by a non-Swede from Marquette, Michigan, Marquette was settled mostly by Swedes who came as a result of the Galesburg Land Company. They generally originated from Småland and Dalarna. The town developed near the mill that was built on the nearby Smoky Hill River. In front of the Riverview Estates, a senior citizens home, is the old mill stone monument.

The large Hans Hanson House (211 East Fifth Street), built in 1888 with eleven rooms, combines Italianate and Carpenter Gothic styles. It has been said the second style reflects a Swedish influence. In 1907, five rooms were added. The Hans Hanson family lived here for 105 years, and it has been restored to its 1888 appearance.

Hanson, an important leader in the development of broom corn, came to the area in 1869 and built a log cabin that spring. Two years later he attached a one-room wood cabin to it. It was in this cabin that fifteen men met in February 1874 and signed the original charter of Marquette. Now both the house and the 1871 cabin, which still stands northwest of the house, are on the National Register of Historic Places. Hanson was not only an early leader in civic development, but he also helped organize the Elim Lutheran Church.

In 1886 and 1887, the town built what is known as the Opera House Block, which included six stores with the Opera House upstairs. A 1905 tornado, which destroyed the west half of town, severely damaged the Opera House, and only one-third of it was rebuilt. Part of the original cornice can be seen above Olson's Furniture Store (106 North Washington). Inside Marquette Farmers State Bank (205 North Washington), founded in 1906, is an interesting teller's cage. Also in the block is a turn-of-the-century drugstore, still in operation.

Other interesting sights in the city include the town library (121 North Washington), built in 1887 as a bank. On the corner of Fifth and Lincoln is Elim Lutheran Church (403 North Lincoln), which was erected in 1906. The sanctuary's stained glass windows memorialize those who died in the 1905 tornado. Paintings by G. N. Malm hang in the sanctuary and a small chapel. On Sixth Street, west of town, is the Lutheran Cemetery, where a number of stones bear Swedish inscriptions.

FALUN

The first Swedish settler in the vicinity of Falun arrived in 1868. Others followed, including a group from the Bishop Hill Colony and another from Galva, Illinois, led by Major Eric Forsse (1819–89). Forsse became postmaster, justice of the peace, and a member of the Kansas legislature and named the town Falun in 1871 for the city in Dalarna where he had served in the infantry. In 1875 and 1876 organizers initiated the Falun Christian Association and built a frame building on what is now Falun Cemetery. Lutherans organized a church in 1887, purchased the association's building, and moved it to town, where it still stands. Sandzén provided the altar painting. A flagpole and marker in the cemetery commemorate the church's original site.

The Falun State Bank's red brick building was constructed between 1905 and 1909. The original fascinating wooden teller's cage and a marble-topped desk are still part of the bank's fixtures.

SMOLAN

Two and one-half miles north of the Salemsborg Church is the small community of Smolan, the birthplace of John Carlin, former Kansas governor of Swedish ancestry. Two cemeteries, the Smolan Lutheran Cemetery (one-half mile north of the city on Burma Road) and the Smolan Mission Covenant Church Cemetery (two miles south on Burma Road and one-quarter mile east), contain graves of the nineteenth-century settlers. The Covenant cemetery has the oldest graves, including some dating to the 1870s. A small white frame Covenant church still stands in the town.

SALEMSBORG

Salemsborg is home to the second oldest Swedish Lutheran congregation in the Smoky Valley, which was organized 16 June 1869. The first church, built the same year, was a dugout with rock walls on which a roof was placed. Today's Gothic-style brick church with two towers, built in 1926, is the congregation's fourth sanctuary. Over the door of the north tower is carved in stone, *"Salemsborgs Sv. Ev. Lutherska Kyrka."* Over the south door is the same inscription in English. Above the north door is a stained glass window with the words, *"Vår Gud är oss en väldig borg."* The English translation, "A mighty fortress is our God," appears on the window over the south door. On the south corner of the building is a plaque—"1869 The Sod Church; 1874 The Frame Church; 1893 The Spire Church; 1926 The Two Tower Church." In the south vestibule's stained glass window is the inscription, "In memory of the charter members of the Salemsborg Lutheran church by the congregation." Four exceptional stained glass panels on the building's east side may best be viewed from the church office interior. Carl Lotave was the artist of the sanctuary's central altar painting. It was originally in the third church, but it was saved from the 1925 fire. The side chancel paintings are by G. N. Malm.

Some of the older stones in the adjacent cemetery have Swedish inscriptions. A monument, in the shape of a pulpit with a Bible, has the inscription: "In memory of the Pioneers who builded the sod church on this place in the year of Our Lord 1869. Erected by the children of Salemsborg 1935."

ASSARIA

Founded in 1875, the Assaria Lutheran Church was an outgrowth of Salemsborg Lutheran. On First Street, the red brick Gothic-style sanctuary was begun in 1913 next door to the 1877 church and finished two years later. The old sanctuary was subsequently razed. On the altar is the Swedish inscription, *"Helig, Helig, Helig"* ("Holy, Holy, Holy"). Immigrants from the Swedish province of Blekinge settled on farms and rasied crops outside Assaria.

SALINA

Swedes helped settle this city some twenty miles north of Lindsborg, establishing businesses and organizing Immanuel Lutheran and First Covenant churches, but both churches have sanctuaries of recent origin.

OGALLAH

Out in the middle of the western Kansas plains is the small limestone Immanuel Lutheran Church (seven miles south of the Interstate 70 Ogallah exit, on the west side of the road) with its short, clipped steeple. Lightning claimed the original wood steeple in the early 1920s. Located on a small hill surrounded by cedar trees planted in the 1940s, the church welcomes visitors with its attractive interior featuring an altar painting done by Sandzén in the 1930s. The original wooden pews, pine floor (raised when the basement was dug), and a pressed metal ceiling remain.

PAGE CITY, SHARON SPRINGS, AND WESKAN

Swedes also settled in Page City, Sharon Springs, and Weskan. The sanctuaries of Bethesda Lutheran Church Page City and Sharon Lutheran in Sharon Springs are of recent construction. On the frame Bethany Lutheran Church in Weskan are the dates 1888, when the congregation was organized, and 1954, when the country sanctuary, at least seventy-five years old, was moved into town from Stockholm in the south. The congregation modernized the sanctuary but retained the old wooden pews.

CONCORDIA

A former congressman, governor, and U.S. senator, Frank Carlson was born in 1893 to Swedish immigrants who farmed in nearby Scandia. At the corner of Seventh Street and Broadway, a Concordia public library bears his name.

North of Concordia is Saron Cemetery where many of the early Swedish settlers are buried and where the cornerstone of the Swedish Evangelical Lutheran Saron Church, built in 1888, rests. The church no longer exists. The cemetery is about three miles north of the Republican River and about one mile east of U.S. Highway 81.

SCANDIA

The Scandinavian Agricultural Society of Chicago initiated in 1868 a colony it called New Scandinavia. That settlement became Scandia. Because the settlers were fearful of Indian attacks, they built Colony House, a stronghold that no longer stands but has been recreated (erected for the 1961 Kansas Centennial). This replica of Colony House stands on the south side of U.S. Highway 36, one-half mile west of Cloud Street. Thure Wohlfort (1835–1916), an early member of the Scandinavian Agricultural Society, was one of the twelve founders of New Scandinavia. Three months after his arrival in 1869, Wohlfort began homesteading land one mile south of Scandia, where the large stone house he shared with his wife, Louise Erickson, still stands. Known as the Wohlfort Home, the house was the center of a large livestock enterprise that made Wohlfort a man of influence in the area. Louise was the daughter of Andrew Erickson, one of the first settlers. The Scandia Library and Museum at 409 Ninth Street (913/335-2271) displays items of local historical interest.

COURTLAND

In 1873 Swedes organized the Swedish Evangelical Lutheran Church of Ada, and five years later, with the arrival of a group from Bucklin, Missouri, the congregation built first a parsonage and then a light sandstone sanctuary. Each family donated and delivered a certain amount of building material. The church was dedicated in 1884 and the tower added four years later. The sanctuary has an attractive chancel featuring an altar painting (1910) by Sandzén surrounded by wood panels with floral designs. Under the altar painting are the words, "*Se Guds Lamm!*" ("Behold the Lamb of God!"). In the basement is a glass cabinet with historic memorabilia. In the adjacent cemetery is a ship's anchor on the grave of S. A. Hagman.

BRANTFORD

Organized in 1874, the Zion Lutheran Church stands out in the country, white stucco over stone. Built of untrimmed limestone, quarried and hauled by oxen from hills three miles away, the structure took nearly four years to build. The church dedicated the building on 6 June 1900 and hung in the belfry a half-ton bell with a Swedish inscription in 1916.

The Brantford Evangelical Covenant Church was organized in 1882, and its present sanctuary was dedicated in 1948.

CLAY CENTER

North of Clay Center is the First Lutheran Church ("Swedesburg"), whose congregation was organized in 1871. Its former striking building was destroyed by a disastrous tornado that hit the area in September 1973. After the tragedy, the congregation purchased a former Roman Catholic church sanctuary, slightly south of the old church. A monument to the congregation's one hundredth birthday rests in the front lawn, and nearby is the congregation's old bell inscribed in Swedish. In the sanctuary in special niches on both sides of the altar are communion vessels and altar crosses rescued after the tornado. A Swedish cemetery, left largely undamaged by the tornado, is west of the church.

The Clay Center Covenant Church, organized in 1890, was originally next to the cemetery, which is north of the city. The church and parsonage were built in 1892. The sanctuary was moved to town in 1949 and the parsonage in 1956.

ENTERPRISE

From the 1860s through the 1880s, several hundred Swedes settled just east of Enterprise, where they built stone structures. A prominent Swedish pioneer was Lars Jäderborg, who came to the area in 1858. Jäderborg obtained considerable acreage, and in 1873 built a large stone house. By 1890 more than fifty stone farmhouses dotted the area, mostly on eighty-acre homesteads. Some of the stone houses and barns still stand. Swedes became known for their skillful stone masonry, and their work was in demand regionally. They were responsible for constructing Stony Point School (built 1872) in the north section of the Enterprise settlement, the Pleasant Hill School (built 1878) in the center, and the Lutheran (built 1877–78) and Mission Covenant (1881) churches. Both of these stone churches are vacant now. In a cemetery adjacent to the Covenant church are buried Swedish members of both the Covenant and Baptist churches.

To see these landmarks, take Factory Street south from Enterprise to Fifth Street. Go east on Fifth, and turn right (south) at first gravel road. The former Covenant Church is on the right side less than one mile from Fifth. At the next crossroads (also gravel), turn left (east) and the Pleasant Hill School will be on the right in one-quarter mile. Retrace your route to Fifth Street, turn right (east), and take the next road going left (north). About three-quarters of a mile on the left (west) is the former Lutheran Church. Also on the left further north on this road is the Stony Point School.

MANHATTAN

The First Lutheran Church of Manhattan was officially organized in 1879. In the fall of 1930, a church was built near the corner of Tenth and Poyntz, which is part of the present church complex (930 Poyntz). In 1963 and 1964, a striking, modern sanctuary was erected. In it is the altar from the former Mariadahl Lutheran Church, and the impressive altar cross is made from walnut obtained from Mariadahl. Outside is the Mariadahl Memorial Bell Tower with the church's old bell. Mariadahl's large Olof Grafström altar painting (1895) hangs in a stairwell.

The Riley County Historical Museum (2309 Claflin Road, 913/537-2210) displays memorabilia belonging to early regional Swedish settlers, and there the altar rail from the Mariadahl Church is exhibited.

OLSBURG

The first Swede to settle in Kansas came to the area northwest of Olsburg along the Big Blue River on 29 June 1855. John A. Johnson (d. 1893) was joined shortly thereafter by other members of his family, including his mother Maria, for whom the settlement of Mariadahl ("Maria's Valley") was named after her death. A thriving hamlet, Mariadahl boasted a stone schoolhouse, a blacksmith shop, a grange store, and the nearby Mariadahl Children's Home. Two stone churches—a Swedish Methodist church built in 1878 and Mariadahl Lutheran built between 1866 and 1871—graced the town. Mariadahl Lutheran, the oldest Swedish Lutheran house of worship west of the Missouri River, was made of native limestone and topped with a central steeple. The controversial razing of this church in 1961 to make way for water impounded by the Tuttle Creek Dam still evokes considerable consternation from local residents.

Parts of the Mariadahl Lutheran Church were saved (see Riley County Historical Museum and First Lutheran Church, Manhattan, above), and the entire Swedish cemetery was relocated to nearby Olsburg. At the Mariadahl Cemetery are monuments to the accomplishments of this community, parts of the church, and artifacts from the cemetery. A stone monument with historic plaques notes that John A. Johnson was the first Swede to settle in Kansas and that the Mariadahl congregation was the oldest Swedish Lutheran church west of the Missouri River. A four-foot bas-relief depicts the historic church, and before it on the ground is the church's cornerstone, originally located on the church's steeple. At the main gate are two stone pillars from the old cemetery, which was begun in 1863, and at the east end is a monument to the Children's Home. The graves of Johnson, his wife, and his mother and other Mariadahl Swedish settlers are marked.

A gravel road leads to the Mariadahl community site. Visible on a nearby hill are the Mariadahl Lutheran Church's steeple, moved to higher ground after the church was razed, and, near the reservoir, old stone barns and the former Ekblad farm.

Across the road from the Mariadahl Cemetery is the cemetery of Olsburg Lutheran Church, where most names on markers are Swedish. Olsburg Lutheran, a red brick building, has a cornerstone indicating that it was organized in 1881 and its most recent sanctuary erected in 1939. Olof Grafström produced the altar painting.

RANDOLPH In 1886 Swedish immigrants settled Cleburne, near Randolph, and on the opposite side of the Tuttle Creek Reservoir from Olsburg. To the north is the Bellegarde Cemetery, where many of the early Swedes are buried. On high ground overlooking the Blue Valley, the cemetery offers a lovely view.

LEONARDVILLE Although not in Leonardville but four miles northeast of the town, the Walsburg Lutheran Church was rebuilt after a 1918 fire destroyed the wooden steeple and roof. Olof Grafström made the altar painting (1918). Nearby is an old stone bridge built by the early Swedish settlers. In Leonardville is the former Swedish Baptist Church, a stone structure built in the early 1890s, which is now abandoned.

AXTELL Founded by Swedes, the white frame Evangelical Mission Covenant Church was built in 1910, but the congregation had been organized in the early 1880s. Over the front door is the inscription, *"Svenska Evangeliska Zion Missions Kyrka."*

LAWRENCE At the Elizabeth M. Watkins Community Museum (1047 Massachusetts at Eleventh Street, 913/841-4109) is a model of a large windmill, a landmark in Lawrence from 1863 to 1905. It was built by John H. Wilder of Massachusetts and Andrew (Anders) Palm (formerly Palmquist) of Killeröd, Skåne. Palm moved to Lawrence in 1862 and became associated with Wilder, possibly as a blacksmith, in his carriage and plow business. Palm fashioned the windmill after those of Skåne. He had returned to Sweden to learn how to construct it and brought back to the United States machinery to propel it, which was subsequently mounted on the windmill by Swedish-American mechanics. Built of native timber, the octagonal windmill powered a mill and Palm and Wilder's machine shop where they made wagons and plows from 1864 to 1885. Though long gone, the windmill appears from time to time as the city's symbol. Also in the museum's collection is the wooden key that locked the windmill's shaft.

Another museum in the city, the Helen Foresman Spencer Museum of Art on the University of Kansas campus (1301 Mississippi, 913/864-4710), has in its collection etchings by Anders Zorn and lithographs and woodcuts by Birger Sandzén.

In Lawrence, Swedes built or owned stone houses in the vernacular style, including one at 1500 West Ninth that probably went up before 1867. Made of native stone, this was one of the "mill houses" built by and for Swedish workmen who constructed and operated the windmill that stood nearby at Ninth and Emery Road. Built in the 1860s, possibly as a hotel for the Swedish workers who constructed the windmill, was the house at 800 Louisiana. Other stone houses include those at 905 Michigan, 900 Pennsylvania, and 1008 Ohio.

OSAGE CITY

Second-stage immigrants, most of them from Illinois, settled this town twenty-five miles south of Topeka beginning in 1869. The next year twenty-two charter members formed the Swedish Evangelical Lutheran Church (now Grace Lutheran). The congregation now meets in a brick sanctuary built in 1912.

VILAS

Eighty miles south of Topeka, Vilas got its start when Swedes, led by Nils Person, arrived in 1869. Bethel Lutheran Church, organized in 1872, lost its original sanctuary to a Kansas tornado, and the congregation replaced it with the red brick structure now standing. The altar painting is by Birger Sandzén.

SAVONBURG

The Friends Home Evangelical Lutheran Church (316/754-3314), three miles west of Savonburg, was organized in 1872. The first church building (see below) was constructed in 1879. In 1898, a new white frame church with a central steeple and Gothic-style windows designed by Olof Z. Cervin of Rock Island, Illinois, was completed. The altar painting is by Olof Grafström. The bell in the steeple is one of the largest in Kansas. The adjacent parsonage was built in 1907. The pioneer Swedes came mainly from Blekinge between 1869 and 1872. Approximately 80 percent were from the parish of Jämshög.

The first building of the Friends Home Lutheran congregation was sold to the Evangelical Covenant Church in 1898 and moved to its present location, one-quarter mile east of the Lutheran church. It is still used by this Covenant congregation, which was organized in 1883.

NEBRASKA

Swedes generally settled in five main locations in Nebraska—the Omaha area; the northeast corner (Oakland, Wakefield, and Wausa); Saunders County (Wahoo, Swedeburg, and Malmo); the Stromsburg area in Polk County; and Kearney, Phelps, and Harlan counties in the south-central part. Some Swedes settled in Gothenburg along the Platte River and around Chappell in western Nebraska. Among the institutions they founded are the Immanuel Deaconess Institute in Omaha, the Luther Academy (now part of Midland Lutheran College in Fremont), and the Bethphage Mission in Axtell. One Nebraska governor—Victor E. Anderson—was of Swedish background as was twentieth-century composer, conductor, and educator Howard Hanson of Wahoo. Noted theologian Conrad Bergendoff of Shickley is also of Swedish descent.

OMAHA

The beginnings of the Immanuel Medical Center (6901 North Seventy-second Street, 402/572-2121) and the adjoining Immanuel-Fontenelle Home (402/572-2595) date from 1887 when the Immanuel Deaconess Institute was founded by Pastor Erick Albert Fogelstrom. Not only was he interested in organizing a hospital but also institutions for the elderly, for orphans, and for invalids. In 1894, a Deaconess Home was founded. With the assurance of support from the Nebraska Conference of the Augustana Synod, in 1901 construction was begun on a children's home. A school of nursing was also established.

Today the modern medical center is affiliated with the Nebraska Synod of the Evangelical Lutheran Church in America, and Swedish support is still strong. In the comfortable and well-equipped Immanuel-Fontenelle Home are displayed Fogelstrom memorabilia.

Another minister, the Rev. Sven Gustaf Larson, first Lutheran home missionary to Nebraska, organized in 1868 the Immanuel Lutheran Church, the first Swedish Lutheran congregation in Nebraska. Subsequently Larson established the Oakland church in 1869, and the Swedeburg, Malmo, Mead, and Lincoln congregations the following year. In 1936 Immanuel Lutheran merged with Zion Lutheran, forming the Augustana Lutheran Church (now at 3647 Lafayette Avenue, 402/551-4728). Its twentieth-century Gothic building was constructed in 1951.

OAKLAND

By 1930, about two-thirds of the foreign-born in Burt County were of Swedish stock. From Oakland, Swedish settlers fanned out to other areas of northeast Nebraska as well as parts of the Far West, including Idaho.

The First Lutheran congregation, organized in 1869, is the second oldest Swedish Lutheran church in Nebraska. A church was built in 1878, but it burned in 1892. The present large Gothic-style brick edifice was constructed the following year (201 North Davis). About the same time the Lutheran church was organized, a Swedish Baptist congregation was also established. On the cornerstone of the First Baptist Church (202 North Fried) are the dates 1869 and 1918, the second date indicating when the present brick sanctuary was built. The Salem Evangelical Covenant Church is a white clapboard building out in the country on Route 1. The congregation was organized in 1877. West of Oakland, Stanton County was settled by Europeans, Swedes among them, and a historical marker on U.S. Highway 275 three miles west of Pilger commemorates their efforts.

In 1989 the Swedish Heritage Center opened in the former Swedish Covenant Church building at 301 North Chard (402/ 685-6161). Both a museum and a gift shop, the center is open every day April through September but closed except on weekends October through March. Since the early 1980s, Oakland has made a commitment to identifying with its Swedish heritage, using the Dala horse motif throughout the community. In 1983 the community reintroduced the tradition of the Swedish Festival, which had been dormant for about twenty-five years, featuring musical performances, folk dancing, a smörgåsbord, and an antique show in early June.

WAKEFIELD

The Salem Lutheran Church (northeast corner of Winter and East Fifth) is a white clapboard structure with a tall dark wood steeple erected in 1905. The exterior has a similar appearance to that of Tabor Lutheran Church in Wausa (see below).

WAUSA

The town's name is an anglicized form of *Vasa*. The Tabor Lutheran Church congregation was organized in 1885. It built its first church in 1886, and its most recent one in 1903.

WAHOO

In front of the Saunders County Courthouse is a historical marker noting that Swedish settlers in Wahoo established Luther Junior College and that one of the town's native sons was composer and conductor Howard Hanson, who was of Swedish extraction.

Luther Academy opened 10 November 1883, the four hundredth anniversary of the birth of Martin Luther. In 1925, it became a junior college, offering courses in liberal arts, teacher training, commerce, and music. Following the 1962 merger of several Lutheran bodies (including the Augustana Lutheran Synod, which operated the college), Midland College in nearby Fremont merged with Luther, creating Midland Lutheran College. Luther's library went to the Midland campus, and today the library is identified as Luther Library (402/ 721-5480). Luther's facilities were sold to another educational institution, which shortly thereafter closed its doors, and the campus stood silent and vacant into the 1990s. Among the decaying structures are a stone monument, which was part of the first building destroyed by fire in 1917, and an old stone gate.

The Howard Hanson House, 1163 Linden, is the birthplace of Dr. Howard Hanson (1896–1981), perhaps the foremost American composer of Swedish parentage. Many of his works emphasize his Swedish ancestry, such as his Third Symphony written in honor of the three hundredth anniversary of the Swedish settlement on the Delaware. From 1924 to 1964, he directed the Eastman School of Music at the University of Rochester, New York As a guest conductor, he worked with orchestras in Europe and the United States.

The white frame Victorian house where he was born and reared, which is on the National Register of Historic Places, was probably built in the 1880s. Restored in the 1960s, the house was opened by the county in 1967, and exhibits also emphasize the contributions of four other Wahoo natives. The piano where Hanson first took lessons and where he composed his first music at the age of seven remains in the house.

Bethlehem Lutheran Church, at 504 West Eighth, is a frame church topped by a tall steeple. Over its front door is inscribed, "Sw. Ev. Lutheran Bethlehem Church October 7, 1906."

MEAD

Founded in 1870, the Alma Lutheran Church erected its white clapboard building at 219 West Fifth in 1886.

MALMO

The Edensberg Lutheran congregation dates from 1870. The church was originally in the country, but when Malmo was founded in 1886, the old church was torn down and a new church constructed in town in 1890. The white frame Covenant Church has the date 1905 on its cornerstone. Malmo's Victorian-style homes are attractive enough to draw visitors.

SWEDEBURG

Located about six miles south of Wahoo, Swedeburg at one time was a lively Swedish settlement. Grace Lutheran Church, organized in 1870, was known as the Swedish Evangelical Lutheran Swedeburg Congregation. Its present white frame Gothic-style church was completed in 1916. Olof Grafström painted Christ in Gethsemane for the altar painting. The original Swedish Mission Church, which was organized in 1876, was about two miles southwest of town at the Fridhem Cemetery. In town, the Swedeburg Covenant Church has a cornerstone that is inscribed, *"Sw. Ev. Luth. Miss. Kyrkan 'Fridhem' 1909."*

STROMSBURG   Called the "Swede Capital of Nebraska," Stromsburg prides itself on its Swedish history. In March 1872, twenty-eight Swedes arrived from Illinois, and their sod houses and dugouts were soon ready. The community persevered despite devastating grasshopper infestation, disease, and (on 20 October 1878) a horrible prairie fire. The Swedish royal insignia over the front door of the modern Stromsburg Bank is only one of the many reminders of Stromsburg's deep Swedish roots. Other evidence includes early twentieth-century mercantile buildings around the town square—the Carlson and Olson Building, the Victor Anderson Building, and the Old Opera House. In the square Lewis Headstrom, a Gästrikland native who died in Stromsburg in 1892, is honored with a plaque. Headstrom found no public service job too small or too large. He served as mayor, postmaster, and town and school board member. Headstrom also constructed the first residential and commercial buildings in Stromsburg.

In July of 1873 northwest of town the pioneers founded the Swede Home Church, now identified as the Calvary Evangelical Lutheran Church of Swede Home (402/764-5981) and the mother congregation of Lutheran churches within the city and in Hordville and Osceola, Nebraska, and Salem, Oregon. The congregation built its present red brick sanctuary, with two silver steeples, in 1914, replacing the original constructed 1881–83. Calvary is located on Rural Route 2, one mile south and one-half mile west of the junction of State highways 92 and 39. In the cemetery across the road from the church are the graves of Johan and Kajsa Hult, victims of the 1878 prairie fire. Surviving members of the family went to the Pacific Northwest and became successful in lumbering.

Another Stromsburg landmark is the Salem Lutheran Church, a daughter congregation of the Swede Home church, which owns a Signe Larson altar painting. Both Salem Lutheran and a Covenant congregation in Stromsburg worship in modern sanctuaries.

In Buckley Park, created with a donation from Swedish Americans John B. and Christine Buckley, is a gazebo made from the steeple of the former Covenant church, built in 1900. The Midwest Covenant Home is on the north side of Ninth Street in town. Many early Swedish pioneers are buried in the Stromsburg Cemetery (on Ninth Street, about one mile east of Main Street).

The white clapboard Swede Plain Methodist Church (congregation established in 1876; building constructed in the 1880s), was moved to the Covenant Cedars Bible Camp twelve miles west of Stromsburg and three miles north of Hordville. The congregation has disbanded.

WAVERLY

Peter Peterson, who emigrated from Småland, first settled in Waverly in 1879, and between 1893 and 1900 eight structures went up on his farmstead, which is listed on the National Register of Historic Places. On the farmstead, which is privately held, are two exceptional buildings—the Queen Anne–style house and the barn, which has two octagonal cupolas and a steep gambrel roof with flared eaves. The National Register protects the private owners by not releasing the farmstead's location.

LINCOLN

The first sanctuary of First Lutheran Church, built by Swedes in 1870, stood originally where the state capitol now stands. The congregation's 1965 sanctuary is located in east Lincoln at 1551 South Seventieth (402/488-0919).

KEARNEY

Built in 1886, the Hanson-Downing House (723 West Twenty-second Street) has been described as a one and one-half–story ornamented cottage of frame construction with a front recessed curved porch, gable roof, and dormer windows. Carved floral and sun decorative motifs adorn the entire house. Charles E. Hanson, who immigrated to Chicago in 1869 and came to Phelps County in the spring of 1878, opened a farm implement business in Kearney in 1882 and built the house four years later. It is listed on the National Register of Historic Places.

KEENE

The congregation of the Evangelical Free Church was organized in 1880. Its white frame church, constructed in 1921, was renovated in 1953.

AXTELL

An inspiring institution of mercy for the mentally and physically handicapped, Bethphage Mission of the Great Plains, on North Second Street (308/743-2401), was founded in 1913 by the Rev. K. G. William Dahl (1883–1917) from Skåne. While at Augustana Theological Seminary in Rock Island, Illinois, Dahl was asked to translate from German a book on the colony of epileptics at Bielefeld, Germany. He was so moved by its story that he decided to build a similar institute in this country. After working for the Immanuel Deaconess Home in Omaha, Dahl accepted a call to come to the Axtell church. In 1914, forty acres of land were bought for the Bethphage Mission site. The first cottage for "guests" was dedicated Midsummer Eve 1914. Tabor cottage, a home for women (today it is the visitor's center), was opened in 1916. Unfortunately, Dahl died in 1917, reportedly having overworked himself in developing the mission. But in the following years, despite many struggles, additional buildings were constructed, notably Sarepta (The Sister's

Home) in 1917, Emmaus Cottage for Men (1919), Bethel Home for Children (1929), Zion Chapel (1930), and Kidron (the home for women and children with tuberculosis) in 1938.

The architect was Olof Z. Cervin of Rock Island. Of Swedish heritage, Cervin designed the buildings in a stepped gable style with red tile roofs, reminiscent of the architecture found in Skåne and Denmark. Of all the buildings, the masterpiece is Zion Chapel. Cervin described it as reflecting Klintian style (after P. V. J. Klint of the famous Grundtvig Cathedral built in the 1920s in Copenhagen). Zion Chapel is of buff-colored brick enhanced by beautiful stained glass windows. The altar window depicts Jesus in the center surrounded by individuals with various handicaps. The chapel's interior is known for its dramatic cloister effect. The wide aisles are designed to facilitate the attendance at services of people who are confined to beds and wheelchairs. Dr. Emmy Evald, daughter of the Rev. Erland Carlsson, spearheaded the building of the chapel by getting the Augustana Lutheran Synod's Women's Missionary Society, which she headed, to support its construction. In the chapel's tower is a mechanical clock donated in 1931 by a Swedish American from Smolan, Kansas.

Zion Chapel at Bethphage Mission of the Great Plains was designed by Swedish-American architect Olof Z. Cervin.

Soaring in the distance on the flat Nebraska landscape is the tall steeple of Bethany Lutheran Church. The white frame church with Gothic-style windows was built in 1885, the second church of the congregation that had been established ten years earlier. The altar painting, "He Dwelt among Us," was produced in 1900 by Olof Grafström. An identical painting is in the Saron Evangelical Lutheran Church in Saronville.

The first church was a sod structure. In the adjacent cemetery in the southwest corner is a historic marker describing the original twenty– by forty-six–foot house of worship. Inside St. Paul Lutheran Church, located in the Pioneer Village museum in Minden on U.S. 6 and U.S. 34 (308/832-1181), is a model of the original Bethany sod church used by the congregation from 1878 to 1885. John and Helga Warp, Norwegian parents of Harold Warp, who founded the extensive Pioneer Village, were married in the sod church in December 1880.

West of Axtell on the Kearney-Phelps county line is the former Salem Methodist Episcopal Church, built in 1898, which has been described as a Carpenter Gothic Revival–style structure. In 1878, Swedish Lutheran pioneers built a sod church, but by 1882 theological disputes within the congregation prompted the Swedish Methodists to send the Rev. Carl Charnquist to organize the dissenters. In 1883 the Methodists built a parsonage, and in 1884, they erected a small church, which served the congregation until the 1898 building was constructed. Near the church is a small cemetery begun in 1882.

The Fletcher Christian Academy (308/263-3209), which occupies the church, moved to its campus a small schoolhouse that had been erected in 1910 in Carter, about forty miles southwest. The church, parsonage, and schoolhouse are all included on the National Register of Historic Places.

FUNK

Fridhem Lutheran Church, the second oldest Swedish Lutheran congregation in Phelps County, still meets in a building constructed in 1890. This structure replaced its sod predecessor, which had cost only about $130 to build. First built adjacent to Fridhem Cemetery, the building was moved in 1910 to its present location (401 Lake). A Grafström altar painting is dated 1909. At the Fridhem Cemetery in the northeast corner is a monument commemorating the pioneer meeting house.

HOLDREGE

"Early settlers," reads a Nebraska historical marker near the Phelps County Courthouse, "lured by government homestead lands and cheap railroad lands, were mainly of Swedish descent. Excellence in education, religion, and agriculture was their goal." One of the oldest buildings in Holdrege surviving from the pioneer days is the bank and opera building, at the northwest corner of West and Fourth, which was built in 1889.

The Phelps County Historical Museum (308/995-5015) on U.S. 183 north of Holdrege tells the story of the county's communities, including Funk, Loomis, Bertrand, and Atlanta. The Swedish artifacts, most of which have been donated by Swedish families, dominate the collection. Many of the early settlers came from Småland. On the grounds of the museum is the former Immanuel Memorial Lutheran Church, originally located in Ragan (Harlan County), an area known as Scandinavia Township that predates Holdrege. The Immanuel congregation was the first religious group to be organized in Harlan County, having been founded in 1879. Its original building, sold to another congregation and moved to Minden where it still stands, was superseded by this sanctuary built in 1903. Most of the congregation lived in Phelps County, and it was they who raised the money to finance the move to the museum, to restore the church, and to establish an endowment for its perpetual upkeep. The church cemetery is next to the church's original site in Ragan. Also located on the museum grounds is the Snowball School, originally constructed eleven miles north of Holdrege and three miles west. The school was built in 1888 and opened in 1890 to serve a student body primarily of Swedish background. The last class was in 1954, and in 1990 the school building was moved to the museum grounds.

Religion found a home inside and outside the city limits. Bethel Lutheran, Phelps County's oldest Lutheran congregation (established in 1877) first built a sod church, commemorated in Bethel's cemetery three miles east of Holdrege. Its sanctuary in town (704 West Avenue) is of recent construction and has a Grafström altar painting.

Eight miles northwest of Holdrege near Loomis is the Moses Hill Evangelical Covenant Church and cemetery. Organized in 1877 as the Swedish Lutheran Mission Church of Wannerburg, it is the oldest Covenant church in Phelps County. The congregation built its white clapboard church in 1904. The congregation claims that the proposal for creating what would become North Park College and Seminary originated at the 1891 Midwest Regional Conference of the denomination, which was held in the first frame Moses Hill sanctuary.

North of Moses Hill is a historic marker commemorating the Christian Children's Home, founded in 1888 by the Evangelical Free Church of America. That denomination's Christian Home, two miles west of Holdrege on the south side of State Highway 23, is a residence for the elderly.

GOTHENBURG

Olof Bergstrom, a Baptist preacher from Delsbo in Hälsingland, who in the early 1870s had helped establish Stromsburg, became in 1881 the founder of Gothenburg in the Platte River Valley. The community's first church was built in 1886 by Swedish Baptists. Today the congregation has a new sanctuary.

Another Swede, Ernest A. Calling (Carlson), after emigrating in 1889 made a name for himself in ranching, business, local government, and land development. About 1907 he built at

1514 Lake Avenue a small-scale Queen Anne–style residence known as the Ernest A. Calling House, now on the National Register of Historic Places.

SOUTH DAKOTA

In the late 1860s Swedish homesteaders began arriving in Clay and Union counties not far from Vermillion in southeast South Dakota (see map, page 168). Minnehaha County, near Sioux Falls, mainly attracted Swedes from Småland and southern Halland. Immigrants from Närke settled farther west in McCook County where the Salem Lutheran Church was organized. In the northeast (Grant County) were founded the towns of Stockholm (in 1884) and Strandburg (1888). Swedes moved from Chisago County, Minnesota, to Marshall and Brown counties in northeast South Dakota, where they tended to settle singly rather than in groups as in other parts of the state. The first shelters were sod structures, but they were soon replaced by log and wooden frame homes.

VERMILLION

On Forest Avenue and Lewis Street is the Forest Avenue Historic District, a residential area of interesting turn-of-the-century homes that have been placed on the National Register of Historic Places. A number of homes are identified with local Swedish builders. Swedish immigrant Eric Matson's work is evident in the mansion built for the president of the University of South Dakota on East Main Street.

At the University of South Dakota in Vermillion (414 East Clark) is the Carl A. Norgren Hall in the W. H. Over Museum. Norgren, son of pioneers in the Dalesburg community (see below), had a number of interests, including natural history, but was best known as a designer, inventor, and manufacturer and owner of the C. A. Norgren Company in Denver.

MISSION HILL

Although Yankton County, west of Clay County, was settled mainly by Norwegians, a number of Swedes also homesteaded in the area.

Swedish immigrants Lars and Anna Johnson, who had come through Wisconsin and Iowa, settled northeast of Mission Hill in 1869 and 1870, building a house where descendants were still living in the 1990s. According to the family, the couple's fourth child was born while Lars traveled to and from Sioux City by wagon to procure materials for building the house.

The one and one-half–story cottonwood Lewis Olson log house west of Mission Hill was constructed in the late 1870s by a Swedish pioneer. It is included on the National Register of

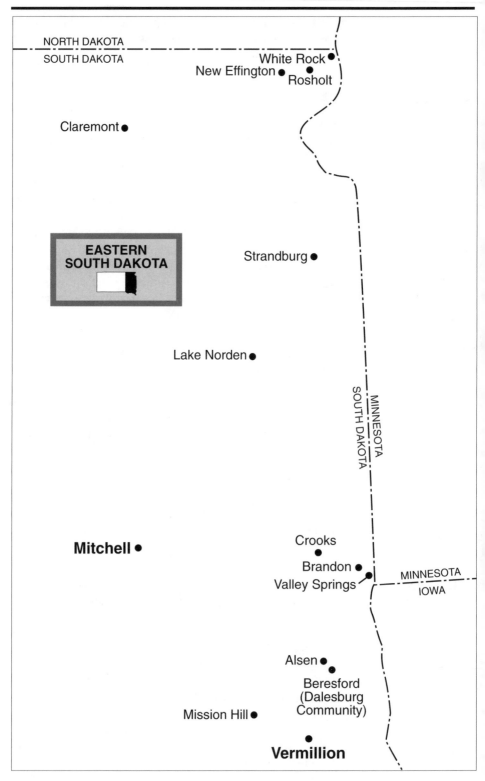

Historic Places. Unfortunately, most of the other log structures in the county have disappeared.

BERESFORD (DALESBURG COMMUNITY)

Although few remnants remain, the Dalesburg Community southwest of Beresford and north of Hub City) was one of the oldest and largest of the Swedish settlements in the Dakotas. Settlers chose the name because many of them were from Dalarna. The community included almost one hundred square miles in northeastern Clay County in the state's southeast corner, and its focal point, Dalesburg Village, was 13.5 miles north of Vermillion on University Road in central Clay County. For one hundred years the doors of the Dalesburg school were open to the community's children. Though the name Dalesburg was first given to the Lutheran and Baptist churches founded in 1871, the village itself took shape around the general store and post office, which Swede Andrew Lyckholm from Leksand, Dalarna, operated on his farm in the 1890s. Hub City was not founded until the 1920s when Bill Inberg, a grandson of Swedish immigrants, opened a garage across from the Dalesburg Lutheran Church.

Daniel Peter Brown, born in Stockholm in 1827, was the most widely known Swedish settler in the area. He was somewhat of a mystery man because he seldom revealed anything about himself or his origin. He was the son of a minister of the Swedish state church and was educated for the ministry. But something happened that degraded his standing. He immigrated to America, taking the name Brown. He enlisted in the Civil War and participated in the siege of Vicksburg in July 1863. Six years later, he was in Clay County, filing a homestead application in Vermillion. A dugout on his claim in Riverside Township served as the first home until he had a log cabin, which is still standing, built in the early 1870s.

The twelve- by seventeen-foot one-room cabin, located fifteen and one-half miles north of Vermillion on State Highway 19 and one-half mile east, is presumably patterned after those in Dalarna. It was constructed of hardwood logs found along the bluffs of the Vermillion River running through Brown's claim. In the corner of the room is a ladder stairway leading to a loft that was used as a sleeping room. A mixture of mud and straw filled the spaces between the logs. The original roof was thatched. The Swedish Historical Society of Clay County and the Clay County Historical Society have worked on its preservation.

The cabin served many important functions in the area's early history. Here the Rev. Brown taught school, held Lutheran services, baptized infants, performed marriages, conducted funerals, and befriended Native Americans. He also served as the government agent for those needing advice in selecting a claim.

Early Swedish pioneers came to this log cabin to seek the Rev. Brown's counsel on a wide variety of subjects. In 1882, Brown sold his farm to a Norwegian and then moved on to Nebraska near the South Dakota border. On a trip to Yankton, he mysteriously disappeared. The Brown Log Cabin stands as a memorial to a man who aided directly or indirectly hundreds of early Swedish pioneers. To get to the cabin, go north on State Highway 19 past State Highway 50, and turn right (east) at the first gravel road. On this bending road travel one-half mile, until you see the cabin on the left (north) side.

Ten Swedish congregations were organized, in or near the Dalesburg Community, in Clay, Union, and Lincoln counties between 1869 and the early 1900s. All but two (the Free Church Ansgar Meeting House and the Ahlsborg Lutheran Church) continue to exist.

The Swedish Baptists organized first, forming the Big Springs Baptist Church (605/547-2816) in 1869 in Union Creek Community in Union County. The congregation built a church in 1874, one they worked to restore for the celebration of the 125th anniversary in 1994. Not far away, the First Swedish Baptist Church of Alcester, which was built in 1902, still stands. In 1871, a Baptist church was founded in the Dalesburg settlement, the congregation being originally known as the Swede Baptist Church of Bloomingdale. The present white frame sanctuary was constructed in 1919 just northeast of the Lutheran church (go south on University Road only three miles, and then travel east on a gravel road for one mile). A cemetery is to the immediate south.

The first Swedish Lutheran congregation in the Dakota territory was organized at Ahlsborg, in Union County, east of Clay County, in January 1870. One year later, the Dalesburg Lutheran congregation was started in an early Swedish settler's dugout. The congregation either met in the dugout or in the open air until a church was built in 1874. The present modest white frame church with Gothic-style windows was constructed in 1897 by Swedish immigrant Eric Matson from Alunda Parish, Uppland. In the twentieth century, another Swede, named G. Anderson, directed the building of the two towers now a part of the church. To get to the church, go east on State Highway 50, turn right (south) on University Road, and go four miles. The church is on the right (west). The church's cemetery is two miles away.

About one-half mile northwest of the former community of Komstad is the Komstad Covenant Church and Cemetery. The congregation dates from 1874. The present white clapboard edifice with a central tower and Gothic-style windows was erected in 1905. Two large attractive stained glass windows were installed in 1924. The north window is in memory of Carolina and Gustavus Norgren.

Norgren, an outstanding local farmer, was from Dalarna, and his wife, Carolina, from Östergötland. Their son, Carl August Norgren, was born in 1890 in South Dakota and became a well-known engineer, inventor, and manufacturer in Denver. Just north of the church at the Southeast South Dakota Experiment Farm (three miles east on State Highway 50 from its intersection with State Highway 19, and two to three miles north on University Road) is a state historic plaque in memory of Gustavus Norgren and "dedicated to the early pioneers of South Dakota."

Peter Norbeck (1870–1937), the first native-born governor of South Dakota and a U.S. Senator, was born in 1879 to a Swedish father and Norwegian mother in a dugout whose remains still stand. The dugout is approximately one and one-half miles southwest of the Norwegian St. Peter's Lutheran Church, which was organized in 1869 by Norbeck's father, a pastor. Norbeck's father, Göran, came to the United States in 1868 by way of Norway. He married a Norwegian in Sioux City, homesteaded, and built the dugout.

ALSEN

The village of Alsen, in western Union County, was named by Olof Erickson, the first blacksmith in the area, for his birthplace—Alsen Parish, Jämtland. In 1871, Erickson took out a land claim and settled on what is today the Anderson Farm. He erected a house that same year, a one and one-half–story white clapboard structure that still stands behind the large, imposing main house.

Solomon Anderson, also a Swede from Jämtland, came to Alsen in 1875 from Omaha, married Erickson's daughter, and purchased the farm in 1878. Their granddaughter—Olof Erickson's great-granddaughter—still owns the homestead, which has earned a place on the National Register of Historic Places. The site, near Beresford (or one-half mile west of Interstate 29 and one-half mile north of State Highway 46) is remarkable for the large number of outbuildings (twenty-one) still standing. The main house is a large clapboard, neo-Classical–style structure with Georgian characteristics, built in 1901. Of five creameries in the area, Anderson's was the most successful.

BRANDON

The Swedona Evangelical Covenant congregation was organized in rural Brandon in 1877, and the first sanctuary, a sod church, was constructed two years later (it stood until 1943). A stone marker notes the spot where the sod church stood. Today's white twentieth-century Gothic frame building dates from 1913. Across the road is the Swedona Cemetery, where there are several interesting gravestones, including that of Israel Granström, an early pioneer who perished in a blizzard. A number of church members came from Västerbotten, including Axel Alexius Anderson, whose gravestone has the province's coat of arms.

Reach the church by going north on Route 11 from Interstate 90 about two and one-half miles to 130 Minnehaha County Road, where you turn left (west). Travel three miles to a county road and turn left (south). The church is about one-half mile from the turn.

During the 1976 Bicentennial, the Sioux Falls Bicentennial Commission identified the most significant homesteads and historical sites in Minnehaha County (Brandon is nine miles east of Sioux Falls). Based on this work, the commission published *Our Heritage,* a complete list of the sites and a detailed map of the county. Of the 105 historic homesteads identified and marked with special bicentennial plaques, at least ten are of Swedish origin. On the Split Rock River between Garretson and Brandon is an old stone house, built in 1880 by O. D. J. Olson (1834–1927), who was born in Mora, Dalarna. He and his wife, Lena (1832–1915), also from Mora, are buried in the Beaver Valley Cemetery in Valley Springs.

CROOKS

Although the first church organized in Minnehaha County was the Nidaros Norwegian Lutheran Church in 1868, Swedish congregations were soon established. The early pioneers of the late 1860s and early 1870s experienced a series of hardships, including drought, grasshoppers, hail and winter storms, and prairie fires. Despite these threats, twenty-five settlers, mainly from Halland, met in May 1878 to organize the Swedish Evangelical Lutheran Church of Benton (now called the Benton Lutheran Church) in Crooks. The church built its first sanctuary in 1885, but lightning destroyed it in 1913. The 1,325-pound bell, which had been purchased in 1894 by the Ladies Sewing Society, fell from the steeple during the fire and cracked. In 1914, the Luther League restored and remounted the bell in a special structure in the cemetery behind the present church sanctuary. The same year a new church bell was installed in the steeple. It is the custom to toll the bell at 10 A.M. the day after the death of a member of the congregation. Swedish pioneers are buried in the cemetery. The first burial was that of Peter Byg, a Dane, who died in April 1880 while trying to save his family and home from a prairie fire.

The white clapboard church with its central steeple and Gothic-style windows was designed by a Sioux Falls architect.

The striking interior features a lovely Gothic-style altar painted white with gold trim and inscribed, *"Jag har bedt för dig."* ("I have prayed for thee"), an excerpt from Luke 22:32. Olof Grafström created the altar painting of Christ in Gethsemane. A cabinet in the back of the sanctuary holds historic memorabilia.

VALLEY SPRINGS

The Beaver Valley Lutheran Church (two and one-half miles east of Brandon) was organized in 1873. The present large brick church building dates from 1922. Birger Sandzén, the well-known Lindsborg, Kansas, artist executed the altar painting of the Ascension.

MITCHELL

At the original site of the New Home Lutheran Church, seven miles south and two miles west of Mitchell, the bell of the old church remains, as does the cemetery. In 1883, a group of Swedish homesteaders organized the Swedish Evangelical Lutheran Nyhem Church and two years later constructed a small frame sanctuary. When the congregation in 1958 erected a new church in nearby Mitchell (1023 South Minnesota Street), the old church building was sold to a farmer, who moved it and then rebuilt it to use as a home. Lightning struck before the remodeling was complete, and the structure was erased by fire.

LAKE NORDEN

Lake Norden in Hamlin County is a predominantly Finnish community, though many of the Finns are of Swedish background. The Lutheran cemetery contains the graves of both Finnish and Swedish-Finnish names and a historic stone indicating where the Lake Norden Suomi Synod Evangelical Lutheran Church stood from 1903 to 1944. Some church services were still being conducted wholly in Finnish in the 1980s.

Several Swedish families contributed, in part, the land for the town site. Charles Larson, with his business partner, bought the first lots of Lake Norden that went on sale. Larson, and later his son, served as mayor. The Lake Norden Baptist Church was established by five Swedish families in 1888, and the church building still used for worship was constructed in 1909. The small white frame Covenant church, organized as the Scandinavian Christian Mission Congregation, was founded by Swedes and Norwegians. The building dates from 1901 and, though now in town, had originally been located two miles east and one-half mile south of town.

STRANDBURG

The beautiful red brick Swedish Lutheran Church of Strandburg (605/676-2414) has been designated a landmark on the National

Register of Historic Places. The congregation's original frame structure, erected in 1892, was struck by lightning in 1905 and burned to the ground. Nothing was saved. The congregation decided to rebuild, and it constructed a second sanctuary between 1905 and 1910. Designed by the Rev. Erick Schöld and a church committee, the church is considered late Victorian Gothic. A tall Gothic-style steeple towers over dark shingling and white wood trim.

The intricate Gothic-style altar and raised pulpit of Swedish Lutheran Church of Strandburg are part of an interior that has changed little since the church was constructed in 1910.

Since 1910, the church's interior has remained very much the same. The raised pulpit with its intricate canopy suspended from the ceiling is of natural hardwood. On either side of the Gothic-style altar are stained glass windows with Swedish inscriptions. The congregation's well-maintained cemetery lies to the east.

Another Grant County church with Swedish roots is the Evangelical Free Church in Stockholm, organized in 1891 and its building constructed in 1905. The Covenant church in Labolt was erected in 1900.

NEW
EFFINGTON

The rural Walla Lutheran Church was organized in 1894 as the Swedish Evangelical Lutheran Walla Church. The congregation built its sanctuary, where it still worships, in 1902. Early pastor K. G. William Dahl, who later founded Bethphage Mission in Axtell, Nebraska, served the church 1907 to 1909.

ROSHOLT

Congregants organized the rural St. Joseph Lutheran Church in 1894 and built its sanctuary in 1902. With the Walla Lutheran Church, St. Joseph shared a pastor, who lived in a parsonage at St. Joseph. Dahl also pastored this church early in his career (1907–09) and wrote a book based on his experiences in Rosholt and New Effington. Swedish was spoken in the services and Sunday School at St. Joseph until 1925. Walla and St. Joseph celebrated their centennials in 1994.

WHITE ROCK

The Augustana Lutheran Church in White Rock, which is in the extreme northeastern corner of the state, was founded in 1887, and in recent years the same pastor has served the Walla, St. Joseph, and Augustana congregations.

CLAREMONT

In 1881, Swedish settlers, many of them from Chisago County, Minnesota, came to South Dakota near Claremont and began to homestead the land. In 1884, they held in a home the first service of what they named the Swedish Evangelical Lutheran Augustana Church, and in 1899 they built a church under the supervision of Swede William Carlson from Center City, Minnesota. Church sources say that Carlson did a handstand on top of the tower the day the building was completed. It was dedicated in 1900. Now called the Augustana Evangelical Lutheran Church, the church celebrated its one hundred tenth anniversary in 1994.

HERMOSA

Far to the west, in Custer State Park (605/255-4515), is the Peter Norbeck Summer House known as Valhalla, which is open to the public by appointment only. The large one and one-half–story log structure with an open front porch was built in 1927 and has been named to the National Register of Historic Places. Peter Norbeck (1870–1937), a well driller, served South Dakota as governor and as a U.S. senator. Having an intense interest in the Black Hills, Norbeck was instrumental in setting aside 127,000 acres as Custer State Park. East of the Game Lodge, at the intersection of State Highway 36 and U.S. 16A, is an official state historic plaque noting the achievements of this man whose father was Swedish and mother Norwegian. Norbeck also was responsible for designing bridges on Iron Mountain Road, which takes visitors to the Mount Rushmore National Memorial. There the faces of four presidents—Washington, Jefferson, Lincoln, and Theodore Roosevelt—are carved in the side of the 5,600-foot mountain in the Black Hills National Forest, a short drive from Hermosa.

NORTH DAKOTA

Since Swedish pioneers tended to settle singly rather than in groups in North Dakota, their influence tended to be diluted, and relatively few landmarks have been preserved. Generally, the Swedish-born population was fairly evenly distributed throughout the region, though a considerable number moved into the Red River Valley. On U.S. Highway 81 five miles west of Grafton and then five miles west on State Highway 9 is an official state marker for the Sweden Post Office, which was established in 1879 and served the community until 1882 when the railroad reached nearby Grafton.

By the early 1960s, twenty-eight Augustana Lutheran Synod congregations were scattered throughout North Dakota. The oldest one, Maple-Sheyenne, was founded in 1878 five miles southwest of Harwood near Fargo. Others included First

Within two miles of the Canadian border, the former Zion Lutheran Church near Souris is open daily to visitors, though it no longer serves a congregation.

Lutheran (1883), Bismarck; Elim (1891), Fargo (the church was built in 1905 and rebuilt in 1939); Herby Lutheran (1891), about nine miles north of Mapleton near Argusville; Sunne (1893), Wilton; Nebo (1895), Valley City; Augustana and Grace (both 1896), Sheyenne; Klara (1897), six miles north of Heimdal; Augustana (1897), Grand Forks; Gustavus Adolphus (1902), Adam; Augustana (1906), Minot; and Gustavus Adolphus (1912), Gwinner.   Immanuel Lutheran of Jamestown is another old congregation.

Members at North Trinity Lutheran, established about seven miles west of Grafton, merged with two Norwegian groups; however, the old clapboard church building from the 1890s is maintained and a yearly service is held there. Covenant congregations include one in Fargo and one in Drayton.

Two miles south of the Canadian border in central North Dakota and six miles northeast of Souris is the former Swedish Zion Lutheran Church. The stone church, built in 1903 and 1904 by members of the congregation, is maintained by local residents. The area's farmers donated one cent per bushel of wheat harvested in 1903 to pay for the church's masonry work. Although the sanctuary no longer serves a congregation, it is open every day for visitors. There to greet them are some of the original furnishings, including the altar, a step-up pulpit, a pump organ, the pews, and a pot-bellied stove.

3 Minnesota

I n 1850, Fredrika Bremer, in writing about her two years in
the United States, commented, "What a glorious new
Scandinavia might not Minnesota become! Here the Swede
would find his clear, romantic lakes, the plains of Skåne, rich in
grain, and the valleys of Norrland." Sixty years later, the Swedes
were the largest ethnic group in Minnesota, having surpassed
the Germans and Norwegians.

Jacob Fahlstrom, or Fahlström (c. 1795–1859), is presumed
to be the first Swede to have settled in Minnesota. As a young
lad, he went to Canada but was separated from his party.
Subsequently adopted by the Chippewa Indians, he later chose
his bride from the tribe. By about 1813, Fahlström had arrived
in the area that would become the Twin Cities of St. Paul and
Minneapolis. Though a guide for the fur-trading companies, he
became a Methodist and acted as a missionary to the Native
Americans. In the 1850s, Fahlström settled on a farm near Afton
in Washington County where he spent his last years.

In the fall of 1850, three Swedes—Oscar Roos, Carl
Fernström, and August Sandahl—came to Washington County
and built a log cabin near Hay Lake, just south of present-day
Scandia, one of the best known Swedish settlements in the St.
Croix Valley. During the following decades, thousands of

179

Swedish settlers came up the St. Croix River, most motivated by economic reasons to leave their native land, disembarking at various points in Washington County, and then remaining in the county or heading to Minnesota's interior or northwest Wisconsin.

Because most modern travelers will begin their exploration of Minnesota from the metropolitan Twin Cities area, Minneapolis and St. Paul open this chapter on places in Minnesota with noteworthy Swedish-American historic landmarks. Using the Twin Cities as an axis on a clock, this chapter will begin with points north, as though the sweep of the hands begins at noon, and circle clockwise to examine east-central, southeast, south, central, and northwest Minnesota. Travelers arriving at the Minneapolis–St. Paul International Airport will not be surprised to see one of Minnesota's most famous native sons, Charles Lindbergh, Jr., remembered by a replica of the *Spirit of St. Louis* hanging from the ceiling near the Northwest Airlines international ticket counter. A terminal also bears his name.

Next to Chicago, the Twin Cities of Minneapolis and St. Paul constitute the most important Swedish-American center in the United States. Swedish influence continues to be greater in Minneapolis, where the number of foreign-born Swedes has been as high as three times greater than in St. Paul.

THE TWIN CITIES

MINNEAPOLIS   Minneapolis is the home of the American Swedish Institute, a private, nonprofit organization, which strives to preserve the Swedish heritage brought to this country by Swedish immigrants and to promote cultural bonds between the United States and Sweden. Over sixty years old, the ASI boasts more than five thousand members who participate in activities organized by numerous auxiliaries and affiliates.

In the Twin Cities, Swedes founded three hospitals, two academies, and two colleges. Early Swedish centers were the Cedar-Riverside area of Minneapolis and Swede Hollow *(Svenska Dalen)*, near Payne Avenue in St. Paul. Since 1933, Swedish Day, or Swedes' Day *(Svenskarnas Dag)*, the largest annual gathering of Swedish Americans in the United States, is held in late June in Minneapolis's Minnehaha Park. The largest Lutheran congregation (Mount Olivet) and one of the largest Covenant congregations (First Covenant) in the United States are in Minneapolis.

INSTITUTES AND MUSEUMS
The American Swedish Institute—2600 Park Avenue at Twenty-sixth Street (612/871-4907). The institute's museum is open

Tuesday through Saturday noon to 4 (Wednesday until 8) and Sunday 1–5.

This imposing mansion built in French Chateau architectural style and made of Indiana limestone was the former home of Swan J. Turnblad (1860–1933), a Swedish newspaper owner who was born in Småland. In 1887, he became manager of the *Svenska Amerikanska Posten*, a struggling Swedish-language weekly in Minneapolis. By 1897 he owned 95 percent of the newspaper's shares, and by the turn of the century, Turnblad had turned around the paper's sagging fortunes. It claimed to be the largest Swedish newspaper in the United States.

In 1903, Turnblad acquired property on exclusive Park Avenue and began the construction of this thirty-three–room mansion. Designed by Minneapolis architects Christopher A. Boehme and Victor Cordella, it took about four years to build. With its exterior turrets and interior first floor mahogany ornamentation, the edifice was one of the most grandiose mansions in the Twin Cities and is now on the National Register of Historic Places. One-third of the rooms contain large stoves *(kakelugnar)* with glazed tiles (each stove is of different design) made in Sweden. After his wife died in 1929, Turnblad surprised the Minneapolis Swedish-American community by announcing that he would establish a new organization, the American Institute of Swedish Arts, Literature and Science (in 1949 the name was changed to the American Swedish Institute) and would endow it with his mansion and other properties. The institute aims to promote the Swedish cultural heritage by presenting lectures, concerts, exhibits, and educational and travel opportunities throughout the year.

Now the mansion's major rooms house the institute's permanent exhibits. Richly decorated and paneled in African and Honduran mahogany, the Grand Hall includes a beautiful fireplace and a portrait of Turnblad by Christian von Schneidau. The Drawing Room, with its made-in-Sweden chandeliers, is used primarily for special exhibits. A museum shop, also on the first floor, is housed in the former den.

The Dining Room is easily the most ornate room in the mansion. Above the mantel of the marble fireplace is the carving of a scene from a Swedish legend showing elves and trolls luring people to live a life of splendor in the enchanted world. This carving is on the official seal of the institute.

The *kakelugn* (a tiled stove) from the Breakfast Room won first prize at the 1900 Paris Exposition. The room also contains furniture from the era of Gustav III (reigned 1771–1792) and a painting by Gustavus Hesselius, one of a number of paintings by Swedish and Swedish-American artists that are owned by the ASI. Hesselius (1682–1755) came to the United States when he was thirty, becoming a noted portrait painter of the colonial

The American Swedish Institute, quartered in a thirty-three room mansion built for newspaper owner Swan J. Turnblad in the early 1900s, hosts Swedish and Swedish-American exhibits, lectures, concerts, and other cultural events.

period. Still used for musical performances and recitals, the Music Room hosts gatherings most Sunday afternoons during the winter months. Visitors pass to the second floor by way of the grand stairway. Above it is a stained glass window, made in Sweden and installed about 1908, that depicts the ransom of Visby, Gotland, in 1361 by Valdemar Atterdag, the conquering Danish king.

On the second floor visitors will find the Library, the Reading Room, and other display areas. The Library features a large collection of Swedish books printed in the United States, and the Reading Room includes many books Turnblad purchased in Sweden. Other rooms on the second floor include a former bed chamber, which contains a collection of glass from various Swedish glass companies. Two other areas—the Blue Room, which displays traveling exhibits, and another small exhibit room—also draw visitors.

The centerpiece of the third floor was originally a ballroom, and it now is used for temporary exhibits of the institute's permanent collection, including immigrant items and Dala paintings. It is surrounded by a number of smaller rooms. In the Värmland Room are about one hundred fifty items sent in 1952 as a token of friendship between the people of Värmland, with its scores of parishes, and the United States. The Peasant Room contains furniture from the nineteenth-century peasant era. A large collection of textile and weaving implements given to the institute by Swedish-American textile artist Hilma Berglund is featured in the Weaving Room. Other third-floor rooms offer additional exhibits—children's toys, immigrant trunks, and a sideboard hand-carved by a Swedish immigrant.

The lower level of the mansion invites visitors with a large lounge furnished with tables, chairs, and a reading materials' rack. The entrance to the ASI's book store, the Bokhandel, is from this lounge. The Bokhandel offers a wide variety of books about Sweden and Scandinavia and also sells cassette tapes, greeting cards, and Carl Larsson print reproductions. Another doorway from the lounge leads to the Kaffestuga, a small but attractive dining area for afternoon coffee.

In 1983 the institute completed construction of a new auditorium off the lounge, and it provides additional exhibition space and serves as the social center for most museum activities. The area can seat more than two hundred fifty for a meal and provides space for lectures, concerts, and other cultural events. Dala paintings by Bengt Engman (1925–87) from Dalarna that depict early Swedish immigration and settlement in Minnesota tell a story as well as decorate the room's walls. Outside in front of the mansion is a statue of Selma Lagerlöf, the Swedish author who won the Nobel prize for literature in 1909.

The Swedish Council of America—2600 Park Avenue at East Twenty-sixth Street (612/871-0593).
Housed in the American Swedish Institute Turnblad mansion, Swedish Council of America leads more than 140 Swedish-American affiliate organizations in working cooperatively to strengthen the cultural relationship between the United States and Sweden and to preserve the Swedish-American heritage. It publishes *Sweden & America*, a quarterly magazine with a circulation of 28,000, and it gives modest grants to further its aims and other awards to recognize distinguished contributors to cultural exchange between Sweden and the United States.

HISTORIC PLACES
Cedar-Riverside Area.
Cedar Avenue was known as Snoose Boulevard from the word *snus* (meaning "snuff"). Its rows of tenement buildings were inhabited by Swedish immigrants who spoke Swedish in the stores and other businesses in the area. Seven Corners, at Cedar and Washington avenues, was the district's hub. Here the famous Swedish American Olle i Skratthult (Olle in Laughterville) entertained his countrymen. Dania Hall, at 427 Cedar Avenue near Riverside, hosted cultural events in which various Scandinavians performed. Built in 1886, the massive red brick edifice was damaged in a fire in the summer of 1991. The Minneapolis Community Development Agency, which has owned the aging building since 1986, replaced the roof. The building had been placed on the National Register of Historic Places in 1975.

Restored Homes on Milwaukee Avenue between Franklin Avenue and Twenty-fourth Street—private residences. Milwaukee Avenue is reserved for pedestrians only.
In the Seward neighborhood near Franklin Avenue are two-story houses dating from the 1880s that were inhabited by so many Swedish and other Nordic working-class residents that for a short while the area was known as "Copenhagen Avenue." Many of the early immigrants in the area worked in the flour mills and the nearby Milwaukee Railroad yards. An unusual feature of the houses is the lovely lattice work on the front porches. In 1974 the entire four-block area was placed on the National Register of Historic Places.

Hennepin County Medical Center's Medical Specialty Center (former Swedish Hospital)—main entrance 900–914 Eighth Street at Ninth Avenue South (612/347-2121).
Swedes from several denominations cooperated in founding the Swedish Hospital in 1898. In 1970, this hospital and St. Barnabas

Hospital combined to create Metropolitan Medical Center using part of the facilities and land of the Swedish Hospital. In early 1992 Metropolitan Medical Center was closed, and the building was sold to Hennepin County Medical Center for a medical specialty clinic.

The name Swedish Hospital can be seen on the Eighth Street facade of the older of the two buildings. Between the two double doors of the main entrance on Eighth Street, one can see the old cornerstone with "Swedish Hospital 1901," an inscription that unfortunately is partially blocked from view by a radiator.

The Swedish Hospital Nurses' Home, established in 1899, was built on the east side of the medical complex facing the Central Free Church. At the top of the building can still be seen the nurses' home inscription.

Floyd B. Olson House—1914 West Forty-ninth Street (between Morgan and Logan Avenues South).

This unpretentious house, listed on the National Register of Historic Places, was the home of Floyd B. Olson, governor of Minnesota from 1931 to 1936, whose father was Norwegian and whose mother was Swedish. A governor popular with the farm and labor movements, he was reelected by many of the same people who voted for Franklin D. Roosevelt in 1932. Olson died while in office after having been nominated to run for the U.S. Senate.

CHURCHES
Augustana Evangelical Lutheran Church—Eleventh Avenue South and Seventh Street (612/332-8595).

In December 1857, the first Swedish Lutheran sermon was preached in Minneapolis by the Rev. Peter Carlson. Nine years later Pastor Carlson joined with eleven Swedes and Norwegians to organize the Evangelical Lutheran Augustana Church of Minneapolis, Minnesota, at a meeting in Knickerbocker Church at Hennepin Avenue and Fourth Street South. In 1867 the new congregation, now numbering twenty-nine communicants, joined the fledgling Augustana Synod and bought a lot on the corner of Washington Avenue and Thirteenth Avenue South, just west of the nearby Scandinavian settlement around Seven Corners. A year later the new church building was sufficiently finished to house the first service.

The enormous increase in Swedish immigrants in Minneapolis soon forced the congregation to look for new and larger space. By 1882 the present sand-colored church building was finished on the corner of Eleventh Avenue South and East Seventh Street. On 24 June 1883, it was dedicated by the Rev.

Erland Carlsson, who together with pastors Lars Paul Esbjörn and Tuve Nilsson Hasselquist, is considered a "pilgrim father" of Swedish Lutheranism in North America.

Between 1874 and 1910, seven daughter congregations were spun off from the mother Augustana congregation. They were Bethlehem (1874) at 2200 Fremont Avenue North; Emanuel (1884) at 697 Thirteenth Avenue NE; St. Paul's (1887) at 2742 Fifteenth Avenue South; Ebenezer (1892) at 2720 East Twenty-second Street; Zion (1893) at 128 West Thirty-third Street; Messiah (1908) at 2501 Columbus Avenue South, and Grace University (1910) at Southeast Harvard and Delaware streets.

Two schools were founded by the church, but no longer exist. In 1887, Emanuel Academy was started in the church basement, but it closed in 1894 when attempts to raise money for the school failed. In 1904, the Minnesota Conference of the Augustana Lutheran Church founded Minnesota College, and for the school it purchased a building at Harvard and Delaware streets. More than eight hundred students were enrolled in the school in the 1923–24 school year, but the school was saddled with heavy debts. In 1930, financial problems forced it to close, and fifteen years later the University of Minnesota bought the property.

Central Free Church—707 Tenth Avenue South (612/332-7722).
The Central Free Church, an Evangelical Free church, is on the same block and directly west of Augustana Evangelical Lutheran. The cornerstone on the red brick structure is labeled, *"Svenska Missions Templet 1895"* (Swedish Mission Temple). The headquarters of the Evangelical Free Church of America is in Bloomington, Minnesota, at 901 East Seventy-eighth Street (612/854-1300).

First Covenant Church—810 South Seventh Street (across from the Metrodome) (612/332-8093).
Carved on the Seventh Street facade of the large red brick building is the inscription, *"Svenska Missions Tabernaklet 1886"* (Swedish Mission Tabernacle). In December 1874, the congregation was officially organized with thirty-one charter members. After the dynamic Rev. E. August Skogsbergh (1850–1939) (sometimes called "the Swedish Dwight L. Moody") assumed his post here in 1884, a larger church building was needed. A lot was purchased on the corner of Seventh Street and Chicago Avenue, and in 1886 the foundation for the present structure was laid. The following year, the building was completed with a seating capacity of twenty-five hundred. Svenska

Tabernaklet was perhaps the liveliest place in Minneapolis, considering Skogsbergh's forceful preaching and A. L. Skoog's powerful singing. (Skoog was called "the Swedish Ira Sankey" in reference to Moody's organ-playing revival singer.) The membership rapidly expanded until the church became, for a while, the largest Covenant church in the United States. It has now been surpassed by the Rolling Hills Covenant Church of Rolling Hills Estates, California.

Through the years, the main sanctuary has been altered. In the large impressive auditorium hang a number of lovely stained glass windows. Downstairs is an interesting archival room where among the items displayed are the organ used by Skoog and the silk hat worn by Skogsbergh when he received the Order of Vasa from the Swedish king. In the small Skogsbergh-Skoog Chapel near the main sanctuary is Skogsbergh's round pulpit, a copy of the original one kept at the Covenant Archives at North Park College in Chicago, which began at First Covenant. The reception room in the church office has a Swedish folk decor.

In Minneapolis's Lakewood Cemetery at 3600 Hennepin Avenue is a reddish granite marker on the Rev. Skogsbergh's grave (lot 194, section 4, grave 4 1/2) which is shaded by oaks at the base of a small hill. To the Värmland native, the church inscribed: "In memory of Erik August Skogsbergh 1850–1939. A faithful pastor, a zealous evangelist, and a courageous leader who fulfilled his ministry."

Mount Olivet Lutheran Church—5025 Knox Avenue South (612/926-7651).

The largest Lutheran congregation in the United States worships in a very spacious light stone Gothic-style church designed by architect Hugo Hansen. The main sanctuary features a beamed ceiling and spectacular stained glass windows depicting various biblical figures.

The church honored the Rev. Reuben K. Youngdahl by naming its chapel for this dynamic pastor who served the church 1938–1968. In the hallway on the lower level of the administration building is a statue of Lina Sandell (1832–1903), who composed hymns, including the favorite *Tryggare kan ingen vara.* Sculpted by Axel Wallenberg of Stockholm, it is similar to one on the campus of North Park College in Chicago.

Bethlehem Baptist Church (formerly First Swedish Baptist)— 720 Thirteenth Avenue South (612/338-7653).

Bethlehem Baptist Church is the oldest Swedish Baptist congregation in Minneapolis. Elim Baptist Church at 685 Thirteenth Avenue NE (612/789-3591) also has Swedish roots.

SCHOOLS
University of Minnesota, Curtis L. Carlson School of Management—271 Nineteenth Avenue South (612/625-0027).
In 1986 the University of Minnesota honored Curtis L. Carlson, the most generous benefactor the school has ever had, by naming its school of management in his honor. Carlson, chairman of Minneapolis's Carlson Companies and a University of Minnesota alumnus, is a former Swedish Council of America board chairman.

Minnehaha Academy—kindergarten through eighth grade, 4200 W. River Road (612/721-3359); ninth through twelfth grade, 3107 Forty-seventh Avenue South (612/729-8321).
Minnehaha Academy is a private coeducational school that was founded in 1913 under the auspices of the Evangelical Covenant Church of America. In the mid-1990s, the school in all its grades had an enrollment of approximately nine hundred students.

OTHER POINTS OF INTEREST
Gustavus II Adolphus Society Hall—1628 East Lake (612/729-9698).
Gustavus II Adolphus Society, a Swedish fraternal organization, constructed this two-story brick building in 1924. Meetings are still held once a month on the second floor of the hall by the society.

Good Templar Center—2922 Cedar Avenue (612/722-8535).
The Good Templar Center is owned by the International Order of Good Templars (IOGT), an international temperance society. A museum and archives, built in 1983, houses items and documents from chapters that have been dissolved. Attached is Enigheten Hall, meeting site of the Enigheten Chapter of IOGT.

SCULPTURE AND OTHER ART
Gunnar Wennerberg Statue—Minnehaha Park (Minnehaha Parkway and Minnehaha Avenue).
Gunnar Wennerberg (1817–1901) was a Swedish poet, composer, educator, and statesman. In Minnehaha Park is a monument to him, a copy of a statue by Carl Eldh that stands outside the Uppsala University library in Uppsala, Sweden. The statue portrays the famous Swede holding his student cap, and inscribed on the monument is a poem by Wennerberg. Near the statue the annual Swedish, or Swedes', Day *(Svenskarnas Dag)* is held.

ST. PAUL

HISTORIC PLACES

The State Capitol—75 Constitution Avenue. Open Monday through Friday 8:30–5; Saturday 10–4; Sunday 1–4. Free admission. Guided tours on the hour by the Minnesota Historical Society (tour information, 612/297-3521; tour reservations, 612/296-2881).

Minnesota has had two governors, Adolph Olson Eberhart and John Lind, who were born in Sweden and ten others who were of Swedish ancestry. Immediately in front of the capitol is a statue of John Albert Johnson (1861–1909), born near St. Peter of Swedish parentage. A similar one is located on the front lawn of the Nicollet County Courthouse in St. Peter. At the monument's base are smaller statues representing miners, farmers, and traders. On Constitution Avenue, just southwest of the capitol, is a statue honoring Floyd B. Olson, governor from 1931 to 1936.

Other monuments celebrate feats of daring. West of the capitol in a park across Constitution Avenue is a monument commemorating Leif Eriksson and his discovery of North America in A.D. 1000. Aviator Charles A. Lindbergh, Jr., is depicted as both a young boy and as a mature navigator in Paul Granlund's 1985 statue of him on the mall, south of the capitol. Other casts of the sculpture are at Lindbergh Field in San Diego, California, and Le Bourget Field in Paris.

Inside the capitol, which the Minnesota Historical Society describes as "grand in design, splendid in detail, and great in its telling of Minnesota history," are portraits of all the governors. On the first floor opposite the Governor's Reception Room is a plaque in memory of Olson. South of the capitol is the History Center of the Minnesota Historical Society (for special events at the center, call 612/296-6126, or outside the Twin Cities, 800/657-3773). At 345 Kellogg Boulevard West, the center offers free admission to its museum and draws visitors with its restaurant and gift shops.

CHURCHES

The First Lutheran Church—463 Maria Avenue (612/776-7210). The First Lutheran Church was the first Swedish Lutheran congregation in Minnesota, having been organized in 1854 by Pastor Erland Carlsson of Immanuel Lutheran in Chicago. Originally the congregation was made up of both Swedes and Norwegians, but in 1870 the two groups separated, the Swedish congregation being known as the First Swedish Evangelical Lutheran Church. The present brick structure, built in 1917, is the third building of the congregation. A unique marble baptismal font supported by four columns has the Swedish inscription,

"Den der tror och blivit döpt, han skall varda salig" ("Whosoever believes and is baptized, he shall be blessed"). In the entrance of the adjacent Norelius Hall is a plaque in memory of Swedish Lutheran leader Eric Norelius (1833–1916). In the lobby are glass cases containing a number of historical items associated with the congregation.

To the west of Norelius Hall can be seen part of Swede Hollow *(Svenska Dalen)* where many Swedes first settled before they moved on to other places. The old houses are gone; the area is now a city park. Nearby Payne Avenue was a major commercial center for St. Paul's Swedish population. Swedish settlers began to arrive in St. Paul in 1852, two years after Fredrika Bremer had made her visit. By 1930, almost eighteen thousand people born in Sweden or of Swedish ancestry lived in Ramsey County.

SCHOOLS

Bethel College and Seminary—3900 Bethel Drive (612/638-6400) in Arden Hills.

In 1871, Dr. John Alexis Edgren from Värmland launched in Chicago's Morgan Park a Swedish Baptist theological seminary. During its early years the seminary moved to several locations, including to St. Paul (1884–86); to Stromsburg, Nebraska (1886–88); and back to Morgan Park in 1888. The seminary was connected with the Baptist Union Theological Seminary of Chicago, and in 1892 was united with the Divinity School of the University of Chicago as the Swedish Department. In October 1905, Bethel Academy was founded in Minneapolis. There were twenty-nine regular academic students in that year, the first class sessions being held in the Elim Baptist Church.

At the 1913 annual meeting in Duluth of the Swedish Baptist Conference (today known as the Baptist General Conference), the decision was made to bring the academy and seminary together in St. Paul under the name of Bethel Academy and Seminary. The first campus was at 1480 North Snelling Avenue. The first two brick structures were built between 1914 and 1916. Bethel College (the high school curriculum was dropped in 1936) became a four-year college in 1947 after a number of years as a junior college, and the seminary remained at that location until 1972 when it was relocated to modern facilities in suburban Arden Hills. On a building at the southeast corner of Snelling and Nebraska avenues can be seen the inscription "Bethel Theological Seminary." The former campus is now the Hubert H. Humphrey Job Corps Center.

In 1994 Bethel College was a four-year liberal arts school with an enrollment of more than twenty-one hundred. The seminary has five hundred students. The college offers courses in Swedish and Scandinavian culture and civilization. The college and the seminary are owned and operated by the Baptist General Conference of America headquartered in Arlington Heights, Illinois.

The Bethel Seminary Archives contains written historical materials related to the various churches of the Baptist General Conference. The archives owns Fredrik O. Nilsson's desk and a number of portraits of early leaders. Nilsson founded the first Baptist congregation in Sweden and brought to Minnesota the Swedes who held the first Baptist service in Minnesota.

On the campus is the Scandia Baptist Church building, the second Swedish Baptist sanctuary in Minnesota and the oldest still in existence. In 1854, F. O. Nilsson cofounded a Baptist congregation in Burlington, Iowa. But a year later, that church disbanded, and most of its members moved to Minnesota. In the summer of 1855, the group reached the eastern shore of Lake Waconia, in Carver County, west of Minneapolis. Soon after their arrival, fewer than a dozen people, including Nilsson, organized the Scandia Baptist Church, and in 1857 built a small log church, what some claim was the first house of worship in

Built in 1857, the Scandia Baptist Church is the oldest Baptist sanctuary in Minnesota and is preserved on the Bethel College campus.

Carver County. In 1910, a porch and small steeple were added. In 1973, the edifice was moved to the Bethel College and Seminary campus, where it is preserved as a symbol of the faith of the early Swedish Baptists in Minnesota. It is still used for weddings and by seminary students who practice their preaching in the sanctuary. (The church is kept locked, but visitors can ask for the key at the seminary administration office across the road.)

Inside, the visitor can see the handmade pews and the old organ. On the exterior left side of the church, the log construction and dovetailing (the logs have been covered with clapboard) are visible. Among the original communicants was Andrew (Anders) Peterson who became famous as a horticulturist in Carver County. From 1850 until his death in 1898, Peterson kept extensive diaries totaling twelve volumes and wrote numerous letters to Sweden. These manuscripts were a source for Vilhelm Moberg's novels, including *The Emigrants, Unto a Good Land, The Settlers*, and *Last Letter Home*, and the two movies based on Moberg's work. In fact, Moberg used Peterson as his prototype for Karl Oskar. The Minnesota Historical Society (345 Kellogg Boulevard West, 612/296-6126) in St. Paul has the original diaries. Microfilm copies are in the University of Minnesota Immigration History Research Center, 826 Berry Street, in St. Paul (612/627-4208).

OTHER POINTS OF INTEREST

Jacob Fahlstrom Historic Plaque—at Kellogg Boulevard and Robert Street, at north end of Robert Street Bridge.

The Jacob Fahlstrom Historic Plaque, embedded in a seven-foot dark stone monument in a park in front of the America Center Building, honors the first Swedish settler in Minnesota. It was unveiled in 1948 by Prince Bertil of Sweden. Fahlstrom once owned eighty acres in what is now downtown St. Paul, but he is said to have given up his claim because the land was too hilly.

SCULPTURE AND OTHER ART

"Vision of Peace" by Carl Milles—Memorial Hall of St. Paul City Hall and Ramsey County Court Building (15 Kellogg Boulevard West) (on the south side of Fourth Street between Wabasha and St. Peter).

A towering thirty-six–foot–high sculpture, "Vision of Peace" is of an Indian god of peace, who holds in one hand a peace pipe and extends the other in a gesture of friendship. The powerful sculpture is made of cream-colored Mexican onyx and is reportedly the largest carved figure of that variety of quartz in the world.

EAST-CENTRAL MINNESOTA

After the initial arrivals in Washington County, Swedes made their first sizable settlement in what is now known as the Chisago Lakes area (encompassing Chisago City, Lindstrom, and Center City) in Chisago County (see map, page 194). Chisago County and neighboring Isanti County have one of the highest percentages of Swedish-American inhabitants of any comparable area in the United States. In the early 1900s, at least 75 percent of Chisago County's population was of Swedish descent. The leader of the first Swedes to come to Chisago County in 1851 was Peter (Per) Andersson (or Joris Pelle Andersson). During the next two years, other families settled near Center City, thus forming the nucleus of the Chisago Lake Lutheran Church, the county's oldest Swedish congregation.

In the Chisago Lakes area are the towns of Chisago City, Center City, and Lindstrom—all Swedish strongholds. The last community was named for Daniel Lindstrom, a half-brother of Per Andersson. Northwest of Taylors Falls, the oldest town in the county, is Almelund, named for John Almquist, one of the first Swedish settlers in the area. Other communities in the county—North Branch, Harris, Rush Point, and Rush City— also have a high percentage of Swedish-American inhabitants.

Chisago County's landscape of lakes, rivers, and forests is similar to parts of Sweden. This similarity, as well as its good soil, made it an attractive place for the early Swedish settlers. Their letters home also drew more Swedes to the area. Vilhelm Moberg's novels, based on the fictitious Karl Oskar and Kristina from Småland, continue to make Chisago County a popular tourist attraction for Swedes.

Isanti County has been identified as the "Dalarna of America" because of the large number of settlers from that central Swedish province. The first Swedish settlers who came in 1857 were mainly Swedish Baptists, settling south of the town of Cambridge.

In 1864 a Lutheran congregation was organized in Cambridge by people who had moved from Chisago County and Wisconsin. Two years later about one hundred families from Rättvik, Orsa, and other villages in the Lake Siljan region of Dalarna arrived, establishing the communities of Dalbo, Walbo, and Athens.

Kanabec County, established in 1858, is directly north of Isanti County. Swedes, mainly from Dalarna, settled in 1871 in and around Brunswick, in the southern part of the county, having been attracted by hardwood and pine logging. Mora, the county seat, is named for Mora, Dalarna, its sister city. Both are known for annual cross-country ski races.

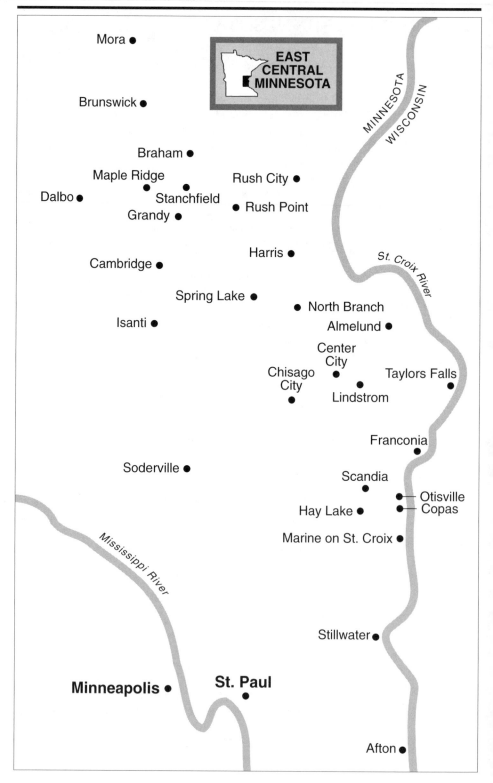

Mora ●

EAST
CENTRAL
MINNESOTA

MINNESOTA
WISCONSIN

Brunswick ●

Braham ●

Maple Ridge
●

Rush City ●

Dalbo ●

Stanchfield

Rush Point ●

Grandy ●

St. Croix River

Harris ●

Cambridge ●

Spring Lake ●

North Branch ●

Isanti ●

Almelund ●

Center
City

Chisago
City

●

Lindstrom

Taylors Falls
●

Franconia
●

Soderville ●

Scandia
●

Otisville
Copas

Hay Lake ●

Marine on St. Croix ●

Mississippi River

Stillwater ●

Minneapolis ●

St. Paul
●

Afton ●

AFTON

Afton is located in the southern part of Washington County and was named for a poem by Robert Burns. On South Indian Trail Road (about four miles northwest from the center of town) is the Jacob Fahlstrom Farmhouse, which is a private residence. The house was a way station along the St. Croix River for early Methodist missionaries. It is a log house, though the logs are hidden by clapboard siding. On the property is a small cemetery where Fahlstrom, his wife, and some of their descendants are buried. At the far end of the cemetery is a stone marker placed in 1964 by the Minnesota Methodist Historical Society. Since Fahlstrom's wife was a Native American, this is regarded as the first Christian Native American cemetery in Minnesota.

A quarter of a mile west of the bend in State Highway 95 is Memorial Lutheran Church (612/436-1138). The small white clapboard sanctuary, built in 1882, is now used only occasionally for weddings and funerals, having been replaced by the new sanctuary complex finished in 1992. The cemetery around the old sanctuary contains numerous graves, many of them belonging to the original Swedish members.

STILLWATER

A number of Swedes were attracted to Stillwater on the St. Croix River, considered for a number of years the logging capital of Minnesota. Large historic Victorian homes built on the bluffs watch over the business district of this quiet community only about twenty minutes east of St. Paul. Several were built or owned by Swedes, including the Andrew Olson House (107 East Laurel), the John G. Nelson House (220 West Olive), and the Frank Berry House (102 School Street).

The Trinity Lutheran congregation was founded by Swedish immigrants in 1871. In the same year they built a sanctuary at Oak and Fourth streets, which was sold in 1882 to another congregation. The congregation erected the present sanctuary in 1883 on the west side of Third Street near Myrtle, but when it renovated the entire church complex in 1983, it created a new entrance at 115 North Fourth Street.

At the north end of Stillwater is the Washington County Historical Society Museum (602 North Main Street, 612/439-5956), where there are a number of artifacts from the early settler and lumbering eras on display. Three miles north of Stillwater on State Highway 95 along the St. Croix River is the Boom Site, where there is a good view of the lovely St. Croix Valley, now designated the St. Croix National Scenic Riverway.

In 1977, Valley Tours, Inc., of Stillwater, began offering several group excursion tours of Washington County, including a Välkommen Swedish Settlement Tour. Call the tour office (612/439-6110) for more information.

MARINE ON ST. CROIX

Marine on St. Croix boasts a designated historic district listed on the National Register of Historic Places and was home to many early-arriving Swedes who disembarked here. A steep dirt road behind the general store leads to the landing site on the St. Croix River where many Swedish pioneers disembarked. A scene from the film based on Vilhelm Moberg's *The Emigrants* was shot at this site. Liv Ullmann and Max von Sydow starred in the Svensk Filmindustri production.

Christ Lutheran Church, organized by Swedes in 1872, is a daughter congregation of the Scandia church (see below). The church building was constructed between 1872 and 1875 of rough lumber planed by hand and was originally located north of the present site. On the chancel wall above the altar painting of the Ascension is Matthew 28:20, which includes Christ's promise, "And, lo, I am with you alway, even unto the end of the world," inscribed in Swedish.

In Township Hall, or the Stone House Museum, at Fifth Street between Oak and Pine streets, is a building considered one of the best examples of early Swedish stonework in Minnesota. Constructed in 1872, the building has sandstone walls made of hand-tooled ashlars with uniform height, depth, and course. Gustaf Carlson, a Swedish immigrant stonemason from Småland built it of locally quarried sandstone. Originally the three rooms served as township offices and a jail. After 1896, the building was used for a variety of purposes, including a church activity center. In 1963 it was converted into a museum with a wide assortment of memorabilia.

The Marine on St. Croix Historic District includes nearly fifty significant structures and sites, many of which are homes built by Swedish immigrants. Many Swedes were employed by the local lumber companies, though some developed their own businesses as harness makers, boat builders, stonemasons, cabinet makers, wagon makers, saloon keepers, and blacksmiths. Generally the Swedish immigrants built their homes in the western part of the village on top of the bluff and behind the mansions of the New Englanders who had arrived first.

Historically, the most important commercial structure is the two and one-half–story Marine General Store at the corner of Maple and Judd streets. This business played an important role in attracting Swedes because one of the early owners advertised widely that he would grant them liberal credit if they settled in Marine. The Marine Village Hall, south of the general store, was built in 1888.

COPAS

In the small community of Copas on State Highway 95 one and one-half miles south of U.S. Highway 97 near Scandia is the former general store, now the Crabtree Kitchen, a restaurant serving some Swedish-style cooking; the old schoolhouse; and across State Highway 95 just south of the restaurant, the former Ames House, a hotel where many of the early Swedish settlers stayed, halfway between Stillwater and Taylors Falls. It is now a private residence.

OTISVILLE

Although no signs lead travelers to Otisville, it lies just north of Copas on County Road 53. Loghouse Landing, today a public landing on the St. Croix River, is the site where early Swedish immigrants disembarked. A log house stands near the site.

SCANDIA

The small community of Scandia, founded in 1855, can boast having the oldest existing Swedish Lutheran Church building (1856) for the third oldest Swedish congregation in Minnesota, the oldest Swedish Lutheran parsonage (1868) in the state, and a monument honoring the first Swedish pioneers to the region.

One of the loveliest Swedish-American historic sites that has been developed is the complex of six pioneer structures called Gammelgården, or The Old Farm. It is open 1–4 Friday, Saturday, and Sunday from 1 May through the last weekend in October (612/433-5053). The two most important structures historically are the old church *(gammelkyrkan)* and the parsonage *(prästhuset)*. In addition, there are an authentic Swedish red *stuga*, the immigrant house, barn *(ladugård)*, corn crib, windmill, and work shed *(arbetsbod)* that has been converted into a gift shop.

In 1867, the Elim Lutheran congregation purchased forty acres of the Ola Hansson farm, and the following year built the parsonage. In 1884, another parsonage was constructed, and the old one was sold to the Nelson family. The parsonage belonged to that family until 1970 when the house and six acres were purchased by the church. Two years earlier, five acres of the farm had been bought to be converted into the Barton Johnson Memorial Park (Johnson died in Vietnam in 1968), lying to the immediate north of Gammelgården. In the 1970s and 1980s, thanks to monetary gifts from several sources, the structures have been repaired and restored. The parsonage, barn, and work shed have always remained in their present locations; the *stuga*, immigrant house, and old church have recently been moved to the site.

Elim Lutheran Church was founded in 1854 by the Rev. Erland Carlsson of Chicago at nearby Hay Lake (see below). Two years later, the congregation erected this *gammelkyrka*, their first church, made of hand-hewn logs. But the congregation soon outgrew the building and a second church was erected on the present cemetery site, north of Gammelgården. The first church was then converted into a school and remained one until

1899 when a new brick school was constructed. The old church was sold to a school board member who moved it to his farm where it became a hay barn. In 1980 it was relocated to Gammelgården and rededicated in 1982 with many dignitaries, including Sweden's Prince Bertil and Princess Lilian, in attendance. Inside the church the visitor can see one original pew (the others are reproductions). On the pulpit is the church's original folding key (made so that it could fit into a person's pocket). The candelabra is from the fourth church that burned in 1907.

The *prästhus* is a large house (five rooms downstairs and two upstairs), particularly for its age (built in 1868). The rooms are fully furnished, many of the items having belonged to the Nelson family. There are a number of significant items from the late nineteenth and early twentieth centuries.

Originally the *stuga* was located on the Gottlieb Magney estate near the St. Croix River. Magney was the architect who designed Foshay Tower in Minneapolis, and he had used the *stuga* as a guest house. Built in 1930 and moved to Gammelgården in the late 1970s, the structure is divided into two rooms, one with built-in cabinets and a Swedish corner fireplace and the other with two built-in beds. Currently the building is used as a place to register guests at Gammelgården and to serve refreshments.

An annual event at Gammelgården on the second Saturday of August is a fiddling contest featuring Swedish music. Midsummer Day, the fourth Saturday in June, is celebrated with dancing around a maypole. Luciafest in December includes a prayer service in the old church.

The present red brick Gothic-style building that is Elim Lutheran Church is the Scandia congregation's sixth building. The fifth was gutted by fire in 1930, but the altar, pulpit, pews, and some furnishings were saved, as were the exterior walls. The sanctuary is noted for its dark wood–beamed ceiling, Gothic-style altar (with a copy of a Thorvaldsen sculpture), chancel rail, pews, and balcony. The sanctuary has a considerable amount of stained glass. Over the main entrance, an inscription reads, "Swedish Lutheran Elim Church Scandia."

Across the street in the cemetery are graves dating to 1860 of a number of former pastors as well as many of the immigrants. To the south is the former Methodist Church cemetery (the sanctuary no longer exists). Elim Lutheran purchased the property in 1917.

About one and one-half miles south of Gammelgården near Hay Lake is a twenty-two–foot obelisk that is a historic monument to the first Swedish settlers in Minnesota. The monument commemorates the arrival of Oscar Roos, Carl Fernström, and

August Sandahl from Västergötland who came to this area in October 1850. They walked from Marine on St. Croix about four miles to the east and built a cabin by the shore of Hay Lake. The monument, erected in 1902, replaced a wood monument that had been dedicated two years earlier.

HAY LAKE

In 1855, a year after the church was established, the early settlers organized a school district. The one-story brick Victorian Hay Lake School was constructed in the 1890s and used as a school until the early 1960s. Eleven years later, it came under the ownership of the Washington County Historical Society and has been declared a national historic site. In the school building, eight grades were taught by a single teacher. On display are various interesting school items from earlier days. The chandelier was rescued by one of the last teachers who found it under the schoolhouse.

The nearby Johannes Erickson Log House is also owned and operated by the Washington County Historical Society. Both are open 1 May through 31 October on Saturday and Sunday 1:30–4:30. Built in 1868, the twenty- by twenty-eight–foot log house is of hewn oak logs with a shingled gambrel (hip)

The Johannes Erickson Log House, built in 1868, is opened to visitors between May and October by the Washington County Historical Society.

roof. This roof allows for a full headroom space in the upstairs area. The log house is fully furnished with nineteenth-century items, but the cupboard is probably the only piece original to the dwelling. The Johannes Erickson family emigrated from Dalsland to Scandia in 1866.

Both the Hay Lake School and the Johannes Erickson Log House are historic landmarks listed on the National Register of Historic Places.

SODERVILLE   In 1872, the Swedish Evangelical Lutheran Church of Ham Lake in Anoka County was organized (the name was later changed to Our Saviour Evangelical Lutheran Church of Ham Lake). It is on County Road 22, less than one-half mile east of State Highway 65 at 2200 Swedish Drive NE. Although the present congregation worships in a sanctuary completed in 1964, located at 1562 Viking Boulevard NE in East Bethel (612/ 434-6117), the old white frame church dating from 1872 still stands, and services continue to be held there on Monday evenings, June through Labor Day. A unique feature of this church listed on the National Register of Historic Places is the central pulpit above the altar. On the altar is a portrait of Christ with the crown of thorns and the inscription, *"Se Guds Lamm"* ("Behold the Lamb of God").

FRANCONIA   Today a community of less than one hundred souls, Franconia is on the flat land of the old St. Croix River bottom, three miles south of Taylors Falls. During its most prosperous years in the 1870s, it was in the center of a timber area with extensive river traffic. The historic district, bounded by Cornelian, Summer, and Henry streets and listed on the National Register of Historic Places, includes ten frame residences (approximately half the number of houses in today's community), seven of which were built between the 1850s and the 1880s. At least four of the homes—the Eric Ostrom, Jonas Lindall, Hans Hanson, and Olof Swanlund homes—are closely associated with early Swedish settlers. The community has erected a stone monument honoring its pioneers.

TAYLORS FALLS   Located on the scenic St. Croix River, Taylors Falls was a tiny village of six houses when the first Swedish settlers disembarked from a riverboat in the 1850s. Oscar Roos, who arrived from Sweden with two friends in 1850 and became a prominent banker, real estate investor, and government official, made Taylors Falls his home. The Munch-Roos house, 360 Bench Street, was built in 1854 by the Munch brothers who emigrated from Prussia. This Greek Revival house was the home of the Roos family who lived in it for about a century (until 1965). The house, a private residence, is listed on the National Register of Historic Places.

The First Lutheran Church was organized in 1860. The present Gothic-style brick structure with its high steeple was built in 1903. The interior hass beautiful natural woodwork.

Kahbakong Cemetery is the only cemetery in Taylors Falls containing the remains of early Native Americans and Swedish, Yankee, and other settlers.

ALMELUND

Almelund, populated with fewer than 150 citizens, opens the Amador Heritage Center at County Road 12 and State Highway 95 every Sunday 1–5, June through September. Visitors who come at other times can visit by appointment (612/583-2883 or 612/583-2203). The center is a nicely organized local museum housed in the former school building of Almelund, constructed in 1910. It contains a number of items from Almelund's first Lutheran church and the former Almquist General Store.

The Immanuel Lutheran congregation was organized in 1887, mainly by people from Småland, and its original building was constructed the same year. In 1926, the present large handsome Gothic-style brick building was erected.

CHISAGO CITY

Chisago City was with Center City and Lindstrom one of the trinity of cities that was the hub of Chisago County. Zion Lutheran Church at 279th and Old Towne Road (612/257-2713) was organized in 1874, and the present church, clad in white aluminum siding, dates from 1908, succeeding the first sanctuary, which was destroyed by fire. The building has a tall central steeple and Gothic-style windows. The Margaret S. Parmly Residence replaced the Bethesda Old People's Home, established by Swedish Lutherans in 1904, the first such home built by Swedes in Minnesota. In the lobby of the modern Parmly Residence is the cornerstone from the Bethesda home.

LINDSTROM

Lindstrom has managed to preserve several homes and churches built about a century ago. The white frame Trinity Lutheran Church at Newell Avenue and Elm Street was built in 1902, the congregation being an offshoot of the Chisago Lake Lutheran Church. On the southeast corner of Lake Boulevard and Elm Street is the former Swedish Methodist Church, constructed in 1892. It is now a Masonic Lodge. Also on Lake Boulevard is St. Bridget of Sweden Roman Catholic Church.

At 13045 Lake Boulevard is the two-story red brick Gustaf Anderson House, designed in the Italianate style and built about 1879. Gustaf Anderson emigrated from Sweden in 1864 and settled in Minnesota, though later he speculated for gold in Montana. He returned to Minnesota to farm in Chisago County and built this house for his retirement. In more recent times it has housed a gift shop.

The two and a half–story frame C. A. Victor House (30495 Park Street) was constructed about 1905. Charles A. Victor was born in Sweden and after settling in Lindstrom in the 1880s became one of its earliest merchants, operating the C. A. Victor General Mercantile Store behind this residence. He was involved in the milling industry and politics, and in 1898 founded *Medborgaren—The Citizen,* one of several area Swedish newspapers.

After the building of the railroad, Lindstrom became a resort area. Fridhem ("Home of Peace") (on Newell Avenue on the north side of South Lindstrom Lake) is a frame structure built about 1898 for use as a summer home. One and a half stories tall, the house is topped by a roof broken by a central gabled dormer. A large porch supported by columns welcomes visitors. It was owned by another newspaperman, Frank A. Larson, a Chicago publisher and owner of the *Svenska Amerikanaren Tribunen.* The Larson family purchased the house in 1911 and spent most of their summers there until 1932. It is still a private residence. All three of these homes are listed on the National Register of Historic Places.

The Swedish heritage of Lindstrom is recognized by monuments and by other points of historical interest. Honoring the founder of the town, Hälsingland native Daniel Lindstrom, and other Swedish immigrants who settled the area is a plaque by the flagpole in Fairview Cemetery. Just south of the Lindstrom City Hall at 12670 Lake Boulevard is a statue of Karl Oskar and Kristina, a replica of one in Karlshamn, Blekinge, by Swedish sculptor Axel Olsson. The figures, characters from Vilhelm Moberg's immigration novels, dramatize the dream of the new and the grief of losing the old. Karl Oskar is looking toward the new land, and Kristina is taking a last look back at Sweden. Annually in early July the town of Lindstrom celebrates Karl Oskar Day. Near Lindstrom at County Road 20 and Red Wing Avenue is a milestone similar to those found in Sweden, and according to the late local historian and tour guide Theodore A. Norelius, it is the last milestone of many that once marked the way between Taylors Falls and the Chisago Lakes area. The town's water tower is decorated like a Swedish coffee pot.

One and one-half miles south of Lindstrom on Glader Boulevard, one mile east of State Highway 95, on the south shore of South Center Lake is the small Glader Cemetery named for Anders Peter Nilsson Glader who came from Furuby, Kronobergs Län 1853. Of all the Swedish cemeteries in Minnesota, Vilhelm Moberg was most impressed by this one. Nearby on the other side of the road is the Jerry Holt Farm. The old wood farm house is of the type Moberg envisioned being built by Karl Oskar and Kristina after they settled in the new land.

CENTER CITY

It has been said that the Chisago Lake Lutheran Church (612/257-6300), a buff-colored brick building dating from the 1880s, is the largest and probably finest rural church in Minnesota. It has been compared with the church in Madesjö Parish, Småland, a province from which a majority of the members of the congregation have their roots. On 12 May 1854, the Rev. Erland Carlsson of Chicago organized the congregation of approximately one hundred members, and the first meeting was held in a haymow. The site is now marked by a monument in the Chisago Lake Cemetery, which lies east of the present church. During the summer of that year, Carlsson had a "meeting house" built as a place of worship and a public school. Eric Norelius, then a twenty-year-old theological student, preached and taught that first summer. He and his brother Anders (Andrew) had left Sweden with the Peter Andersson group (see page 193).

The first resident pastor arrived in the spring of 1855 and the following year a small frame church was begun on the location of the present church. In 1858 the church was the site for the organization of the Minnesota Conference of the Augustana Lutheran Church, an event marked by an obelisk in front of the present sanctuary. Between 1868 and 1873, the membership of the congregation doubled from four hundred to eight hundred. By 1897, the number would increase to 1,495 adults and 816 children, the highest membership in the church's history. As a result of the rapid growth in membership, it was necessary to construct a larger sanctuary with a greater seating capacity. A few weeks after the building was completed in 1882, a bolt of lightning struck the steeple and a fire ignited. The fire gutted the church, but work to rebuild began immediately. The present edifice, completed in 1889, is identical in size to the former church. Since the late nineteenth century, the interior has been remodeled several times.

This building is of Romanesque style with round arched stained glass windows. A soaring steeple, containing clocks on each side above the belfry, is capped by a gold cross. Above the main door is the inscription, "Swedish Ev. Lutheran Church Erected AD 1882." The spacious sanctuary contains a large raised canopied pulpit. The words *Helig, Helig, Helig* ("Holy, Holy, Holy") appear on the altar under the statue of Christ.

The church contains an interesting Heritage Room. In the Fireside Room (lower lounge) is a lovely and dramatic tapestry by Marjorie Pohlmann depicting the history of the Chisago Lake Lutheran congregation (see the cover). The agrarian roots in the immigrants' homeland, the sailing ships that brought them to the United States, the Civil War, the lightning that struck the church building in 1882 and the fire that resulted, the transformation from horse and buggy (or horse and sled) to automobiles and vans, and the metamorphosis from an agricultural-based economy to an industrial and urban one—all are recorded in the tapestry's history-telling threads. On the north side of the sanctuary near the entrance to the adjacent Parish Building, is a flagpole with a plaque in memory of the Swedish pioneers who organized and built the church. The church cemetery to the east contains the graves of the early Swedish pioneers of the area.

Immediately south of the church is a historic district. This residential area on the east side of Summit Avenue is situated on a rise overlooking North Center Lake. The lots making up this district were laid out in 1888, and most of the nineteen residences were constructed during the late 1890s or the first decade of the twentieth century. Many of the frame houses were constructed by William Carlson, the owner of the local lumberyard, who was also the town's resident carpenter and builder. Carlson was responsible for much of the woodwork in the Chisago Lake Lutheran Church. The houses feature classical detailing, gable ornamentation, extensive use of windows, and front porches. The owners were Swedish merchants, tradesmen, politicians, retired farmers, and professionals, reflective of the growing prosperity of the area. The oldest houses are those nearest the church.

HARRIS

Fish Lake Evangelical Lutheran Church and Cemetery in Harris (612/674-4252) was organized in 1867. It is the second oldest Swedish Lutheran congregation in Chisago County. The first church was built between 1874 and 1879, but in 1886 lightning struck the tall steeple, and the structure burned to the ground. The congregation immediately decided to build a new sanctuary, constructing it from 1886 to 1889, and the white frame edifice with a central steeple and Gothic-style windows still serves the congregation.

The church is in a lovely setting among maple trees, making it a beautiful sight in autumn. In the sanctuary is an unusual fresco on the chancel wall. Painted by J. Blomquist, it portrays Christ in Gethsemane with an angel. Billowy clouds are seen behind. Outside the church is a granite Centennial Memorial stone. A particularly interesting section of the adjacent cemetery is where pastors are buried. Gravestones of the Revs. P. A. Philgren and N. J. Brink note they were from Sweden.

RUSH CITY

The First Evangelical Lutheran congregation was organized in 1876 and the present Gothic-style brick church was built in 1909. It replaced a wood structure built in 1877. The large two-story Queen Anne J. C. Carlson House, at Bremer and Sixth, constructed in 1899, is probably the most impressive residence in town and is listed on the National Register of Historic Places. J. C. Carlson, a leading entrepreneur of Rush City, came to the community in 1882, and thirteen years later was president of State Bank of Rush City.

RUSH POINT

Calvary Lutheran Church, organized in 1870 in Rush Point, is the third oldest Swedish Lutheran congregation in Chisago County. The present church was built in 1913. It is made of light-colored brick, similar in color to that of Chisago Lake Lutheran Church, and has Gothic-style windows.

GRANDY

Union Church in Grandy was built in the 1880s as a Swedish Adventist church. It was first located southeast of town. When the church was moved into Grandy in 1905, it was a union church for all faiths, but it later served residents as a community center.

CAMBRIDGE

In the pioneer era, Cambridge, some forty-five miles north of downtown Minneapolis, was at the southern end of a great pine forest. During the 1850s the town site served as a stopping place for loggers on their way to the pineries that lay farther north. With the influx of Swedish immigrants in the 1860s and 1870s, the town gradually developed into a major service center, and it became the county seat of Isanti County.

INSTITUTES AND MUSEUMS
Pioneer Cabin and West Riverside Museum School—West Riverside Historical Grounds (go west on State Highway 95 out of Cambridge and then north on County Road 14 for one-half mile).
Operated by the Isanti County Historical Society (612/689-4229), the Pioneer Cabin is a replica of the Edblad Cabin in which the Cambridge Lutheran Church was organized in 1864. Isak and Christina Edblad and their children came to Wisconsin from Jämtland in 1856. But in 1859 there was a conflict with the Native Americans, and the family decided to move on to Isanti County. They built a two-room log cabin (later a lean-to was added) on a high bank close to the Rum River. The many alterations that were made on the cabin through the years caused considerable problems when efforts were undertaken to restore the cabin. However, another cabin practically identical

to that of the Edblad family was discovered in Spring Lake, a small community east of Cambridge. It had been built in the 1860s by the Carl H. Youngquist family, which had immigrated to the United States in 1854. This cabin was purchased and moved to its present location. The home that one sees is mainly the Youngquist cabin, though the lean-to was completed in 1981 of logs salvaged from other local pioneer buildings. It has two floors and numerous pioneer items, many donated by the Edblad family, including a homemade weight-driven clock.

By 1880 there were twenty-one Swedish families who had cleared land and built log cabins on the west side of the Rum River near Cambridge. Shortly thereafter they petitioned to establish a school district. School was first held in a wooden structure west of the present building. In 1898, a special $800 bond issue was approved allowing construction of the brick structure. In the early 1970s, as a result of consolidations, the West Riverside School ceased to exist, and the property was leased to the Isanti County Historical Society, which, along with the West Riverside Restoration Committee, has restored the building as it would have looked in 1900. Listed on the National Register of Historic Places, the school hosts old-time school sessions for several weeks each summer.

In the West Riverside School, children were taught for more than seventy years. Here Swedish immigrants learned English, and the community gathered for social and cultural events.

An important purpose of the rural schools was to help the Swedish immigrants learn English and to prepare them to take the examination to become American citizens. Thus a number of people over twenty-one years of age attended school. Also in these schools, from four to six weeks during the summer, "Swede Schools" were held, and Swedish and religion were taught. The rural schools were also the community center for social and cultural events.

HISTORIC PLACES

Former Residence of D. Olof Anderson (today the Carlson Funeral Home)—southwest corner of Ashland and Third Avenue.

This large white clapboard house with numerous varied gables was the home of D. Olof Anderson, one of the founding fathers of the Cambridge business community. Anderson came from Rättvik, Dalarna, in 1867. By age 23 he had enough capital to enter into a partnership for general merchandising with Hans J. Gouldberg, a fellow Swede from Dalarna.

CHURCHES

Cambridge Lutheran Church and Cemetery—621 North Main (612/689-1211).

The congregation of Cambridge Lutheran Church was organized in the log cabin of the Isak Edblad family, which had become a place for Sunday meetings. In 1868, a frame church was completed, forty feet long and twenty-six feet wide. In May 1880, the present large edifice was started, but not completed until 1884. While most churches of the time had two-tiered towers, a distinctive third tier was added to the Cambridge spire, making it unique among American Lutheran churches. It is made of heavy timber. Through the years the impressive church building has been altered several times, yet amazingly it has retained a unified composition. In the main sanctuary, the nave is original, but the chancel is a later addition. The stained glass windows are from the 1950s except for two over the rear doors, dating from the 1930s.

Inside the east entrance of the church's narthex is a granite date marker with a brief history of the church and a Swedish inscription. The most impressive feature of the narthex is the lovely pioneer window. The eight- by twelve-foot leaded stained glass window, installed in 1979, traces the history of Christianity from medieval Sweden to twentieth-century Minnesota. In the lower left-hand corner is the introduction of the faith into Sweden by St. Ansgar about A.D. 830. Then the window shows the Swedish immigration to America, including the arrival at Taylors Falls on the St. Croix River and the pioneer settlement on Rum River in Isanti County. In the upper left-hand corner is a pioneer couple walking from their cabin (it is the restored pioneer cabin near Cambridge) to the first Lutheran church located on the site marked by the Centennial Monument in the adjacent cemetery. In the bottom center of the window is the present Cambridge Lutheran Church surrounded by today's community. Christian symbols on the right depict the future. Dominating the window is a Christ figure with outstretched hands. The church also has an impressive pioneer archive with a number of unique items from the congregation's history. Because the congregation was made up largely of immigrants from Rättvik in Dalarna, Sweden, the church figures prominently in Swedish immigration studies.

The cemetery is located west of the church. The Centennial Monument was dedicated in 1964 in commemoration of the area's pioneer Swedish Lutheran immigrants. There is a monument to Peter Andersson who helped establish the Chisago Lake Lutheran Church in Chisago County. The inscription notes incorrectly that he and his family along with three other families "founded the first permanent Swedish Lutheran settlement in Minnesota, at Chisago Lake" (the first was Scandia in Washington County). In the cemetery are the graves of Isak Edblad, his wife, and daughter; Oscar Viotti, who served in the early years as the "Swede School" teacher and assistant pastor of the Cambridge congregation; and several former pastors, whose graves are located in the northwest corner.

First Baptist Church—304 Main Street South (612/689-1173). This Swedish congregation was organized in 1883 and the present church constructed in 1930.

OTHER POINTS OF INTEREST
Commissioned by the city in 1990 as a tribute to its sister city Rättvik, a Rättvik horse stands in Cambridge's City Park, one block south of State Highway 95 along the Rum River.

ISANTI

Three-quarters of a mile east of State Highway 65 on County Road 43 north of Isanti is the site of Tamarack Church, which was the first Swedish Baptist congregation in the county. The founders were from Hälsingland. The original church building was torn down in 1910, but in the present church building is a painting of the former one. South of the church site is the North Isanti Baptist Cemetery, which includes the graves of several Baptist ministers.

Nearby is an unusual design in farm architecture—Linden Barn, found 2.6 miles east of State Highway 65 on the south side of County Road 19. The large round structure is a unique landmark in Isanti County. Olof Linden who came from Sweden in 1874 constructed the barn forty years later of ten-inch concrete blocks with four-inch tile facing on the inside. The barn is on the National Register of Historic Places.

At the intersection of State Highway 65 and County Road 56 south of Isanti is the Erickson Farmstead, which was first developed by Otto Erickson who with his family came to Isanti County in 1868 from Hudiksvall, Hälsingland. His son, Edward Erickson, replaced the original farm buildings with the present ones after his farming operations prospered. The farm features a large three-story frame farmhouse, constructed in 1915, and a number of red outbuildings built between 1915 and 1930. The farmstead is associated with Isanti County's important potato-growing industry. Privately owned, the farmstead is on the National Register of Historic Places.

SPRING LAKE

The congregation of Spring Lake Lutheran Church was organized in 1874 and the present brick church built in 1942. In front of the church is Danielson Memorial Swedish Bell Tower, a replica of the bell tower at the Vextorps Church in Värnamo, Jönköpings Län. Across the road is a lovely cemetery in a wooded area with rolling terrain. Nearby is a centennial monument in the shape of a runestone.

STANCHFIELD

Stanchfield Baptist Church's modern red brick building, built in 1966, is a continuation of the Swedish Baptist congregation organized in 1866. People from Orsa, Dalarna, settled this town and the surrounding area.

BRAHAM

Rice Lake Cemetery, west of Braham near the junction of State Highway 65 and County Road 4, is particularly lovely in late June or early July when the peonies are in bloom. The cemetery has a monument near the flagpole with an inscription noting the site of the church in which the Rice Lake Swedish Lutheran congregation worshiped from 1879 until 1932, when the congregation merged with Braham Lutheran. Dr. Amandus Johnson, noted Swedish-American scholar, was confirmed in the Rice Lake church.

At 309 Beechwood is the Oscar Olson House. Constructed in 1914 by Fred Soderberg, a local pharmacist, the large clapboard house is an example of classical revival design. Oscar Olson, a prominent banker and leader of Braham, lived in the house for over fifty years. The house is on the National Register of Historic Places.

BRUNSWICK   The Immanuel Lutheran Church of Brunswick (on Route 70 east of State Highway 65) was founded in 1885. The present congregation worships in an attractive red brick, Gothic-style church built in 1920 in the west end of town.

MORA   Annually since 1973, on the second Sunday of February, Mora has hosted the Vasaloppet Cross Country Ski Race, which is patterned after the one in Mora, Dalarna. The thirty-six–mile (fifty-eight–kilometer) race is the second longest in the United States, beginning just north of Warman on State Highway 65 and ending in downtown Mora. It is open to all contestants eighteen years of age and over. Two shorter routes, one a twenty-mile (thirty-two–kilometer) race and the other a "tour," are open to those less than eighteen years of age. The "Ole" Statue represents a race participant and is a replica of a statue in Mora. In a park overlooking Lake Mora is the thirty-nine–foot bell tower, whose bell tolls to greet skiers who have completed the Vasaloppet. Nearby is the Kranskulla Statue (girl with a wreath) by which the contestants ski. The Vasaloppet headquarters is in the former railroad depot in downtown Mora.

The county courthouse at 18 North Vine Street, completed in 1894, is a historically significant brick Romanesque building. Nearby Dala horses decorate the lampposts in the business district. Also indicative of the Swedish influence in Mora is the twenty-two–foot–high, three thousand–pound replica of a *Dalahäst* presented to the community in 1972 by the Jaycees (west of State Highway 65 at the fairgrounds on Union Street).

DALBO   Built in 1910, the Dalbo Grange Hall's frame building has been the home of the Dalbo Swedish Unitarian Society and the Dalbo Church of Jesus Christ of Latter Day Saints. More recently it has served as the Dalbo township town hall. The structure is known for its good acoustics.

Salem Lutheran Church, with its central steeple, was completed in 1901 (the congregation was organized in 1874). Many of the charter members came from Venjan, Dalarna. Testimony to that heritage is found in every stained glass window—each displays a Bible verse or some other religious quotation in Swedish.

MAPLE RIDGE   The South Maple Ridge Covenant Church, a simple Gothic Revival frame building, was constructed in 1897. The unadorned interior includes original woodwork and benches. The building is no longer being used, but it is maintained by the Maple Ridge Cemetery Association and is listed on the National Register of Historic Places. The Swedish Mission Church of

The thirty-nine–foot bell tower in Mora overlooks Lake Mora, and its bell tolls to greet skiers who complete the annual Vasaloppet Cross Country Ski Race. The race is patterned after one in Sweden that commemorates Gustav Vasa's return to Sweden in 1520 to lead a rebellion against Danish oppression.

South Maple Ridge was organized in 1884 and is located just south of the intersection of County Roads 1 and 3.

NORTHEAST MINNESOTA

HINCKLEY   Opened 4 July 1976 in the old railroad depot of the St. Paul and Duluth Railroad, the Hinckley Fire Museum (612/314-7338) is dedicated to those who lost their lives in a tragic afternoon fire of 1 September 1894. The fire ravaged this part of Minnesota, destroying six villages, including Hinckley. It was one of the worst fires in history, killing 418 people, 258 in Hinckley alone. This fiery cyclone swept over central Pine County, devastating about four hundred square miles of country. A significant share of the victims were Swedish and Norwegian settlers. Probably the best eyewitness account, published in 1894 under the title

Eld-Cyklonen or Hinckley Fire, was originally written in Swedish by Gudmund Emanuel Åkermark. It was translated into English by William Johnson of Hinckley and published in 1976 by the Pine County Historical Society.

The museum is open 1 May through mid-October 10–5 daily and other times by appointment. The former men's waiting room is now the museum's reception area. In the women's waiting room is a large diorama portraying the fire. In the former freight room is a one hundred–seat auditorium featuring a fifteen-minute slide and audio presentation. A model of the old town, partially burned items, and various lumbering tools are displayed. There are posted accounts of the fire, many of which were written by Swedish pioneers. There is also a display of immigrant letters and Swedish linen.

Approximately one-quarter mile east of Interstate 35 is a large granite monument, fifty feet in height, dedicated to the memory of the 418 men, women, and children who died in the fire. The monument was dedicated in 1900. In the adjoining cemetery are a number of stones with Swedish names. Some of those Swedes buried here were victims of the fire.

KERRICK

The Louis Hultgren House on State Highway 23, southwest of the business district, was built in the mid-1890s. Hultgren was born in Sweden in 1863 and immigrated to the United States twenty-five years later. When Kerrick was a logging town on the recently constructed Eastern Minnesota Railroad line, Hultgren discovered a fine molding sand south of town while working for the railroad. In 1892 he bought land, extracted the molding sand, and began a Pine County industry that supplied foundries as far away as central Canada. The house, a private residence, is listed on the National Register of Historic Places.

AITKIN

Bethlehem Lutheran Church, off County Highway 12, is the oldest Lutheran congregation in Aitkin County that has had continuous worship services since its founding. Organized in 1891, the church was formed by Swedes from Klövsjö in Jämtland. The white Gothic-style wood church with its central steeple was built in 1897, set on more than eight acres, and paired with a cemetery. Much of the lumber was hand-hewn. In 1982, the church was placed on the National Register of Historic Places.

DULUTH

The city of Duluth and the mining area of the Mesabi Range to the northwest were settled by large numbers of Scandinavians, particularly Finns and Swedes. They began arriving in the 1850s and 1860s. An example of a Swedish immigrant who settled in this area was Carl Eric Wickman (1887–1954), the founder of the Greyhound Corporation. The nearby city of Superior, Wisconsin, also attracted Swedes. With the completion of the Northern Pacific Railroad in the mid-1880s, many Swedes came to the northern part of Minnesota to work as lumbermen. Unfortunately, there are relatively few Swedish historical landmarks that have survived from the early pioneer days.

The greatest concentration of Swedes in Duluth was in the West End. The center of the Swedish residential area with its older houses and tall trees was along West Third Street. There are a number of Swedish congregations in this section, including Bethany Lutheran Church at 2308 West Third Street (218/722-5108). It was organized in 1889, and the present sanctuary was constructed in 1903. First Covenant Church, 2101 West Second Street (218/722-5451), at the northwest corner of Twenty-first Avenue West and Second Street, and Temple Baptist, 2202 West Third Street (southwest corner of West Twenty-second Avenue and West Third Street, 218/722-4141), were also early churches. Temple Baptist, organized in 1884, is a red brick classical building with a dome over the auditorium. The cornerstone reads, "First Swedish Baptist Church AD 1910."

South of Duluth on Midway Road is the little white frame Augustana Lutheran Church and Cemetery (218/628-1306). The cornerstone notes that the "Sv. Ev. Luth. Midway Church" was organized in 1874 and built in 1917. There were also a number of Swedish settlers in the town of Cloquet, southwest of Duluth, but none of the old church buildings survive. The First Swedish Lutheran Church of Duluth (now Gloria Dei Lutheran Church, 219 North Sixth Avenue East, 218/722-3381) was organized in 1870 by the Rev. P. A. Cederstam, who was serving as a traveling missionary for the Augustana Lutheran Minnesota Conference.

In downtown Duluth in a park overlooking Lake Superior stands a statue of Leif Eriksson on London Road. The statue was erected in 1956 by the Norwegian American League of Duluth and by popular subscription.

HIBBING

Andrew G. Anderson, nicknamed "Bus Andy," was a Swedish immigrant born in 1882 who settled in this northern Minnesota community in the Mesabi Iron Range. Along with two other men, Anderson in 1914 founded a transportation service between Hibbing and Alice. The business grew, and in 1916 the Mesabi Transportation Company, the forerunner of the nationally known Greyhound Corporation, was founded. Another early Hibbing resident, Swedish American Carl Eric Wickman, is recognized as Greyhound's founder, but he later moved to Chicago. Unlike Wickman, Anderson stayed in Hibbing until his death in the mid-1960s. Erected in 1920 and listed on the National Register of Historic Places, the large two-story brick Anderson House, a combination of Georgian Revival and Spanish architecture, still stands at 1001 East Howard Street and remains a private residence. The Greyhound Bus Origin Center (Twenty-third and Fifth Avenue East) tells the bus line's history. Call the Hibbing Chamber of Commerce (218/ 262-3895) for information.

SOUTHEAST MINNESOTA

In 1853, a group of immigrants led by twenty-one–year–old Hans Mattson founded a community in Goodhue County (southeast of the present Twin Cities). It was first called the Mattson Settlement, but it was renamed Vasa in honor of Gustav Vasa. Like Hans Mattson, many of the early settlers came from northern Skåne. He was a prominent immigrant promoter of Swedes to Minnesota and founder of three Swedish-language weekly newspapers. By 1854 at least ten Swedish families were living in the Vasa community, and by 1880 almost 4,300 foreign-born Swedes lived in the county.

Southeast of Vasa are Millville (Wabasha County), where a church erected in 1874 still stands, and Houston (Houston County), where Swedish Baptist leader F. O. Nilsson is buried.

NININGER

The two-story Good Templars Hall at 9965 124th Street was constructed in 1858 by the Nininger chapter of the Independent Order of Good Templars. One year later, financial problems forced the group to sell the hall to the local school district. After serving the community as a school until 1949, the building became the town hall and later the community center. The last remaining structure from the original town, the building was placed on the National Register of Historic Landmarks in 1980.

VASA

Vasa Historic District in Vasa, southwest of Red Wing and ten miles east of Cannon Falls, is listed on the National Register of Historic Places because it has been described as "the most intact, unchanged of the original Swedish colonies of Minnesota," remaining "one of the most representative of an immigrant people from which Minnesota derives so much of its national cultural image." There are nineteen buildings dating from the nineteenth century.

At the entrance to the Vasa Swedish Lutheran Church park grounds is a plaque commemorating the 135th anniversary of Vasa's founding and the 350th anniversary of the Swedes' landing in Delaware. Early immigration promoter Hans Mattson,

Minnesota's first commissioner of immigration and a secretary of state, is recognized for outstanding public and military service (he led a company of Swedish volunteers in the Civil War). Eventually knighted by the Swedish king for his work, Dr. Eric Norelius (1833–1916) initiated many efforts in Minnesota's history. He not only worked within the church, establishing the Augustana Synod and about a dozen Lutheran churches, but also helped found Minnesota's first private children's home and first private high school, published the state's first Swedish newspaper, and helped create Gustavus Adolphus, one of the state's first colleges. Norelius settled in Vasa in 1855.

The red brick Vasa Swedish Lutheran Church with a tall wood spire and Gothic-style windows was built in 1869 and dedicated the following year. It is built on a high knoll and is the focal point of the settlement. It is the congregation's third sanctuary. Along the stone wall in front of the church are iron rings formerly used for fastening horses' reins. To the right of the church are a monument and the graves of Norelius and his wife, Inga Charlotte (1838–1924). In the adjacent cemetery are the graves of the parents of Swan J. Turnblad, the Swedish-born newspaper publisher whose former home now houses the American Swedish Institute in Minneapolis.

The sanctuary features a unique pulpit envisioned by Dr. Norelius. It has been said that he thought for some time about a suitable pulpit for the church. One night as he was sleeping, the inspiration for its design came to him in a vision. It was a closed Bible under an open one, the inside of the latter facing the pastor and the outside facing the congregation. The Vasa congregation was organized in 1855, and Norelius was its first pastor. A small log church that also served as a school was built in 1856. The second church, a frame structure, was erected in 1862, but the congregation quickly outgrew it. In 1865, the building was moved to its present location where it was first used as a schoolhouse and now serves as the Vasa Museum. From the end of May to the end of September, the museum is open Sundays 1–5.

Both the old church and the adjacent caretaker's house, while basically Greek Revival in character, have been described as containing distinctly Swedish stylistic overtones. The museum features a large collection of memorabilia, including items brought from Sweden and some made in the early days of the settlement. Built around 1877, the caretaker's house was first used as a boarding house (named the Vasa House) and later as a girls dormitory for the Vasa school.

Other landmarks in or near Vasa include the town hall, also built about 1877, which has interior benches that came from the old church and were made locally by Swedish craftsmen. The W. F. Peterson Farmstead, one-half mile south on County

Built in 1862, this building first served Vasa as a church. Later it was a schoolhouse, and now it shelters the collections of the Vasa Museum.

Road 7, is the site of the first Vasa Lutheran Church, but the building is no longer standing. It also has one of two special cabins found only in Vasa, reputedly examples of Swedish vernacular rural architecture. The Lutheran parsonage was built in 1869 of the same locally fired red brick as the Vasa Lutheran Church. The Eric Norelius House dates from approximately 1870.

The Vasa Children's Home was one of the first private institutions of its kind in Minnesota. It was begun by Norelius in 1865 when four orphan children were brought to Vasa. The original building, which was constructed in 1899, is now a private farmhouse. The home was relocated in 1926 at the junction of state highways 61 and 19, between Vasa and Red Wing (directly across the road is the farm of A. P. Anderson, the inventor of the cereals known as puffed wheat and puffed rice). The present facility is the fourth building. It is under the direction of the Lutheran Social Service of Minnesota and houses children with special learning handicaps.

In the valley known as Jemtland, south of Vasa on what is now County Road 7, some of the settlers in 1857 built their homes. In a small cemetery known as Gravbacken is a memorial stone honoring the pioneers who were laid to rest between 1859 and 1881. Other markers in the cemetery include crosses made from pipes. To get to Gravbacken drive one and one-half miles south on County Road 7 from the Vasa Lutheran Church. Take a sharp right at 315th Avenue, and drive one mile to White Rock Trail. Turn left and travel about one-half mile, past houses on either side. Gravbacken, with its unique markers, is on a knoll behind a field to the right.

Eight miles southwest of Vasa is a marker at the site of Norelius's first home near Spring Garden Lutheran Church. Over the door of the white frame church with a central steeple is the inscription, "Sw. Ev. Luth. Kyrkan Spring Garden 1876."

WELCH

Among the congregations organized by Norelius is Welch Lutheran Church (now known as Cross of Christ Lutheran), which was organized in 1873. At the corner of U.S. Highway 61 and County Road 7, the church has in its sanctuary a replica of the pulpit made by Norelius for the Vasa Lutheran Church. Other congregations organized by Norelius include the Cannon River Lutheran Church, which was organized in 1857; St. Ansgars Lutheran Church in Cannon Falls (1869); Zion Lutheran Church in Goodhue (1869), whose present congregation is the result of a merger; and the First Lutheran Church in Red Wing (1855). St. Ansgars worships in a building completed in 1970.

RED WING

The First Lutheran Church congregation in Red Wing, founded in 1855, constructed in 1895 an impressive Gothic-style building with a high steeple. The buff limestone structure, at Fifth Street and West Avenue in the historic mall district, was built on the same site as the second church. In the 1950 remodeling, a chapel was created and dedicated to Norelius's memory.

The congregation of the First Covenant Church of Red Wing, organized in 1874, now worships in a church built in 1978 at Twin Bluff Road and Pioneer. Its former church building, constructed in 1874 and 1875 at the corner of Sixth Street and West Avenue, is owned by another congregation.

MILLVILLE

The simple Swedish Evangelical Lutheran Church in Millville was built in 1874, constructed of fieldstone with Gothic-style windows. It is no longer used, but it was deeded by the Minnesota Synod of the Lutheran Church in America to the village of Millville and is maintained by the Millville Historical Association. Ask at Francis Apple's gas station for directions. The church is listed on the National Register of Historic Places.

HOUSTON

The Swede Bottom Cemetery in Houston is important in the history of Swedish Baptists because it contains the grave of F. O. Nilsson (1809–1881), early leader of the denomination. The first Swedish Baptist congregation organized in Minnesota was in Houston in 1853, but the old sanctuary no longer exists.

SOUTH MINNESOTA

Finding efforts to expand the settlement in Goodhue County difficult, Swedes who had come to Minnesota from Indiana in the summer of 1857 moved on to south-central Minnesota in search of land. They called their settlement Vista in memory of their native Småland community. Other Swedes began to arrive in Nicollet County, some fifty miles southwest of Minneapolis, in 1854, coming in covered wagons or riverboats from Illinois and Wisconsin. The first group also had its origins in Småland and settled in the farming areas south, north, and west of St. Peter, which is now a city of about nine thousand nestled on the winding Minnesota River.

NEW RICHLAND	The Vista Lutheran Church (507/465-3539) was organized as early as 1858 by Dr. Eric Norelius, but the attractive red brick Gothic-style building still standing six miles northeast of New Richland on County Road 20 was constructed in 1908. The sanctuary is unique because of the Swedish inscriptions stenciled on the walls. The church is listed on the National Register of Historic Places. One-quarter mile west of Vista Lutheran are two cemeteries—Lutheran and Covenant—on either side of the road. Just west of the cemeteries is the Vista Evangelical Covenant Church (507/465-8365), which was organized in 1876. The members of this church constructed the present sanctuary in 1964.
MANKATO	Born in Värmland in 1870 and an immigrant to the United States in 1882, Adolph Olson Eberhart was an early twentieth-century public servant. His house, at 228 East Pleasant Street, remains a private residence. The two and one-half–story Georgian Revival structure, built around 1903, is distinctive in its irregular roofline featuring attic dormers and Palladian windows and in its open-entrance porch. The house is listed on the National Register of Historic Places. A Blue Earth County resident, Eberhart was a state senator (1901–06), lieutenant governor (1906–09), and governor (1909–15). He was a student at Gustavus Adolphus College in St. Peter before coming to Mankato in 1895 to study law.
ST. PETER	In 1857, a Swedish Lutheran congregation was established in St. Peter (the present church—First Lutheran—was built in 1965 at 1114 West Traverse Road at Sunrise Drive, 507/931-3060). One of the first Swedes to settle just north of St. Peter was Gustaf Johnson of southern Östergötland. His son, John A. Johnson, was governor of Minnesota from 1905 to 1909.

SCHOOLS

Gustavus Adolphus College—800 West College Avenue (507/933-8000).

The Swedish Lutherans in Minnesota began a school in Red Wing in 1862. In the following year, it was moved to East Union, Carver County, and renamed St. Ansgar's Academy. In October 1876, the school opened in St. Peter under its present name. This liberal arts institution has grown to more than 2,300 students and a faculty of about 160. Situated on a hill on the west end of St. Peter, the lovely campus has a number of buildings and historical markers underscoring its Swedish heritage.

Near the center of campus is a bust of Gustavus Adolphus (1594–1632), the Swedish king and defender of Lutheranism, which was unveiled 6 November 1932 on thethree hundredth anniversary of his death at the Battle of Lützen. Nearby is Old Main. This stone building, dating from 1876, is the oldest structure on the campus, and it has been placed on the National Register of Historic Places. Near the front of Old Main is the millstone used in the mill at East Union, Carver County, from 1865 to 1875 as a means of support of St. Ansgar's Academy.

The modern Folke Bernadotte Memorial Library (507/933-7556), opened in 1972, has a picture and plaque of Count Folke Bernadotte (1895–1948) near the information desk. On the third floor of the library are the archives of the college and

Old Main, dating from 1876, is the oldest structure on the 255-acre Gustavus Adolphus College campus. Swedish Lutheran immigrants founded the school in 1862.

the Minnesota Synod of what was formerly the Lutheran Church in America.

The Nobel Hall of Science was dedicated in 1963 in honor of Alfred Nobel by Dr. Glenn T. Seaborg, then chairman of the U.S. Atomic Energy Commission and the 1951 cowinner of the Nobel Prize in Chemistry (Seaborg's Swedish parents immigrated to Ishpeming, Michigan, and then to California). Also present at the 1963 dedication were twenty-seven other Nobel prize winners. In the lobby is a Foucault pendulum and four panels with a summary of Alfred Nobel's life, its significance, and an excerpt from his will. Each fall the college hosts the Nobel Conference, attended by many world-famous scholars.

In the lobby of the Jussi Björling Recital Hall is a bust of the renowned Swedish operatic tenor to whom the hall is dedicated. There is also a photograph of Björling (1911–60) and a poem by Swedish poet Bo Setterlind (1923–91). The Björling Recital Hall is part of the Schaefer Fine Arts Complex, which includes the Anderson Theater named in honor of Evan Anderson (1892–1969), professor of speech, and his wife, Evelyn, associate professor of speech and director of the theater.

Dedicated in 1962, Christ Chapel is an impressive modern structure in the center of the campus with a soaring spire 187 feet high and a seating capacity of twelve hundred. In the narthex are plaques honoring P. A. Mattson, who served as president 1904–11, and O. J. Johnson, president 1913–42.

Throughout the campus are various sculptures by artist-in-residence Paul Granlund. The son of a Lutheran pastor, Granlund (b. 1925) has cast nearly six hundred bronze sculptures for public spaces in the United States and in international cities, including Hong Kong and Paris. Those on campus include "Masks of the Muses" outside the Anderson Theater, "Sonata" in the lobby of the Jussi Björling Recital Hall, "Luna Moth Matrix" east of Christ Chapel, "Palindrome" west of Christ Chapel, "Apogee" near the Carlson Administration Building, a bust of Linnaeus at the arboretum, and various sculptures and friezes in Christ Chapel representing the history of the church. The artist's studio is located in Schaefer Fine Arts Center.

Within Minnesota, other selected Granlund works include the following: in LeSueur, "The Mothers Louise," located in a small park adjacent to the W. W. Mayo House (North Main Street); in Minneapolis, "Sprites," in the main building of Hennepin County Medical Center's Medical Specialty Center; also in Minneapolis, "Birth of Freedom," in front of Westminster Presbyterian Church (Nicollet Mall at Twelfth Street South); in St. Paul, "Anthrosphere," at the World Trade Center; in Faribault, "Adolescence," at the Constance Bultman Wilson Center; and in Northfield, two works at St. Olaf College.

Other Gustavus Adolphus College buildings honoring Swedish Americans include the Carlson Administration Building, named for Edgar Carlson, president from 1944 to 1968; the Lund Ice Arena and Lund Physical Education Center, named for Minnesota grocer Russell T. Lund and his first and second wives; Norelius Hall, a student residence hall named for the college's founder, Eric Norelius (1833–1916); Rundstrom Hall, named for Inez Rundstrom (1869–1953), the first woman graduate of Augustana College, Rock Island, Illinois, and a professor of mathematics at Gustavus Adolphus for forty-eight years; Edwin J. Vickner Hall, named for the linguist and Scandinavian scholar (1878–1958); Matthias Wahlstrom Hall, named for the college's fifth president (1881–1904); Johnson Student Union, built as a gymnasium in 1921 and dedicated to the college's seventh president, Oscar J. Johnson, in 1987; and the arboretum's Melva Lind Interpretive Center, named for a former women's dean.

The Linnaeus Arboretum, a 135-acre tract of trees with a formal garden, prairie areas, and an interpretive center, was created under the leadership of Biology Professor Charles Mason and in honor of the Swedish immigrants who in 1862 founded Gustavus Adolphus. The arboretum was initiated with the planting of five thousand trees in 1974 and named for Swedish botanist Carl von Linné, who is responsible for the binomial biological nomenclature used today. Set in the arboretum is an example of Swedish folk architecture, the pioneer home of the Carl J. and Clara C. Borgeson family, who came from Sweden and settled in Minnesota. Made with twenty-five–foot white oak logs held in place by dovetail notching, the cabin has a single room with a narrow staircase leading to a sleeping loft, a plan typical of the Swedish *stuga*. It was built in the 1860s or 1870s and originally located in Norseland.

In addition to the Nobel conference mentioned above, the college annually sponsors the Bernadotte Institute on World Affairs and the Raoul Wallenberg Lecture. Gustavus Adolphus was the first American school of higher education to confer a degree on Wallenberg in absentia. Scandinavian studies are a formal program of academic study within the curriculum.

HISTORIC PLACES
John Albert Johnson (1861–1909) was governor of Minnesota between 1905 and 1909 and widely regarded as the likely Democratic nominee for president in 1912 (he died in 1909 in his third term as governor). He was born near St. Peter in 1861. In front of the Nicollet County Courthouse (507/931-6800) stands a statue of Johnson. The Johnson House, listed on the National Register of Historic Places, may be found at 418 North

Third Street (private residence). His grave is in the southeast quadrant of the Klein Cemetery off Sunrise Drive. Citizens have named the highway leading into St. Peter from the north the John A. Johnson Memorial Highway.

In 1855, twelve miles northwest of St. Peter on State Highway 22, several Swedish families bought land and called the place Scandian Grove. Three years later, the Rev. P. A. Cederstam from Chisago Lake presided at the organizing of the Scandian Grove Lutheran Church (507/246-5195). A sanctuary was built in 1888 and preserved for ninety years, but a fire destroyed it in 1978. A new church has been built on the same site. In the sanctuary is the old baptismal font, and in the library are two walls made from brick of the former church, some of which bear marks from the fire.

In the adjacent church park is the log house built in 1855 by Andrew Thorson, a leader of the Scandian Grove community and one instrumental in persuading Lutheran church leaders to relocate Gustavus Adolphus College to St. Peter. It was in his house that the Scandian Grove Lutheran congregation was organized. The cabin was moved to the park in 1952 and dedicated as the congregation's Pioneer Building. In the nearby cemetery are the graves of five church pastors.

BERNADOTTE

The red brick Gothic-style Bernadotte Evangelical Lutheran Church on County Road 10 five miles east of Lafayette (507/228-8380) was built in 1897 (the congregation was organized in 1866). In front of the church and to the left is a Bicentennial plaque presenting a brief history of the church and explaining the origin of the name Bernadotte, which the town took to honor the ruling house in Sweden. The family derived from Jean-Baptiste Bernadotte (1763–1844), one of Napoleon Bonaparte's field marshals, who after election as crown prince by the Riksdag, adopted the Lutheran faith and became known as Karl XIV Johan. The town was originally called New Sweden.

In the church basement is a framed telegram from King Gustav VI Adolf and a letter from the king's secretary on the one hundredth anniversary of the founding of the congregation. In a glass case is a leather-bound book on the life of Gustav V presented in 1933 on the visit of Count Folke Bernadotte. A descendant of Jean-Baptiste Bernadotte, Count Folke Bernadotte (1895–1948) was leader of the Swedish Red Cross and served as a Swedish diplomat. During his appointment by the United Nations to help mediate the Palestinian conflict between Arabs and Jews, he was assassinated in Jerusalem.

GIBBON

Organized in 1871, the Clear Lake Lutheran Church built a Gothic-style white frame place of worship in 1890. About four years later, the congregation merged with the Augustana Lutheran Church in Gibbon, located about five miles north. The old sanctuary now belongs to the Clear Lake Cemetery Association and is used for one service a year, usually near midsummer. Down the road to the west is the Clear Lake Baptist Church, which was also organized in 1871. Its sanctuary formerly belonged to a German Methodist congregation and was moved to its present site in 1934.

NEW ULM

John Lind (1854–1930) was born in southern Småland and came to the United States in 1868 with his parents. He was the first man of Swedish birth to be elected to the U.S. Congress (he served three terms, 1887–1893), and he was governor of Minnesota from 1899 to 1901. In 1902 he was elected to a fourth term in Congress and served after reelection until 1905. At the corner of North State and Center streets, at 622 Center Street, Lind built a Queen Anne–style mansion, constructed primarily of local red brick, in 1887. It is owned by the Lind House Association, which opens it 1–4 Monday through Friday and by special arrangement (507/354-8802). The house is listed on the National Register of Historic Places.

LAKE BENTON

In this southwestern Minnesota community is the Ernest Osbeck House (106 South Fremont), which is listed on the National Register of Historic Places. Osbeck, born in Alvesta, Sweden, in 1859, arrived in Lake Benton in 1884 and helped organize the Lake Benton Co-op Creamery Association, the local bank, and the Lake Benton Opera House. His home, built in 1887 in the Queen Anne style, remains a private residence.

CENTRAL MINNESOTA

The first Swedes came to the area west of the Twin Cities in 1854 by flatboats on the Minnesota River (see map, page 224). They founded King Oscar's Settlement in the southeastern part of Carver County, which later divided into the East Union and West Union settlements. The following summer, a party of sixteen people from central Västergötland arrived. In 1858, a Lutheran congregation was founded that divided in the same year into the East Union and West Union parishes. In northern Carver County, two miles south of Watertown (directly west of Minneapolis and St. Paul), a group of Swedes named their community Götaholm. In between these northern and southern sites, Swedish Baptists settled around Lake Waconia, having come from Burlington, Iowa, and Galesburg, Illinois, in 1855. This colony was called Scandia.

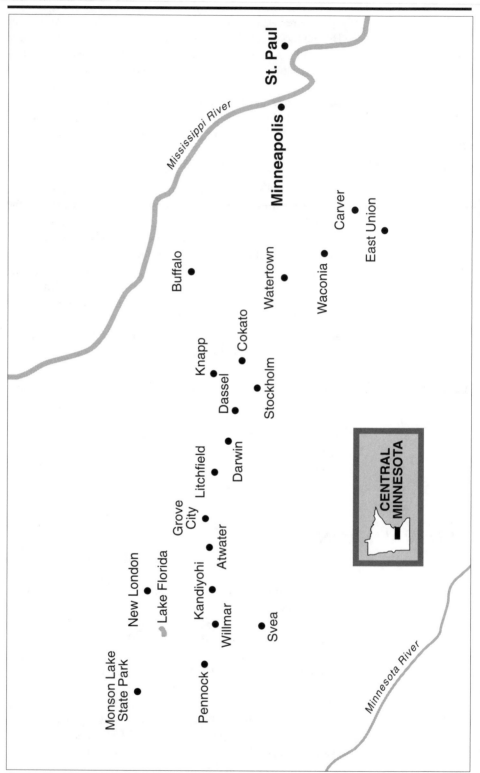

St. Paul

Mississippi River

Minneapolis

Carver

East Union

Buffalo

Watertown

Waconia

Cokato

Knapp

Stockholm

Dassel

Darwin

Litchfield

Grove City

Atwater

New London

Lake Florida

Kandiyohi

Willmar

Svea

Monson Lake State Park

Pennock

Minnesota River

CENTRAL MINNESOTA

Swedish settlement west of the Twin Cities in Wright, Meeker, Kandiyohi, and Swift counties came in the 1850s and 1860s. Most of the early Swedish settlers who initially arrived in Wright County in 1862 came from parishes in western Värmland. The first Swedes settled in the present-day town of Buffalo in the center of the county. In the late 1860s, Cokato and Stockholm in southwest Wright County became Swedish centers. The Rev. John S. Nilson of the Götaholm (Watertown) congregation organized the earliest Swedish Lutheran churches in this county, including Stockholm Lutheran in 1866; Carlslund (now the Zion Lutheran Church, Buffalo) in late 1866; and Swedesburg (which later merged with Zion in Buffalo) in 1873.

Swedes began arriving in Meeker County, west of Wright County, in 1856. Both Eric Norelius and Peter Magnus Johnson, a Methodist minister, preached in the area in 1861. After 1869, the year the St. Paul and Pacific Railroad was built through Meeker County, Swedish congregations were established in several communities, including Dassel, Swan Lake, Beckville, Ostmark, Litchfield, and Grove City (formerly Swede Grove)—all built near the tracks.

The railroad not only meant that people and goods would come in but also that an employer—the railroad—was ready at hand. Hans Mattson, who had helped settle Vasa and who from 1866 to 1871 was a promoter of immigration for Minnesota and a land agent for the railroad, was instrumental in bringing Swedes into these central Minnesota counties. The railroad traced the line at the interface of two regions, the prairie and the timberlands.

EAST UNION

East Union Lutheran Church, Cemetery, and Parish Hall at 15180 County Road 40 (612/448-4591) form an attractive church facility located about three and one-half miles southwest of Carver. The brick church with a central steeple and green shutters on Gothic-style windows was built in 1866, though the congregation was organized eight years earlier. The church welcomes guests with a stone plaque over the front door bearing a Swedish inscription. The sanctuary has a raised canopied pulpit. In the narthex are portraits of all the former pastors, including Pehr Carlson, the congregation's founder. The Salem Lutheran congregation, which once thrived in downtown Carver but dissolved in 1952, placed the bell from its church in front of East Union.

The cream-colored clapboard East Union Parish Hall has a sign over the front door noting that it was the pioneer building of the Union Settlement church (1856–66) and St. Ansgar's Academy (1863–76), forerunner of Gustavus Adolphus College. The East Union congregation purchased the St. Ansgar school property in 1883 and renovated the old building into a parish hall. It is probably the oldest building of the Minnesota Conference of the former Augustana Synod, dating to the pre–Civil War period.

CARVER

The West Union Lutheran Church, founded about six months after East Union Lutheran Church so that churchgoers in this part of the settlement would not have to travel so far to worship, stands at 15820 Market Avenue at its intersection with County Road 50 (612/466-5678). (Take County Road 40 south out of Carver, and then go west at County Road 50.) The church's cemetery lies beside it in a lovely wooded rise above the cornfields. To the right of a tree-lined path leading to the church is the original parish hall built in 1904. A new parish hall was constructed in 1960. The sanctuary was built in 1868, and the spire was added in 1871. The church was beautifully remodeled in 1973, its ceiling and walls covered with attractive light wood, giving the effect of an inverted ship's hull. Graves in the cemetery date from 1858.

WACONIA

On the northeast shore of Lake Waconia was a settlement called Scandia, near the present-day town of Waconia. Andrew Peterson (1818–98) was one of the first settlers (most came from Iowa); by 1860 there were some thirty families in the area. Peterson was a careful horticulturist and researcher, and had a farm, now identified as the Andrew Peterson, or Rock Isle, Farmstead, which has been included on the National Register of Historic Places.

The Swedes at Scandia organized a Baptist congregation in 1855 in Peterson's log house, and a log church was built in 1857. In the early 1970s, it was moved to the Bethel College campus near St. Paul. The Scandia Baptist Cemetery where Peterson is buried is directly across the road from the former site of the Scandia Baptist Church. That site is now part of the Island View Country Club.

WATERTOWN

The community at Swede Lake was for many years called Götaholm, but today it is part of Watertown township. In December 1858 the settlers organized a Lutheran congregation. A small church was built near Swede Lake in 1859 and was used until 1870, when a new sanctuary was constructed in Watertown, two and a half miles farther north. A third church was built in 1890 and the present structure in 1950. In 1948 the church's name was changed to Trinity Lutheran (612/955-1891). A monument on County Road 10 marks the site of the original church. Behind the marker are a few gravestones.

BUFFALO

Near Buffalo is the Marysville "Swedesburg" Lutheran Church. The red brick building with Gothic-style clear windows and a dark wood steeple was built in 1891 and is listed on the National Register of Historic Places. The congregation merged with Zion Lutheran in Buffalo (1200 South Highway 25, 612/682-1245), and the last regular Sunday service was held in 1950. However, during the summer season, meetings are held Monday evenings in the old church. The sanctuary contains the old furnishings.

KNAPP

Five miles north of Cokato and one and one-half miles west of County Road 3 is the North Crow River Lutheran Church (612/286-2354). With Gothic-style windows and a central bell tower, the church bears the inscription, "Sw. Ev. Luth. Church North Crow River 1903." The congregation was organized thirty-three years earlier. In the adjacent cemetery is a granite stone with an inscription to the pioneers. In the nearby community of South Haven is Grace Lutheran Church and a Swedish cemetery, founded 1890, at County Road 37 and County Road 2.

COKATO

At the Cokato Museum at Fourth and Millard (612/286-2427) (open 9–4:30 Monday through Friday) "To a New Land . . . a New Life" features various memorabilia of the Swedish immigrants. An interpretive exhibit explains the settling of Cokato. In the museum is a restored eighteen– by twenty-four–foot log cabin (three sides have been reconstructed) built by Nils Lans. Lans had been an officer in the Swedish army before he emigrated to America, where he served during the Civil War and homesteaded south of Cokato. This cabin was moved in 1940 to Peterson Park across the street from the museum where it served as a warming house in the winter. When the museum was built in 1976, the cabin was moved log by log to its present location. The fourth side of the cabin is open so that visitors may see the furnished interior containing numerous artifacts donated by area Swedes.

Displayed in the museum are a spinning wheel and loom, farming tools, and surveying equipment. Exhibits feature old Cokato shops, a turn-of-the-century house, and a school. There is also a display of the Swedish and Finnish *psalmodikon*—a stringed musical instrument.

Also owned by the Cokato Historical Society and adjacent to the Cokato Museum is the Gust Akerlund Photography Studio, 390 Broadway Avenue at Fourth. It is a simple single-story wood frame building that combines the photography studio and a residence. It was constructed in 1905 and remains relatively unaltered. It is listed on the National Register of

Historic Places. Gust Akerlund was born in Sweden and came to this country as a young man, first living in Wisconsin. He arrived in Cokato in 1902, purchased a photography studio, and went into business.

STOCKHOLM

About four miles southwest of Cokato is Stockholm and the Stockholm Lutheran Church and Cemetery. The area, originally called Mooers Prairie, was settled by Swedes in 1862, the first having arrived from Kandiyohi County after being driven from that county by the Dakota (Sioux) Indian uprising of that year.

When the township was organized in 1868, it acquired the name Stockholm. The Stockholm Lutheran congregation was the first church in the county, organized in 1866. Built in 1876, the interior has been modernized; the exterior is faced with light and dark bricks. On the steeple is the inscription, "Sw. Ev. Lutheran." To the west of the church is a Swedish cemetery; another one is on the other side of the road to the east.

DASSEL

Gethsemane Lutheran Church (formerly First Lutheran), 211 East Atlantic Avenue (612/275-3852), was organized in 1873, and the present Gothic-style brick church with bell tower was built in 1886. The sanctuary has a raised canopied pulpit. A three-crown motif has recently been stenciled near the ceiling.

Seven and one-half miles north of Dassel is a small white frame church, built in 1899 by a congregation organized in 1873 and called Swan Lake Lutheran Church. Although the sanctuary was sold in about 1985 to the Finnish Old Apostolic Lutheran congregation, the old cemetery is still owned by Gethsemane Lutheran in Dassel.

DARWIN

North of Darwin is the congregation of the Ostmark Lutheran Church (32721 680th Avenue, 612/693-8450), now within the boundaries of Watkins, which was organized in 1894 and the white clapboard church built in 1911.

About five or six miles south of Darwin is Lake Jennie Covenant Church and Cemetery. The congregation was organized in 1886 and the white frame church built in 1921.

LITCHFIELD

Trinity Episcopal Church, at Sibley Avenue North and Fourth Street (612/693-6035) was built of vertical board and batten construction in 1871 and has been placed on the National Register of Historic Places. It began as an American Episcopal church. Its second rector became interested in the Swedish people in the community and learned the Swedish language in order to hold services for them. He organized a Swedish Mission, later known as Emmanuel Church. In 1929, the two parishes merged. The old altar in Trinity Episcopal is from the former Emmanuel Church. Nearby is the Meeker County Historical Society (308 North Marshall Avenue, 612/693-8911), which displays a collection of artifacts from pioneer days. One mile south of town on State Highway 22 is the Litchfield Cemetery.

Also seven miles south of Litchfield at 20521 600th Avenue is Beckville Lutheran Church and Cemetery (612/693-2519). A white frame church with a bell tower built in 1901, the building is on a gravel road that can be reached by going south from Litchfield on State Highway 22 for 5.6 miles, traveling west on County Road 28 for 2.5 miles, and then turning north on the gravel road. The congregation was organized in 1869. At the bottom of the stairwell to the lower level is a glass case with former communion vessels and early church documents. Bishop Herbert Chilstrom, who was baptized in this church, was named the first national bishop of the Evangelical Lutheran Church in America (a denomination formed in 1988 by the merger of the American Lutheran Church, the Lutheran Church in America, and the Association of Evangelical Lutheran Churches). Bishop Chilstrom, born in 1931 in Litchfield, is a third-generation Swedish American.

GROVE CITY

Originally called Swede Grove, Grove City is home to Trinity Lutheran Church at 54384 Highway 12 (612/857-2001), which has the date 1922 on its cornerstone. Originally called First Evangelical Lutheran, Trinity was formed from a merger of Immanuel and Amdahl Lutheran churches.

ATWATER

Immanuel Lutheran Church at 300 Third Street South (612/974-8695) was organized in 1868. The white frame church has Gothic-style windows and a central steeple and dates from 1876.

KANDIYOHI

Two and one-half miles south of Kandiyohi stands Tripolis Evangelical Lutheran Church and Cemetery, 3249 County Road 8 SE (612/382-6264). This is a white frame church, built in 1881, with a central steeple and Gothic-style windows. This congregation was organized in 1868. In Kandiyohi itself on Atlantic Avenue is Ebenezer Evangelical Lutheran Church (612/382-6264), a white frame structure, built in 1907, originally as a chapel of Tripolis Lutheran.

WILLMAR

One-half mile north of downtown Willmar at 610 U.S. Highway 71 is the Kandiyohi County Museum (612/235-1881). The museum contains an interesting and very comprehensive collection of early immigrant artifacts portraying the prairie life of the settlers. The displays are not sorted according to ethnicity, though Norwegians and Swedes are predominant in the county. A two-day Willmar Fest, featuring home-baked cakes and cookies, takes place annually in June.

SVEA

Another old Swedish congregation is Svea Lutheran in Svea, about eight miles from Willmar. Organized in 1870, the congregation built its present sanctuary in 1920. Adjacent to the church is an old cemetery.

PENNOCK

According to Lena A:son-Palmqvist in an unpublished study, "Building Traditions among Swedish Settlers in Rural Minnesota," the best preserved rural "Swedish" church in Kandiyohi County is the old Mamrelund Lutheran Church (612/599-4548). The congregation was organized in 1869; the first two buildings were destroyed by fire and storm. In 1883 the present old Mamrelund Lutheran church was erected on Seventy-fifth Avenue about four miles north of the town of Pennock. (To reach the church, take Kandiyohi County Road 1 north 3.4 miles. Turn east on a gravel road, travel less than one-half mile [a lake is on the right], and then turn south on another gravel road. The church is on the west side.) In 1915, a church in town was built, but the congregation decided to maintain the country church. It still uses the church for three special summer services and one Christmas service.

The sanctuary in this wonderful old church still has the original elaborately designed wall stenciling. In the chancel are Gothic-style windows. In the center the empty cross is depicted; below the cross is the inscription, *"Se Guds Lamm"* ("Behold the Lamb of God"). There are other Swedish inscriptions stenciled on the walls to the left and right of the altar. Over the back door is the quotation from Luke 11:28: *"Saliga äro de som höra Guds ord och gömma det"* ("Blessed are they that hear the word of God, and keep it").

Three miles north of Mamrelund Lutheran Church is the Lundby Covenant Cemetery, maintained by the Salem Covenant Church. (To reach the cemetery, go north four miles on County Road 1. Turn east on County Road 27, travel 2.1 miles, and then turn north on a gravel road, on which the cemetery rests on the east side one-half mile north.) Salem Covenant (612/599-4574) is the oldest existing congregation of the Evangelical Covenant Church of America in Minnesota. Although the congregation worships in a new red brick church built in 1968, the cornerstone notes that the church dates from 1871. It formerly met in a building that stood next to the Lundby Covenant Cemetery.

LAKE FLORIDA   The Lake Florida Covenant Church was organized in 1870 as a Lutheran congregation known as the Swedish Evangelical Lutheran Church of Norway Lake. The small white frame building, located near Lake Florida on County Road 29, one and one-half miles east of County Road 5, and about ten miles from Willmar, was built between 1873 and 1876. In 1879, the congregation voted to leave the Augustana Synod and affiliate with the Mission Friends, becoming one of the earliest Covenant parishes in Minnesota. It served as a parish church until 1955 but now is owned and maintained by a private association of local citizens. A special service is held once a year on the first Sunday in August. The interior has been nicely restored and contains many old furnishings. From 1890 to 1907, the Rev. Nils Frykman, also known as a hymn writer, served as pastor to this church and three other central Minnesota congregations.

NEW LONDON   The former Lebanon Lutheran Church was the oldest congregation in Kandiyohi County, having been organized in 1859 as the New Sweden congregation in a log cabin of one of the early Swedish settlers. In 1865, this congregation, known as the Nest Lake Church, was reorganized after the fighting against the Dakota (Sioux) Indians had ended. In 1896, the name of the congregation was changed to Lebanon. The third church building of the congregation, which presently houses the Monongalia Historical Society and Museum (612/354-2990), was constructed in 1873. It is a white frame neo-Gothic building, and it is open 1–5 Thursday, Friday, and Sunday and 10–5 Saturday.

In the former church sanctuary is an altar painting completed in 1901 by Olof Grafström (1855–1933). Also displayed are various furnishings of the old church. In the balcony are memorabilia from the former Trinity Lutheran Church, New London. (This was a Norwegian congregation that merged with Lebanon Lutheran to form the present Peace Lutheran Church. The sanctuary is located on the other side of the adjoining cemetery—see below.)

The West Lake Massacre Historical Inclosure at Peace Lutheran Church Cemetery in New London includes the memorial markers to the victims of the 20 August 1862 Dakota (Sioux) Indian massacre. Visitors first notice the tall metal Broberg-Lundborg Monument listing the thirteen people, all members of the New Sweden Church, who were killed by the Dakota (Sioux) Indians near West Lake while on their way home from a religious meeting held at the home of Andreas Lundborg. The monument was erected 20 August 1891 by a special act of the Minnesota Legislature. The remains of the settlers were removed from West Lake (today called Monson Lake) in June 1891 and now rest where this memorial is erected.

The inclosure contains plaques describing the tragic event, based on the eyewitness story of Anna Stina Broberg, the lone survivor, as related to Victor E. Lawson, Kandiyohi County historian.

MONSON LAKE STATE PARK

Two historic markers note the location where members of the Anders P. and Daniel P. Broberg and Andreas L. Lundborg families were killed during the 1862 Dakota (Sioux) uprising. Beyond one stone marker are two depressions where the original settlers' dugouts were located. Every other August, the park holds a ceremony to commemorate those lost in the massacre.

Visitors may obtain a pamphlet entitled "Historical Sites in Kandiyohi County" from the Kandiyohi County Museum in Willmar. The pamphlet lists, locates, and explains additional markers in the county relating to the events of August 1862. Mainly Norwegian and Swedish pioneers were victims of the uprising in Kandiyohi County.

NORTH-CENTRAL MINNESOTA

North-central Minnesota's Morrison County attracted numerous Swedes who settled down to farming and lumbering. Here the most famous Swedish name was Lindbergh.

West of Morrison County is Douglas County, where land seekers began arriving in 1863 as a result of the newly enacted Homestead Act. In 1878, the first railroad came to Alexandria, the county seat. Some Swedish settlements prospered in the county, particularly in the Holmes City–Lake Oscar area. The county has declared itself the "Birthplace of America," referring to the 1898 discovery of the Kensington Runestone, whose authenticity is dismissed by most scholars, on the farm of Olof Ohman, an early Swedish settler.

Otter Tail County was established in 1858, and Swedish immigrants began arriving in the 1870s when the railroad was built. Swedish Lutheran churches were established in Fergus Falls, Christine Lake, Battle Lake, Henning, Eagle Lake, and Parkers Prairie. In Fergus Falls a Swedish Baptist congregation was organized.

LITTLE FALLS

The Charles A. Lindbergh House at 1200 Lindbergh Drive South (612/632-3154) welcomes visitors from May through October. From 1 May through Labor Day, the site is open all week (10–5 Monday through Saturday and 12–5 Sunday). In September and October, visitors may come only on Saturdays (10–4) and Sundays (12–4). Call the house for information about guided tours.

The Charles A. Lindbergh House, completed in 1906, in Little Falls was where Charles Lindbergh, Jr., spent his boyhood summers. His father, an attorney, served in the U.S. Congress 1907 to 1917.

The house built by Charles Lindbergh, Sr., is set near the banks of the Mississippi River on over one hundred acres of land he bought in 1898. It replaced a three-story thirteen-room house he had built that was lost in a fire. Though simpler in style than the first, the present house is built on the same foundations. Used primarily as a summer home, the house is where Charles Lindbergh, Jr., spent his boyhood summers. After 1924, the Lindbergh family rarely used the house, and in 1931, the family donated it to the state of Minnesota, which designated the site a state park. The Minnesota Historical Society has restored the house as closely as possible to its earlier appearance and has constructed a history center nearby to tell the story of the Lindbergh family. It is listed on the National Register of Historic Places.

Dedicated in 1973, the history center introduces the Lindberghs with a brief film, which is shown in an auditorium that shares the ground floor with a bookstore. The family tree decorates a wall next to the ramp to the second floor, where memorabilia of both father and son are exhibited. On the third floor one can listen to voice recordings of Charles Lindbergh, Jr.

Ola Månsson (1808–1893), grandfather of Charles Lindbergh, Jr., had a farm near Simrishamn, Skåne. He also was a member of the Riksdag before he immigrated to America in 1860. The family homesteaded near Melrose, Minnesota, and Månsson began identifying himself as August Lindbergh, the surname having been previously adopted by a brother in Sweden. Månsson's son, Charles August Lindbergh (1858–1924), attended the University of Michigan Law School and practiced law in Little Falls. He was a Republican member of the U.S. Congress from 1907 to 1917 and was nominated for governor of Minnesota on the Farmer-Labor ticket in 1924, but he died during the campaign. He requested that no grave marker be erected in his memory.

Charles A. Lindbergh, Jr. (1902–74), attended high school in Little Falls, graduating in 1918. He spent two years running his father's farm and then went on to the University of Wisconsin to study civil engineering. But he dropped out during his sophomore year to enter a flying school in Lincoln, Nebraska. After being a pilot for an airmail line, Lindbergh decided to try for the $25,000 Orteig Prize for the first nonstop New York–France flight. Financed by a group of St. Louis businessmen, Lindbergh helped design a plane—the *Spirit of St. Louis*—which was used in the historic 20–21 May 1927 flight.

The Charles A. Lindbergh House contains furniture and other articles contributed by the Lindbergh family. In the rear of the house, toward the Mississippi River, is a lovely garden. Along the garden path is a plaque noting that the 110-acre park was a gift from members of the Lindbergh family in honor of the memory of Charles Lindbergh, Sr. Below the house can be seen the rock foundations of the original house.

NELSON

The impressive Fahlun Lutheran Church (612/762-0140), a white frame rural church with a tall steeple, has the inscription "*Sv. Ev. Luth. Fahlun Kyrka*" on the stained glass window above the main door. The sanctuary has an altar painting (1909) by Grafström and various symbolic stained glass windows with Swedish inscriptions. The church lies two miles north and one mile east of Nelson.

ALEXANDRIA

In front of the Douglas County Courthouse may be found a plaque honoring Theodore A. Erickson (1871–1963), who was Douglas County Superintendent of Schools 1907–15 and founder of the 4-H movement in Minnesota.

Another plaque outside the Calvary Evangelical Lutheran Church at 605 Douglas was dedicated in 1977 to commemorate the one hundredth anniversary of the founding of the Svea

Swedish Evangelical Lutheran congregation by six Swedish couples. Although the church's current building dates from the 1950s, a stained glass window is among items taken from the first church built in the 1880s that are now displayed in the church's library lounge. Likewise, the altar and baptismal font from the 1909 church are in the chapel. The church changed its name in 1948.

In the Runestone Museum (206 Broadway, open 9–5 Monday through Saturday and 12–5 Sunday) can be seen the Kensington "runestone." Above the display is a map showing the alleged route taken by the Scandinavians in 1362. Other displays include "Viking" memorabilia that have been excavated, including a battle axe found near Mora in 1933. One mile east of the Runestone Museum, where U.S. Highway 52 and Sixth Avenue merge, is a large replica of the Kensington runestone, erected in 1951 by the local Kiwanis Club. Near the museum is a twenty-eight–foot Viking statue, weighing twelve thousand pounds, which the town claims to be the world's largest Viking statue. It should be noted that the town of Alexandria emphasizes the Kensington runestone to attract tourists. The claim that Nordic people visited Minnesota in the fourteenth century has been disputed by most scholars.

About 15 miles west of Alexandria in Runestone Park (Ohman Farm), just south of State Highway 27, is a plaque identifying the site where the Viking runestone was found in 1898. Upon entering Runestone Park, the Olof Ohman white frame farmhouse can be seen as well as a barn displaying pictures of Ohman and various newspaper clippings describing the discovery. The park was dedicated in 1973. The road from Fergus Falls to Sauk Center is identified as Viking Trail.

HOLMES CITY

In the small village of Holmes City is the former Swedish Baptist Church, now the town hall; a mill; and the remains of an old blacksmith shop and a creamery. The congregation of the Trinity Lutheran Church (612/886-5532), which merged with Oscar Lake Lutheran Church, was organized in 1875. The town cemetery is on the north side of State Highway 27.

OSCAR LAKE

About three miles west of Holmes City is Oscar Lake, where the Oscar Lake Lutheran Church is located near the lake named in honor of King Oscar II. The white frame church and steeple were built in 1884. The congregation, which merged with Trinity Lutheran of Holmes City, was organized in 1866, making it the oldest Swedish Lutheran church in the Red River Valley. The sanctuary has been modernized, but some of the old furnishings have been retained. A cemetery south of the church contains the graves of some of the first settlers in the area who came in the 1860s.

Almost two miles north and two miles west of Kensington is the cemetery of Wennersborg Lutheran Church, where a large stone with a plaque commemorates this historic church built in 1880 but destroyed by fire in 1948.

HOFFMAN

The Elk Lake Pioneer Cemetery, dating from 1870, was one of the first burial grounds in Grant County. A plaque in the small cemetery explains that in 1872 residents of the Elk Lake Township built a schoolhouse and the following year the Rev. Laurits Carlson organized Grant County's first religious congregation.

FERGUS FALLS

In 1900, local Swedish Lutherans founded Northwestern College at 420 Alcott Avenue East. It existed for thirty-two years (closed in 1932 for financial reasons) as an academy and business school; it never became a four-year college. Some fifteen hundred individuals attended Northwestern College during its existence. Today the Broen Memorial Home, an institution for the elderly, uses the former school building.

It should be noted that there were other Swedish Lutheran educational academies in northwestern Minnesota. The Red River Valley Conference of the Augustana Lutheran Church was not only involved with Northwestern College, but also North Star College in Warren, about 140 miles north of Fergus Falls in Marshall County. It was founded by the Rev. E. O. Chelgren in 1908 and was in existence until 1936. A Swedish Lutheran pastor named S. J. Kronberg organized the Lund Academy at rural Christine Lake in Otter Tail County in 1898, but it closed after the 1900–01 school year. Hope Academy in Moorhead was founded in 1888. An economic depression in the early 1890s severely felt in the Red River Valley forced the school to close in 1896.

DETROIT LAKES

Although the area around Detroit Lakes was more heavily settled by Norwegians than Swedes, the Upsala Lutheran Church was founded by the latter. The white frame building with a belfry, built in 1876, has an attractive rural setting. The congregation was organized in 1871. The church was closed in 1964, but a midsummer service is still held every year. Among the trees to the east is the church cemetery. Ten miles northeast of Detroit Lakes are the Lund Lutheran Church, constructed in 1903, and its cemetery. The congregation was founded in 1884. The attractive red brick Eksjo Lutheran Church of Lake Park has a cornerstone noting "Sw. Ev. Luth. Church of Eksjö AD 1901." There is an adjacent cemetery.

MOORHEAD

The Bergquist Pioneer Cabin, at Eleventh Avenue North and the Red River, is identified as the oldest house in Moorhead on its original site and has been on the National Register of Historic Places since 1980. John Gustav Bergquist built the log cabin, originally a one-story structure, in 1870, two years after coming to America. In 1873 his brother, Peter, joined him, and together they added a second floor. John farmed and developed a brick manufacturing business, while Peter started a grocery store. After Hank Peterson, a later resident, added many rooms to the log structure, the original was lost to view but protected from the weather. In 1976 Peterson donated the building and the lot to the Bergquist Pioneer Cabin Society and restoration commenced. In 1991, the society donated it to the Clay County Historical Society, which opens it during the annual Scandinavian Hjemkomst Festival the third weekend in June or by appointment (218/233-4606).

Bethesda Lutheran Church, Fortieth Avenue and Eighth Street South (218/236-1420), occupies a building constructed in 1971. Its previous sanctuary was built in 1905 and still stands at the southwest corner of Sixth Street and Second Avenue South, where it shelters Churches United for the Homeless. The Bethesda congregation, founded in 1880, was responsible for finding funding for Hope Academy. Prior to 1905, the congregation worshiped in a frame building, now an apartment building, located at 316 Seventh Avenue. It was built in 1874 and used as the Moorhead's first schoolhouse until it was purchased by the Lutherans in 1880.

The Bergquist Pioneer Cabin, the oldest house in Moorhead on its original site, was built by nineteen-year-old Swedish immigrant John Gustav Bergquist in 1870. Bergquist's descendants, including his great-grandson, helped restore the cabin more than one hundred years later.

NORTHWEST MINNESOTA

Kittson, Marshall, and Roseau counties are located in the extreme northwest corner of Minnesota. The oldest Lutheran church in Kittson County is the Red River Lutheran Church (218/674-4421), twelve miles southwest of Hallock, organized in 1881. The first services were held in the log house of Lars Mattson, brother of Hans Mattson. The community is called Mattson. There are several other townships and communities in Kittson County with Swedish names—Skane, Tegner, Karlstad. Bethel Lutheran in Karlstad (218/754-2491) and Maria Lutheran in Kennedy (218/674-4311) are of Swedish origin. Settlers in Kittson County were more likely to be Swedish than any other nationality.

In Warren, seat of Marshall County, the Swedes established North Star College in 1908, which was open until 1936. Swedish Lutheran churches in the county include Bethesda in Strandquist (218/436-2641) and First Lutheran and Immanuel in Warren (both 218/745-4221). In Roseau County, First Lutheran and Bethel (both 218/463-2547) in Roseau were Augustana Lutheran churches.

4 The South 🏴󠁅

With the exception of Texas, the South has attracted relatively few Swedish immigrants. Small organized colonies sprang up in Florida (New Upsala, Pierson, and Hallandale), and in Silverhill, Alabama, but in Georgia, Louisiana, the Carolinas, and Virginia, there are few landmarks.

The largest concentration of Swedes in the South is in Texas, particularly in and around the state capital of Austin. The first Swedish group arrived in Texas in the late 1840s under the leadership of Swen Magnus Swenson, who came from near Jönköping.

This survey of the South first explores sites in Virginia and then turns to North and South Carolina, Georgia, Florida, Alabama, and Louisiana before considering migration into Texas.

VIRGINIA

FALLS CHURCH   It took twelve years of labor for Swedish-born Carl Milles (1875–1955) to complete the monumental sculpture "The Fountain of Faith" at National Memorial Park, a private cemetery on Lee Highway (703/560-4435 or 560-6600). The sculpture was dedicated in 1952 in the presence of more than twenty-five thousand people. Its twenty-nine figures portray the joyful reunion after

239

death of people the sculptor, who became an American citizen in 1945, had known in the United States, Sweden, and France. The figures were cast in bronze in an art foundry in Stockholm. Also located in the National Memorial Park is Milles's "The Sun Singer." (Another casting of "The Sun Singer" is in Allerton Park, near Champaign, Illinois.)

RICHMOND

Carl Milles's "Small Triton Fountain" in front of the Virginia Museum of Fine Arts, 2500 Grove Avenue (804/367-0844), shows Triton seated on waves holding a conch shell to his lips.

FORT MONROE AND NEWPORT NEWS

The Fort Monroe Casemate Museum, at 20 Bernard Road (804/727-3973) and the Mariners' Museum, 1 Museum Drive in Newport News (804/595-0368), are museums that contain sizable collections of John Ericsson memorabilia. Most of it relates to the Civil War battle between the *Monitor* and the *Merrimac* in Hampton Roads, a channel through which the Elizabeth and James rivers empty into Chesapeake Bay. Ericsson (1803–89), an engineer and contributor to the invention of the propeller, designed the *Monitor*. When the *Monitor* defeated the *Merrimac* of the South, it marked not only a significant day in Civil War naval history but also a new epoch in world warship design and construction. Ericsson was born in Sweden and served in the Swedish army before leaving for London where he spent twelve years working as an engineer. In 1839 he brought his expertise to the United States, where he lived and worked for fifty years.

DAHLGREN

Dahlgren is the site of the Naval Weapons Laboratory and the Naval Weapons Factory and is named in honor of American-born Rear Admiral John Dahlgren (1809–1870), the son of a Swedish merchant who came to New York in 1806 and who eventually served as Swedish consul at Philadelphia.

NORTH CAROLINA

FLAT ROCK

It was on Connemara Farm that writer Carl Sandburg, the son of Swedish immigrants, spent his last twenty-two years (1945–1967). Connemara, meaning "country estate" in Gaelic, is today the Carl Sandburg Home National Historic Site (704/693-4178) on Little River Road. The twenty-two–room house had originally been built about 1838 by Christopher Gustavus Memminger of Charleston, South Carolina, who in 1861 became the first secretary of the treasury of the Confederacy. The 266-acre farm consists of the main house and twenty-five outbuildings. When the Sandburgs moved to Flat Rock in 1945, three daughters and

*Connemara Farm in
Flat Rock,
North Carolina,
was for twenty-two
years the home of
Swedish-American
writer Carl Sandburg.*

two grandchildren accompanied them along with a library of ten
thousand books and Mrs. Sandburg's Chikaming goat herd.
While at Connemara, Sandburg wrote his only novel, *Remembrance
Rock* (1948), and published his autobiography, *Always the Young
Strangers* (1953).

Former CBS reporter Edward R. Morrow once interviewed
Sandburg at Connemara, and viewing a short film clip of this
interview is an option to visitors to the main house. The house
is said to have the same appearance as it did when the Sandburgs
lived there. On the wall of the music room is a photo of Sandburg
with his Swedish tulip-shaped guitar (unfortunately, the instrument has been lost). The downstairs study includes many of the
family's books and a life mask of Sandburg made by a dentist.
Outside is a rock under a hemlock tree where Sandburg frequently sat drinking coffee and writing. His study on the second

floor is a small, cluttered room where his typewriter sits on a fruit crate. Across the street from the entrance to the Carl Sandburg Home National Historic Site is the Flat Rock Playhouse, where the Vagabond Players, during the summer, present *The World of Carl Sandburg* and Sandburg's *Rootabaga Stories.*

ASHEVILLE   The Biltmore Estate, a 255-room mansion in French Renaissance Chateau style, was built by George W. Vanderbilt at the end of the nineteenth century on grounds that include gardens and wineries. In the second-floor Living Hall is a painting by Anders Leonhard Zorn entitled "The Waltz." The works of Zorn (1860–1920), a Swedish painter, etcher, sculptor, and portrait painter who lived and worked in Mora, Sweden, are found in many European and American collections. The entrance to the estate is one mile north of the intersection of Interstate 40 and U.S. Highway 25 (800/543-2961 or 704/255-1776). The site is open year-round except New Year's Day, Thanksgiving, and Christmas. Call for fee schedule.

SOUTH CAROLINA

MURRELLS   "The Fountain of the Muses," a fifteen-piece group by Swedish
INLET   sculptor Carl Milles, can be found at Brookgreen Gardens on U.S. Highway 17 South, midway between Georgetown and Myrtle Beach (803/237-4218). It was relocated here from the Metropolitan Museum of Art in New York.

GEORGIA

AMERICUS   North of Americus on State Highway 49 is a state historic marker indicating the site where Charles Lindbergh, Jr., who flew the first transatlantic flight in 1927, first flew solo. In 1923, the young aviator came to Souther Field, a World War I training center, and purchased a Curtiss JN4 "Jenny" with which he planned to begin his barnstorming career. Lindbergh bought the plane after a new engine and an extra twenty-gallon fuel tank had been added. With fewer than twenty hours' instruction, Lindbergh soloed for the first time, and then he spent a week at the field practicing his aviation skills. His record-setting nonstop solo transatlantic flight from New York to Paris was still four years away.

At Souther Field a twelve-foot monument by sculptor William Thompson depicts Lindbergh as a wing walker in his early barnstorming days. Evoking the exuberance of youth, the sculpture honors the record-setting Swedish-American pilot. Thompson is Professor of Art Emeritus at the University of Georgia.

FLORIDA

In recent years, many retired Swedish Americans have settled in Florida. In turn, they have organized a number of churches. The Evangelical Covenant Church of America has a large retirement center called Covenant Village of Florida in Plantation, near Fort Lauderdale.

In earlier days, there were three main Swedish settlements in the state, the first and largest being New Upsala. Swedes were also drawn to Vero Beach, beginning in 1904, where they organized the Evangelical Mission Covenant Church of Vero Beach in 1942.

NEW UPSALA AND SANFORD

New Upsala, an agricultural settlement north of Orlando and near Sanford in east-central Florida, was founded in 1870 by the Rev. William Henschen (1842–1925), his brother Esaias, and a group of friends. It was named for Uppsala, Sweden, the town from which the Henschens came. About this time, General Henry Shelton Sanford, a wealthy entrepreneur, purchased twelve thousand acres of land in the area. He was advised by the Rev. Henschen that many Swedes would be eager to work the land if they had the means to pay for the transatlantic voyage. Sanford agreed to pay the cost in return for a period of labor in the citrus groves.

In Sweden, Josef Henschen, a brother of William and Esaias, recruited the first laborers and led about one hundred immigrants to Florida in 1871. In 1875 Sanford donated a tract of one and a half acres of land for a Swedish church and cemetery. In the early years, the church was served by Swedish Baptist and Presbyterian ministers, but in 1892 it became a Lutheran congregation. The church disbanded in 1946 and the sanctuary was torn down. A bronze tablet on a block of granite erected in 1951 marks the location of the former sanctuary. Nearby is the Swedish cemetery amidst giant live oaks draped with Spanish moss.

At the entrance to the General Sanford Memorial Library and Museum in Sanford, there is a bronze plaque that notes in the inscription that "much of the labor in the groves was performed by Swedish immigrants who settled in nearby New Upsala." A street in Sanford where the early Swedes had their homes is named Upsala Avenue.

After Josef Henschen immigrated to Florida, he became a large citrus grower and landowner himself. He is probably responsible for having the former Pinellas Point on the western coast renamed St. Petersburg in honor of a Russian business associate. In 1880 he founded Forest City, now part of the greater Orlando area, in Seminole County.

PIERSON

Pierson, in Volusia County northwest of De Land, was named for Peter Pierson (Per Persson) (1857-1926), who arrived in 1876 with his brother Nels. Another brother was a horticulturist in Cromwell, Connecticut. In the mid-1880s, the Pierson Colonization Society was organized to induce Swedes to relocate in Florida. Ebenezer Lutheran Church, 139 South Volusia Avenue, was founded in 1884, and the congregation erected a sanctuary in 1894 that was enlarged three years later. Though the 1894 sanctuary still stands, it has been remodeled.

HALLANDALE

Hallandale in Broward County was founded in the late nineteenth century as a daughter colony of the Halland Settlement in Southwest Iowa. Named for Lutheran pastor Bengt Magnus Halland, the Halland Settlement of Stanton, Iowa, had three Lutheran congregations formed in 1870, and even one hundred years later more than one-half of Stanton's population claimed to be of Swedish ancestry. Bethlehem Lutheran Church, 26 N.W. Third Avenue, in Hallandale was organized by the Swedish settlers.

ALABAMA

SILVERHILL

In Chicago, the Svea Land Company was organized in 1890 for the purpose of establishing a Swedish colony. After years of research, it was decided that the settlement would be located in Baldwin County in southern Alabama. During the economic depression of 1893, five men, including Oscar Johnson, of the Svea Land Company went to Baldwin County to look over the land. The first family arrived in Silverhill before the end of 1896.

The early years were extremely difficult. Over eleven thousand peach trees were planted, but they all were killed by insects and disease. The settlers turned to raising dairy cattle and established the first creamery in Alabama. They were aided by Dr. Oscar Winberg, originally from Västergötland before he moved to Chicago and then Silverhill. Winberg was a veterinarian and horticulturist who introduced modern farming methods to the settlement. He became a recognized authority on the cultivation of oranges and developed a sweet variety of kumquat and the satsuma. Gradually the area began to prosper.

The Silverhill Public Library building at 21961 Sixth Street South was formerly the land office. It was also used for a period of time as a school and church. The building and the People's Supply Company are the only two important structures still standing from the early settlement. They both date from the 1890s. The Silverhill library is listed on the National Register of Historic Places.

Oscar Johnson Park is named for the man who was the first manager of Silverhill. Across the street from the Lutheran church is the former schoolhouse, which is now a private residence.

In 1902, the Covenant congregation was organized as the Svenska Evangeliska Mission Församling, or the Swedish Evangelical Mission Congregation. One month after its founding, the Silverhill Land Company gave the congregation two lots on which to build a church. It was a small white frame building with a steeple. In 1957, a new sanctuary was dedicated next to the old one. In 1978, the congregation offered the old building to Blakely Historic Park, about twenty-six miles north in Spanish Fort. The plan was to move the church building in four parts— remove and airlift the steeple and then cut the sanctuary into three parts and truck them to the new site. The airlift was successfully accomplished on 26 August 1978. But the following May, the attempt to move the sanctuary was not successful, and the part of the sanctuary that did survive the move was subsequently destroyed by a hurricane. The steeple has been placed on top of the park pavilion, which was dedicated as the Church Pavilion in September 1982.

In Silverhill, there is also a Lutheran congregation—Zion Lutheran Church at 15875 Fourth Avenue—formed by Swedes that meets in a white frame Gothic-style church. A few third- and fourth-generation Swedish families still attend this church as well as the Evangelical Covenant church at 16096 Silverhill Avenue. The Baptist congregation, founded in 1899, has for the most part lost its Swedish heritage. It meets in a building constructed in 1970.

Silverhill Cemetery, though not exclusively devoted to Swedes, has numerous Swedish graves.

LOUISIANA

HAMMOND

The graves of Peter Hammond and his family are on the south side of the 500 block of East Charles Street between North Holly and North Olive streets in Hammond. Located under an enormous live oak tree, the graves are marked with a historical plaque. Hammond, from the parish of Hammerdal in Jämtland, arrived in the state of Louisiana about 1815 and founded this town, in Tangipahoa Parish, some sixty miles northwest of New Orleans. He purchased a considerable amount of timberland from the government and produced pitch, turpentine, tar, and mast timbers for ships. In 1830, he married a cousin of Mrs. Ralph Waldo Emerson. During the Civil War, the family lost most of its wealth.

TEXAS

To a great extent, the early history of Swedish immigration to Texas focused on Swen Magnus Swenson. Born near Jönköping in 1816, Swenson emigrated to New York as a young man of twenty. In 1838, he made his way to Texas and at twenty-five became overseer of a large cotton plantation near Richmond, southwest of Houston. With his uncle, Swante Palm, who arrived in Texas in 1844, Swenson became involved in a mercantile business in La Grange, between Houston and Austin. In 1848, Swenson married the Richmond plantation owner's widow. In the years to follow, Swenson, always having a keen business sense, made a fortune in cotton production, commerce, and real estate. He became one of the richest men in Texas, owning large tracts of land in Travis, Williamson, and Jones counties. (Jones County, home to part of Abilene, is about two hundred miles northwest of Travis and Williamson counties.)

In the 1840s, Swenson made two visits to Sweden to encourage people to immigrate to Texas. He as well as a brother in Småland and Swante Palm were responsible for promoting the migration of young Swedes. In 1848, twenty-five of Swenson's relatives as well as farm laborers and single women left Småland for Texas. Swenson paid their passage and in turn the Swedes worked for him until the debt was paid. Frequently after one year the young Swedes were able to buy their own land. Many engaged in cotton production and became prosperous farmers. Fully two-thirds of the Swedes came from the Jönköping area and generally settled in central Texas in Travis and Williamson counties (see map, page 248), though some also went to West Texas to McCulloch County and Jones County (to Ericksdahl near Stamford) and to the coastal areas of Willacy County (Lyford) as well as Galveston and Houston. In Austin, the Travis County seat, a historical marker dedicated in 1990 marks Swedish Hill, home to many early immigrant Swedes.

Because Swenson was a convinced Unionist, he opposed slavery and secession. Holding these beliefs endangered his life and the lives of his family members and forced him to flee to Mexico before the war was over. After the war he settled in New Orleans as a cotton exporter. In 1867, he relocated to New York City and established a banking firm. Swenson remained in New York until his death in 1896 (he is buried in Brooklyn). After his death, Swenson's sons and daughters continued to run the Texas ranches. Today the heirs own four ranches totaling about two hundred sixty thousand acres.

MONTE ALTO   Stockholm Cemetery, the only reminder of a Swedish community promoted by the Wallin, Johnson & Matson Land Company of Minnesota, lies northwest of McAllen and Edinburg, between Monte Alto and Lyford. On FM 491 about one mile west of FM 1425, the cemetery holds some of these early settlers who came from 1912 to 1914, attracted by the abundance of inexpensive and fertile farmland and the long growing season of the Rio Grande River Valley.

CORPUS CHRISTI

Swedish native Kent Ullberg, a sculptor whose works have been shown in Asia, Europe, and Africa as well as North America, now calls Padre Island his permanent home. Though his monumental works stand in diverse public and private spaces worldwide, Corpus Christi claims several outstanding examples. These include the twenty-four–foot "Leaping Marlin" at the Coastal Bend Community Foundation on North Padre Island; "Wind in the Sails," a bronze on red granite that is more than twenty-three feet and stands at the *Corpus Christi Caller-Times* headquarters; and a five-foot bronze casting called the "Great Blue Heron," made for the Texas State Aquarium. Since 1975 Ullberg has been winning awards from the National Academy of Design, the National Academy of Western Art, the National Sculpture Society, the Society of Animal Artists, and other various arts organizations.

OLIVIA

Along the Texas coast across the bay from Port Lavaca is Olivia, namesake of the wife of the Rev. Carl J. E. Haterius of Galesburg, Illinois, who in 1892 acquired the land for the town, which was laid out the next year. Swedes established a cemetery and church, later called the Eden Lutheran Church, but Hurricane Carla destroyed much of the small community in 1961 with gusts of 175 m.p.h. and a high tide of more than eighteen feet in Port Lavaca.

DAYTON

Brought by the railroad and out-of-state developers, Swedish immigrants helped settle the community of Stilson, which is remembered by an official Texas historical marker two and one-half miles west of Dayton on the U.S. Highway 90 right-of-way. Northwest of Houston, Dayton lies in Liberty County.

ROUND TOP

Swede Anders Oxehufwud emigrated to the United States in 1923, and he and his wife spent almost twenty-five years of retirement in La Grange, a contemporary stopping point for travelers between Austin and Houston. But it was to the International Festival-Institute at Round Top (409/249-3129), fifteen miles northeast of La Grange, to which Oxehufwud left in 1987 his collection of Swedish heirlooms. His family's furniture, ceramics, textiles, and other examples of the decorative

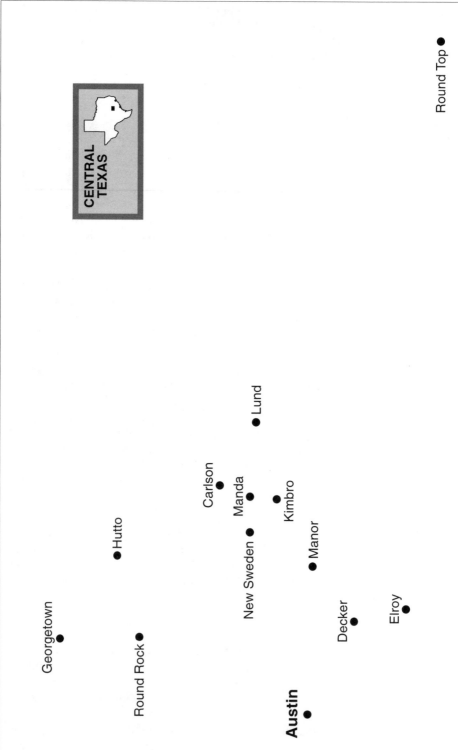

CENTRAL TEXAS

Round Top ●

● Lund

Carlson ●

Manda ●

● Kimbro

New Sweden ●

● Hutto

● Manor

Georgetown ●

Decker ●

Round Rock ●

Elroy ●

Austin ●

arts, some of which date to the sixteenth century, are now displayed in the institute, a place where international musicians gather to study and perform.

SAN ANTONIO

The University of Texas Institute of Texan Cultures, at Bowie Street and Durango Boulevard on HemisFair Plaza (512/226-7651) is open 9 to 5 Tuesday through Sunday without an admission fee. The institute contains unique displays of more than two dozen ethnic groups that contributed to Texas history and culture. The Swedish section gives a good overall glimpse of the achievements of Swedes in Texas. Displays include Swedish pioneer items and artifacts and memorabilia from the Palm Valley Lutheran Church in Round Rock. A large wall board notes the more important events and people in the history of Swedish immigration to Texas.

AUSTIN

HISTORIC PLACES
Swedish Log Cabin—Garden Center of Zilker Park, Barton Springs Road, Garden Center 10–4:30 daily.
S. M. Swenson bought a large tract of land east of Austin in 1850 and named this ranch Govalle from the Swedish dialect *god vall*, meaning "good pasture." A park in East Austin to this day is called Govalle. Around 1840 a log cabin was constructed on the land. Gustaf Palm, Swante Palm's brother and S. M. Swenson's uncle, arrived with his family in 1848, and until after the Civil War lived in this log cabin. Later when the Gustaf Palm family built a home at Fourteenth and San Jacinto streets in Austin, the log cabin was moved to that location and for many years served as a wash house. Later it was relocated to Round Rock in nearby Williamson County. In May 1965, the cabin was moved to Zilker Park. Now restored, the cabin holds a number of artifacts associated with the early Swedish pioneers and is maintained by the Austin Parks and Recreation Department and the Texas Swedish Pioneers Association. The TSPA donated materials and tools to the park's replica of an 1860s Swedish blacksmith shop. The board and batten siding was supplied by John Rolf whose parents lived in New Sweden, near Manor.

The Old Bakery and Emporium—1006 Congress Avenue, one block south of the state capitol, 9–5 Monday through Friday (512/477-5961).
In 1863, Charles Lundberg emigrated from Sweden to the United States, and nine years later he moved to Austin. He went into the bakery business as a journeyman. Shortly thereafter, he bought out his employer's business and, according to his newspaper obituary notice, "from that day on he conducted the largest and most successful bakery in Austin."

Constructed east of Austin about 1840 for S. M. Swenson, this Swedish log cabin now stands in Austin's Zilker Park.

After Lundberg died, the business was sold. About seventy-five years later, the building had to be rescued from deterioration. Today the two-story brick bakery is listed on the National Register of Historic Places and owned by the City of Austin. Lundberg's seventeen-foot bakery paddle still hangs on the wall, and his name, carved in stone, is visible near the roof line.

The Johnson Home—West First Street at Loop 1 (MoPac Expressway).
Erected in 1858 by Sam Houston's friend Charles Johnson, this home was built of native stone from Johnson's own quarries by fellow Swedes. The long porch and Ionic columns were added later. In 1924, it became the home of the Travis County American Legion.

Swedish Hill (Svenska Kullen)—bounded by Red River, Fourteenth, Eighteenth, and Navasota.
This community was home in the 1870s to Swedish immigrants who erected homes and churches in the area, now divided by Interstate 35 yet tied together by a mix of neighborhood, government, and university interests. Placed on the National Register of Historic Places in 1986, the Swedish neighborhood is remembered by an official state historic plaque on the east frontage road of Interstate 35 between Fifteenth and Sixteenth streets.

Former Palm School—northwest corner of Interstate 35 and East First Street.
This tan stucco building was named in honor of Swante Palm. At the First Street entrance are plaques describing the history of the school, which was named in his honor in 1901. Though originally used as a school, the building was converted in 1976 into a business office complex known as Palm Square. Nearby is Swante Palm Park.

CHURCHES
Former Gethsemane Lutheran Church—1510 Congress (three blocks north of the Texas State Capitol).
The former Gethsemane Lutheran Church building, dedicated in November 1883, served its congregation as a place of worship until purchased by the State of Texas and transformed into a state historic site in 1965. The structure is rich with Gothic Revival–style decorative elements and contains such rural Swedish church architectural characteristics as a curved hood-shaped base for the carpentered cupola. A light tan brick building with Gothic-style stained glass windows, the church has a tall front central bell tower protruding beyond the rectangular sanctuary. Stone retrieved from the 1852 Texas

capitol that burned in 1881 and doors from the Old Main building at The University of Texas found new use in this structure.

In 1868, the first Swedish Lutheran service was held in Austin. It was then decided to organize a Lutheran congregation, making Gethsemane the second oldest Lutheran church in Texas (a German group formed the first). Swante Palm chaired this organizational meeting. In 1875, the congregation became an official member of the Augustana Synod.

In 1950, Gethsemane Lutheran found itself becoming engulfed by the expanding state government complex. Church leaders decided to purchase property at 200 West Anderson Lane on the north side of Austin, and a new sanctuary was built and dedicated in 1963. During the previous year, however, the old church was recorded as a Texas historic landmark. In 1965, the Texas Legislature passed a bill, signed by Gov. John Connally, acquiring the 1883 structure. The church building was restored in 1970 and 1971 and has been listed in the National Register of Historic Places. A plaque recounting its history is to the right of the front door. Office workers now toil within the church walls, and the Texas Historical Commission has made plans to set up a library there.

Still visible are the lovely stained glass windows. The Bergstrom family (see below) donated a few of them along with the natural wood Gothic altar and steeple bell. The pulpit, altar painting, and baptismal font are noteworthy.

The former Gethsemane Lutheran Church, which was constructed by a Swedish congregation and dedicated in 1883, is built of stone retrieved from the Texas Capitol that burned in 1881 and has doors that once were used in the Old Main building at The University of Texas.

The new sanctuary of the Gethsemane Lutheran congregation at the northeast corner of West Anderson Lane and Purnell Drive has a contemporary design with impressive modern stained glass windows. In the narthex is the original cornerstone from the downtown church's steeple.

Near the old Gethsemane Lutheran Church were two other Swedish congregations. As the government complex expanded in the 1950s, both church sanctuaries were sold and torn down. Although the congregations moved elsewhere in Austin, state historic plaques were erected where the original buildings had been located.

Swedish Central Methodist Church—plaque located on the south side of West Fourteenth Street at Colorado, directly north of the State Supreme Court building.

The Swedish Central Methodist Church congregation was organized in 1873 by the Rev. Carl J. Charnquist, a minister who came to Texas from Michigan. His preaching started revivals, resulting in the formation of several Methodist congregations in the Austin area. From 1896 to 1900, the pastor was Dr. O. E. Olander, later to organize Texas Wesleyan Academy and to serve in the Texas State Legislature. During his pastorate, a Gothic-style church building was acquired at the corner of Thirteenth and Colorado. The congregation worshiped in this building until it was sold to the state government in 1956, at which point a new church was built at 6100 Berkman. The new church has the bell, organ, and stained glass windows from the former one.

Swedish Evangelical Free Church—plaque is on the southwest corner of West Fifteenth and Colorado streets.

The first Evangelical Free church in the Austin area was organized in 1891 in Decker in eastern Travis County. In Elroy, in southeast Travis County, another Evangelical Free church was organized thirteen years later. By the 1920s, however, the children of these early immigrants were moving to Austin. In 1925, a church was built at the corner of West Fifteenth and Colorado streets, and into the 1930s Swedish was spoken in the services. It was known as the Swedish Evangelical Free Church until 1952 when *Swedish* was replaced with *First* as a result of a merger with a Norwegian group. When a new sanctuary was completed in 1962 at 4425 Red River, the former sanctuary was torn down.

St. David's Episcopal Church—304 East Seventh Street (512/ 472-1196).

S. M. Swenson, a member here in the late 1850s and early 1860s, was senior warden from 1859 to 1863 and chairman of the building committee. The main entrance was given in his memory by his grandchildren.

SCHOOLS
The University of Texas at Austin— 512/471-3434.

The University of Texas at Austin is the largest university in the South. On the fifth floor of the Geology Building are a plaque and photo of Johan August Udden (1859–1932). After teaching natural science at Bethany College in Lindsborg, Kansas, and Augustana College in Rock Island, Illinois, Udden came in 1903 to Texas, where he was director of the Bureau of Economic Geology from 1911 to 1932. Among his accomplishments was to conduct oil explorations, whose success greatly improved the financial position of the university. In the basement of the Geology Building is the Sedimentation Research Laboratory, named in his honor.

Swede Swante Palm (1815–1899), known as a Renaissance gentleman of the Southwest, served as vice consul for Sweden and Norway from 1866 until his death. A justice of the peace, alderman, postmaster, and bibliographer, Palm gathered the largest private book collection in nineteenth-century Texas. In the 1850s, Palm built a small house on Ash Street (now Ninth) near Congress Avenue, which served as the Swedish consulate. His growing book collection forced him to enlarge it in 1879. Palm donated most of his approximately twelve thousand–volume collection to The University of Texas in 1897. The remainder went to the university on permanent loan in 1953. On campus, an oil portrait of Palm hangs in the Harry Ransom Humanities Research Center and a bust is displayed in the Eugene C. Barker Texas History Center.

His three thousand–volume collection of books in Swedish has been described as a "private public library" because it encompassed a broad range of subjects and genres. In explaining to critics why he chose The University of Texas rather than a Swedish-American institution as his collection's depository, he said, "Texas is my second fatherland." The collection was split among different campus libraries, but most of the books are stored in the Collections Deposit Library. In 1990, a historical marker was added to his restored grave site in Oakwood Cemetery, and in 1991 the State of Texas dedicated an official historical marker on West Ninth Street at Congress Avenue where Swante Palm's home once stood.

In 1912, the Texas Wesleyan College/Academy, organized by O. E. Olander, opened. It operated until 1936 when the twenty-one–acre campus was sold to The University of Texas. Renamed Wesleyan Hall, the building survived until the late 1970s when it was torn down to make way for a new building for The University of Texas School of Law. A plaque near the site commemorates the Swedish Methodist school.

Swante Palm Elementary School—7601 Dixie Drive (512/280-1890).

This elementary school was dedicated in Palm's honor 26 April 1987. Other schools in Austin honoring Swedish-Americans are the Carl T. Widén Elementary School (5605 Nuckols Crossing) and the Linder Elementary School (2800 Metcalf). Widén was a leader in the Texas Swedish community for many years before his death in 1986 at the age of 101.

OTHER POINTS OF INTEREST

Oakwood Cemetery—bounded by Navasota, Martin Luther King, Jr., Boulevard, and Bob Harrison.

Near the corner of East Sixteenth and Navasota is a state marker describing the history of this noteworthy cemetery. Swante Palm, Johan August Udden, and O. E. Olander are buried in this cemetery. At Swante Palm's grave, an official Texas historical marker highlights his life's contributions.

Lester E. Palmer Auditorium and Convention Center—400 South First Street (near intersection of Barton Springs Road and Riverside Drive).
This civic building was named for Lester E. Palmer, mayor of Austin in the 1960s, who was a second-generation Swedish American.

Seaholm Water Works—East First near North Lamar.
The installation is named for Walter Seaholm (Sjöholm), former superintendent of Austin's Water Department. His father emigrated from Sweden.

Bergstrom Air Force Base—2500 block of State Highway 71 (512/389-0444).
Formerly called Del Valle Air Base, the base was renamed 12 November 1942 partially at the suggestion of then-Congressman Lyndon B. Johnson in honor of Capt. John August Early Bergstrom, who is believed to have been the first Austin casualty in World War II. Bergstrom, whose father and mother were of Swedish ancestry, was born in Austin in 1907. He was assigned to Clark Field in the Philippines where he lost his life in a Japanese air attack.

ELROY

In the town of Elroy, southeast of Austin, an official Texas historical marker in front of the Elroy library notes that Swedish and German immigrants settled the area in the 1890s. Three Swedish churches served the settlers.

DECKER

The white building of the Decker United Methodist Church on the west side of Farm Road 3177, two miles south of U.S. Highway 290, is the congregation's second sanctuary. It dates to the turn of the century. The early Swedish Methodist immigrants in Decker attended church in Austin in the late 1860s and early 1870s before they erected their first church in 1879. The sanctuary is noted for its dark wood paneling and beamed ceiling. The interior has remained practically unaltered since it was built. The church cemetery is nearby.

MANOR

The impressive white clapboard New Sweden Evangelical Lutheran Church has the highest steeple in eastern Travis County—104 feet. Set four and one-half miles north of Austin on U.S. Highway 290 (two miles northeast on Farm Road 973), the church and nearby New Sweden Lutheran Cemetery (two miles southwest) are all that remain from a Swedish settlement. It had been developed by a group of young men sponsored by S. M. Swenson. The church was organized in 1876 and first

Northeast of Manor, Swedish settlers formed the New Sweden community and organized in 1876 an Evangelical Lutheran congregation. They completed this building, the New Sweden Evangelical Lutheran Church, in 1922.

known as the Swedish Evangelical Lutheran Congregation of Manor. In 1879 the first church was completed. The present edifice was constructed in 1921 and 1922. It is tradition for the Easter service to be held at the cemetery. The congregation also hosts a *julotta* every Christmas.

LUND

The small settlement of Lund includes a few houses, a water tower, a church, and a cemetery. On the Monday after Easter in 1980, the old Bethlehem Lutheran Church, twelve miles east of the New Sweden Lutheran Cemetery, was destroyed by a tornado, and the present plain light-colored brick structure was constructed the following year. North of Elgin, this small Lutheran church contains items saved from the former sanctuary, including stained glass windows, the altar painting, and pews. A separate structure was built for the old church bell. The congregation was organized in 1897, and the first church was built across the road near the cemetery in 1898.

CARLSON, MANDA, AND KIMBRO

The Swedish presence in Carlson, Manda, and Kimbro, all small communities northeast of Manor in Travis County, is recorded on official historical markers. At the intersection of Carlson and Lund roads, a marker notes that Swedish brothers Pete and John Carlson came to the United States in 1869 and settled in the community in 1881. Pete opened the community's first store, and John operated the local cotton gin. Nearby Manda was founded by Swedish immigrants also in the 1880s and named for Amanda Bengtson Gustafson, sister of the town's postmaster. Organized in 1892, the Manda Swedish Methodist congregation was active until 1962. Its historical marker rests at the intersection of Manda and Wells Ranch roads. Another nearby community, Kimbro, had been settled earlier—in the 1870s—by Swedes, Danes, and Germans. A Swedish Evangelical Free church founded in Kimbro was moved to nearby Elgin in 1954. Kimbro's marker stands on North Kimbro Road at the Free Church's cemetery.

ROUND ROCK

Round Rock is seventeen miles north of downtown Austin. The area was originally settled by Swedes, but the Swedish influence diminished as Round Rock assumed the role of an Austin suburb. The 100 and 200 blocks of Round Rock's East Main Street have been designated a commercial historic district and added to the National Register of Historic Places.

HISTORIC PLACES
Andrew J. Palm House Museum—212 East Main Avenue (between Lampasas and Sheppard), opposite the City Hall Annex. Open 9–5 Monday through Friday.
The Andrew J. Palm House Museum is a one-story clapboard house believed to have been built in 1873. The house was recorded as a Texas historic landmark in 1978. To the right of the front door is a historic plaque. Andrew Palm was the fourth son of Anna Palm. A farmer and rancher, he arranged for other

Swedish families to come to Central Texas and settle in Palm Valley.

The house was originally one mile from the Palm Valley Lutheran Church on land that S. M. Swenson had sold to Palm. The house was moved in 1976 to Round Rock. The house's interior contains a central hall and one large, high-ceilinged room on either side. The rooms, one a Victorian parlor and the other a pioneer kitchen, are furnished, but nothing displayed was owned by the Palms. Except for an addition at the rear, the house has been restored to its original appearance. The museum was dedicated in 1977.

Nelson Mercantile Store—201 East Main Avenue.

This early commercial building, erected in the late nineteenth century and used for a variety of businesses, has been designated a Texas historic landmark. On top of the ornate facade is the inscription, "Lumber J. A. Nelson & Co. Hardware." Nelson developed a successful business in lumber, hardware, and agricultural implements. In 1970, a local bank became the owner of the building, which had deteriorated badly. Plans are under way for its restoration.

Nelson-Crier House (Woodbine Mansion)—405 East Main Avenue at Burnet Street (private residence).

The large brick house with six Ionic columns on its East Main Avenue facade is an official state historic site. The house has three floors, a basement, an attic, and a widow's walk. The Arvid Nelson family came to Texas in 1854. One of the sons, Andrew, was then nineteen years old, and his younger brother, August, seventeen. The family settled in Williamson County and at first rented land from S. M. Swenson before purchasing their own farm. Andrew, known as A. J., built several wagons, bought oxen, and engaged in hauling flour and cotton to the Gulf ports and returning with supplies. During the Civil War, he continued to haul supplies and lumber while his brother, August, served in the Confederate Army. After the war, A. J. had extensive farming enterprises in Williamson County. When he died in 1895, his widow with her sons and daughters started the construction of this impressive residence that took five years to build using material from Austin homes that were being dismantled. After Mrs. Nelson's death in 1923, two sons continued to live in the mansion (three generations of Nelsons resided there) until it was sold in 1960.

Telander Heritage House—off U.S. Highway 79 east of Palm Valley Lutheran Church.

The two-room house, built in 1885 of limestone, was one of the first homes in the area. It remains a private residence.

Palm House—east of Palm Valley Lutheran Church on U.S. Highway 79.

This two-story white frame house, which belonged to the Andrew J. Palm family, rests on land designated as a Round Rock city park. Restoration is under way.

T. E. Nelson Homestead—nearly four miles north of U.S. Highway 79 on the east side of Route 1460.

The large house, built by Andrew J. Nelson, has walls that are two feet thick. Nelson brought Swedish families to the area, and in return for their passage, they worked on his ranch. T. E. Nelson was his son.

The house is marked by a state medallion—"Home of A. J. Nelson, rancher-banker from Sweden. Swedish masons, paying voyage costs, built this house, 1860. Recorded Texas historic landmark, 1965."

CHURCHES

Palm Valley Lutheran Church—2500 Palm Valley Boulevard (2.25 miles east of Round Rock on U.S. Highway 79) (512/255-3322).

The area was originally called Brushy Creek, but it was renamed Palm Valley in honor of the Palm family. Swedes arrived in the Brushy Creek district as early as the 1850s. Among the early Swedish immigrants was Anna Palm, who arrived along with her husband, Anders Andersson Palm, and their six sons. She was encouraged to settle here in 1853 by Swante Palm, her brother-in-law, and S. M. Swenson, her nephew. After only a few months in Texas, her husband died, and in 1863, Henning, her youngest son, succumbed to pneumonia. She asked Swenson that the land where Henning was buried be designated a cemetery. Henning was the first to be buried in what became the Palm Valley Lutheran Cemetery.

The congregation was organized in 1870 and a wooden church built. Earlier there had been a log church building. Under Pastor Gustaf Berglund's leadership, the decision was made in 1894 to construct a new sanctuary. The present church is a red brick Gothic-style structure with a high steeple. The sanctuary has twelve outstanding stained glass windows. One of these is dedicated to the memory of the Palm family and another to the early pioneers. In the narthex is a glass case containing the old communion vessels and the communion wine jug that was regularly carried to the Palm Valley railway station one-half mile to the east from which it traveled to San Antonio to be filled with wine. In 1955 a parish hall was added, and fifteen years later the Centennial Hall was dedicated. Between the church sanctuary and the social hall is the old bell from the former Trinity Lutheran College in Round Rock. In the center of the west end of the large adjacent cemetery are the oldest graves, some with Swedish inscriptions.

SCHOOLS

Trinity Lutheran College—1000 East Main Avenue at College Street on the property of Trinity Lutheran Home.

This college was founded in 1906 with Dr. J. A. Stamline serving as its first president. In 1929, financial problems forced its closing. It merged with Evangelical Lutheran College, becoming known as the Texas Lutheran College, which was located in Seguin. North of the plaque that marks the site is a square stone building that is the only surviving structure from the former college campus. In 1929, the Lutheran Welfare Society opened Trinity Lutheran Homes for the care of children and the elderly.

OTHER POINTS OF INTEREST

Swedish Methodist Cemetery—one and one-half miles north of the T. E. Nelson homestead on FM 1460, on west side.

The small cemetery contains the graves of early Swedish pioneers of the Union Hill area. The Brushy Methodist Church was adjacent to the cemetery. The congregation moved to nearby Georgetown in 1906 (see below).

HUTTO

Incorporated in 1911, Hutto prospered after Swedish immigrants made cotton production a major agricultural enterprise there. A historical marker on U.S. Highway 79, one-half block east of its intersection with FM 1660, attests to their efforts.

The Hutto United Methodist Church at 605 East Street (the southwest corner of Liberty and East Streets) was founded when Swedish Methodists organized the congregation in private homes in 1892. Nineteen years later the present sanctuary was dedicated. In 1938, this congregation merged with an American Methodist group, but the old Swedish church building continues to be used by the congregation. The interior features a pressed metal ceiling painted in white and gold.

The white clapboard Hutto Evangelical Lutheran Church at the northeast corner of Live Oak and Church streets was organized in 1892.

GEORGETOWN

As early as 1871, Swedish settlers near Union Hill, three and one-half miles south of Georgetown, began holding Methodist worship meetings in homes. Through 1880, the Rev. Carl Charnquist served as a circuit preacher. In 1883 a church was built, one year after the Swedish Methodist-Episcopal Brushy Church congregation was officially organized. As the years passed, Swedes bought land east and north of Georgetown, making the distance to and from the country church inconvenient. In 1906, the present white limestone Gothic-style St. John's United Methodist Church was built at 311 East University Avenue (northeast corner of State Highway 29 and Myrtle Street) (512/863-5886) by Swedish carpenters and formally dedicated. The old church was then torn down. In the rear of the present sanctuary, which has been listed on the National Register of Historic Places, are twelve pews from the old church. The lighting fixtures (originally fueled by kerosene) in the rear of the sanctuary also were from the Brushy church.

The former Brushy Evangelical Free Church built a sanctuary in 1892 southeast of Georgetown, but the congregation dedicated a new building in 1963 at 1322 East University Avenue.

TAYLOR

Tenth Street United Methodist Church was founded by the Rev. Carl Charnquist in 1900. The white frame church building at 410 West Tenth (northeast corner of West Tenth and Hackleberry streets) (512/352-2244) was formerly owned by a disbanded Presbyterian congregation. The Methodists moved the building to its present location in 1911, where an official marker attests to its significance.

MASON

The three-story Victorian Reynolds-Seaquist Home at 400 Broad Street was constructed of sandstone in the 1880s for a wealthy banker. The house was completed by Oscar Seaquist (Oscar Edward Johnson Sjökvist), who purchased it in 1919. Seaquist, who was born in Oslo and emigrated at the turn of the century, had developed a successful boot-making business in Mason.

The house features exterior galleries surrounding the entire first and second floors and small balconies on the third. On the top are a profusion of gables, turrets, and chimneys. The twenty-two–room mansion, still owned and occupied by Seaquist's heirs, has fifteen fireplaces and five indoor stairways. In 1972 and 1973, the house was totally restored. In 1974 it was placed on the National Register of Historic Places. It is open daily 9–11 and 2–6.

BRADY

The first Swedes came to Brady, 110 miles northwest of Austin, in the 1880s and 1890s. Carl Hurd, a cousin of S. M. Swenson, had emigrated earlier in the century from Sweden to Texas. In 1885, four young Swedes including Dan and Lee Hurd, sons of Carl Hurd, arrived in McCulloch County, and each bought one-half section of land five miles east of Brady. Shortly thereafter

*This obelisk near
Brady honors Swedes.*

other Swedish families arrived, and the settlement was called East Sweden. A schoolhouse was built as well as a church. Since the first minister was Presbyterian, the East Sweden Church was identified with that denomination. A marker five and one-half miles northeast of Brady on U.S. Highway 190 and one-quarter mile east on a county road officially commemorates the East Sweden Presbyterian Church.

A second migration of Swedish settlers took place between 1900 and 1908. The Rev. E. Severin became a land agent, bringing parties from Williamson and Travis counties to an area seven miles west of Brady. Sixteen families settled there in 1905 and 1906 and called it West Sweden. A third group of Swedish families moved to Melvin Valley, sixteen miles west. Many of these families made their living from the land, but others brought skills in carpentry, stonemasonry, and blacksmithing to the community.

The ninety-five early Swedish families who helped populate McCulloch County between 1886 and 1912 in East and West Sweden and Melvin are honored on a thirteen-foot stone obelisk at the East Sweden Community Center (4.5 miles northeast of Brady on State Highway 190). Leaders of the first ninety-five Swedish families to settle the area are specifically identified.

The community center, once the schoolhouse, serves as a meeting place for those interested in preserving the area's history. Official state historical markers stand at the East Sweden Church and the Free Church in Melvin (on FM 2028, one mile south of U.S. Highway 87).

NORSE

Norse is a small community approximately one hundred miles north of Austin where a number of Norwegians settled. In the cemetery of Our Savior's Lutheran Church is the grave of Gustaf W. Belfrage (1834–1882), a Swedish-American naturalist noted for his work on insects. Belfrage came to Texas shortly after the Civil War. Between 1868 and 1873, he sent valuable collections of insect specimens to various educational institutions in New England, Sweden, England, and Russia. Students from Southern Methodist University, Texas A&M University, and Baylor University honored Belfrage with a special grave marker.

DALLAS

The Dallas Museum of Art, 1717 North Harwood (214/922-1200), holds Claes Oldenburg's "Stake Hitch" in its collection.

ABILENE

Built in 1910 for Swen Mangus Swenson's great-nephew William Gray Swenson and his wife, Shirley McCollum Swenson, the Swenson House, 1726 Swenson, reflects the Prairie and Mission styles popular during the early part of the century. The house, distinctive in its split staircase, oval dining room, and preserved woodwork, was home to the founder of Abilene's third bank, Citizens National Bank of Abilene. Swenson held financial interests and leadership positions in railroad, utility, real estate, and oil enterprises. The Abilene Preservation League, which owns the property, hosts the June Festive Swedish Smörgåsbord there annually, celebrating those of Swedish ancestry who helped settle this part of the West. For information about the annual Swedish festival, contact the Abilene Preservation League, 174 Cypress, Suite 302, Abilene, Texas 79601 (915/6767-3775).

AVOCA

Avoca, approximately two hundred miles northwest of Austin, is near Stamford. The Ericksdahl Community, located four and one-half miles northeast of Avoca, was organized between 1905 and 1909 for the most part by Swedes and their descendants from Travis and Williamson counties. The first Swedes in the area, however, were banker S. M. Swenson and his sons. As early as 1854, Swenson had secured one hundred thousand acres in the region. After the turn of the century, he authorized his sons, who had operated under the name of the S. M. Swenson Land and Cattle Company, to sell land to settlers of Swedish descent.

In 1906, Pastor J. A. Stamline formally organized the Bethel Lutheran Church, four and one-half miles northeast of Avoca on FM 600. This Ericksdahl Community congregation held worship services in private homes until the "Little White Church on the Hill" was completed by the fall of 1907 on land previously part of the Swenson ranch. The present stone church with a high steeple was completed in 1941 to replace the older one. The church contains a Heritage Room in the balcony of the sanctuary with a model of the previous sanctuary as well as numerous photographs. In front of the Bethel Lutheran Church is a state historic marker honoring the Swedes who settled the Ericksdahl Community.

5 The West

NEW MEXICO

Only a handful of Swedes migrated to the American Southwest, and generally it was mining and farming opportunities that attracted them. Among those few was Carl Eklund, who came to the United States from Sweden in 1885. An adventurous young man with a free spirit suited to the West, Eklund was, at various times, a cattleman, farmer, sheep man, saloon keeper, stonemason, miner, railroader, civic leader, and hotel operator. His skill as a card player must have also been an asset. Drawn to Clayton in New Mexico's northeastern corner, Eklund found there grasslands that stretch into three states and are preserved by the federal government. He became a rancher and ultimately owned about one hundred fifty thousand acres of ranch land north of the city, which he called the JE Ranch, using the initials of his father, Johannes Eklund. In 1894, Eklund purchased a two-year-old building in Clayton at 15 Main Street and turned it into the Eklund Hotel, Dining Room and Saloon. Enlarged in 1898 and again in 1905, it was known to travelers as the fanciest hotel between Dallas and Denver. When the hotel went up for sale in 1990, the history-minded Eklund Association purchased it and reopened it in 1992 as the Eklund Dining Room and Saloon.

265

COLORADO

Swedes initially came to Colorado to search for minerals, particularly gold, and to claim free land under the Homestead Act of 1862. They worked in the lead and silver mines around Leadville, and in forestry. By 1890, almost ten thousand Swedes lived in the state, making them the fourth largest of the foreign-born nationalities.

LONGMONT

In 1869, a group of Swedes founded a settlement near the present city of Longmont and named it Ryssby after a parish in Småland. Sven Johan Johnson was the acknowledged leader of the first Ryssby settlers, having arrived in 1869 with his younger brother and five other young men, to be followed by their respective families. They built one-room cabins from logs cut in the foothills of the Rockies some eight miles to the west. They worked as hired men on other farms, as lumberjacks, or as miners. Gradually they acquired more and more land, eventually encompassing about two thousand acres. Other settlers arrived, and in 1875 a schoolhouse was built.

In early 1877, the Rev. Frederick Lagerman, fresh from the Augustana Theological Seminary in Rock Island, Illinois, helped to organize in Boulder County what was called the Swedish Evangelical Lutheran Congregation-Ryssby. Although

The Ryssby church, modeled after a church in Ryssby, Småland, was built in 1881.

Lagerman left shortly thereafter, plans went ahead to build a church. On Reformation Sunday 1881, Pastor Johannes Telleen of Denver laid the cornerstone. The Ryssby church (on Sixty-third Street, one mile south of Nelson Road) sits on a knoll in rolling farm country near the foothills of the Rockies. Modeled after a church in Ryssby, Småland, it is a simple structure of sandstone. The entryway is surmounted by a short steeple constructed in 1924. The original was hit by lightning ten years earlier, and the steeple was never rebuilt to its former height. The simple interior has a fir floor, hard-backed pews (six are original), ornate chandeliers, a pot-bellied stove, and the original pump organ. Above the altar is the Swedish inscription, *"Ära vare Gud i höjden"* ("Glory be to God on high"). The church completed an extensive interior restoration in 1992.

By 1900, booming employment was making nearby Longmont an important regional municipality. As a result, young people left, and the Ryssby congregation declined. The last regular service was held in 1906, and eight years later the congregation merged with the Elim Lutheran Church of Longmont. However, two pastors from Longmont and Loveland were determined to preserve the legacy of the historic Ryssby church.

In 1924, a midsummer service at the old church was reinstituted, and it has become an annual event. Held the fourth Sunday of June, the service includes a Swedish liturgy. Also very popular are the annual candlelight services on the second weekend in December (three on Saturday and three on Sunday). These services, which feature seasonal music and a Bible reading in Swedish, have become so popular that those who wish to attend are advised to contact the Lutheran church in Longmont (see below) in early November. Couples also rent the church for wedding ceremonies.

In 1933, the church officially was made a state historic site, and a marker was erected. It is also on the National Register of Historic Places. Outside the church, large locust, elm, and maple trees planted by the original settlers still shade the grounds. To the east is the cemetery, where the oldest graves are in the southeast corner.

The congregation of First Evangelical Lutheran Church, 803 West Third Avenue (at Terry) (303/776-2704), was originally called Elim Lutheran and was organized in the late 1880s. In 1902 the old Methodist church on Terry between Third and Fourth avenues was purchased and was used by the Lutheran congregation for about thirty-five years. Today the building is a funeral home. After Ryssby and Elim were organized into a "joint parish," the name was changed to First Lutheran Church. Later the present Gothic-style church made of red sandstone was dedicated. The architect was Hugo Hansen, also responsible for designing Mount Olivet Lutheran Church in Minneapolis, the largest Lutheran congregation in the country.

Adjacent to the main sanctuary is the Ryssby Chapel with a number of items related to the Ryssby church, including its pulpit, bell, and altar candelabra. The altar rail is a re-creation of the original one. A pen and ink sketch portrays the original church with its tall steeple. In July 1966, forty parishioners from Ryssby, Sweden, came to worship at First Lutheran and presented a painting of their church.

In the basement is a glass case containing Ryssby church memorabilia as well as brass candlesticks from the Värnamo Association for Industry and Craftsmanship.

DENVER

INSTITUTES AND MUSEUMS
Swedish Medical Center—501 East Hampden Avenue, Englewood (303/788-5000).
The most outstanding name among Swedes in Denver regarding health care in the early part of the twentieth century was Dr. Charles A. Bundsen (1872-1956), who was from Holma, a village near Lysekil, Bohuslän. As a young man, Bundsen went to sea, eventually coming to Canada and the United States. After serving with the Medical Corps in Manila during the Spanish-American War, Bundsen came to Denver to attend medical school. One night, as the story goes, Bundsen dreamt of founding a sanatorium in Denver where Swedish people could be treated for tuberculosis. Colorado with its high altitude, low humidity, and considerable sunshine was regarded as an ideal climate for the cure of pulmonary tuberculosis. A plan for the establishment of such an institution was presented to a group of Denver businessmen who in 1905 agreed to its incorporation. It was to be known as the Swedish Consumptive Sanatorium (name changed in 1909 to Swedish National Sanatorium), and Bundsen was to be its chairman. The Swedish Ladies' Consumptive Aid Society was formed in June 1905 to promote the idea of a sanatorium, and in October 1906 a committee was authorized to purchase five acres of land in nearby Englewood. The first building was begun the following year, and twenty-five patient cottages and an administration building soon went up. Five Swedish denominations and five fraternal organizations joined forces in supporting the project.

In 1921, the board decided to expand the facilities further, resulting in the adoption of the mayflower program. The "mayflower" was an artificial replica of a little flower grown in Sweden. A considerable amount of money had been raised in Sweden since 1907 in the fight against tuberculosis with the sale of *majblomman*, an idea begun by Beda Hallberg of Gothenburg.

As a result of a visit to Sweden in 1921 by Bundsen and John Osterberg, a businessman from Providence, Rhode Island, the mayflower idea was adopted in the United States as well. An organization known as Majblomman, Inc., was formed in Providence. The net proceeds from the distribution and sale of the mayflowers were used exclusively by the Swedish National Sanatorium. Meanwhile in 1923 and 1924, three additional buildings were completed. An iron fence with plaques noting the donors was constructed. In 1927, Prince Wilhelm visited the sanatorium, greatly encouraging its further expansion. Groundbreaking ceremonies for the Mayflower Pavilion were held in April 1930; the building was completed the following year, and Beda Hallberg delivered the principal speech at the dedication.

In the mid-1940s, Bundsen resigned as medical director, and in 1952 a new wing of the Mayflower Building, known as the Bundsen Addition, was completed. In recent times, two other hospitals have joined forces with the sanatorium. Today the entire complex is known as the Swedish Medical Center, one of Denver's largest hospitals.

HISTORIC PLACES
The Colorado State Capitol—Broadway and East Colfax Avenue (303/866-2604).
Near the main rotunda, in a niche to the right of the main stairway, is a bronze bust of Edwin Carl Johnson (1884–1970), former Colorado governor (1933–37, 1955–57) and U.S. Senator (1937–55) of Swedish ancestry (George A. Carlson, Colorado governor 1915–20, was also of Swedish background). Johnson was born on a farm near Scandia, Kansas, and later moved to Colorado to improve his health. Initially a supporter of Franklin D. Roosevelt, Johnson gained a reputation as a critic of the president and was considered a party maverick.

CHURCHES
Augustana Lutheran Church—5000 East Alameda Avenue (303/388-4678).
The congregation was organized in 1878. Two years later, Dr. Johannes Telleen took charge of the congregation. From a group of eleven active members in that year, the congregation has grown to become one of the largest Lutheran churches in the United States with a current baptized membership of nearly twenty-one hundred. In 1881, the first service was conducted in a sanctuary on Broadway, Welton, and Nineteenth streets. Telleen remained with the congregation until 1884, serving also as Swedish vice-consul in Denver. He then went to the West Coast, establishing congregations in California. A new sanctuary

was built at Twenty-third and Court Place in 1889. Augustana Lutheran grew rapidly in the 1920s and 1930s. During the pastorate of Dr. Paul H. A. Noren in the 1950s, five and a half acres were purchased and the present strikingly modern sanctuary was constructed. In 1965 Christ Chapel and the Paul H. A. Noren Educational Building were dedicated.

In the patio is the first building's cornerstone. An Archives Room contains memorabilia. The impressive church is on high ground with good views of parts of Denver and the Rocky Mountains, including Mount Evans and Pikes Peak.

IDAHO SPRINGS

Area gold strikes brought Swedes to the community of Idaho Springs, some thirty-five miles west of Denver. At the eastern end of town is the small Gothic-style Zion Lutheran Church, 1921 Virginia (303/567-4378). The congregation was organized and the church built in 1896, and in the 1940s the frame church building was renovated.

GYPSUM

At one time, Swedes, Norwegians, and Finns made up 75 percent of Gypsum Valley's population. First Lutheran Church was most likely built in the 1890s by the local Nordic settlers. Across the street is the former Upper Gypsum School, originally three miles south of town, and also probably built by local Nordic immigrants. The area has diversified farming, including the raising of grain, potatoes, and livestock. Old Swedish congregations in other towns include Trinity Lutheran Church in Loveland, Mount Calvary Lutheran Church in Boulder, and Tabor Lutheran Church in Pueblo.

COLORADO SPRINGS

At the 14,110-foot summit of Pikes Peak near Colorado Springs is a plaque commemorating Swedish-American artist Carl Gustafson Lotave, born in Jönköping in 1872. He studied under Swedish artist Anders Zorn, spent some time in Paris, and then in the 1890s came to the United States to accept a position in the art department at Bethany College, Lindsborg, Kansas, where he was an associate of Birger Sandzén. Later Lotave moved to Colorado Springs where he was noted for his landscapes, portraits, and frescoes.

It has been reported that Lotave wanted his ashes to be deposited on Pikes Peak. On his deathbed in 1924, he made a request that Richard Wagner's "The Ride of the Valkyries" be played on the phonograph. As the music began, Lotave staggered to his feet and stood at attention until it was finished. A friend, J. Alden Brett, was so moved by the scene that he scribbled on a piece of paper an ode to the painter, the last words of which were, "Farewell, O soul on starlit seas adrift" (the ode is written on the plaque on Pikes Peak). After Lotave died, his ashes were brought to the summit and a special ceremony was held in late October 1925 with five hundred people in attendance. Colorado Springs Pioneers Museum at 215 S. Tejon Street (719/578-6650) is in possession of several of Lotave's paintings, including "The Riding Master."

An early Colorado Springs church, Bethany Lutheran at 1401 South Eighth (719/632-9017) was organized in 1897.

Peterson Air Force Base, which is southeast of Colorado Springs (call base operator at 719/554-7321), was constructed in 1942 and named for Lieutenant Edward J. Peterson, Jr., who lost his life at the airfield during that summer. He was born in 1917 on a farm in Harlan County, Nebraska, his grandfather having come from Blekinge.

VICTOR

Many Swedes involved in mining were attracted to such places as Leadville, Cripple Creek, and Victor. In Victor is the former Swedish Lutheran Church, opposite the Roman Catholic Church of Our Lady of the Mountain Shrine. At the northwest end of town is the cemetery. In this large graveyard, the visitor will be interested to observe the graves of a wide range of ethnic groups, including Swedes, who were attracted by Victor's mining opportunities.

TELLURIDE

This southwest Colorado community was one of the many gold rush boom towns of the late nineteenth century. Finnish and Swedish immigrants (mainly Swede-Finns) came to work as miners, blacksmiths, or boarding house employees. Telluride's east side was known as Finn Town, and there Finns and Swede-Finns each formed their own tight-knit communities and each had their own social halls. Finn Hall, built in 1896, served many of the town's five hundred Finns. Swede-Finn Hall, built in 1899 by the Royal Order of Runeberg, a social fraternity, was after thirty years opened to the public for social activities. At 472 West Pacific (303/728-2085), it has become a public restaurant and club that hosts many of the skiing enthusiasts who come to this former mining community turned year-round resort.

UTAH

Between 1850 and 1905, about thirty thousand Nordic immigrants, converts to the Church of Jesus Christ of Latter Day Saints (LDS), arrived in Utah. Of this number, the Danes were the most numerous, though over a third were Swedish, the largest contingents coming from Skåne, and Stockholm and the surrounding area. By 1900, Scandinavians formed about a third of Utah's foreign-born population. The first pioneer Swedish Mormon was John Eric Forsgren (1816–90) from Gävle. After serving in the Mormon Battalion in California during the Mexican War, Forsgren came to Salt Lake City in 1847, only three months after the arrival of Brigham Young. Three years later, Forsgren was sent to Sweden as a missionary. In Gävle, his brother, Peter, accepted Mormonism, becoming what is believed to be the first baptized LDS convert in Scandinavia. Eventually Peter Forsgren came to Brigham City, Utah, where he became a patriarch in the church. After being banished from Gävle, John Forsgren found his way to Copenhagen where he and other LDS missionaries successfully proselytized in Denmark and nearby Skåne.

The first large party of Nordic immigrants—about three hundred (approximately one-third Swedish)—arrived in Salt Lake in October 1853. They were advised by Brigham Young to settle in the Sanpete Valley west of the Wasatch Mountains and south of Salt Lake City. Communities including Mount Pleasant and Spring City were subsequently populated by Swedish immigrants. Other Swedes settled in Salt Lake City (by 1885 there was a "Swede Town") and in Cache County, north of Salt Lake City, particularly in Brigham City and Logan. It was the Scandinavian farmers who helped make Sanpete and Cache counties the granaries of Utah.

The Mormon leadership pushed the immigrants to learn English quickly and put away as much as possible their European cultural differences. Despite rapid assimilation, Nordic meeting groups, auxiliary to the regular Mormon congregations, did exist. Resenting Danish domination, Otto Rydman made a bid for Swedish meetings within the church and became editor of *Utah Korrespondenten*, founded in 1890.

Swedish Lutherans arrived after the Mormons, but Lutheran congregations were largely confined to the larger urban areas. Because Swedish settlers came first to Salt Lake City and because it remains the political, religious, and cultural focus of the state, this survey begins there and then moves from north to south, including Brigham City, Ogden, Mount Pleasant, and Ephraim.

SALT LAKE CITY

The Daughters of Utah Pioneers erected on the grounds west of the state capitol (350 North Main, 801/538-3000) a plaque honoring the eighty-six thousand pioneers who settled the valleys of the Rocky Mountains between 1847 and 1869. Hilda Anderson Erickson is recognized as being at her death in 1968 (in her 108th year) the last of the early Utah pioneers. Born in Västergötland, she came at the age of six to Utah on foot and by ox cart from Nebraska with her mother and two brothers.

On the grounds east of the capitol is a plaque honoring the Mormon battalion that served during the Mexican War. John Eric Forsgren had been a private in the battalion's Company D, and his name is listed on a plaque near the monument dedicated in 1927 (see the introduction to Utah for more information on Forsgren).

A large museum, the Daughters of Utah Pioneers Memorial Museum at 300 North Main (across the street from the state capitol, 801/538-1050), is dedicated to the memory of the Latter Day Saints pioneers. Open without admission charge Monday through Saturday 9–5 year-round and on Sundays 1–5 June through August, the museum contains a considerable variety of memorabilia, a great part of which is of Swedish origin or belonged to early Swedish Mormons. Names of Nordic pioneers may be found throughout the museum.

In the early years, the Mormon Church maintained a works program in Salt Lake City to help the immigrants find employment and to take advantage of their skills. Nordic carpenters and builders were involved in the construction of such structures as the Mormon Temple, the Mormon Tabernacle, and Brigham Young's Beehive House.

In July 1882, the Rev. Johannes Telleen of Denver with five charter members organized the Zion Lutheran Church, the first Lutheran church in Utah. Leaders of the Augustana Synod were of the opinion that there was sufficient support in Salt Lake City for a congregation, believing that a number of Swedes nominally converted to the Latter Day Saints would be willing to rejoin a Lutheran church. Despite much zeal, Lutheran success was very limited.

The Zion Lutheran congregation constructed its first church in 1885. Six years later a second structure was built, and it remained the sanctuary until 1956 when the present building at 1070 Foothill Drive (801/582-2321) was completed. At the northwest corner of Second South and Fourth East is a plaque noting the location of the earlier churches.

BRIGHAM CITY

In the Brigham City Cemetery are buried a number of Swedes, including Mormon John Eric Forsgren (1816–90); his father, John O. Forsgren (1793–1880); and other members of the family. The cemetery's entrance is on Third East near Fourth South.

OGDEN

The second oldest Lutheran congregation in Utah is Ogden's Elim Lutheran Church, which was organized in 1888. The Rev. F. A. Linder, its founder, met with some hostility from the Mormons who did not welcome his missionary efforts. The first church was constructed in 1889 and 1890, but the sanctuary used now at 575 Twenty-third (801/394-5543) dates from 1948.

MOUNT PLEASANT

The oldest building in the Mount Pleasant Historic Commercial District is Liberal Hall at 51 West Main Street, which was constructed in 1874 and 1875. A stucco building with a gable roof, it was in the 1870s a meeting place for locals who became disenchanted with either the authoritarian style of the local Mormon leadership or unhappy over the ban on Swedish in the church services. In 1875, a Presbyterian minister from Illinois arrived and subsequently secured the building and established a Presbyterian church and mission school. In 1881 the Presbyterian Board of Home Missions purchased the building, and since then it has changed hands several times, serving recently as a senior citizens center. Although this and other Presbyterian schools were never very successful in encouraging people to leave the LDS church, they were important in stimulating the growth of a public education system throughout the state of Utah.

Two other nineteenth-century buildings, the N. S. Nielson House at 179 West Main Street and the Sanpete County Cooperative Store at 160 West Main Street, were built in whole or in

N. S. Nielson built his home in the 1890s in Mount Pleasant, which he served as mayor in 1896 and 1897. An example of Victorian eclecticism, the home combines in its exterior Second Empire, Queen Anne, and Beaux Arts classical motifs.

part by Swede N. S. Nielson (1848–1925) who had come to Mount Pleasant in 1869 after converting to the LDS church. Becoming disenchanted with the faith, Nielson and his two brothers joined other disaffected Mormons as stockholders in the Sanpete County Cooperative Store, which was known as the "Swedish" or "Gentile" store. Until the depression, the store was one of Sanpete Valley's most prominent establishments. N. S. Nielson was a successful banker, sheep man, and entrepreneur who took on the duties of mayor in 1896 and 1897.

The N. S. Nielson House, constructed in the early 1890s, is an example of Victorian eclecticism combining Second Empire, Queen Anne, and Beaux Arts classical external motifs. Included on the National Register of Historic Places, the house reflects the prosperity that a growing livestock industry brought to Mount Pleasant.

EPHRAIM

Nordic Mormons, particularly Danes, settled in this Sanpete County community. Two early houses built by Swedes still stand and are listed on the National Register of Historic Places. The small square Niels Ole Anderson House (308 South 100 East) with Federal-style and Greek Revival detailing was built in two stages. The oldest part is two rooms built of fired brick in the late 1860s. Owners expanded the house with a two-room adobe addition in the early 1880s. Since then the house, typical of the area's pioneer architecture and craftsmanship, has remained relatively unaltered.

Anderson, part owner in a sawmill and active in church and community life, had emigrated to Utah from Sweden in the mid-1850s when he was about ten. He came with his family, whose members had converted to the LDS faith. He kept a journal of pioneer life and his Indian encounters and became known as a folklorist and an expert craftsman. He returned to Sweden between 1880 and 1882 as a Mormon missionary.

The Johnson-Nielson House (351 North Main Street), a large Victorian-style home, was also associated with early Swedes in the community. Scandinavian Americans built homes in other communities in Sanpete County, including Spring City, in the late nineteenth century. Many are built in the style described by Swedish folklife scholar Sigurd Erixon as a pair house, which features a large central unit flanked by a single room on each side.

WYOMING

Starting as early as the 1870s, Nordic Mormons also helped to settle Wyoming along with Arizona, Colorado, Idaho, Nevada, and New Mexico. In Wyoming, three Swedish Lutheran congregations were organized—St. Luke's (in Buffalo), St. Paul (in Cheyenne), and Trinity (in Sheridan).

MONTANA

Most Swedish settlers in Montana were engaged in mining and cattle ranching. Montana's Swedes generally lived in the state's western mountain regions. Five Lutheran congregations were established before World War I in Helena (St. John's, 1895), Missoula (Immanuel, 1898), Butte (Emanuel, 1898, and later renamed Gloria Dei), Anaconda (First, 1904), and Barber (Grace, 1911). After the First World War, two Augustana Lutheran churches were started in Great Falls (Bethel and First English).

Three Montana governors (J. Hugo Aronson, John E. Erickson, and Forrest H. Anderson) have been of Swedish ancestry (neighboring Idaho has had one—Donald W. Samuelson). Aronson was born at Gällstad in Älvsborg. Malmstrom Air Force Base in Great Falls is one of three Air Force bases in the United States named for pilots of Swedish ancestry. Colonel A. Malmstrom, born of Swedish parents in Chicago, died in an air disaster in 1954 near Great Falls.

IDAHO

Although Swedes never came in large numbers to Idaho, there was a significant settlement named New Sweden near Idaho Falls. Important church landmarks are to be found in Boise and near Moscow. In 1905, Idaho's Swedish Lutherans organized a college—Coeur d'Alene—in northwestern Idaho, but it closed after only fifteen years.

IDAHO FALLS

In the 1890s, Chicago's Swedish Land Company encouraged a number of Swedes, mainly from the Oakland area of northeast Nebraska, to homestead in the Upper Snake River Valley west of Idaho Falls. Later settlers from Småland were attracted to the region. By digging irrigation canals, settlers transformed the sagebrush valley gradually into a rich agricultural land that today grows potatoes and grains, including barley and oats.

The New Sweden Mission Church was organized in 1894, and a sanctuary was built the following year. But the New Sweden church had trouble maintaining membership, and in September 1928 the church building was sold and subsequently torn down. Only the parsonage and the graves of the early Swedish settlers in the well-maintained New Sweden Cemetery remain. Facing the cemetery on a monument made of flat lava rock is a historical marker dedicated in 1974 to the New

Sweden pioneers: "In loving memory . . . for their many hardships to give us our proud heritage in this thriving and prosperous community." The cemetery is on Pioneer Road near its intersection with New Sweden School Road.

The Alliance Covenant Church, now at 557 South Boulevard, dates from the merger in 1929 of the New Sweden and Idaho Falls (organized in 1899 as the Swedish Evangelical Mission Church of Idaho Falls) congregations. It was called the Mission Covenant Church, but that name has been changed to Alliance Covenant. The congregation is a member of the Christian Missionary Alliance.

In April 1898 the Scandinavian Evangelical Lutheran Gustaf Adolphus Church was organized. The congregation in 1939 adopted the name First Evangelical Lutheran Church and began the construction of the present-standing red brick sanctuary, completed two years later. The Gothic-style lanterns in the sanctuary, obtained from a Boise bank, are made of Swedish iron. The stained glass windows are in memory of former Swedish members of the congregation. The former altar painting is by Gustav Nathanael Malm (1869–1928), a student of Olof Grafström.

BOISE

In Boise the Immanuel Evangelical Lutheran Church at 707 West Fort (three blocks north of the state capitol) (208/344-3011) was organized in 1906. Between 1908 and 1913, a lovely sandstone Gothic-style sanctuary was built, today on the National Register of Historic Places and known as the Augustana Chapel. Charles F. Hummel, the architect, was also involved with the construction of the state capitol. The chapel's twentieth-century Gothic features include a cruciform plan with an off-center tower. It has its original wooden pews, chancel rail, baptismal font, pulpit, and gold-trimmed white Gothic-style altar. Augustana Chapel is still used by the congregation for early morning Sunday worship service, although a newer adjacent edifice, built in 1980, is employed for most church functions. In the foyer of the new church is the old pump organ.

MOSCOW

In Moscow's city cemetery are the graves of the Rev. and Mrs. Peter Carlson. During his pioneer ministry, Carlson, the first pioneer Swedish Lutheran pastor in the Pacific Northwest, established Lutheran congregations throughout Idaho, Oregon, and Washington. Carlson was born in Småland in 1822, emigrated in 1854, was ordained in 1859, and initiated his pioneer ministry in 1879.

In 1884 Carlson organized First Lutheran, a Swedish group that built a white clapboard sanctuary in 1906, which still stands on the corner of Second and Van Buren. In 1961, it and a

Simple and stately, the Cordelia Lutheran Church is the oldest Lutheran building in Idaho. Built in 1883, it belonged to the first Swedish congregation in the state.

Norwegian congregation merged to form Emmanuel Lutheran (1036 West A Street).

Organized by Carlson four years earlier, in 1880, was Cordelia Lutheran Church, which built a sanctuary in 1883 that still stands. The first Swedish congregation in the state and the oldest Lutheran building in Idaho, Cordelia Lutheran also claims to be the site of the first confirmation in the West. Southeast of Moscow, Cordelia is about one mile east of Genesee-Troy Road, in between its intersection with Eid Road and Lenville Road.

Originally and officially known as "The Swedish Evangelical Lutheran Congregation, Cordelia, Nez Perce County, Idaho Territory," the church persevered until 1913, when the congregation merged with that of a forerunner of Moscow's Emmanuel Lutheran Church. A modest eighteen– by twenty-four–foot structure that must have suited the church's eighteen founding members, the church lay dormant until 1948, when restoration was initiated but unfinished. Restoration was undertaken again in earnest in the early 1990s by volunteer labor provided by the Friends of Cordelia Committee, a committed group that sprang from Emmanuel Lutheran in Moscow. Behind the church is a small cemetery with some Swedish inscriptions. In the cemetery is a granite stone with a reference to the Rev. Carlson.

TROY

In Troy, the Rev. Carlson organized the Westdala Lutheran Church in 1886, and its members built a sanctuary in 1891. In 1902, it was moved to Main Street, where members had it remodeled several times. In 1949 the church was renamed Troy Lutheran Church (208/835-3641).

COEUR D'ALENE

The Swedish Lutheran Coeur d'Alene College was founded in 1905 by J. Jesperson, who had been the business manager at Augustana College in Rock Island, Illinois. The Rev. Carl J. Renhard (1870–1946), pastor of Immanuel Lutheran Church in Portland, Oregon, and founder of Emanuel Hospital in that same city, was chosen as the college's second president. Between 1905 and 1920 several buildings were constructed, including dormitories and a gymnasium. In 1908, this coeducational institution had 120 students; however, the Swedish-American Lutheran constituency in Idaho was not large enough to support it, and it was forced to close. The property was purchased by the Norwegian Lutherans and converted into a home for the aged, which still exists, but the buildings have been greatly altered during the intervening years.

WASHINGTON

The Pacific Northwest, particularly Washington, attracted numerous Swedes, the first sizable group arriving in the 1880s. The largest number were attracted to the Puget Sound area (see map, page 280), seeking opportunities in farming, fishing, and lumbering. By the turn of the century, businessmen, builders, mechanics, and engineers were arriving. Larger communities with significant Swedish-American populations are Seattle (particularly the Ballard section), Tacoma, Everett, and Bellingham. Preston near Seattle was at one time almost totally Swedish. Smaller towns in western Washington with many Swedes include La Conner, Hockinson, Mount Vernon, and Enumclaw. Hoquiam and Aberdeen had many Swede-Finns. Swedes also settled in other parts of the state, including Selah in the Yakima Valley and Spokane. This review of cities moves, generally, north to south, from Ferndale in the northwest to Skamokawa and Chinook, which lie across the Columbia River from northwestern Oregon. It concludes with Spokane, the city in this survey most removed from the western coast.

FERNDALE

In Hovander Homestead Park at 5299 Nielsen Road (south of Ferndale off Hovander Road) (206/384-3444) stands the Hovander Home, a fine example of turn-of-the-century frame construction that was built between 1901 and 1903. Håkan

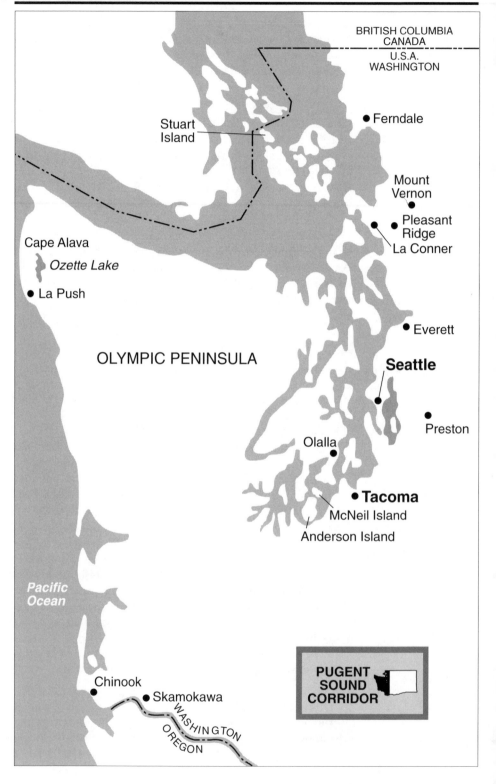

BRITISH COLUMBIA
CANADA
U.S.A.
WASHINGTON

● Ferndale

Stuart
Island

Mount
Vernon
●

Pleasant
Ridge
La Conner

Cape Alava

Ozette Lake

● La Push

● Everett

OLYMPIC PENINSULA

Seattle

●
Preston

Olalla
●

● **Tacoma**
McNeil Island
Anderson Island

*Pacific
Ocean*

Chinook
●

● Skamokawa

WASHINGTON
OREGON

PUGENT
SOUND
CORRIDOR

Hovander (originally named Håkan Olsson Håvander), an architect, was a native Swede who immigrated twice to the United States. In 1969 the Hovander Homestead was purchased by Whatcom County, and in 1974 it was placed on the National Register of Historic Places.

Hovander was born in 1841 in Sallerup, Skåne. As a teenager, he came to the United States where he worked as a mason's helper and bricklayer. He returned to Sweden, and in 1879 married in Stockholm. As a result of failing health, he immigrated again, spending some time in New Zealand but finally arriving on the U.S. West Coast, first in San Francisco and then in Seattle. In 1898, Hovander purchased one hundred acres of homestead land and three years later began the house, for which he himself laid the brick for the foundation. A high peaked roof with many gables tops the lovely home, which is accentuated with a white scalloped trim. The large rooms with high ceilings contain many pieces of the Hovander family's furniture brought to Washington around Cape Horn. In the parlor and along the hallway are portraits of King Oscar II. In the Architect's Room (formerly Hovander's sons' bedroom) are some of his plans, including drawings of a building in Stockholm. The second floor is a storage area that was never completed.

In addition to the main house are several structures, including a large red barn, milk house, and water tower. In the

Håkan Hovander, an architect and native Swede, built his home, now the main attraction in Hovander Homestead Park, between 1901 and 1903.

barn, built in 1911, are numerous pieces of farm equipment and an old stagecoach. The nearby water tower was constructed in 1916. The milk house also has been restored and is furnished with equipment needed by the Hovanders for making butter and cheese. The farm became almost totally self-sufficient, producing meat, eggs, other dairy products, fruit, grains, and silage.

After Hovander died in 1915, his wife continued to live on the farm until 1936. Otis, one of the seven children, oversaw the farm until Whatcom County purchased it in 1969.

MOUNT VERNON

The Salem Lutheran Church (1005 South Third Street at Snoqualmie) was organized in 1913 as a result of the merger of the Swedish Finnish Evangelical Bethesda congregation of Cedardale and others. The Bethsaida congregation of Pleasant Ridge joined in 1925. The light-colored brick sanctuary was constructed in 1916. In the Fireside Room on the second floor of the education building is a 1918 Olof Grafström painting of the Last Supper.

An early home is the Magnus Anderson House at 2018 Dike Road. Also along Dike Road, at 1775, stands another hand-built reminder of earlier times, a windmill constructed by Axel E. Carlson in 1906. For many years windmills with elevated tanks were a common sight on Skagit County farms.

PLEASANT RIDGE

In this community near La Conner can be seen the old Bethsaida Lutheran Church parsonage (1754 Chilberg Road), which is on the National Register of Historic Places, and the church cemetery. The Bethsaida Lutheran Church, begun in 1881, was the first Swedish Lutheran congregation in Washington. In 1892, a sanctuary was built, but it burned in the late 1960s. What was left was torn down. In 1925 the congregation merged with Salem Lutheran Church of Mount Vernon (see Mount Vernon).

In the Pleasant Ridge Cemetery on Valentine Road is the reddish granite stone of Magnus Anderson (1836-1926) and his wife and son. Anderson was a pioneer of 1869, and an anchor is carved on the stone. A cabin he built still stands in La Conner. On the grave of Charles William Rosenquist (1857-1920) is the inscription, "Here rests a woodman of the world."

A noteworthy historical home is the Peter Downey House (1880 Chilberg Road).

LA CONNER

Many Swedes, Norwegians, and Swede-Finns were attracted to the rich Skagit Valley noted for its dairy and vegetable farms. To the east are the Cascade Mountains, including Mount Baker.

The town of La Conner covers a rocky hill on the east bank of Swinomish Channel. This picturesque community is the oldest in northwest Washington and has a number of well-preserved buildings from the 1870s to 1910, some of which have Swedish connections. La Conner was founded as a trading center in 1867, and it became an important fishing center. Fish canneries and vegetable processing plants are located in and around the town. The La Conner Historic District, which has earned a place on the National Register of Historic Places, is roughly bounded by Second, Morris, and Commercial streets and the Swinomish Channel.

A one-story cabin, twelve by twenty feet, stands in La Conner as a reminder of pioneer days. Magnus Anderson, a native Swede and ship's carpenter, built the cabin and helped settle Pleasant Ridge after coming to the area in the 1860s. Built of squared hewn logs, the cabin's gabled roof extends over the front porch. Originally located near the north fork of the Skagit River, the cabin was moved to La Conner in 1952. Anderson and his family are buried at Pleasant Ridge Cemetery.

Another noteworthy building in La Conner is the Nelson-Pierson Grocery on First Street at the end of Washington. Erected in 1908, the grocery was run by Swedes in the early part of the century. At 212 Morris Street stands the Ole Wingren House, home to Ole Wingren, an early La Conner photographer and stationer whose shop stood next door. The house dates from the 1890s. The Perry Polson House, at Third Street and Benton, was home to Polson, who immigrated with his father, Olof Polson (or Pålsson) (1833–1903), from Sweden. The Polsons along with Carl John Kilberg (or Chilberg) were among the first settlers in the La Conner area and came from Halland in the 1870s. At first a surveyor, construction worker, and farmer, Perry Polson in 1884 moved to La Conner and started a hardware store that he successfully expanded into a farm implement business.

Helping visitors appreciate the history of La Conner and the surrounding area is the Skagit County Historical Museum at 501 South Fourth (206/466-3365), which is open Tuesday through Sunday 11–5. Available there is a pamphlet outlining a walking tour of La Conner. Scattered throughout this attractive museum are numerous items used and donated by Swedes of the area. The museum also owns an extensive oral history collection of interviews with early area settlers.

Other early homes also of interest include the Olof Polson House (Fir Island), the Nels Larson House (at 1895 Bradshaw Road), and the Charlie Nelson House (at 1836 Chilberg Road).

EVERETT

Zion Lutheran Church was organized in 1900, but the old church building has been replaced with one built in 1963.

SEATTLE

Swedes in Seattle made their way in medicine, retailing, and the steel, fishing, construction, and lumber industries. The city has a strong Nordic element, especially evident in Ballard, where signs proclaim "Velkommen til Ballard" and shops fly Nordic as well as U.S. and Washington state flags. The Ballard Avenue Historic District (along Ballard Avenue between Northwest Market Street and Northwest Dock), a four-block commercial stretch typifying modest turn-of-the-century commercial buildings, boasts the former Scandinavian-American Bank building (5300–5304 Ballard), for a time the second largest bank in Seattle.

INSTITUTES AND MUSEUMS

Nordic Heritage Museum—3014 Northwest Sixty-seventh Street (206/789-5707). Open Tuesday through Saturday 10–4 and Sunday 12–4.

Housed in a public school built in 1907 where children of Nordic immigrants were formerly taught, the Nordic Heritage Museum is the largest ethnic museum in the Pacific Northwest. An effort by the Heritage Museum Foundation, founded in 1979, to develop a collection focusing on the origins of the Nordic immigrants and their experiences in American society, the museum presents collections from all five Nordic countries. Exhibits include one featuring the development of the Ballard community, where the early immigrants' influence can still be

A part of the "The Dream of America" exhibit at the Nordic Heritage Museum tells the story of the departure of the Nordic immigrants who left their homes to find a new life. Housed in a former school where immigrants' children were taught, the museum is the largest ethnic museum in the Pacific Northwest.

felt. "The Dream of America," the museum's major historical exhibit, acquaints visitors on the first floor with the immigrants' struggle to create a new life in a raw land. It follows them as they arrive as innocent immigrants, work in deplorable conditions, move to the Midwest, and then push on to the Northwest. On the second floor, exhibits tell the story of Scandinavians in the Northwest, including their role in the fishing and logging industries, focuses on their contribution to its development, and explains the strong ties binding these groups. The third floor devotes its five galleries to highlighting the five Nordic countries, and the Swedish gallery traces a typical immigrant along the journey to the United States.

The 51,000-square-foot museum, some of which has undergone extensive renovation, hosts international exhibits and offers a large reading area to those who use its library. On the main floor are facilities for language and rosemaling instruction. At Christmastime the museum recreates Scandinavian cultural events and in summertime holds an annual festival. In addition to a language school and an education program linked to area schools, the museum sponsors various performing arts events and other cultural activies such as film series. More than sixty-five thousand visitors come to the Nordic Heritage Museum each year.

Swedish Hospital Medical Center—747 Summit Avenue (206/386-6000).

Opened in 1910, the Swedish Hospital was founded in 1908 by a group of Seattle's Swedish residents under the leadership of Dr. Nils August Johansson (1872–1946) who was from Lund, Sweden. Desiring to become a physician and believing that opportunities were too limited in Sweden, Johansson arrived in 1893 in Boston. After working in the Colorado mines, Johansson studied medicine at the University of Denver, and then he moved to Washington. After working at St. Luke's Hospital in Denver, Johansson resolved that someday he would start his own hospital. This became a reality in Seattle when ten Swedish men promised him one thousand dollars each. When the founder of a private hospital at Summit and Columbia was tragically killed in a car accident in 1912, Johansson was able to buy this facility.

As a result of Johansson's interest in cancer research, in the early 1930s, the hospital's tumor institute was opened (1221–1225 Madison Street, 206/386-2323). On the second floor of the Arnold Medical Pavilion are several plaques, including one honoring the institute. In the main lobby of the hospital is a portrait of Johansson. The hospital's library is named in his honor, and the Katherine Brown Johansson Chapel for his wife.

The Swedish colors are in evidence in the hospital's flag and the hospital's color scheme.

In 1980, two of Seattle's hospitals—the Doctors and Seattle General—merged with Swedish, making it the largest private hospital in the Pacific Northwest.

CHURCHES

Ballard is dotted with churches, several of which began as Swedish congregations. Though their ownership has sometimes shifted out of Swedish hands, the old sanctuaries constructed shortly after the turn of the century still survive. These include the Free Swedish Evangelical Mission Covenant Church (1723 Northwest Sixty-first Street) and Swedish Bethel Lutheran Church (Sixty-Fourth Street and Twenty-second Avenue NW). The Ballard Baptist Church at 2004 Northwest Sixty-third (the original church was at the southwest corner of Twentieth Avenue NW and Northwest Sixty-first) is a daughter congregation of First Baptist, which became known as Central Baptist, Seattle. Originally known as First Scandinavian Baptist and then First Swedish Baptist Church, the Central congregation was organized in 1883. It had its roots in the pioneer work of Olaus Okerson, who arrived in Portland, Oregon, in 1880. Central Baptist no longer exists, but its building was located at Ninth and Pine. Artifacts from that church are at First Baptist Church of Seattle at Seneca and Harvard. Another daughter congregation of First Baptist (Central Baptist) is Elim Baptist at 2410 North Fifty-sixth Street in the Sunnyside section of Seattle. The congregation of Elim Baptist constructed its building in 1913.

First Covenant Church—400 East Pike (northwest corner of Bellevue and Pike streets) (206/322-7411).
Built in 1910 and 1911, the large sandstone edifice, constructed in the Classical style, is the third for this congregation, which was organized in 1889. The building is one of two of the Rev. Erik August Skogsbergh's tabernacles still surviving. Skogsbergh (1850–1939), a Minneapolis pastor recognized for outstanding preaching, worked for several years in Seattle and built monumental auditoriums in both cities. It was dedicated in 1911 and originally seated twenty-five hundred. Since then several renovations, including the addition of a sizable lobby, have reduced the number of seats. Nonetheless, the oval high-domed auditorium remains impressive, its balcony encircling three-fourths of the sanctuary. Stained glass windows depicting lilies grace the building throughout. Though formerly "Swedish Tabernacle" appeared on the pediment on the Pike Street side, one bearing "First Covenant Church" has replaced it.

Gethsemane Lutheran—911 Stewart Street (southeast corner of Ninth Avenue and Stewart) (206/682-3620).
A daughter church of First Lutheran in Tacoma, Gethsemane was established in 1885 by the Rev. Peter Carlson. Its modern sanctuary was completed in 1961.

Columbia Lutheran Home—4700 Phinney North (206/632-7400).
Formerly Columbia Conference Home for the Aged, Columbia Lutheran Home was founded in 1920 by Dr. C. R. Swanson as a home for indigent Swedes. Gradually the home's purpose changed, and today it is a skilled care nursing home operated by the Pacific Northwest Synod of the Lutheran Church in America. A new building replaced the old one in 1980.

Former Emmaus Lutheran Church—169 Northwest Sixty-fifth Street.
A Swedish congregation, organized in 1906, built the frame structure with Gothic-style windows between 1910 and 1915.

SCHOOLS
University of Washington—(206/543-2100; information center, 206/543-9198).
The impressive Alfred H. Anderson Hall, a nineteenth-century Gothic-style building, honors Alfred H. Anderson (1854–1914), the son of a Swedish immigrant and himself a prominent lumberman, member of the Washington Legislature, and a leader in establishing the present campus of the university. Another building, the Warren G. Magnuson Health Sciences Center, is named in honor of the former U.S. Senator who was born in Minnesota and reared in a Swedish-Norwegian family. One of the largest of its kind in the United States, the Department of Scandinavian Languages and Literature saw unprecedented growth under the chairmanship of Professor Walter Johnson in the late 1960s and early 1970s. At Suzzallo and Allen Library, the front facade on the Suzzallo entrance bears emblems of various European universities, including one from Uppsala University.

From 1905 to 1918, a Swedish Baptist school known as Adelphia College existed, having been organized the same year as Bethel Academy in Minneapolis. Its founder and president was Dr. Emanuel Schmidt (1868–1921) from Hälsingland. A number of its graduates became missionaries in China. Because of financial problems during the First World War, the school was forced to close. The red brick Adelphia Hall, built in 1905, remains and continues to be identified by that name. It is owned by the Seattle Preparatory School (2400 Eleventh East, 206/324-0400), which is run by Jesuits, who have added a gymnasium in front of the building.

OTHER POINTS OF INTEREST

Nordstrom—1501 Fifth Avenue (main retail outlet and corporate headquarters) (206/628-2111).

Nordstrom, now a nationwide department store chain whose stock is traded on the New York Stock Exchange, began in 1901 as a shoe store in downtown Seattle. The original store at Fourth and Pike no longer stands. John W. Nordstrom and two sons expanded the business. Nordstrom, with over fifty stores and other smaller specialty stores and leased shoe departments, has grown into one of the largest fashion specialty retailers in the West and has expanded into East Coast markets, employing over thirty-one thousand in the early 1990s with net earnings of more than $140 million. A third generation of Nordstrom family members holds executive management positions.

Founder John Nordstrom (1871–1962) was born in Luleå, Sweden. At age sixteen, he left his native land for the United States, where at first he worked in the iron mines in Michigan's Upper Peninsula. In 1889, he headed west, arriving in San Francisco. After working in the redwood forests of California as a logger, Nordstrom in 1897 went on to the Klondike in Alaska, where he struck it rich. From there he and a partner opened a shoe store in Seattle. The present main store and corporate headquarters on Fifth Avenue was built in 1938. Its colored terrazzo skin hides the old structure except near the top of the southernmost end.

Former Frederick and Nelson Department Store—Fifth and Pine.

One of the original partners of Frederick and Nelson was Nels B. Nelson (born Nils B. Nilsson in Kristianstad, Skåne, in 1854). After emigrating, he first went to Colorado, where he farmed and mined for gold. In 1891 he came to Seattle, where he became partners with Frederick (a Dane) in the department store business. Nelson died in 1907, and the business was sold in the 1930s to Marshall Field.

Lake View Cemetery—1554 Fifteenth East (206/322-1582).

The earliest Swedish settlers of Seattle are buried in this cemetery.

Nils A. Johansson House—2800 Broadway East (near East Hamlin Street).

The Swiss Chalet–style Nils A. Johansson House, in the North Capitol Hill area, was built in 1909.

Swedish Club—1920 Dexter Avenue North (business office, 206/283-1090; restaurant, 206/283-1077).

With a membership of about four thousand, the Seattle Swedish Club is probably the most active organization of its kind in the United States. Founded in 1892 by Nels B. Nelson and others and at first meeting in halls and private homes, the club ten years later began meeting at its own clubhouse on Eighth Avenue. For almost sixty years that location remained its home. Members banded together to improve opportunities for Swedes in the city. The Dexter Avenue facilities, acquired in 1960, feature a restaurant on the upper floor overlooking Lake Union and meeting rooms and classrooms where members gather throughout the week. Originally open only to men, the club expanded to include women as members in 1989.

In the main lobby, Swedish dolls in various provincial folk costumes, Swedish glass, photographs of various organizations, and the charter of the Swedish Club interpret the club's background. The dolls come from the internationally known doll and folk dress factory of Charlotte Weibull in Åkarp, Skåne. A small statue of Selma Lagerlöf is a replica of one in Karlstad, Sweden. In the second floor stairwell is a Mora clock dated 1843 in front of a Dala folk painting. The second floor bar features the insignias of six Swedish provinces as well as portraits of the Swedish monarchs from Gustav Vasa.

A block of iron ore from Sweden, displayed at the 1962 Seattle World's Fair, stands in front of the club near where an inscription on the Memorial Fountain greets visitors with the saying, "Happy is the house which shelters friends and treasures their memories." The club celebrated its centennial in 1992.

SCULPTURE AND OTHER ART
At the Shilshoe Bay Marina (7001 Seaview NW, 206/728-3385), the Leif Eriksson statue, erected in 1962, commands an impressive view of the Olympic Mountain range in the distance and a large marina to the east.

PRESTON

In 1888, a group of Swedish Baptists came to Washington State from Minnesota to work in lumber camps and mills near Snoqualmie Pass east of Seattle. In 1892, they bought a shingle mill near Lower Preston, which began to flourish under the leadership of August Lovegren (1861–1917), who was from Värmland and one of the original owners. Later an additional shingle mill and sawmill were built in Lower Preston, attracting additional Swedish Baptist immigrants.

Swedish Lutherans from Jämtland settled in nearby Upper Preston. They held services in the Vasa Hall founded in 1902. The present lodge was built in 1948, replacing one that burned.

In Lower Preston in 1900, twenty people, including Lovegren donated a plot of land, and in 1902 the present white frame Preston Baptist Church was built. In 1954 the sanctuary was remodeled.

Lovegren built a planing mill on a site next to the general store. His three-story white frame house with blue trim still stands. In the cemetery are buried many of the early Swedish settlers, but Lovegren and his wife, Hilma (1863–1954), are buried in nearby Fall City Cemetery.

OLALLA

In Olalla across from Vashon Island is the Charles F. Nelson House, built in 1913 and now a national historic site. It was home to Swede Charles F. Nelson, a merchant. The large two and a half–story frame house at Nelson and Crescent Valley roads, still a private residence, has a five-sided steeple. With a long veranda running nearly the entire front length of it, the house sits on a knoll overlooking Puget Sound's Colvos Passage. During the Alaska gold rush, Nelson traveled to the Yukon where he operated a store. In 1904, he returned to Olalla, opened a store, and soon became the town's principal merchant.

OLYMPIC PENINSULA

In the spring of 1888, K. O. Erickson, a legendary Swedish pioneer of the Pacific Northwest settled on the Olympic Peninsula as a fur trader among the Native Americans, whose language he learned and whose leaders named him an honorary chief. One of his fur stores was in a settlement named Mora near La Push on the Olympic Peninsula Pacific coast. Erickson also founded a successful savings and loan association at Port Angeles. He gave money to his native city, Mora, Dalarna, for the construction of a park across from the Zorn Museum and to the Swedish Boy and Girl Scouts. Author, newspaperman, and merchant Svante Lofgren recorded Erickson's life in his book *Vita Björnen (The White Bear)*. Lofgren lived on Washington's Stuart Island, the most northwesterly island in the continental United States.

Another settler on the Olympic Peninsula was Lars Ahlstrom, who homesteaded near Ozette Lake. Much of his plank trail survives and is used by tourists on their way out to Cape Alava, site of a prehistoric Indian village. This trail, with its crosswise puncheon plan, represents a long tradition in northern Sweden.

TACOMA

Nicholas Delin (Nikolaus Dalin), it is said, was the first white man to settle on land within the present city limits of Tacoma. In 1852, the Gotland native built a water-powered sawmill, and for his contributions to early Tacoma, the city named a street in his honor. Another street bears the name of one of the Swedish kings, Karl XIV Johan, who was king from 1818 to 1844.

The Washington State Historical Society Museum and Library (315 North Stadium Way, 206/593-2830) commends itself to Tacoma visitors as a helpful partner in understanding the historic development of the state. The museum holds a Swedish corner cupboard, formerly owned by an early settler.

Of the churches, First Evangelical Lutheran Church at the northwest corner of South Sixth and I (across from Wright Park) was one of the earliest, organized in 1882 by Pastor Peter Carlson. The following year a small sanctuary was completed. Until 1887, Norwegians were also worshiping with the Swedes, but then they organized their own congregation.

In 1889, the second church building, on South Eighth and I streets, was constructed by well-known Tacoma contractor Edward Young, a Bohuslän native who had immigrated to the United States the year before. Pastor Johannes Telleen, Columbia Conference President of the Augustana Lutheran Synod, who was present at the dedication, called the second church the "Swedish Lutheran Cathedral of the West Coast," but a fire in 1924 destroyed it. Three years later the church dedicated the red brick building in which it still worships. Young was also responsible for the construction of the First Church of Christ Science, 902 Division, and Lincoln High School, 701 South Thirty-seventh Street.

Two former Swedish churches are the red brick Covenant church (corner of South I and South Tenth streets) with the date 1909 on its cornerstone and First Swedish Baptist Church (southeast corner of South Twelfth and I streets). First Swedish Baptist was organized in 1893 by Olaus Okerson, and the Gothic-style white frame building was dedicated in 1902. The current congregation, known as Central Baptist Church of Tacoma, meets at 5000 Sixty-seventh Avenue W.

The oldest Swedish lodge west of the Mississippi and the first Swedish secular organization in the Pacific Northwest was the Swedish Order of Valhalla, first called Freya Lodge and organized in Tacoma in 1884. Still meeting monthly in the Valhalla Building at 1216 South K (on the west side of K Street between Twelfth and Thirteenth) (206/272-0277), the lodge has a current membership that still boasts many native-born Swedes. The three-story building, constructed in 1906, holds many turn-of-the-century furnishings and has an auditorium with a curved balcony on the second floor and a dining room on the third. The society was organized for social and benevolent purposes.

Pacific Lutheran University at 121st South at Park Avenue South (206/531-6900) was founded by Norwegian Lutherans, but with the demise of Coeur d'Alene College in Idaho in 1920, both Swedish and Norwegian Lutherans in the Pacific Northwest gradually became convinced that cooperation was necessary. The college invited the Columbia Conference of the Augustana Lutheran Synod to place a professor on the staff and also to elect an advisory member to its board of trustees. By 1933, the Columbia Conference was ready to enter into cooperation with the Norwegian Lutherans. The following year the Columbia Conference representation on Pacific Lutheran's board was increased to three members. The coming together of these two groups is one of the strengths of this university.

The largest cemetery in the city, Tacoma Cemetery, or Old Tacoma Cemetery, at South Tacoma Way and South Forty-eighth Street, is also the final resting place of many of the early Swedish settlers.

Southwest of Tacoma and accessible by ferry from Steilacoom are Anderson and McNeil islands. In 1896, twenty-one Swedish adults and their children organized the Swedish Evangelical Lutheran Sunne Congregation of Anderson and McNeil islands. A small frame church was built near the south coast of McNeil Island; nearby was a cemetery. Unfortunately, the congregation no longer exists. Though today there is a federal penitentiary on McNeil Island, many descendants of the early Swedish settlers continue to live on neighboring Anderson Island.

SELAH

East of the Cascade Range and north of Yakima is Selah. Today descendants of the five Swedish families who came to Selah as second-wave immigrants from Sioux City, Iowa, in 1908 own and operate large orchards and fruit processing plants in the Yakima Valley. All adults in the immigrating families had been born in Sweden and educated there, but all the children had been born in the United States. These and other Swedish immigrants soon organized the Swedish Mission Covenant Church, and by 1910, they had built a church where eventually many community functions were held, simply because it was the city's largest public auditorium. Until 1928, services were conducted in Swedish. The church still stands (103 North First, 509/697-6116), though it has been altered architecturally over the years. The property of the church now also encompasses what was formerly the Methodist church, which was built in the same year.

SKAMOKAWA

The rural community of Skamokawa in southwestern Washington is on the north side of the Columbia River estuary, some thirty miles from the Pacific Ocean and offers to visitors the Skamokawa Historic District, which is on the National Register of Historic Places. Swedes and Norwegians began coming to the area in the late 1860s and 1870s, attracted by fishing, farming, and logging opportunities. Part of Skamokawa was called "Swede Town," where there are several frame houses dating from the 1880s and 1890s. In 1887, the Swedish Evangelical Lutheran Bethany congregation was organized in Skamokawa, but it has disbanded.

Further west in Deep River, the Finns organized the Finnish Holy Trinity Evangelical Lutheran Church (or Deep River Pioneer Lutheran Church). The white frame structure, constructed in 1902, eight years after the congregation was organized, is a national historic landmark. A nearby cemetery has both Finnish and Swedish names on the gravestones. Nearby Rosburg Cemetery also has a number of Swedish names on the markers.

CHINOOK

The fishing community of Chinook near the mouth of the Columbia River attracted Scandinavians after it was established in the late 1870s. At the turn of the century, the congregation of the Evangelical Lutheran Church, more Norwegian than Swedish, was organized and a church built. It was designed by a carpenter from nearby Astoria, Oregon, and was built by local Scandinavians. On occasion, Swedish pastors from Astoria came across the wide Columbia River to serve the congregation. The white frame church with a central steeple has Gothic-style windows and a barrel vault wood ceiling.

SPOKANE

In 1888 the Salem Lutheran congregation was organized by the Rev. Peter Carlson. The following year, the church constructed a building with a brick veneer at Broadway and Walnut. In 1949, during work on an adjoining Sunday School building and gymnasium, a spark from a cutting torch ignited a disastrous fire. Saved were many of the stained glass windows, most of the pipe organ, and the Olof Grafström 1924 painting of the Good Shepherd. The windows were incorporated in the new sanctuary. Other notable churches include the former Swedish Baptist Church at the southeast corner of Broadway and Adams and the First Covenant Church (5212 Division), whose new building houses in the narthex the cornerstone of the former Covenant Tabernacle (Svenska Tabernaklet).

OREGON

As was the case with Washington, Swedes first arrived in Oregon in significant numbers during the 1880s. The 1905 Lewis and Clark Exposition in Portland and the work of the Oregon State Commission of Immigration attracted considerable numbers so that by 1910 there were about ten thousand Swedish-born in the state, representing nearly 10 percent of all foreign-born. Swedes were largely "second-stage" immigrants, having settled first in other states.

The largest contingent of Swedes lived in Portland where they tended to be builders and carpenters or employees of various sawmills. The oldest Swedish Lutheran congregation in the Pacific Northwest was organized in Portland by pioneer missionary Peter Carlson. The first important Swedish settlement in the state was Powell Valley, fourteen miles east of Portland. Swedes also lived in considerable numbers in Astoria, Warren, Colton, The Dalles, Ione (north-central Oregon), and along the Pacific Coast, particularly in and around Coos Bay. This survey of Oregon cities begins with Astoria at Oregon's northwestern corner, moves generally southward, juts to central Oregon for Ione and The Dalles, and ends with coastal landmarks near Florence and Coos Bay.

ASTORIA

Salmon fishing and opportunities in lumbering first attracted Swedes to Astoria along with a greater number of Finns, and a midsummer festival draws them back annually. Several of the outstanding historic homes in Astoria have Swedish connections. These include the Captain Eric Johnson House at 960 Franklin Avenue, the Albin W. Norblad House at 1625 Grand, the Benjamin Young House and Carriage House at 3652 Duane Street, and the Dr. Toivo Forsstrom House at 726 Seventh Street. Norblad was first elected governor of Oregon in 1929, and Walter, his son, served as a congressman from 1946 to 1965. Young was one of the leading salmon packers on the lower Columbia, and he expanded his operations, opening canneries in Alaska and on the Fraser River in British Columbia. For a complete description of these homes, many of which are built on steep slopes near the wide mouth of the Columbia River and all of which are privately owned, visitors may consult the brochure, "Walking Tour of Astoria," which may be purchased at the Flavel House at Eighth and Duane (503/325-2203) or at the community's Heritage Museum at 1618 Exchange (503/325-8395).

Swedish Lutherans in Astoria organized the First Swedish Evangelical Lutheran Church in 1880 under the guidance of the Rev. Peter Carlson, making it the second oldest congregation of the former Columbia Conference of the Augustana Lutheran Church. In 1929, this congregation merged with a neighboring German church. The new Trinity Lutheran congregation disposed of the old properties and in 1930 built a sanctuary on the corner of Sixteenth and Franklin. This edifice is now the Performing Arts Center of Clatsop Community College. The old organ and stained glass windows may still be found in the building.

In 1974, Trinity Lutheran consolidated with Zion Lutheran, a Finnish congregation, to form Peace Lutheran Church. This congregation uses the former Zion Lutheran sanctuary, built in 1947 and modernized, at 565 Twelfth Street. In the narthex is a stained glass window from the Trinity church. Also in the narthex are two glass cases with memorabilia from the two congregations—one with Finnish items, the other with Swedish. A cornerstone made of Finnish marble has been placed near the front entrance with an inscription noting the merger of the two churches.

In 1919 plans began to be made for what would eventually become Columbia Memorial Hospital with which many Swedes would be involved over the years. Two years after the Astoria Finnish Brotherhood began to consider providing a hospital for Astoria, the Fraternal Hospital Association, Inc., composed of numerous Astoria fraternal organizations, was organized. It eventually sought support for its hospital proposal from the Columbia Conference of the Augustana Lutheran Church, and with its support, groundbreaking for the facility took place in 1927. Today that structure is a nursing home, and the hospital now serves the community in a building constructed in 1978.

MIST

Swedes began coming to this wooded hill country in 1877. A Swedish Lutheran congregation was organized in 1886, but neither the colony nor the church flourished. The little white frame church is at least ninety years old, and since the early 1960s has been owned by the Community Church of nearby Birkenfeld. On U.S. Highway 30, near the turnoff for Mist, is a sign noting Swedetown Road.

WARREN

Bethany Lutheran Church, a white frame church with a central steeple and twentieth-century Gothic-style windows, features Christ in Gethsemane, one of approximately two hundred altar paintings by Swedish immigrant Olof Grafström, an artist who taught in Lindsborg, Kansas, and Rock Island, Illinois. The building at 34721 Church Road was constructed in 1908, a year after the congregation organized, and has been modernized. North of it is the Bethany Memorial Cemetery. Mount St. Helens is visible to the northeast. Nearby on U.S. Highway 30 is the Warren Baptist Church, which was also organized by Swedes.

PORTLAND

Three active churches in Portland have Swedish roots. First Immanuel Lutheran Church may be called the "mother" church of the former Columbia Conference of the Augustana Lutheran Synod. Established in 1879 as the Scandinavian Evangelical

Lutheran Church, it changed names within a few months to the Swedish Evangelical Lutheran Immanuel Congregation. The Rev. Peter Carlson, its founder and first pastor, was born in Småland in 1822 and emigrated in 1854, first residing in St. Charles, Illinois. Five years later he was ordained a minister.

Immanuel Lutheran's first sanctuary was erected in 1882 at Burnside and Tenth. In that sanctuary the Columbia Conference of the Augustana Lutheran Church was organized in 1893. During the Rev. Carl J. Renhard's pastorate (1904-1910), the present sanctuary was built at the southeast corner of Northwest Irving Street and Northwest Nineteenth Avenue (1816 Northwest Irving Street, 503/226-3659) and dedicated in September 1905. The twentieth-century church in the Gothic style features a tall off-center spire. The sanctuary's stained glass windows represent a number of Christian symbols in memory of various former members of the congregation and include numerous Swedish inscriptions. Adjacent to the church on the Nineteenth Street side is the old parsonage.

The "mother" church of the Pacific Northwest's Swedish Baptists is Temple Baptist Church at 1319 Northeast Seventh (503/233-5953) (opposite the west end of Lloyd Center). Baptists began meeting in 1875, but 1884 is recognized officially as the founding of the First Scandinavian Baptist Church of Portland. In 1878, the Rev. Olaus Okerson, born in Skåne and known as the early leader of Swedish Baptists in the Northwest, had spoken to the group. The sanctuary, built in the Classical style and featuring exterior Ionic columns, was dedicated in 1927 and renovated in 1973.

Another early church, the former Swedish Tabernacle, built in 1912, grew from a congregation formed in 1887 as the Swedish Mission Church. Built at 1624 Northwest Glisan Street (the southeast corner of Northwest Glisan Street and Northwest Seventeenth Avenue), the two-story red brick rectangular tabernacle is said to have been designed by members of the congregation with the idea of its being sold for warehouse use at a later date. The building is now on the National Register of Historic Places. The auditorium features a U-shaped balcony, its face decorated with a repeating motif of plaster rosettes. Eventually called the Swedish Evangelical Mission Covenant Church, the congregation sold the tabernacle in 1953 and now, as First Covenant, meets at 4433 East Burnside. Since the sale, the building has been used as a theater and a union hall.

Immanuel Lutheran's minister the Rev. Carl J. Renhard (1870–1946), was the moving spirit in the founding of Emanuel Hospital & Health Center, now one of the largest health facilities in the Pacific Northwest (2801 North Gantenbein, 503/280-3200). Born in Småland, Renhard immigrated to the United

States at the age of ten. Reared in Nebraska, he was confirmed at the Swede Home Church near Stromsburg and was trained at Augustana Theological Seminary. He came west shortly after the turn of the century. In September 1909, he gathered nine Swedish men (that number shortly increased to twelve) and with them formed the Swedish Lutheran Hospital Board. Three years later, in 1912, Emanuel Hospital purchased a three-story residence on the southwest side of Portland at 209 Southwest Taylor Street.

Four years later, in 1916, the first building at the hospital's present location on the northeast side of the Willamette River (at North Stanton Street and Vancouver Avenue) was opened (this building was razed in 1952 to make way for a 128-bed addition). In 1918, the Nurses Home was opened to serve the Emanuel Hospital School of Nursing, which taught nursing for more than fifty-five years. In 1926, the main hospital was erected at Commercial Avenue and Graham Street, and six years later two more additions were constructed. These parts are the oldest structures still standing at the present site, and numerous additions have been built. In 1977, President Gerald Ford dedicated the Patient Tower, and in 1980, the complex expanded further. The surrounding neighborhood was once known as Swede Hill. At the corner of Rodney and Stanton is the former Augustana Lutheran Church, but now the Lutheran congregation meets at Fourteenth and Knott.

Two blocks west of Immanuel Lutheran Church is Linnea Hall at 2066 Northwest Irving Street (between Northwest Twentieth and Northwest Twenty-first avenues). The Swedish Society Linnea was one of the oldest Swedish societies in the Pacific Northwest and the only independent Swedish lodge in Portland. Organized in 1888 as Svenska Bröderna (The Swedish Brothers), the group four years later changed the name to Svenska Sällskapet Linnéa, and this name appears on the cornerstone laid in 1910. On top of the two and a half–story frame building are a curvilinear gable and square-domed corner pavilions. Wooden pilasters with Corinthian capitals flank a deeply recessed central entrance with double-leaf doors. Above the entrance are two stained glass windows on either side of a painted wood carving of the Swedish national emblem. The rear two-story dance hall was destroyed by fire in 1929.

The society played an important role in the cultural and historical development of Swedish heritage in Portland. It sponsored a variety of activities, such as picnics and parties, and on all occasions Swedish was spoken, Swedish food prepared, and Swedish folk traditions observed. Though the membership reached five hundred in the early 1920s, it declined in the 1930s. By 1946 it had shrunk to 125, and in 1979 the hall was sold. A

Swedish flag continues to be flown over the building, which in 1980 was named a Portland historical landmark.

One thousand feet above the city of Portland in Pittock Acres Park (3229 Northwest Pittock Drive, 503/823-3624) is the Pittock Mansion. On the National Register of Historic Places, this home is open 12-4 daily (except for major holidays). This twenty-two room mansion was built in the French Renaissance style between 1909 and 1914 by Henry L. Pittock, founder of Portland's *The Daily Oregonian* (later called *The Oregonian)*, and showcases fine examples of Swedish craftsmanship. In the first floor library is an intricately detailed wood carving above the fireplace, depicting the family crest, hand executed by William G. Klingenberg, one of Portland's Swedish craftsmen. On the second floor is ornate hand-carved Victorian walnut furniture made in the 1880s by Daniel Wennerberg, a Swedish cabinet-maker. Mrs. Edward Atiyeh, an Oregon governor's wife and granddaughter of Wennerberg, made a gift of the furniture to the mansion. Pictures of Wennerberg and his wife are in the bedroom.

GRESHAM

Swedes came to Gresham and Powell Valley as early as 1875, though a larger number arrived in the 1890s. The Trinity Lutheran Church congregation was organized in 1899, originally being known as the Swedish Evangelical Lutheran Saron Church of Powell Valley. A building was constructed the same year, but no longer exists. A new sanctuary was erected in 1932 at 507 West Powell Boulevard, and it contains the altar painting of the former church.

COLTON

In 1906, the Rev. Carl J. Renhard, the Portland minister who was the leading force in the founding of Portland's Emanuel Hospital medical complex, established the Oregon Swedish Colonization Company in an attempt to encourage more Scandinavian Lutherans to move to the Pacific Northwest. Renhard was looking for people who were Swedish, Lutheran, and Republican. Most of the original settlers came from Nebraska, particularly Oakland, Wakefield, and Omaha. One of the more outstanding families was the Hults from the Swede Home Lutheran Church near Stromsburg, Nebraska. Nels P. Hult became a successful lumberman after building the first lumber mill in the area. Two thousand acres of land were purchased to be made available to the settlers. In 1907 the Swedish Evangelical Lutheran Carlsborg congregation was formally organized in Hult's home. During the following years the white frame church was built. In 1945, the congregation changed its name from Carlsborg Evangelical Lutheran to Colton Lutheran. The church stands on the south side of State Highway 211 next to the local high school. In nearby Colton Cemetery are the graves of the Rev. Renhard (1870–1947); his wife, Anna (1874–1945), who was Hult's daughter; and other members of the Hult family.

On Hult Road, west of town is the Lutheran Pioneer Home, a nursing home begun by the Hults. The Luther Cornay Chapel has the original pews and altar curtain of the Colton Lutheran Church. The Hults also contributed to other Oregon charities and the arts, including the Hult Center for the Performing Arts in Eugene.

THE DALLES

The Fort Dalles Historical Museum at Fifteenth and Garrison streets (503/296-4547) features three late nineteenth-century log structures—the Lewis Anderson house, barn, and granary—all listed on the National Register of Historic Places. Anderson was a Swede and the house was built for him by a fellow Swede. Called "a noteworthy Scandinavia in America vernacular ensemble," the structures were originally on Anderson's homestead on Pleasant Ridge south of The Dalles, overlooking Mount Hood to the west and the rolling Columbia River plateau to the north. The museum commission serving both Wasco County and The Dalles undertook in 1972 to dismantle the structures and move them to the historical museum.

Made of hewn yellow pine logs with dovetailed corners, the rectangular (thirty-four by twenty-four feet) one and a half–story house rested (as did the other farm buildings) on a fieldstone foundation. On the first floor were a parlor, pantry, small bedroom, kitchen, and front bedroom. Stairs led up to a sleeping area. The small hip-roofed shelter for the front entry was added later. The period furnishings include a pump organ and a loom.

The barn (thirty by thirty feet), open only on special occasions, was on a slope at its original location; thus, it has an upper and lower level (hayloft and threshing floor above, central double row of mangers below). Builders used fifty-foot hewn tamarack (evergreen) logs in 1890 for its construction. The granary, which is not open to the public, was built between 1885 and 1890 as a homestead at Rock Prairie. Anderson had it dismantled and moved to his property about 1898. Born in northern Sweden in 1862, Anderson went to sea on an English vessel at age fourteen. After he returned in 1881 to Sweden, he left almost immediately to accompany his sister and a group of settlers to the United States. After marrying in Wisconsin, Anderson went to Minneapolis but then pushed on to Pleasant Ridge in 1885. Although he persuaded other Swedes to follow, Pleasant Ridge's lack of water was a shortcoming that few could overlook. Most drifted on, but Anderson and his family persevered. Finally, after his four children divided the land, he moved to The Dalles and worked in the construction trade.

IONE

Ione is located in a very sparsely populated area of north-central Oregon where the wheat farms are two to four thousand acres each and where some of the last land was available for homesteading in the lower forty-eight states. Swedes first homesteaded land here in 1883, beginning as sheep herders.

The Rev. Erik Norelius, an emigrant from Hälsingland who helped found and lead the Augustana Synod of the Swedish American Lutheran Church, visited this isolated community, then known as Gooseberry, in 1886. In April of that year he conducted the first service of the Lutheran church and organized the congregation. Formerly called Valby Evangelical Lutheran, the small white frame building with its short steeple was dedicated in 1897.

The former Valby Evangelical Lutheran church has stood on the vast farming land of north-central Oregon since 1897.

JUNCTION CITY

For many years an annual Nordic festival has been held mid-August in Junction City. Danes, Finns, Norwegians, and Swedes each have their special day in this four-day festival.

FLORENCE

Heceta Head Lighthouse on U.S. Highway 101 north of Florence is the most powerful beacon along the Oregon coast. The lighthouse and keeper's quarters, now on the National Register of Historic Places, were built by a crew of Swedish-born carpenters between 1892 and 1894. Its location makes it probably Oregon's most photographed coastal lighthouse. Although today it is fully automated, formerly Swedes operated and maintained this lighthouse as they did most of the lighthouses along Oregon's coast.

COOS BAY   In North Bend near Coos Bay, formerly called Marshfield, the former First Lutheran Evangelical Church of North Bend at 777 Florida was built in 1908 by Scandinavian immigrants who worked in the sawmills and logging camps of Coos County. Many were Swedish-speaking men and women who were born in Finland. In 1958, First Lutheran and Trinity Lutheran, a Swedish congregation organized in 1884, merged and constructed a new building at 1290 West Thompson Road in Coos Bay that was dedicated in 1960. Trinity Lutheran's sanctuary at Third and Commercial was torn down.

Coos Bay historic homes owned and/or built by Swedes include three still in private hands. The three-story white frame Nerdrum House at 955 South Fifth, constructed in 1911 and 1912, is considered one of the finest homes in the Coos Bay area. The house was built by Hjalte Nerdrum who emigrated from Finland and was employed by native Swede C. A. Smith at his lumber company. Nerdrum pioneered a new technique for making pulp with salt water from the bay.

The Nasburg-Lockhart House at 687 North Third was constructed in 1884 by Andrew Nasburg who in the early 1860s owned and operated the first general store in Marshfield (Coos Bay). A second-stage immigrant who had first settled in Illinois, Nasburg came to Oregon in 1859. The National Register of Historic Places includes this house.

The Myren-Hillstrom House at 353 South Fifth Street was built about 1889 by Norwegian Robert Myren. His daughter Rose married into the Hillstrom family (Swedish-speaking Finns).

The two-story Queen Anne–style Patrick Hughes House built in 1898 stands in Cape Blanco State Park in Curry County. Designed and constructed by Swede Peter John (Per Johan) Lindberg (1851–1920), a Port Orford building contractor, the house was home to pioneer rancher and dairy farmer Patrick Hughes.

CALIFORNIA

The first Swedes to arrive in California in large numbers came in the 1870s, though gold seekers, fishermen, sailors, traders, and adventurers had arrived as early as the 1840s. A Swedish-Norwegian consulate was established in San Francisco in 1850. This city and Los Angeles became the main centers of the Swedish community in the state, attracting some 40 percent of the Swedish-born. The two most important Swedish rural settlements, both in the San Joaquin Valley, are Kingsburg and Turlock. The former has become known as the Swedish village of California, in somewhat the same way that Solvang, near

Santa Barbara, is identified with the Danes (Solvang, however, is much more developed as a tourist attraction). Swedes settled throughout the northern, central, and coastal parts of the state and in the southern cities of San Diego and Pasadena. By 1970, this most populous state could claim to have more Swedish-born residents than any other state, followed by Illinois, New York, and Minnesota. This survey examines the cities and towns where the Swedes settled, moving from San Francisco in the north to San Diego in the south.

SAN FRANCISCO

CHURCHES

Ebenezer Lutheran Church—678 Portola Drive (415/681-5400).
The church was organized in 1882 by the Rev. Johannes Telleen who was born in Sweden in 1846 and emigrated to the United States as a boy of seven, settling with his parents in Moline, Illinois. In 1872, Telleen was ordained a Lutheran pastor and subsequently held pastorates in several places, including Denver, before coming to San Francisco. Telleen was also important to San Francisco Swedes because he established a church bulletin named *Ebenezer.* In 1887 it developed into *Vestkusten (The West Coast),* which continues to be the Swedish weekly tabloid published in San Francisco.

In 1885, the first church, located on Mission Street between Eighth and Ninth, was dedicated, but in 1903 it was sold to the Salvation Army (the 1906 earthquake destroyed it). The congregation constructed a new church at 208 Dolores, which was saved from the 1906 earthquake. Dedicated only two months before the great earthquake and fire, the church escaped considerable interior damage, thanks to a bucket brigade. Water was carried up ladders on the steeple and poured on the many small fires that broke out on the roof from flying sparks. Unfortunately, fire destroyed the building in August 1993.

The only old item in the modern sanctuary on Portola Drive is the baptismal font. In the narthex is a painting of Telleen and his wife. A glass case in the basement hall contains memorabilia. The old altar painting (1893) by Olof Grafström is in the chapel. Outside the chapel are two historical plaques honoring Telleen and Jonas Auslund, a pioneer Swedish Lutheran missionary in California in the 1870s. In the higher tower is a 1909 bell that had come around Cape Horn. Near the base of the bell tower is the old cornerstone.

St. Mark's Lutheran Church—1111 O'Farrell (between Franklin and Gough) (415/928-7770).
In Pioneer Plaza of this German Lutheran church built in 1894 and dedicated a year later are eight historical plaques commemorating pioneer Lutherans in America and California and

historic congregations of various faiths in San Francisco. The congregation, which was founded in 1849, claims to be the oldest Lutheran church in California. Included among the plaques is one honoring the Rev. Johannes Telleen (see above) and the Rev. Lars Paul Esbjörn. Esbjörn was a pioneer of the Swedish Lutheran church in the United States and was an emissary of Sweden's state church for fourteen years in the Midwest.

First Covenant Church—455 Dolores (between Seventeenth and Eighteenth) (415/431-8755).

In 1877, First Covenant Church was established and called Swedish Evangelical Mission Church of San Francisco. Its first sanctuary was a former German church on Jessie Street. In 1893, the Swedes built a church on the same site, but it was destroyed in the 1906 earthquake. The present tabernacle-style church was completed in 1907. In the 1950s both the exterior and interior were modernized, and the "gingerbread" removed.

Scandinavian Seamen's Mission—2128 Fifteenth (near Market Street and the Swedish American Hall) (415/861-8499).

The Scandinavian Seamen's Mission is run by the Baptists.

Norwegian Seamen's Church—2454 Hyde Street (415/775-6466).

The pastor from a sister church in San Pedro conducts monthly services in Swedish September through June.

OTHER POINTS OF INTEREST

William Matson Residence—1950–1960 Jackson Street (between Gough and Octavia).

This brick Georgian-style U-shaped structure, which has served envoys of both Sweden and Germany, overlooks the Golden Gate area and Marin County. Built by Swede William Matson (1849–1917), the mansion has two wings, which partly enclose a beautiful garden. Matson was born in Lysekil, Bohuslän, but found himself in 1867 in San Francisco as a sailor. In 1901 he organized the Matson Navigation Company. Matson's Pacific cargo ship line thrived, according to Swedish-American author Allan Kastrup, and Matson earned respect as an innovator in shipping: his ships used wireless telegraphy and a gyro pilot and compass before any others on the Pacific. Operating both cruise and cargo lines, he developed commercial trade with Hawaii and expanded his lines' routes eastward as far as the Indian Ocean.

For a while, Matson was president of the San Francisco Chamber of Commerce and honorary Swedish consul general in

San Francisco. In the mid-1940s, the Swedish government bought his mansion and used it as the consular office and residence of the Swedish consul general until 1985, when it was sold to the German government.

Swedish American Hall—2174 Market (415/861-9313).
The Swedish Society was founded in 1875 (previously there had been a Scandinavian society) mainly as a group to benefit the sick. The society met in various locations until Scandia Hall was built, but fire destroyed it in 1906. In 1907 and 1908 the society constructed the hall on Market, enabled financially by Erik O. Lindblom, one of three Swedes credited with discovering gold in Nome, Alaska. Lindblom also founded a Swedish bank in San Francisco, long defunct, and built in the Oakland Hills the Claremont Resort Hotel, a gleaming palacelike hostelry that remains an Oakland landmark today. The four-story Swedish American Hall has several meeting rooms (the main hall is on the second floor) and a library. The building's exterior has scalloped trim protruding from the gable. Today the facilities are used by several fraternal organizations.

Former office of *Vestkusten*—30 Sharon Street (between Fifteenth and Sixteenth streets).
Vestkusten is one of four remaining Swedish-language newspapers in the United States. Begun in 1886 as a bulletin of the Ebenezer Lutheran Church, it was converted the following year into a secular weekly. In 1890, Alexander Olsson from Halland began working for the publication. Four years later, he and Ernst Skarstedt, a well-known writer and chronicler of the Swedish people in the West, purchased the paper, but Skarstedt withdrew and the paper became Olsson's. When he died in 1952, his son, Hugo Olsson, took over. Thirteen years later, Karin W. Person, a journalist from Blekinge, bought the paper. In the early 1990s, she, in turn, sold it to Barbro Sachs-Osher, who continues to publish the long-established periodical. The former office is a highly ornate typical three-story San Francisco townhouse; the current office of *Vestkusten* is at 237 Ricardo in Mill Valley (415/381-5149).

Alexander Olsson was the foremost of five founders of Sveadal, a 110-acre recreation park in the Santa Cruz Mountains near Morgan Hill, south of San Jose, and since 1926, when it was purchased by the Swedish-American Patriotic League, the traditional meeting place for northern California Swedes. The park was dedicated by Crown Prince Gustav Adolf and Crown Princess Louise. A plaque, personally signed by the royal couple, was erected on the front of the clubhouse. It was removed after a clubhouse fire in 1979, but it was restored when

Near San Jose, Sveadal is a 110-acre recreation park in the Santa Cruz Mountains that is the traditional gathering place for Swedish Americans in northern California.

the clubhouse was reconstructed. Another plaque, honoring Olsson, is annually brought to Sveadal during the summer months. Since 1894, when they met in Golden Gate Park at the Midwinter Fair and Exhibition, local Swedes have gathered annually, and now they meet in Sveadal to celebrate the arrival of summer at the Swedish-American Midsummer Festival, which includes the ritual of raising and dancing round the Maypole, the naming of a Midsummer Queen, and a parade.

Raoul Wallenberg Traditional High School—40 Vega (415/ 749-3469).

In the fall of 1981, under the sponsorship of California Congressman Tom Lantos, Rhode Island Senator Claiborne Pell, and others, World War II hero Raoul Wallenberg was made an honorary citizen of the United States, an honor formerly accorded only to the Marquis de LaFayette and Sir Winston Churchill. Wallenberg was personally responsible for saving the lives of thousands of Hungarian Jews during the latter part of World War II. His capture and incarceration by the Russians and his death in a Russian prison stirred an international controversy.

Wallenberg Traditional High School, whose six hundred students specialize in high academics, opened in 1981. It was at that time the only educational institution in the United States named in honor of the Swedish hero.

WOODSIDE

Five miles north of Woodside on Canada Road is the Filoli Estate, built in 1915 and acquired in 1937 by William Matson's daughter and her husband, Lurline and William P. Roth. The mansion was used for the popular television program "Dynasty."

OAKLAND

In 1887, St. Paul's Lutheran Church was organized and the first sanctuary, which no longer exists, was constructed at Ninth and

Clay. The second church was built in 1901 at Tenth and Grove. The congregation now worships in a sanctuary at 1658 Excelsior Avenue that was constructed in 1946.

The Salem Lutheran Home at 2361 Twenty-ninth Street was organized at St. Paul's Lutheran Church in 1924. Through the years it has maintained a close link with this congregation. The First Covenant congregation was organized by Swedes in 1887 and the Swedish Covenant Center at 4000 Redwood Road was constructed in 1971.

BERKELEY

Founded in 1897 as a Sunday School in a rented hall, Berkeley Covenant Church (1632 Hopkins, 510/516-8775) enjoys a long history of religious service and fellowship that grew from a handful of faithful Swedish-speaking families. Not until 1903 was the church officially chartered by sixteen members as Svenska Missionen, or the Swedish Mission Church. In this early fellowship, members incorporated in 1906, built the first church in 1907, and navigated the rough waters of periodic closings between 1917 and 1922, when growth resumed under the pastorate of the Rev. David Sandstrom.

Congregants were reluctant to adopt English, and until 1934 pastors conducted services in Swedish. In the 1950s the church celebrated its fiftieth anniversary with a groundbreaking ceremony for new construction, and at the seventy-fifth anniversary adopted a new constitution.

The Judah L. Magnes Memorial Museum (the Jewish Museum of the West) at 2911 Russell Street (510/849-2710) awards the Raoul Wallenberg Holocaust Hero Medal, which recognizes the selfless efforts of Raoul Wallenberg during World War II to rescue Jews from the Holocaust. Per Anger, who in the 1950s was Swedish consul general in San Francisco, was during World War II an attaché in the Swedish Embassy in Budapest. His assignment was to assist Wallenberg in saving Hungarian Jews from the Nazis.

SACRAMENTO

On the second floor of the state capitol (on Tenth between N and L streets) at the senators' double-door entrance to the State Senate is a portrait, along with other California governors, of Earl Warren (1891–1974), governor of California 1943–53 and chief justice of the U.S. Supreme Court 1953–69. Warren's mother was born in Sweden, and his father, in Norway. His wife, also Swedish, was the daughter of the Rev. Nils Peter Palmquist, an early minister of the Swedish Baptist Church in San Diego. (Call 916/324-0333 for state capitol tour information.)

LAKE TAHOE

Vikingsholm, a thirty-eight–room mansion built between 1929 and 1935 and now in Emerald Bay State Park (916/525-7277), resembles by plan an ancient Norse fortress and chieftain's castle. Designed by Swede Lennart Palme, the two-story stone structure has on each end a tower, one three stories and the other, two. (Palme, trained in civil engineering at the Royal Technical University in Stockholm, was born in Stockholm in 1881 and was a first cousin of the father of Olof Palme [1927–1986], Sweden's prime minister 1969–76 and 1982–86.) An enclosed balcony on the second floor is highly ornamented by carvings, and the house features Swedish antique furnishings. From the living room, visitors may see a panoramic view of Emerald Bay. Also in the Nordic style is a caretaker's log house with wood carvings, a roof overlaid with split logs, and a chimney reminiscent of those in Dalarna.

Though now owned by the California Department of Parks and Recreation and open seasonally for tours, the house was built for Lora J. Knight, widow of an eminent Chicago multimillionaire, who lived in the house until her death in 1945. From a parking lot on State Highway 89, a visitor may reach Vikingsholm following a steep trail (approximately one mile). The grounds are also accessible by boat.

RIPON

North of Turlock in Ripon is the Bethany Covenant Church (209/599-4233), which was organized in 1916 and built in 1920.

TURLOCK

Located in the San Joaquin Valley and famous for its melons, Turlock was to a considerable extent founded by Swedish Mission Friends, many of whom came from Youngstown, Ohio. Probably the most prominent of the early settlers was land agent Nels O. Hultberg from Torrlösa, Skåne. After working in Illinois, he was sent by the U.S. government and the Mission Friends in 1893 to Alaska, where he maintained a mission for the church and carried out tasks for the government. But after staking a claim he struck gold in 1898 on the Seward Peninsula. The same year John Brynteson, Erik Lindblom, and Jafet Lindeberg also struck gold and thus initiated the famous turn-of-the-century rush to Alaska that brought almost twenty thousand prospectors to Nome. According to Helen Alma Hohenthal's *Streams in a Thirsty Land,* Hultberg felt compelled to leave Alaska after two of his children died, and he transferred ownership of his mine to an Eskimo who traded it to another minister. The Covenant Church, which had expanded North Park College and Swedish Covenant Hospital with proceeds from the gold, and the new owner went to court over ownership, and the battle did not end until 1920 when the court found in favor of the minister. In 1902 Hultberg settled in Turlock where he sold land, opened the first dairy, participated in other commercial enterprises, and developed a fruit orchard. He drew many

Swedes to the area with advertisements in Swedish-language religious periodicals in the United States and Sweden.

Turlock Covenant Church (209/667-1191), organized in 1902 as Beulah Covenant, built its first sanctuary, now gone, at West Main and Lander. With growth, the congregation decided in 1923 to purchase the high school on Laurel and High streets. The pastor named the area Beulah Park because of the beauty of the tall palm trees and flowering shrubs on the grounds. In 1927 and 1928 the church built the Beulah Tabernacle on the site, hanging in it the old church's bell, which had been cast in New York and transported by ship around Cape Horn to California in 1888. Into the thirties, the church was known locally as the Swedish Mission Church.

Emanuel Medical Center opened in 1917 under the name Emanuel Hospital at 1318 Canal. That building, now an apartment house, is recognized as a historic site. Brothers Eric and Albert Julien, both doctors, founded the hospital, and they, along with the Rev. A. G. Delbon, pastor of the Turlock Covenant Church, and the Rev. E. N. Train (Covenant Church, Hilmar), promoted it in the early years. A highly respected Covenant-owned institution, Emanuel Medical Center at 825 Delbon (209/667-4200) encompasses the hospital itself, Brandel Manor Convalescent Hospital, and the residential retirement community of Covenant Village.

Another Turlock landmark is the familiar Nazareth Lutheran Church at the corner of Orange and Columbia. It was organized in 1912 and its sanctuary constructed in 1927. At the corner of Columbia and Locust is the former Swedish Baptist Church, which was constructed in 1937 after the congregation was organized in 1908. At 575 North Soderquist Road is Turlock Memorial Park (209/632-1018), a city cemetery with numerous Swedish graves.

HILMAR

The early promoters of the farming community of Hilmar, south of Turlock, were Nels O. Hultberg and Andrew Hallner, minister, author, and journalist. The colony was named for Hultberg's oldest son, Hilmar, and was set on seventeen thousand of the thirty-five thousand acres in the area Hultberg bought in 1902. Hultberg and Hallner advertised in Swedish periodicals principally in the Midwest. Within eight weeks of the first advertisements, twenty-two families had arrived in Turlock. The first came in 1902, and others followed during the next three years. Grasshopper and rabbit plagues and sandstorms tested the colonists and made the early years difficult. Eventually, hard-won irrigation sustained farming efforts, and almond and walnut orchards along with dairy farms and cheese factories predominate today.

Two early congregations built churches in the colony, but they were compelled to move, leaving their cemeteries behind, when the Western Pacific Railroad plotted its course about two miles east of the original settlement. The Covenant congregation was organized in 1902 and is older than Beulah Covenant in Turlock by a few months. The cornerstone has a Swedish inscription with the dates 1903–1921. The Berea Lutheran congregation was organized in 1906. In 1948, it moved its small sanctuary, which was built in 1910, to Bloss and Lander, from a site near the Berea Lutheran Cemetery. In the cemetery is a monument erected to the memory of the Rev. and Mrs. Edward Nelander by the Angelica Swedish Lutheran Church of Los Angeles. Services were conducted in Swedish for more than two decades, and the transition to English was slow.

KINGSBURG

The town of Kingsburg in the grape country (home of Sun Maid Raisin Growers, the largest raisin production facility in the world) of the San Joaquin Valley, midway between San Francisco and Los Angeles, prides itself on being California's Swedish village. Although the Swedish population today is probably no more than 30 percent of the total seven to eight thousand, Kingsburg's pioneers were predominantly Swedish. In 1921, a survey showed that 94 percent of the population within a three-mile radius of Kingsburg was Swedish. Frank D. Rosendahl of Närke and Andrew Erikson from Ishpeming, Michigan, made efforts that beginning in 1886 brought Swedish settlers to Kingsburg. The following year the first Swedish Lutheran church in the San Joaquin Valley was founded. Eventually five Swedish churches were organized in Kingsburg.

The community is making efforts to give the downtown business district a Swedish look, which translates architecturally to facades with steeply peaked shingled roofs, windows in gables and dormers, and side paneling with cross boards and used bricks. The Dala horse appears on the town's light poles. Annually on the third Saturday of May the town hosts the Swedish Festival.

INSTITUTES AND MUSEUMS
Kingsburg Historical Park—east of Kingsburg on East Sierra between Madsen and Eighteenth Street.
Historic structures from other Kingsburg locations give a sense in this park of early life in the Kingsburg community. Typical is the three-room Clay Elementary School, which was built in 1913 and originally stood at Saginaw and Smith. Built in 1908 was the Peter Olson House (also known as the Olson-Ball House), constructed by Swedish immigrant Peter Olson who was born in Ängelholm, Skåne, in 1857. Olson arrived in Chicago

in 1880 but continued on to Minnesota, where he worked as a logger and learned the carpenter's trade. After twelve years in Minnesota, Olson moved to Kingsburg where he took up farming and became a rancher and fruit grower who was especially successful in growing grapes. Olson built several houses in and around Kingsburg. Three other structures—an old barn with handmade agricultural tools, a tank house (typical of early San Joaquin Valley water storage structures), and the Olson Brothers Welding Building—indicate the agricultural ingenuity of the community. Also open is a building featuring a doctor's office, a pharmacy, and the Rieffle Grocery Store.

The Kingsburg Chamber of Commerce (209/897-2925), which is housed in Kingsburg's former railroad depot, welcomes visitors to Kingsburg and can provide additional information about the city or the historical park. A Dala horse stands atop the depot's roof.

CHURCHES

The oldest congregation in town, Concordia Evangelical Lutheran Church at 1800 Sierra Street (Sierra and Eighteenth) (209/897-2165), was organized in 1887. Six years later, in 1893, the California Conference of the Augustana Evangelical Lutheran Church was founded in Kingsburg. In the narthex of the twentieth-century Gothic red brick building is the original communion service set and other memorabilia significant in the congregation's history. Organized by the Rev. Telleen, who was prompted to action by correspondence from Andrew Erikson, the congregation built its first sanctuary in 1888 on Lincoln, just off Sierra. That structure, though now owned by another congregation, still stands.

The First Baptist Church is a reddish brick building of the Romanesque style that has a cornerstone inscribed, "Swedish Baptist Church A.D. 1920." The Evangelical Covenant Church at the corner of 1733 Draper (209/897-3310) was organized in 1907. In 1917, the congregation decided to erect a Romanesque building on the same site as the old one built in 1907. The first Covenant church in the area, built halfway between Kingsburg and Reedley in the midst of peach orchards and vineyards, was Colony Covenant (209/897-3854), a branch of which founded the Evangelical Covenant congregation in Kingsburg. Colony was organized in 1891 and four years later built a small white frame sanctuary.

OTHER POINTS OF INTEREST

The Kingsburg Town Cemetery (South Academy Avenue and East Clarkson Avenue) has in its northeast section graves with Swedish inscriptions.

TEMPLETON

Templeton, a small rural community six miles south of Paso Robles, is home to probably the oldest Swedish church building in California still serving its original congregation. Bethel Lutheran Church at Third and Crocker streets (805/238-2729) was organized by the Rev. Telleen in 1886, and the sanctuary was constructed a year later. This lovely old brick church has nineteenth-century windows in the Gothic style and a central wood steeple, which was a later addition. The congregation retains many of the old features in the sanctuary—the original altar cloth and pulpit, wooden offertory plates carved by a member, and the pastor's kneeling stool that is made of deer antlers.

In another part of town is the church's attractive cemetery, which has a lovely rose garden display at its center. Underscoring the community's Swedish heritage is the multitude of graves with Swedish names and inscriptions. Early settlers were attracted by the region's lumbering opportunities. A couple of wooden markers, including that of Anders Anderson, bear Swedish inscriptions.

SANTA BARBARA

At the north end of the city are the Earl Warren Showgrounds (Las Positas Road and U.S. Highway 101). The Covenant Church's Samarkand Retirement Center is also located here. About one hour northwest of Santa Barbara is the attractive community of Solvang, a Danish tourist town near the base of the Santa Ynez Mountains.

PASADENA

The Messiah Lutheran congregation at 570 East Orange Grove Boulevard was founded in 1912, and the twentieth-century Gothic-style sanctuary was constructed in 1924. The altar painting (1921) is by Olof Grafström. The Evangelical Covenant Church, organized in 1912, erected its sanctuary at 539 Lake Avenue North in 1947.

Also in Pasadena on East Villa between Oak and Linda Rosa is the Vasa Temple–Skandia Lodge (818/585-0134), a stucco building with a roof edged in tile. Built in 1928 by Swedes, the building houses a hall with a stage backdrop depicting a Swedish scene. On both sides of the stage, stenciled on the wall, is the symbol of the Vasa Order and its motto, *"Sanning och Enighet"* ("Truth and Unity").

LOS ANGELES

Swedish landmarks in Los Angeles span the gamut from noteworthy churches to locations of commercial and entertainment industry interest. The "mother" church for Swedish Lutherans of Southern California is Angelica Lutheran Church at 1345 Burlington Avenue (the northwest corner of Fourteenth and

Burlington) (213/382-6378). Two years after it was organized by the Rev. Telleen in 1888, the first church, at Tenth and Grand, was dedicated. Twelve years later a second sanctuary was built at Seventeenth and Hope. The Burlington sanctuary was completed in 1925. A large landscape painting by Christian von Schneidau, depicting an idyllic romanticized Los Angeles including the two former Angelica sanctuaries, hangs in the Fellowship Hall.

Roger Dahlhjelm (1881–1950) and Howard F. Ahmanson (1906–68) were men whose grandfathers had emigrated from Sweden and who themselves influenced commercial development in Los Angeles. Dahlhjelm founded in 1934 the Farmers Market at the corner of Fairfax Avenue and West Third where twenty thousand people come every day (open Monday through Saturday 9–6:30, Sunday 11–5; administrative office, 213/933-9211). Dahlhjelm's paternal grandfather, Claes Dahlhjelm, came to the United States from Östergötland in the early 1850s and was one of the first settlers in the Chisago Lake area in Minnesota. Dahlhjelm encouraged farmers during the Depression to locate their stands together. Settling on West Third and Fairfax as the best location, Dahlhjelm and others opened the Farmers Market in July of 1934 with eighteen stalls. Today the market has well over 150 stalls, shops, stores, and restaurants. Above gate 1 is the office and space where formerly Dahlhjelm lived, and there hang photographs of the market in its early days, some featuring actors and actresses from Los Angeles's film colony. Dahlhjelm remained the market's manager until 1949.

Ahmanson, who was the grandson of Jönköping immigrant Johan August Åhmanson, developed the very successful Los Angeles-based Home Savings and Loan Association. Out of that success grew the Ahmanson Foundation, which provides financial encouragement and assistance in education, the arts, and medical research. Named in his honor are the Ahmanson Gallery in the Los Angeles County Museum of Art at 5905 Wilshire and Ogden (213/857-6000), the Ahmanson Theatre at 135 North Grand Avenue (213/972-7401) in the Music Center, and the Ahmanson Center for Biological Research at the University of Southern California.

On the sidewalk at Mann Chinese Theatre, 6925 Hollywood Boulevard (213/464-8111), are the signatures and the handprints and footprints of famous actors and actresses. Included are Gloria Swanson, whose father was of Swedish parentage; Swedish film and stage star Viveca Lindfors; and Swedish-American actress and singer Ann-Margret, whose family (the Olssons) came from Valsjöbyn. In a display of Academy Award winners, Swedish actress Ingrid Bergman is cited for receiving the award for best actress in 1944 *(Gaslight)* and 1956 *(Anastasia)* and for best supporting actress in 1964 *(Murder on the Orient Express).*

CLAREMONT   The Nordic Collections in the Honnold/Mudd Library (909/ 621-8150) of the Claremont Colleges (747 North Dartmouth Avenue) began as a result of a bequest—the private library and residual estate of former Professor of History Waldemar Westergaard (at Pomona College 1916–25 and at the University of California–Los Angeles 1925–50). Westergaard and his colleague David Bjork frequently traveled to Scandinavia, acquiring books, pamphlets, and microfilms. About thirty thousand feet of their microfilm rest in UCLA's library. Other Scandinavian scholars, including former director Franklin Scott and the late Columbia University Professor John H. Wuorinen, have contributed additional works.

RIVERSIDE   Though Eden Lutheran Church's building was constructed in twentieth-century Romanesque style in 1952, the congregation dates from 1888.

RANCHO PALOS VERDES   The all-glass Wayfarers' Chapel at 5755 Palos Verdes Drive South (310/377-1650) stands as a national memorial to Emanuel Swedenborg and is owned by the Swedenborgian Church. The cornerstone was laid in 1949, and the chapel was dedicated two years later. A favorite site for weddings, the chapel was designed by Lloyd Wright, son of architect Frank Lloyd Wright. Visitors standing in the chapel (it is open daily 9– 5) look out on the Pacific Ocean with Catalina Island on the horizon.

Surrounding the chapel is a lovely garden. A Visitors Center, completed in 1958, contains exhibits and literature about the Swedenborgian faith, including a display on Johnny Appleseed (John Chapman), Swedenborgian missionary of the American frontier.

Nearby in Rolling Hills Estates is the Rolling Hills Covenant Church (2222 Palos Verdes Drive North), a huge modern complex with the largest membership of any Covenant church in the United States.

In San Pedro a Swedish service is held monthly at the Norwegian Seamen's Church, which was built in 1951.

SAN DIEGO   In San Diego are several landmarks related to Charles A. Lindbergh, Jr., who flew the first nonstop solo transatlantic flight. Lindbergh, a twenty-five–year–old aviator at the time of his famous 1927 flight, was the son of a Stockholm-born immigrant who came to America in 1860 and became a well-

A national memorial to Emanuel Swedenborg and owned by the Swedenborgian Church, the all-glass Wayfarers' Chapel was designed by Frank Lloyd Wright's son.

known Republican congressman from Minnesota who served five terms. At the San Diego Aerospace Museum (2001 Pan American Plaza in Balboa Park) (619/234-8291) a reproduction of Lindbergh's *Spirit of St. Louis* is featured along with other Lindbergh memorabilia. The museum is open daily 10–4. At 2200 Pacific Highway (at Juniper Street) at Solar Turbines, Inc., is a historical plaque identifying the building as the site where Lindbergh supervised the construction of the *Spirit of St. Louis.* In the lobby of the East Terminal at San Diego's Lindbergh Field is a bust, sculpted by Paul Fjelde, that was a gift of Ryan Aeronautical Company to the citizens of San Diego.

Other San Diego sites of Swedish interest include the House of Sweden in Balboa Park, where coffee and refreshments are served each Sunday afternoon. It is part of the series of stucco buildings known as the House of Pacific Relations (619/ 234-0739). Noteworthy churches include a congregation formed in 1891 that built a Swedish Baptist chapel at the corner of Nineteenth and H (Market). Six years later, its new pastor was the Rev. N. P. Palmquist from South Bend, Indiana, whose daughter would one day marry Earl Warren, U.S. Supreme Court Chief Justice 1953–69. Although the Rev. Palmquist left for Oakland at the turn of the century and the church closed shortly thereafter, the congregation reemerged in 1907 under the name Bethel Baptist Church and met at Sixteenth and E streets. Today that congregation is known as the College Avenue Baptist Church, which has been located since 1940 at the corner of College and Adams. The chapel built in 1891 still stands, though it is used by another congregation. Also in the city were three Augustana Lutheran congregations—Ascension, Bethesda, and Calvary.

ALASKA

As the nineteenth century gave way to the twentieth, Swedes were drawn to Alaska's vast regions mainly by gold; employment opportunities in the forestry, mineral, and fishing businesses; and mission work. Those who came as prospectors included John Brynteson, Erik Lindblom, and Jafet Lindeberg, known as the "Three Lucky Swedes," who discovered gold in Alaska on a tributary of the Snake River. Their strike near the fledgling settlement of Nome on 22 September 1898 brought thousands to Alaska seeking gold. Swedes Charles John Anderson, who made a fortune in Alaska and lost it in the San Francisco 1906 earthquake, and John Erikson, who also successfully searched for gold and later became a newspaper publisher and banker in Seattle, are also well-known players in the gold rush drama. Swedes who stayed in Alaska after gold fever passed often turned to fishing or farming for a livelihood.

SITKA

Before 1867 when Alaska was part of Russia, the Russian-American Company employed Finns, including Swede-Finns, as officers, clerks, carpenters, shipwrights, sailors, and sea captains in New Archangel, the Russian name for Sitka, the principal port. There Captain Arvid Adolph Etholén, a Swede-Finn and an early governor, held Alaska's first Lutheran service—perhaps the first on the North American West Coast—in the governor's residence in 1840. Over the objections of Russian Orthodox leaders, a Lutheran church was dedicated on Lincoln Street in 1843, the first Protestant church in Alaska. Services were conducted alternately in Finnish and Swedish, but occasionally services were held in German. After 1867 when Alaska came under the control of the United States, many members returned to Europe and the congregation was left without a pastor. The building deteriorated until 1888, when it was torn down. The congregation was reestablished in 1940 (there was little if any Swedish influence in this congregation), and in a few years the members built a new church at the old site. A fire claimed the building in 1966, and in 1993 the third sanctuary was also destroyed by fire (the church undertook rebuilding). A Kessler organ built in Estonia in 1844 and thought to be the first one on the West Coast was damaged in the 1993 fire but is being restored. It had been a possession of the first congregation and then held in the Sheldon Jackson Museum until 1983 when it had been returned to the congregation. Buried in the small Lutheran cemetery is Edvard Etholén, son of the early governor.

ANCHORAGE

The small frame Oscar Anderson House (420 M Street, 907/274-2336) is advertised as the oldest wooden house in Anchorage. Overlooking the Knik Arm of Cook Inlet, the house, now on the National Register of Historic Places, was built by a Swedish immigrant in 1915. Anderson first settled in Seattle in 1905, where he owned a restaurant. After coming to Anchorage in 1915, Anderson started a meat market, owned part of an airline, published a newspaper, and worked as a coal company executive. He lived in the house until 1969, and in 1976 his widow donated the house to the city, which completed its restoration in 1982. The house is open afternoons Wednesday through Sunday from May through September for an admission fee.

HAWAII

Avation pioneer Charles Lindbergh (1902–74) spent the last six years of his life in the community of Kipahulu near the eastern tip of Maui, about nine miles from Hana. Lindbergh's grave is in the cemetery of the Palapala Hoomau Congregational Church. Visitors should be careful not to confuse the Hoomau Church, located off the main road at the end of a dirt drive, from peach-colored St. Paul's Church. On his simple grave is the inscription from Psalms 139:9: "If I take the wings of the morning, and dwell in the uttermost parts of the sea." The graveyard is near the edge of an awe-inspiring cliff overlooking the Pacific Ocean with the island of Hawaii visible to the south. To reach this remote location, visitors must drive what is considered to be the most spectacular Hawaiian coastal road—Hawaii State Highway 360—known as the Hana Highway. The road's six hundred sharp turns and fifty-four bridges carry visitors alongside waterfalls and through thick tropical rain forests.

SOURCES OF ADDITIONAL INFORMATION

The first section of this list includes useful works on the history of Swedish America. Inclusion means that scholars acknowledge these works as standard or that they are important as sources of general information or as indicators of new directions in scholarship. Many of the authors cited have contributed additional books and articles to this field of study. In the second section are periodicals whose focus is Swedish America, and in the third are the names and addresses of the most important research centers and libraries with Swedish-American resources.

BOOKS

Anderson, Philip, and Dag Blanck. *Swedish-American Life in Chicago: Cultural and Urban Aspects of an Immigrant People.* Chicago and Urbana: University of Illinois Press and the Swedish-American Historical Society, 1992.

Barton, H. Arnold. *Letters from the Promised Land.* Minneapolis and Chicago: University of Minnesota Press and Swedish-American Historical Society, 1975.
See other works by this author.

Beijbom, Ulf. *Swedes in Chicago: A Demographic and Social Study of the 1846–1880 Immigration.* Translated by Donald Brown. Uppsala: Acta Universitatis Upsaliensis, 1971.

Beijbom, Ulf, ed. *Swedes in America: New Perspectives.* Växjö: The Emigrant Institute, 1993.

Bergendoff, Conrad. *The Augustana Ministerium: A Study of the Careers of the 2,504 Pastors of the Augustana Evangelical Lutheran Synod/Church, 1850–1962.* Rock Island, Ill.: Augustana Historical Society, 1980.
See other works by this author.

Carlsson, Sten. *Swedes in North America, 1638–1988: Technical, Cultural, and Political Achievements.* Stockholm: Streiffert, 1988.

Dahlgren, Stellan, and Hans Norman. *The Rise and Fall of New Sweden: Governor Johan Risingh's Journal 1654–1655 in Its Historical Context.* Stockholm: Almqvist & Wiksell International, 1988.

Hasselmo, Nils. *Swedish America: An Introduction.* New York: Swedish Information Service, 1976.
  See other works by this author.

Holmquist, June, ed. *They Chose Minnesota.* St. Paul: Minnesota Historical Society Press, 1981.

Isaksson, Olov. *Bishop Hill: A Utopia on the Prairie.* Translated by Albert Read. Stockholm: LTs förlag, 1969.

Janson, Florence Edith. *The Background of Swedish Immigration 1840–1930.* Chicago: University of Chicago Press, 1931.

Johnson, Amandus. *Swedish Settlements on the Delaware.* Philadelphia: University of Pennsylvania, 1911; rpt. New York: D. Appleton & Co.
  See other works on the New Sweden Colony by this author.

Johnson, Emeroy. *A Church Is Planted: The Story of the Lutheran Minnesota Conference, 1851–1876.* Minneapolis: Lutheran Minnesota Conference, 1948.
  See other works by this author.

Kastrup, Alan. *The Swedish Heritage in America.* Minneapolis: Swedish Council of America, 1975.

Landelius, Otto R. *Swedish Place-Names in North America.* Translated by Raymond Jarvi. Carbondale: Southern Illinois University Press, 1985.

Lindmark, Sture. *Swedish America, 1914–1932: Studies in Ethnicity with Emphasis on Illinois and Minnesota.* Stockholm: Läromedelsförlaget, 1971.

Lindquist, Emory. *Smoky Valley People: A History of Lindsborg, Kansas.* Lindsborg: Bethany College, 1953.
  See other works by this author.

Ljungmark, Lars. *Swedish Exodus.* Translated by Kermit Westerberg. Carbondale and Chicago: Southern Illinois University Press and the Swedish-American Historical Society, 1979.
  See other works by this author.

Moberg, Vilhelm. *The Emigrants.* Translated by Gustaf Lannestock. New York: Simon and Schuster, 1951.
  See also Unto a Good Land, The Settlers, *and* The Last Letter Home *by this author.*

Moe, M. Lorimer, ed. *Saga from the Hills: A History of the Swedes of Jamestown, New York.* Jamestown: Fenton Historical Society, 1983.

Nelson, Helge. *The Swedes and the Swedish Settlements in North America.* 2 vols. Lund: C. W. K. Gleerup and New York: A. Bonnier, 1943; rpt. New York: Arno Press, 1979.

Nordstrom, Byron, ed. *The Swedes in Minnesota*. Minneapolis: Denison, 1976.

Norelius, Eric. *The Pioneer Swedish Settlements and Swedish Lutheran Church in America 1845–1860*. Translated by Conrad Bergendoff. Rock Island, Ill.: Augustana Historical Society, 1984.

Olson, Adolf. *A Centenary History as Related to the Baptist General Conference of America*. Chicago: Baptist Conference Press, 1952.

Olson, Ernst W., ed. *History of the Swedes of Illinois*. 3 vols. Chicago: Engberg Holmberg Publishing Company, 1908.

Olsson, Christopher, and Ruth McLaughlin. *American-Swedish Handbook*. 11th ed. Minneapolis: Swedish Council of America, 1992.

> *This is particularly useful for information about specific Swedish-American organizations, including historical societies, fraternal orders, and other similar groups.*

Olsson, Karl A. *By One Spirit: A History of the Evangelical Covenant Church of America*. Chicago: Covenant Press, 1962.

Olsson, Nils William. *Swedish Passenger Arrivals in New York, 1820–1850*. Chicago: Swedish-American Historical Society, 1967.

> *See other works by this author.*

Ostergren, Robert. *A Community Transplanted: The Trans-Atlantic Experience of a Swedish Immigrant Settlement in the Upper Middle West, 1835–1915*. Madison: University of Wisconsin Press, 1988.

Scott, Larry E. *The Swedish Texans*. San Antonio: The University of Texas Institute of Texan Cultures, 1990.

Stephenson, George M. *The Religious Aspects of Swedish Immigration: A Study of the Immigrant Churches*. Minneapolis: University of Minnesota Press, 1932.

Swedish-American Historical Society. *Guide to Swedish-American Archival and Manuscript Sources in the United States*. Chicago: Swedish-American Historical Society, 1983.

Vedung, Siv. *A Book Collector on the Texas Frontier: Swante Palm and His Swedish Library at The University of Texas at Austin*. Houston: Texas Swedish Cultural Foundation, 1990.

Whyman, Henry. *The Hedstroms and the Bethel Ship: Methodist Influence on Swedish Religious Life*. Carbondale: Southern Illinois University Press, 1992.

In addition, readers should consult local libraries, historical societies and congregations for publications about a particular site.

PERIODICALS

The Bridge (Bryggan)

> *Published quarterly by* The Emigrant Register *in Karlstad, Sweden, this magazine is a useful source of information.*

Sweden & America
> *Published four times a year since 1987, this magazine is the primary publication of the Swedish Council of America. It contains articles about Swedish Americans and Swedish-American history.*

Swedish American Genealogist
> *Published four times a year since 1981, this journal is an important source of information about people, places, organizations, and a variety of themes in Swedish-American history.*

Swedish-American Historical Quarterly (from 1950 to 1982 *Swedish Pioneer Historical Quarterly*)
> *Published four times each year since July 1950 by the Swedish-American Historical Society, this journal is the most important peiodical in the field of Swedish-American history. Readers will find articles about places, people, themes, and events. Also, in each October issue since 1978 the journal has published a bibliography of publications in this field for the previous year.*

In addition, readers should consult Nordstjernan *(New York) and* Vestkusten *(San Francisco), which are two significant Swedish-American newspapers, and the publications of specific state and local historical societies and other similar organizations for information about particular sites.*

ARCHIVES AND RESEARCH CENTERS

The American Swedish Historical Museum, 1900 Pattison Avenue, Philadelphia, Pennsylvania 19145 (215/389-1776).

The Swedish-American Historical Society Archives, North Park College, 5125 North Spaulding Avenue, Chicago, Illinois 60625 (312/583-5722).

The Swenson Swedish Immigration Research Center, Augustana College, P. O. Box 175, Rock Island, Illinois 61201-2273 (309/794-7443).

Readers may also seek information about specific sites from state, county, and local historical societies; the colleges associated with Swedish America, including Augustana, Bethany, Bethel, Gustavus Adolphus, North Park, and Upsala; denominational archives; the Vasa Order of America archives in Bishop Hill, Illinois; congregations; and other organizations.

NAME INDEX

See also the Subject Index that follows

SUBJECT INDEX

See also the preceding Name Index